W0010820

Java in a Nutshell

A Desktop Quick Reference for Java Programmers

Java in a Nutshell

A Desktop Quick Reference for Java Programmers

David Flanagan

O'Reilly & Associates, Inc.
Bonn • Cambridge • Paris • Sebastopol • Tokyo

Java in a Nutshell

by David Flanagan

Copyright © 1996 O'Reilly & Associates, Inc. All rights reserved.
Printed in the United States of America.

Published by O'Reilly & Associates, Inc., 103 Morris Street, Suite A, Sebastopol, CA 95472.

Series Editor: Mike Loukides

Editor: Paula Ferguson

Production Editor: John Files

Printing History:

February 1996:   First Edition

Nutshell Handbook and the Nutshell Handbook logo are registered trademarks of O'Reilly & Associates, Inc.

Many of the designations used by manufacturers and sellers to distinguish their products are claimed as trademarks. Where those designations appear in this book, and O'Reilly & Associates, Inc. was aware of a trademark claim, the designations have been printed in caps or initial caps.

While every precaution has been taken in the preparation of this book, the publisher assumes no responsibility for errors or omissions, or for damages resulting from the use of the information contained herein.

This book is printed on acid-free paper with 85% recycled content, 15% post-consumer waste. O'Reilly & Associates is committed to using paper with the highest recycled content available consistent with high quality.

ISBN: 1-56592-183-6   [4/96-4th]

Table of Contents

Part II: Programming with the Java API

Part III: Java Language Reference

Part V: API Cross References

How to Use This Book

If you're new to Java, you'll want to take this book off to a peaceful place and learn about the language by reading the first three sections. Later, when you have some free time, you may want to sit down and study the example code in the next six sections. Primarily, though, this book is designed to lie flat on your desk, right next to your keyboard, for quick and convenient reference while you program. Before diving right in, please read this brief overview—it tells you how to get the most out of the book.

Part I: Introducing Java

This first part of the book introduces the Java language. Section 1, *Getting Started with Java*, is an overview of Java, with some samples of Java code to give you the flavor of the language. Section 2, *How Java Differs from C*, documents how Java differs from the C programming language and Section 3, *Classes and Objects in Java*, explains object-oriented programming with Java. Sections 2 and 3 are fairly independent of each other; you can read either one first. If you already know how to program in C or C++, the first part of this book should teach you everything you need to know to start programming with Java. If you do not know C or C++ programming, you may want to find a slower-paced book to introduce you to Java programming. After you have learned Java, you can use this material as a refresher course.

Part II: Programming with the Java API

Sections 4 through 9 form the second part of the book. The bulk of these sections is Java code—practical, real-world examples of programming with Java and Java API. The text provides an overview of the code and the code itself is thoroughly commented. Overall, though, there is not much hand-holding here. Studying the examples on your own is the best way to learn about, and build real understanding of, the Java API. The examples are also an excellent starting point for your own explorations of Java, and you should feel free to adapt them to your own needs and interests.

The sections and their contents are as follows:

Section 4, *Applets*
> Starts with a simple "Hello World" applet and progresses through event handling, animation, imagemaps, and audio.

Section 5, *Graphical User Interfaces*
> Demonstrates the use of each component, and the most important layout managers in the `java.awt` package. Shows how to create custom dialog boxes and custom components.

Section 6, *Input and Output*
> Shows how to read and write files and obtain file information and directory listings. Illustrates the use of streams and the creation of your own filter stream classes. Includes a full-featured example of creating and using pipes.

Section 7, *Networking*
> Demonstrates how to download text files with the URL class and obtain URL information and content with the `URLConnection` class. Shows how to send and receive datagrams and how to implement clients and servers.

Section 8, *Advanced Graphics and Images*
> Illustrates smooth animation with double-buffering and clipping. Shows how to keep track of images that are being loaded and how to process and manipulate image data.

Section 9, *Advanced Threads*
> Demonstrates thread exclusion and notification with `synchronized`, `wait()`, and `notify()`. Shows how to create thread groups, how to set thread priorities, and how to query information about threads and thread groups.

The code presented in Part II can also be found online at:

> http://www.ora.com/catalog/books/javanut/

Part III: Java Language Reference

Part III of this quick reference consists of eight short sections of reference material on the Java language and related topics. The sections are as follows:

Section 10, *Java Syntax*
> A quick reference of Java language constructs: tables of primitive data types, character escapes, operators, modifiers, reserved words, and documentation comments.

Section 11, *Events*
> A table of Java event types, the GUI components that generate them, and the fields of the Event object that are set for each type.

Section 12, *Fonts, Colors, and Cursors*
> Tables of font names, colors, and cursors defined by Java for platform-independence.

Section 13, *System Properties and Applet Parameters*
> Documents the standard system properties, and explains how you can use properties and parameters to allow customization of your programs and applets.

Section 14, *Applet Security*
> Shows what applets can and cannot do. Provides complete list of security restrictions imposed on untrusted applets.

Section 15, *Java-Related HTML and HTTP Syntax*
> Covers the full syntax of the HTML <APPLET> tag that lets you include applets in your Web pages.

Section 16, *The Unicode Standard*
> Everything you need to know about Unicode, the character set used by Java. Provides an outline of the encoding, and explains how to convert Unicode to UTF-8 form for storage and transmission.

Section 17, *JDK Development Tools*
> Full documentation, in UNIX man-page format, for *java* (the interpreter), *javac* (the compiler), *appletviewer*, and the other tools in Sun's Java Developers Kit.

Part IV: API Quick Reference

Part IV is the real heart of this book. It is a *complete* quick reference for every class, method, and variable in the Java API. The first eight sections document the classes in each of the eight packages in the Java API; the ninth section collects and documents the exception and error classes from all of the packages. Except for error and exception classes, the quick reference is organized alphabetically by package and by class. To look up a class, turn to the section that documents the class's package. To look up a method, turn to the documentation for the class that defines the method.

The documentation for each package begins with an overview of the package and a class hierarchy diagram of the classes defined in the package. This material orients you and provides the context for understanding the information on the individual classes.

The documentation of each class begins with a one or two paragraph overview. This is followed by a listing of all the constants, variables, and methods defined by the class. The listing is in almost-legal Java syntax and looks very much like a Java class definition: an extends clause indicates the superclass of a class, and an implements clause lists any implemented interfaces. Similarly, method and variable declarations include public, static, abstract, final, and similar modifiers to indicate the exact type of the method or variable. Methods are listed with their return type and complete argument list. A `throws` clause indicates any exceptions that a method can throw.

The Java syntax of the class listings is augmented by comments that provide additional information about the methods. The *//Overrides* comment lets you know when a method overrides a method defined in a superclass. The *//Defines* comment is similar—that is, it tells you when a method implements an abstract method defined by a superclass. The *//Empty* comment tells you that the method body is empty (i.e., that the method does nothing). This is often a useful hint that the method should be overridden by a subclass. (Note, however, that methods that simply return `null` are also essentially empty, but are not commented in this way.)

Within each class, variables and methods are grouped into categories in order to better show the overall structure of the class. The categories are always listed in the following order:

1. Public constructors

2. Protected constructors

3. Constants

4. Class (or static) variables

5. Public instance variables

6. Protected instance variables

7. Class (or static) methods

8. Public instance methods

9. Protected instance methods

Within each category, fields are listed alphabetically by variable name or method name, and the start of each category is indicated with a comment. If there are no constructors defined by the class, a comment specifies the Java default constructor. If there are no non-private constructors, a comment notes this fact to indicate that the class is non-instantiable.

Unless a method is explicitly mentioned in the class overview, its documentation is limited to the method prototype. Consider, though, all the information contained in this simple and compact form:

- The name of the method, which, in the context of the class that defines it, helps make the method's purpose clear.

- The return type and argument types of the method, which definitively specify how to invoke the method.

- The argument names, which help make the purpose of each argument clear.

- The method modifiers, such as `public`, `protected`, `abstract`, `final`, `static`, and `synchronized`, which specify how the method can be used and how it works.

- The `throws` clause, which specifies any errors or abnormal exit conditions for the method.

Do keep in mind that this is a quick reference, and it cannot provide definitive descriptions of each method and variable in the API. It has the advantage, however, of being about one tenth the size of the official API documentation shipped with Java. If you can't figure out how to use a method from the information given in this book, read about the method in the online documentation. The next time you use the method, this quick reference should be the only memory jogger you need!

Note that the material in Part V of this book is designed to be used in conjunction with this API quick reference.

Part V: API Cross References

This final part of the book cross references the API documented in Part IV. The sections in this part allow "reverse lookup" of information. In Part IV, for example, you can look up the superclass of a class, or the exceptions thrown by a method. In Part V, by contrast, you can look up the subclasses of a class, or the list of methods that throw a given exception. The sections of Part V (and their uses) are as follows:

Section 27, *Class Defined-In Index*
>   Look up a class name and find out the package in which it is defined. Useful when you want to look up a class's documentation but you don't know in which section of Part IV to look.

Section 28, *Method Defined-In Index*
>   Look up a method name and find out what class, or classes, define that method. Useful when you want to look up a method, but you don't know whether it is defined by a class or by one of the class's superclasses.

Section 29, *Subclass Index*
>   Look up a class and find a list of all its subclasses. Useful for figuring out if you are using the right version of a class, or if there is a more specific subclass that would be better suited to your task.

Section 30, *Implemented-By Index*
>   Look up an interface and find a list of classes that implement that interface. Useful when you know you want to use the interface, but don't know what implementations are available.

Section 31, *Returned-By Index*
>   Look up the name of a class and find a list of methods that return objects of that type. Useful when you know that you want to work with an object of a certain type, but don't know how to obtain an instance of that object.

Section 32, *Passed-To Index*
>   Look up the name of a class and find a list of methods that take arguments of that type. Useful when you have an object and want to figure out what you can do with it.

Section 33, *Thrown-By Index*
>   Look up the name of an exception and find a list of methods that can throw it. Useful when planning exception handling strategies, and debugging programs that mysteriously throw exceptions.

Glossary, Contents, Index, and Tabs

This book also contains a glossary following Part V. Use it to look up unfamiliar Java-related terms. Every Java keyword appears in the glossary, often with example usage, so you can use this section as a simple Java language reference. Finally, don't forget that this book has a table of contents and a subject index, which can help you locate whatever information you're looking for. Also, notice the tabs along the edge of the book. Use these to jump quickly to each part of the book.

Preface

This handbook is a desktop quick reference for Java programmers. It also includes introductory and tutorial material for C and C++ programmers who want to learn Java. Everyone who uses this book should be sure to read the *How to Use This Book* section that precedes this one; it describes the structure of the book and explains how to get the most out of it.

Java Books and Resources

O'Reilly & Associates is developing a series of Java books. The series will include an introductory volume, a language reference, a Java Virtual Machine reference, and a complete set of Java API reference manuals (i.e., manuals that document the Java API in more complete detail than is possible with the quick reference format of this book). In addition, the Java series will include volumes covering advanced topics in Java programming, such as: networking, programming with threads, and distributed computing. Refer to *http://www.ora.com/info/java/* for a complete list of current and upcoming titles in the O'Reilly & Associates Java series.

Sun Microsystems has online reference documentation for the Java API that you may find useful in conjunction with this quick reference handbook. You may want to visit *http://www.javasoft.com/* to view or download this API documentation and other useful documents.

Also, the *comp.lang.java* newsgroup is a central location for discussion about Java. The newsgroup may soon split into a number of subgroups, for more specialized discussion, so be sure to read the FAQ list to find out which groups are most appropriate for your needs.

About the Example Programs

The example programs presented in this book are available online. See *http://www.ora.com/catalog/books/javanut/* for more information on how to download them.

Some of the examples assume that you are using tools like *javac* and *appletviewer* from Sun's Java Developers Kit (JDK). If you are using a development environment or tools from some other vendor, simply follow that vendor's instructions for compiling Java code, running applications, and displaying applets.

Please bear in mind that Java is evolving very quickly. The classes in the Java API still have a number of bugs in the Java 1.0 release, and it seems new platforms and development tools are being announced every week. It's not possible to test all the examples on all platforms, and you may sometimes find that the examples don't work correctly because of bugs in the Java class library or in a particular implementation (or port) of Java. In this case, you'll have to try to find a workaround that fixes the problem on your particular platform—this is simply the price of being on the cutting edge of a new technology.

Conventions Used in This Book

Italic is used for:

- UNIX pathnames, filenames, and program names.

- New terms where they are defined.

Boldface is used for:

- Names of GUI buttons and menus.

`Typewriter Font` is used for:

- Java language keywords, classes, methods, and variables and HTML tags in the main body of the text.

- Command-line options in the main body of the text.

`Italic Typewriter Font` is used for:

- Arguments to methods, since they could be typed in code as shown but are arbitrary names that could be changed.

- Variable expressions in command-line options in the main body of the text.

Franklin Gothic Compressed is used for:

- Java and HTML code set off from the main body of the text and class definitions in the API quick reference.

Franklin Gothic Compressed Bold is used for:

- Class, method, and variable names in class definitions in the API quick reference.

- Command lines and options that should be typed verbatim on the screen.

Franklin Gothic Compressed Italic is used for:

- Arguments to methods and comments in class definitions in the API quick reference.

- Variable expressions in command lines.

Request for Comments

We invite you to help us improve the book. If you have an idea that could make this a more useful programmer's quick reference, or if you find a bug in an example program or an error in the text, let us know by sending mail to *bookquestions@ora.com.*

If we find it necessary to issue errata for this book or to release updated examples or reference information, you'll find that updated information at the site *http://www.ora.com/catalog/books/javanut.*

Acknowledgments

I am grateful for the help of all the people who worked on this book. I had the pleasure of working with my friend and colleague Paula Ferguson, who edited this book. Her careful reading and always-practical suggestions made the book stronger, clearer, and more useful. Paula also wrote Section 1, which is an excellent overview of Java and Java programming.

Mike Loukides got this whole project underway. As the series editor for this and other O'Reilly & Associates Java books, he got me started on the book and provided high-level direction and guidance while it was evolving from a rough outline. Eric Raymond and Troy Downing were technical reviewers—they helped spot my errors and omissions, and offered good advice on making the book more useful to Java programmers.

John Files was the production editor for the book. He coordinated the entire production process, entered changes from edited copy, and handled the meticulous task of fixing line and page breaks in the manuscript. Mary Ann Faughan copyedited the book, Cory Willing proofread it, and Kismet McDonough did a final quality-control check. Seth Maislin wrote the index. Norm Walsh and Stephen Spainhour helped to generate the Windows screendumps that appear in the text. Chris Reilley created the figures, including all the detailed class hierarchy diagrams in Part IV. Edie Freedman designed the cover. Nancy Priest designed the interior format of the book and Lenny Muellner carefully implemented the format in *troff.*

Sue Willing arranged a special printing for the book so that it could appear in bookstores much sooner than would otherwise be possible. Sheryl Avruch and Frank Willison, the Production Manager and Editor-in-Chief at O'Reilly & Associates, made this book a priority and expedited its production.

Part I

Introducing Java

Part I is an introduction to Java and Java programming. If you know how to program in C or C++, these sections should teach you everything you need to know to start programming with Java.

Section 1, *Getting Started with Java*
Section 2, *How Java Differs from C*
Section 3, *Classes and Objects in Java*

Getting Started with Java

You've probably already heard a lot about Java; you wouldn't be reading this book if you didn't think Java was an important new technology. By now, you've probably downloaded a Java-enabled version of Netscape Navigator and played around with some of the impressive applets on Sun's Java site (*http://www.javasoft.com*) and Gamelan (*http://www.gamelan.com*). And now you're itching to start writing your own applets.

Before we get started with our first Java example, it's important to give you a bit of background about the language. With all the media hype surrounding Java (and the World Wide Web and Internet in general), it's easy to lose sight of why Java is so interesting. Lots of attention has been focused on using Java to provide interactive content on Web pages. But most of the Java applets I've seen to date are toys, interesting and attention-grabbing proofs-of-concept that don't solve real-world problems.

What's exciting about Java is that it's a language designed for programming on the Internet. It's a lot more important than ultra-hip Web pages. Java enables us to write completely new kinds of applications. With Java it's possible to imagine a true document-centric system, where a colleague can send you a report packaged with the word processing, spreadsheet, and database software you need to work with it. Or a "game broker" that acts as a matchmaker between players, who then communicate directly with each other to play the game, without the server's intervention. The fact that these applications don't exist yet just means that we haven't figured out how to use the full power of Java.

Java offers the promise that the network will become the computer. If the Internet breaks down barriers, Java removes the last and most difficult of these: the barrier that prevents you from taking software from some random site and executing it on any platform.

Why Java?

Java began life as a programming language for software for consumer electronics: devices such as toasters, microwave ovens, and personal digital assistants. Software for consumer devices has some unique design requirements. For instance, the software needs to be able to work on new computer chips as they are introduced — manufacturers often change the chips they are using as new chips become more cost-effective or introduce new features. The software also needs to be extremely reliable, because when a consumer product fails, the manufacturer typically has to replace the entire device.

A small team at Sun, headed by James Gosling, that was working on this problem quickly discovered that existing programming languages like C and C++ were not up to the task. For one thing, a program written in C or C++ must be compiled for a particular computer chip. When a new chip comes out, the program must be recompiled. The complexity of C and C++ also makes it extremely difficult to write reliable software.

As a result, in 1990 Gosling started designing a new programming language that would be more appropriate for consumer electronics software. This language, originally known as Oak, was small, reliable, and architecture-independent. In 1993, as the Java team continued to work on the design of the new language, the World Wide Web appeared on the Internet and took it by storm. The Java developers realized that an architecture-neutral language like Java would be ideal for programming on the Internet, because a program could run on all of the different types of computers connected to the Internet. In fact, all of the design goals of Java made it ideally suited for Internet programming.

At that point, the development of Java took on new importance for Sun. The team wrote a Web browser, called HotJava, that was the first Web browser to support Java applets. An *applet* is a small Java program that can be embedded in another application. You can include an applet in an HTML document to provide interactive, executable content on a Web page. HotJava demonstrated the power of the Java language in a very visible fashion to programmers and to the rest of the world. And the rest is history.

Programmers started tinkering with the Alpha release of Java that Sun made available, creating all sorts of "cool" applets. Their experience and feedback helped refine the language and its application programming interface (API). At the same time that Sun released the first Beta version of the language, Netscape announced that Version 2.0 of its Web browser, Netscape Navigator, would support Java applets. This support served only to increase the already-strong interest in Java technology, both in the computing world and on the Internet. With companies like IBM, SGI, and Oracle licensing the Java technology from Sun, you can be certain that more software and hardware products will be incorporating Java technology. As this book goes to press, even Microsoft has announced its intention to license Java.

What Is Java?

In "The Java Language: A White Paper," Sun describes Java as follows:

> Java: A simple, object-oriented, distributed, interpreted, robust, secure, architecture neutral, portable, high-performance, multithreaded, and dynamic language.

Sun acknowledges that this is quite a string of buzzwords, but the fact is that they all aptly describe the language. In order to understand the full potential of Java, let's examine each of these buzzwords in terms of the design goals Sun was trying to achieve in creating the language.

Simple

Java is a *simple* language. But what exactly do we mean by simple? One design goal was to create a language that a programmer could learn quickly, so the number of language constructs has been kept small. Another design goal was to make the language look familiar to a majority of programmers for ease of migration. If you are a C or C++ programmer, you'll find that Java uses many of the same language constructs as C and C++.

In order to keep the language both small and familiar, the Java designers removed a number of features available in C and C++. These features are mostly ones that led to poor programming practices or were rarely used. For example, Java does not support the `goto` statement; instead, it provides labelled `break` and `continue` statements and exception handling. Java does not use header files and it eliminates the C preprocessor. Because Java is object-oriented, C constructs like `struct` and `union` have been removed. Java also eliminates the operator overloading and multiple inheritance features of C++.

Perhaps the most important simplification, however, is that Java does not use pointers. Pointers are one of the most bug-prone aspects of C and C++ programming. Since Java does not have structures, and arrays and strings are objects, there's no need for pointers. Java automatically handles the referencing and dereferencing of objects for you. Java also implements automatic garbage collection, so you don't have to worry about memory management issues. All of this frees you from having to worry about dangling pointers, invalid pointer references, and memory leaks, so you can spend your time developing the functionality of your programs.

If it sounds like Java has gutted C and C++, leaving only a shell of a programming language, hold off on that judgment for a bit. As we'll see in Section 2, *How Java Differs from C*, Java is actually a full-featured and very elegant language.

Object-Oriented

Java is an *object-oriented* programming language. As a programmer, this means that you focus on the data in your application and methods that manipulate that data, rather than thinking strictly in terms of procedures. If you're accustomed to procedure-based programming in C, you may find that you need to change how you design your programs when you use Java. Once you see how powerful this new paradigm is, however, you'll quickly adjust to it.

In an object-oriented system, a *class* is a collection of data and methods that operate on that data. Taken together, the data and methods describe the state and behavior of an *object*. Classes are arranged in a hierarchy, so that a subclass can inherit behavior from its superclass. A class hierarchy always has a root class; this is a class with very general behavior.

To take an example from the natural world, you might define a "living thing" class to be the root of your class hierarchy. This class could have two subclasses: "animal" and "plant." You might further define the "mammal" class as a subclass of "animal."

Finally, if you defined a "human" class as a subclass of "mammal," the "human" class would inherit behavior from "mammal," "animal," and "living thing".

Java comes with an extensive set of classes, arranged in *packages*, that you can use in your programs. For example, Java provides classes that create graphical user interface components (the `java.awt` package), classes that handle input and output (the `java.io` package), and classes that support networking functionality (the `java.net` package). The `Object` class (in the `java.lang` package) serves as the root of the Java class hierarchy. For more information on the Java API, see Part IV, *API Quick-Reference*.

Unlike C++, Java was designed to be object-oriented from the ground up. Most things in Java are objects; the simple numeric, character, and boolean types are the only exceptions. While Java is designed to look like C++, you'll find that Java removes many of the complexities of that language. If you are a C++ programmer, you'll want to study the object-oriented constructs in Java carefully. Although the syntax is often similar to C++, the behavior is not nearly so analogous. For a complete description of the object-oriented features of Java, see Section 3, *Classes and Objects in Java*.

Distributed

Java is designed to support applications on networks; it is a *distributed* language. Java supports various levels of network connectivity through classes in the `java.net` package. For instance, the `URL` class allows a Java application to open and access remote objects on the Internet. With Java, it's just as easy to open a remote file as it is a local file. Java also supports reliable stream network connections with the `Socket` class, so you can create distributed clients and servers. For more information about Java's networking capabilities, see Section 7, *Networking*, and Section 24, *The java.net Package*.

Interpreted

The Java compiler generates byte-codes, rather than native machine code. To actually run a Java program, you use the Java interpreter to execute the compiled byte-codes, so Java is an *interpreted* language. Java byte-codes provide an architecture-neutral object file format; the code is designed to transport programs efficiently to multiple platforms. A Java program can be run on any system that implements the Java interpreter and run-time system. Collectively, the interpreter and run-time system implement a virtual machine called the Java Virtual Machine.

In an interpreted environment, the standard "link" phase of program development pretty much vanishes. If Java has a link phase at all, it is only the process of loading new classes into the environment, which is an incremental, lightweight process. As a result, Java supports rapid prototyping and easy experimentation, which leads to faster program development. This is in sharp contrast with the more traditional and time-consuming process of compiling, linking, and testing.

Robust

Its origin as a language for software for consumer electronics means that Java has been designed for writing highly reliable or *robust* software. Java certainly doesn't eliminate the need for software quality assurance; it's still quite possible to write unreliable software. However, Java does eliminate certain types of programming errors, which makes it considerably easier to write reliable software.

Java is a strongly typed language, which allows for extensive compile-time checking for potential type-mismatch problems. Java is more strongly typed than C++, which inherits a number of compile-time laxities from C, especially in the area of method declarations. Java requires explicit method declarations; it does not support C-style implicit declarations. These stringent requirements ensure that the compiler can catch method invocation errors, which leads to more reliable programs.

One of the most significant enhancements in terms of reliability is Java's memory model. Java does not support pointers, which eliminates the possibility of overwriting memory and corrupting data. Similarly, Java's automatic garbage collection prevents memory leaks and other pernicious bugs related to dynamic-memory allocation and deallocation. The Java interpreter also performs a number of run-time checks, such as verifying that all array and string accesses are within bounds.

Exception handling is another feature in Java that makes for more robust programs. An *exception* is a signal that some sort of exceptional condition, like an error, has occured. Using the `try/catch/finally` statement, you can group all of your error handling code in one place, which greatly simplifies the task of error handling and recovery.

Secure

One of the mostly highly touted aspects of Java is that it's a *secure* language. Security is an important concern, as Java is meant to be used in networked environments. Without some assurance of security, you certainly wouldn't want to download an applet from a random site on the Internet and let it run on your computer. Java implements several security mechanisms to protect you against code that might try to create a virus or invade your file system. All of these security mechanisms are based on the premise that nothing is to be trusted.

Security actually goes hand-in-hand with robustness. Java's memory allocation model is one of its main defenses against malicious code. As we've already seen, Java does not have pointers, so a programmer cannot get behind the scenes and forge pointers to memory. More importantly, the Java compiler does not handle memory layout decisions, so a programmer cannot guess the actual memory layout of a class by looking at its declaration. Memory references in compiled Java code are resolved to real memory addresses at run-time by the Java interpreter.

Many of the defenses in Java are there to protect you from untrusted applets. The Java run-time system uses a byte-code verification process to ensure that code loaded over the network does not violate any Java language restrictions. Part of this security mechanism involves how classes are loaded from across the network. For example, loaded classes are placed in a separate namespace than local classes, to prevent a malicious applet from replacing standard Java classes with its own versions. For more information about applet security, see Section 14, *Applet Security*.

Of course, security isn't a black-and-white thing. No one can guarantee that a Java program won't contain malicious code of any form; what Sun can claim is that Java makes rogue software more difficult to write. Java anticipates and defends against most of the techniques that have historically been used to trick software into misbehaving. It's impossible to say that Java, or any system, is "perfectly secure." Sooner or later, someone will invent new ways to attack software systems and the ball will be back in Sun's court. In real life, the best you can get is "reasonably safe," where the definition of "reasonably" depends on some tradeoff between functionality and security. The Net is clearly a dangerous environment. Java offers a reasonable middle ground between ignoring the security problem and being paralyzed by it.

Architecture Neutral

As we've already seen, Java programs are compiled to an architecture neutral byte-code format. The primary advantage of this approach is that it allows a Java application to run on any system, as long as that system implements the Java Virtual Machine. Since Java was designed to create network-based applications, it is important that Java applications be able to run on all of the different kinds of systems found on the Internet.

But the architecture neutral approach is useful beyond the scope of network-based applications. As an application developer in today's software market, you probably want to develop versions of your application that can run on PCs, Macs, and UNIX workstations. With multiple flavors of UNIX, Windows 95 and Windows NT on the PC, and the new PowerPC Macintosh, it is becoming increasingly difficult to produce software for all of the possible platforms. If you write your application in Java, however, it can run on all platforms. And using the the Abstract Windowing Toolkit (the java.awt package, described in Section 19, *The java.awt Package*), your application can even have the appropriate appearance and behavior for each platform.

Portable

Being architecture neutral is one big part of being *portable*. But Java goes even further, by making sure that there are no "implementation-dependent" aspects of the language specification. For example, Java explicitly specifies the size of each of the primitive data types, as well as its arithmetic behavior. (These data types are described in Section 10, *Java Syntax*.)

The Java environment itself is also portable to new hardware platforms and operating systems. The Java compiler is written in Java, while the Java run-time system is written in ANSI C. The run-time system has a clean portability boundary that is essentially POSIX-compliant.

High-performance

Java is an interpreted language, so it is never going to be as fast as a compiled language like C. In fact, Java is on the average about 20 times slower than C. But before you throw up your arms in disgust, be aware that this speed is more than adequate to run interactive, GUI and network-based applications, where the application is often idle, waiting for the user to do something, or waiting for data from the network.

Of course, there are some situations where performance is critical. To support those situations, the Java designers are working on "just in time" compilers that can translate Java byte-codes into machine code for a particular CPU at run-time. The Java byte-code format was designed with these "just in time" compilers in mind, so the process of generating machine code is fairly simple and it produces reasonably good code. In fact, Sun claims that the performance of byte-codes converted to machine code is nearly as good as native C or C++.

When you are considering performance, it's important to remember where Java falls in the spectrum of available programming languages. At one end of the spectrum, there are high-level, fully-interpreted scripting languages such as Tcl and the UNIX shells. These languages are great for prototyping and they are highly portable, but they are also very slow. At the other end of the spectrum, you have low-level compiled languages like C and C++. These languages offer high performance, but they suffer in terms of reliability and portability.

Java falls in the middle of the spectrum. The performance of Java's interpreted bytecodes is much better than the high-level scripting languages (even Perl), but it still offers the simplicity and portability of those languages. And while Java isn't as fast as a compiled language, it does provide an architecture neutral environment in which it is possible to write reliable programs.

Multithreaded

In a GUI-based network application such as a Web browser, it's easy to imagine multiple things going on at the same time. A user could be listening to an audio clip while she is scrolling a page, and in the background the browser is downloading an image. Java is a *multithreaded* language; it provides support for multiple threads of execution (also called lightweight processes) that can handle different tasks.

One benefit of multithreading is that it improves the interactive performance of graphical applications for the user. Unfortunately for the programmer, writing code in C or C++ that deals with multiple threads can be quite a headache. The main difficulty lies in making sure that routines are implemented so that they can be run by multiple concurrent threads. If a routine changes the value of a state variable, for example, then only one thread can be executing the routine at a time. With C or C++, writing a multithreaded application involves acquiring locks to run certain routines and then releasing them. Writing code that explicitly handles locks is problematic and can easily lead to deadlock situations.

Java makes programming with threads much easier, by providing built-in language support for threads. The `java.lang` package provides a `Thread` class that supports methods to start a thread, run a thread, stop a thread, and check on the status of a thread. See Section 23, *The java.lang Package*, for more details.

Java's thread support also includes a set of synchronization primitives. These primitives are based on the monitor and condition variable paradigm, a widely-used synchronization scheme developed by C.A.R. Hoare. With the `synchronized` keyword, you can specify that certain methods within a class cannot be run concurrently. These methods run under the control of monitors to ensure that variables remain in a consistent state.

A number of the examples in the various sections of Part II, *Programming with the Java API*, show the use of threads.

Dynamic

The Java language was designed to adapt to an evolving environment; it is a *dynamic* language. For example, Java loads in classes as they are needed, even from across a network. Classes in Java also have a run-time representation. Unlike in C or C++, if your program is handed an object, it can find out what class it belongs to by checking the run-time type information. The run-time class definitions in Java make it possible to dynamically link classes into a running system.

A Simple Example

Enough, already! By now you should have a pretty good idea of what Java is all about. So let's stop talking about abstract buzzwords and look at some concrete Java code. Before we look at an interesting applet, though, we are going to pay tribute to that ubiquitous favorite, "Hello World."

Hello World

Example 1-1 shows the simplest possible Java program: "Hello World."

Example 1-1: Hello World

```
public class HelloWorld {
    public static void main(String[] args) {
        System.out.println("Hello World!");
    }
}
```

This program, like every Java program, consists of a public class definition. The class contains a method or procedure named `main()`, which is where the interpreter starts executing the program. The body of `main()` consists of only a single line, which prints out the message:

```
Hello World!
```

This program must be saved in a file with the same name as the public class plus a *.java* extension. To compile it, you would use *javac*:*

```
% javac HelloWorld.java
```

This command produces the *HelloWorld.class* file in the current directory. To run the program, you use the Java interpreter, *java*:

```
% java HelloWorld
```

Note that when you invoke the interpreter, you do not supply the *.class* extension for the file you want to run.

A Scribble Applet

Example 1-2 shows a less trivial Java program. This program is an applet, rather than a standalone Java application. It runs inside an applet viewer or Web browser, and lets the user draw (or scribble) with the mouse, as illustrated in Figure 1-1.

Example 1-2: A Java applet

```
import java.applet.*;
import java.awt.*;

public class Scribble extends Applet {
    private int last_x = 0;
    private int last_y = 0;
    private Color current_color = Color.black;
```

---

*Assuming you're using Sun's Java Developers Kit (JDK). If you're using a Java development package from some other vendor, follow your vendor's instructions.

Figure 1-1: A Java applet running in a Web browser

Example 1-2: A Java applet (continued)

```
private Button clear_button;
private Choice color_choices;

// Called to initialize the applet.
public void init() {
        // Set the background color
        this.setBackground(Color.white);

        // Create a button and add it to the applet.
        // Also, set the button's colors
        clear_button = new Button("Clear");
        clear_button.setForeground(Color.black);
        clear_button.setBackground(Color.lightGray);
        this.add(clear_button);

        // Create a menu of colors and add it to the applet.
        // Also set the menus's colors and add a label.
        color_choices = new Choice();
        color_choices.addItem("black");
        color_choices.addItem("red");
        color_choices.addItem("yellow");
```

Example 1-2: A Java applet (continued)

```
            color_choices.addItem("green");
            color_choices.setForeground(Color.black);
            color_choices.setBackground(Color.lightGray);
            this.add(new Label("Color: "));
            this.add(color_choices);
        }

        // Called when the user clicks the mouse to start a scribble
        public boolean mouseDown(Event e, int x, int y)
        {
            last_x = x; last_y = y;
            return true;
        }

        // Called when the user scribbles with the mouse button down
        public boolean mouseDrag(Event e, int x, int y)
        {
            Graphics g = this.getGraphics();
            g.setColor(current_color);
            g.drawLine(last_x, last_y, x, y);
            last_x = x;
            last_y = y;
            return true;
        }

        // Called when the user clicks the button or chooses a color
        public boolean action(Event event, Object arg) {
            // If the Clear button was clicked on, handle it.
            if (event.target == clear_button) {
                Graphics g = this.getGraphics();
                Rectangle r = this.bounds();
                g.setColor(this.getBackground());
                g.fillRect(r.x, r.y, r.width, r.height);
                return true;
            }
            // Otherwise if a color was chosen, handle that
            else if (event.target == color_choices) {
                if (arg.equals("black")) current_color = Color.black;
                else if (arg.equals("red")) current_color = Color.red;
                else if (arg.equals("yellow")) current_color = Color.yellow;
                else if (arg.equals("green")) current_color = Color.green;
                return true;
            }
            // Otherwise, let the superclass handle it.
            else return super.action(event, arg);
        }
    }
```

Don't expect to be able to understand the entire applet at this point. It is here to give you the flavor of the language. In Section 2, *How Java Differs from C*, and Section 3, *Classes and Objects in Java*, we'll explain everything you need to know to understand this example. Then in Section 4, *Applets*, we'll present a number of example applets, several of which are a lot like this one.

The first thing you should notice when browsing through the code is that it looks reassuringly like C and C++. The if and return statements are familiar. Assignment of values to variables uses the expected syntax. Procedures (called "methods" in Java) are recognizable as such.

The second thing to notice is the object-oriented nature of the code. As you can see at the top of the example, the program consists of the definition of a public class. The name of the class we are defining is Scribble; it is an extension, or subclass, of the Applet class. (The full name of the Applet class is java.applet.Applet. One of the import statements at the top of the example allows us to refer to Applet by this shorter name.)

Classes are said to "encapsulate" data and methods. As you can see, our Scribble class contains both variable and method declarations. The methods are actually defined inside of the class. The methods of a class are often invoked through an instance of the class. Thus you see lines like:

```
color_choices.addItem("black");
```

This line of code invokes the addItem() method of the object referred to by the color_choices variable. If you're a C programmer, but not a C++ programmer, this syntax may take a little getting used to. We'll see lots more of it in Sections 2 and 3. Note that this is a keyword, not a variable name. It refers to the current object; in this example, it refers to the Scribble object.

The init() method of an applet is called by the Web browser or applet viewer when it is starting the applet up. In our example, this method creates a **Clear** button and a menu of color choices, and then adds these GUI components to the applet. Section 5, *Graphical User Interfaces*, demonstrates the use of these components in much more detail, and Section 19, *The java.awt Package*, contains quick reference documentation for all the GUI classes.

The mouseDown() and mouseDrag() methods are called when the user clicks and drags the mouse. These are the methods that are responsible for drawing lines as the user scribbles. The action() method is invoked when the user clicks on the **Clear** button or selects a color from the menu of colors. The body of the method determines which of these two "events" has occurred and handles the event appropriately. Sections 4 and 5 both contain examples that illustrate event handling with mouseDown(), mouseDrag(), action(), and other methods in great detail. Section 11, *Events*, contains quick reference information about events.

To compile this example, you'd save it in a file named *Scribble.java* and use *javac*:

```
% javac Scribble.java
```

This example is an applet, not a standalone program like our "Hello World" example. It does not have a main() method, and therefore cannot be run directly by the Java interpreter. Instead, we must reference it in an HTML file and run the applet in an applet viewer or Web browser. It is the applet viewer or Web browser that runs the Java interpreter internally to interpret the applet's compiled code. To include the applet in a Web page, we'd use an HTML fragment like the following:

```
<APPLET code="Scribble.class" width=500 height=300>
</APPLET>
```

Example 1-3 shows a complete HTML file that we might use to display the applet. Section 15, *Java-Related HTML and HTTP Syntax*, explains the HTML syntax for applets in full detail.

Example 1-3: An HTML file that contains an applet

```
<HTML>
<HEAD>
<TITLE>The Scribble Applet</TITLE>
</HEAD>
<BODY>
If you're using a Java-enabled browser, please scribble away
in the applet below.  If your browser can't run Java
applets, you're out of luck.  Sorry!
<P>
<APPLET code="Scribble.class" width=500 height=300>
</APPLET>
</BODY>
</HTML>
```

Suppose we save this example HTML file as *Scribble.html*. Then to run this applet, you could use Sun's *appletviewer* command like this:

```
% appletviewer Scribble.html
```

You could also display the applet by viewing the *Scribble.html* file in your Web browser, if your browser supports Java applets. Figure 1-1 showed the `Scribble` applet running in Netscape Navigator.*

---

*Some beta versions of Netscape Navigator can't run applets loaded as local files—in these buggy versions of Netscape, the HTML file must actually be downloaded from a Web server. By the time you read this, chances are good that your version of Netscape will not have this bug.

How Java Differs from C

Java is a lot like C, which makes it relatively easy for C programmers to learn. But there are a number of important differences between C and Java, such as the lack of a preprocessor, the use of 16-bit Unicode characters, and the exception handling mechanism. This chapter explains those differences, so that programmers who already know C can start programming in Java right away!

This chapter also points out similarities and differences between Java and C++. C++ programmers should beware, though: While Java borrows a lot of terminology and even syntax from C++, the analogies between Java and C++ are not nearly as strong as those between Java and C. C++ programmers should be careful not to be lulled into a false sense of familiarity with Java just because the languages share a number of keywords!

One of the main areas in which Java differs from C, of course, is that Java is an object-oriented language and has mechanisms to define classes and create objects that are instances of those classes. Java's object-oriented features are a topic for a chapter of their own, and they'll be explained in detail in Section 3, *Classes and Objects in Java.*

Program Structure and Environment

A program in Java consists of one or more class definitions, each of which has been compiled into its own *.class* file of Java Virtual Machine object code. One of these classes must define a method `main()`, which is where the program starts running.*

To invoke a Java program, you run the Java interpreter, *java,* and specify the name of the class that contains the `main()` method. You should omit the *.class* extension when doing this. Note that a Java applet is not an application—it is a Java class that

---

*Method is an object-oriented term for a procedure or function. You'll see it used throughout this book.

---

is loaded and run by already running Java application such as a Web browser or applet viewer.

The `main()` method that the Java interpreter invokes to start a Java program must have the following prototype:

```
public static void main(String argv[])
```

The Java interpreter runs until the `main()` method returns, or until the interpreter reaches the end of `main()`. If no threads have been created by the program, the interpreter exits. Otherwise, the interpreter continues running until the last thread terminates.

Command-Line Arguments

The single argument to `main()` is an array of strings, conventionally named `argv[]`. The length of this array (which would be passed as the `argc` argument in C) is available as `argv.length`, as is the case with any Java array. The elements of the array are the arguments, if any, that appeared on the interpreter command line after the class name. Note that the first element of the array is *not* the name of the class, as a C programmer might expect it to be. Example 2-1 shows how you could write a UNIX-style *echo* command (a program that simply prints out its arguments) in Java.

Example 2-1: An echo program in Java

```
public class echo {
    public static void main(String argv[]) {
        for(int i=0; i < argv.length; i++)
            System.out.print(argv[i] + " ");
        System.out.print("\n");
        System.exit(0);
    }
}
```

Program Exit Value

Note that `main()` must be declared to return `void`. Thus you cannot return a value from your Java program with a `return` statement in `main()`. If you need to return a value, call `System.exit()` with the desired integer value, as we've done in Example 2-1. Note that the handling and interpretation of this exit value are, of course, operating-system dependent. `System.exit()` causes the Java interpreter to exit immediately, whether or not other threads are running.

Environment

The Java API does not allow a Java program to read operating system environment variables because they are platform-dependent. However, Java defines a similar, platform-independent mechanism, known as the system properties list, for associating textual values with names. A Java program can look up the value of a named property with the `System.getProperty()` method:

```
String homedir = System.getProperty("user.home");
String debug = System.getProperty("myapp.debug");
```

Section 2: How Java Differs from C

The Java interpreter automatically defines a number of standard system properties when it starts up. You can insert additional property definitions into the list by specifying the -D option to the interpreter:

```
%java -Dmyapp.debug=true myapp
```

See Section 13, *System Properties and Applet Parameters*, for more information on system properties.

The Name Space: Packages, Classes, and Fields

As a language that is designed to support dynamic loading of modules over the entire Internet, Java takes special care to avoid name space conflicts. Global variables are simply not part of the language. Neither are "global" functions or procedures, for that matter.

No Global Variables

In Java, every variable and method is declared within a class and forms part of that class. Also, every class is part of a *package*. Thus every Java variable or method may be referred to by its fully qualified name, which consists of the package name, the class name, and the field name (i.e., the variable or the method name), all separated by periods. Package names are themselves usually composed of multiple period-separated components. Thus, the fully qualified name for a method might be:

```
david.games.tetris.SoundEffects.play()
```

Packages, Classes, and Directory Structure

In Java, every compiled class is stored in a separate file. The name of this file must be the same as the name of the class, with the extension *.class* added. Thus the class `SoundEffects` would be stored in the file *SoundEffects.class*. This class file must be stored in a directory that has the same components as the package name. For example, if the fully qualified name of a class is `david.games.tetris.SoundEffects`, the full path of the class file must be *david/games/tetris/SoundEffects.class*.*

A file of Java source code should have the extension *.java*. It consists of one or more class definitions. If more than one class is defined in a *.java* file, only one of the classes may be declared `public` (i.e., available outside of the package), and that class must have the same name as the source file (minus the *.java* extension, of course). If a source file contains more than one class definition, those classes are compiled into multiple *.class* files.

Packages of the Java API

The Java API consists of the classes defined in the eight packages listed in Table 2-1.

---

*We'll use UNIX-style directory specifications in this book. If you are a Windows programmer, simply change all the forward slashes in filenames to backward slashes. Similarly, in path specifications, change colons to semicolons.

Table 2-1: The Packages of the Java API

Package name	Contents
java.applet	Classes for implementing applets
java.awt	Classes for graphics, text, windows, and GUIs
java.awt.image	Classes for image processing
java.awt.peer	Interfaces for a platform-independent GUI toolkit
java.io	Classes for all kinds of input and output
java.lang	Classes for the core language
java.net	Classes for networking
java.util	Classes for useful data types

The Java Class Path

The Java interpreter looks up its system classes in a platform-dependent default location, or relative to the directories specified by the -classpath argument. It looks
up user-defined classes in the current directory and relative to the directories specified by the CLASSPATH environment variable. The directories in a class path specification should be colon-separated on a UNIX system, and semicolon-separated on a
Windows system. For example, on a UNIX system, you might use:

```
setenv CLASSPATH .:~/classes:/usr/local/classes
```

This tells Java to search in and beneath the specified directories for non-system
classes.

Globally Unique Package Names

The Java designers have proposed an Internet-wide unique package naming scheme
that is based on the domain name of the organization at which the package is developed.

Figure 2-1 shows some fully qualified names, which include package, class, and field
components.

The package Statement

The package statement must appear as the first statement (i.e., the first text other
than comments and whitespace) in a file of Java source code, if it appears at all. It
specifies which package the code in the file is part of. Java code that is part of a particular package has access to all classes (public and non-public) in the package,
and to all non-private methods and fields in all those classes. When Java code is
part of a named package, the compiled class file must be placed at the appropriate
position in the CLASSPATH directory hierarchy before it can be accessed by the Java
interpreter or other utilities.

If the package statement is omitted from a file, the code in that file is part of an
unnamed default package. This is convenient for small test programs, or during
development, because it means that the code can be interpreted from the current
directory.

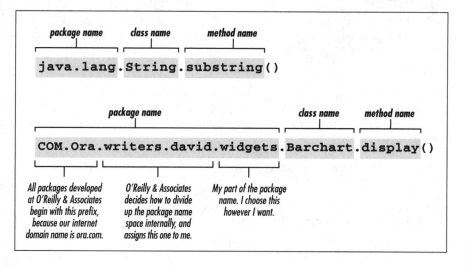

Figure 2-1: Fully qualified names in Java

The import Statement

The import statement makes Java classes available to the current class under an abbreviated name. Public Java classes are always available by their fully qualified names, assuming that the appropriate class file can be found (and is readable) relative to the CLASSPATH environment variable. import doesn't actually make the class available or "read it in"; it simply saves you typing and makes your code more legible.

Any number of import statements may appear in a Java program. They must appear, however, after the optional package statement at the top of the file, and before the first class or interface definition in the file.

There are three forms of the import statement:

```
import    package ;
import    package.class ;
import    package.* ;
```

The first form allows the specified package to be known by the name of its last component. For example, the following import statement allows java.awt.image.ImageFilter to be called image.ImageFilter:

```
import java.awt.image;
```

The second form allows the specified class in the specified package to be known by its class name alone. Thus, this import statement allows you to type Hashtable instead of java.util.Hashtable:

```
import java.util.Hashtable;
```

Finally, the third form of the import statement makes all classes in a package available by their class name. For example, the following import statement is implicit (you need not specify it yourself) in every Java program:

```
import java.lang.*;
```

It makes the core classes of the language available by their unqualified class names. If two packages imported with this form of the statement contain classes with the same name, it is an error to use either of those ambiguous classes without using its fully qualified name.

Access to Packages, Classes, and Fields

Java has the following rules about access to packages, classes, and fields within classes. Note that the public, private, and protected keywords used in these rules will be explained in more detail in the next chapter.

- A package is accessible if the appropriate files and directories are accessible (e.g., if local files have appropriate read permissions, or if they can be downloaded via the network).

- All classes and interfaces in a package are accessible to all other classes and interfaces in the same package. It is not possible to define classes in Java that are visible only within a single file of source code.

- A class declared public in one package is accessible within another package, assuming that the package itself is accessible. A non-public class is not accessible outside of its package.

- Fields (variables or methods) within a class are accessible from a different class within the same package, as long as they are not declared private or private protected. private fields are accessible only within their own class and private protected fields are accessible only within their own class and within subclasses.

- Fields within a class are accessible from a different package as long as the class is accessible, and the field is declared public, or the field is declared protected or private protected and the access is from a subclass of that class.

- All fields of a class are accessible from within that class.

Local Variables

The name space rules we've been describing apply to packages, classes, and the fields within classes. Java also supports local variables, declared within method definitions. These local variables behave just like local variables in C—they do not have globally unique hierarchical names, nor do they have access modifiers like public and private.

Comments

Java supports three types of comments:

- A standard C-style comment that begins with `/*` and continues until the next `*/`. As in most implementations of C, this style of comment cannot be nested.

- A C++-style comment that begins with `//` and continues until the end of the line.

- A special "doc comment" that begins with `/**` and continues until the next `*/`. These comments may not be nested. Doc comments are specially processed by the *javadoc* program to produce simple online documentation from the Java source code. See Section 10, *Java Syntax*, for more information on the doc comment syntax, and Section 17, *JDK Development Tools*, for more information on the *javadoc* program.

Since C-style comments do not nest, it is a good idea to use C++-style `//` comments for most of your short comments within method bodies. This allows you to use `/* */` comments to comment out large blocks of code when you need to do that during development. This is especially important because, as you will see, Java does not support a preprocessor that allows you to use `#if 0` to comment out a block.

No Preprocessor

Java does not include any kind of preprocessor like the C *cpp* preprocessor. It may seem hard to imagine programming without `#define`, `#include`, and `#ifdef`, but in fact, Java really does not require these constructs.

Defining Constants

Any variable declared `final` in Java is a constant—its value must be specified with an initializer when it is declared, and that value may never be changed. The Java equivalent of a C `#define`'ed constant is a `static final` variable declared within a class definition. If the compiler can compute the value of such a `static final` variable at compile-time, it uses the computed value to pre-compute other compile-time constants that refer to the value. The variable `java.lang.Math.PI` is an example of such a constant. It is declared like this:

```
public final class Math {
    ...
    public static final double PI = 3.14159.....;
    ...
}
```

Note two things about this example. First, the C convention of using CAPITAL letters for constants is also a Java convention. Second, note the advantage Java constants have over C preprocessor constants: Java constants have globally unique hierarchial names, while constants defined with the C preprocessor always run the risk of a name collision. Also, Java constants are strongly typed and allow better type-checking by the compiler than C preprocessor constants.

Defining Macros

The C preprocessor allows you to define macros—a construct that looks like a function invocation but that is actually replaced directly with C code, saving the overhead of a function call. Java has no equivalent to this sort of macro, but compiler technology has advanced to a point where macros are rarely necessary any more. A good Java compiler should automatically be able to "inline" short Java methods where appropriate.

Including Files

Java does not have a #include directive, but it does not need one. Java defines a mapping of fully qualified class names (like java.lang.Math) to a directory and file structure (like *java/lang/Math.class*). This means that when the Java compiler needs to read in a specified class file, it knows exactly where to find it and does not need a special directive to tell it where to look.

Furthermore, Java does not make the distinction between *declaring* a variable or procedure and *defining* it that C does. This means that there is no need for C-style header files or function prototypes—a single Java object file serves as the interface definition and implementation for a class.

Java does have an import statement, which is superficially similar to the C preprocessor #include directive. What this statement does, however, is tell the compiler that the current file is using the specified classes, or classes from the specified package, and allows us to refer to those classes with abbreviated names. For example, since the compiler implicitly imports all the classes of the java.lang package, we can refer to the constant java.lang.Math.PI by the shorter name Math.PI.

Conditional Compilation

Java does not have any form of the C #ifdef or #if directives to perform conditional compilation. In theory, conditional compilation is not necessary in Java since it is a platform-independent language, and thus there are no platform dependencies that require the technique. In practice, however, conditional compilation is still often useful in Java—to provide slightly different user interfaces on different platforms, for example, or to support optional inclusion of debugging code in programs.

While Java does not define explicit constructs for conditional compilation, a good Java compiler (such as Sun's *javac*) performs conditional compilation implicitly—that is, it does not compile code if it can prove that the code will never be executed. Generally, this means that code within an if statement testing an expression that is always false is not included. Thus, placing code within an if (false) block is equivalent to surrounding it with #if 0 and #endif in C.

Conditional compilation also works with constants, which, as we saw above, are static final variables. A class might define the constant like this:

```
private static final boolean DEBUG = false;
```

With such a constant defined, any code within an if (DEBUG) block is not actually compiled into the class file. To activate debugging for the class, it is only necessary to change the value of the constant to true and recompile the class.

Unicode and Character Escapes

Java characters, strings, and identifiers (e.g., variable, method, and class names) are composed of 16-bit Unicode characters. This makes Java programs relatively easy to internationalize for non-English-speaking users. It also makes the language easier to work with for non-English-speaking programmers—a Thai programmer could use the Thai alphabet for class and method names in her Java code.

If two-byte characters seem confusing or intimidating to you, fear not. The Unicode character set is compatible with ASCII and the first 256 characters (0x0000 to 0x00FF) are identical to the ISO8859-1 (Latin-1) characters 0x00 to 0xFF. Furthermore, the Java language design and the Java `String` API make the character representation entirely transparent to you. If you are using only Latin-1 characters, there is no way that you can even distinguish a Java 16-bit character from the 8-bit characters you are familiar with. For more information on Unicode, see Section 16, *The Unicode Standard*.

Most platforms cannot display all 34,000 currently defined Unicode characters, so Java programs may be written (and Java output may appear) with special Unicode escape sequences. Anywhere within a Java program (not only within character and string literals), a Unicode character may be represented with the Unicode escape sequence \u*xxxx*, where *xxxx* is a sequence of one to four hexadecimal digits.

Java also supports all of the standard C character escape sequences, such as \n, \t, and *xxx* (where *xxx* is three octal digits). Note, however, that Java does not support line continuation with \ at the end of a line. Long strings must either be specified on a single long line, or they must be created from shorter strings using the string concatenation (+) operator. (Note that the concatenation of two constant strings is done at compile-time rather than at run-time, so using the + operator in this way is not inefficient.)

There are two important differences between Unicode escapes and C-style escape characters. First, as we've noted, Unicode escapes can appear anywhere within a Java program, while the other escape characters can appear only in character and string constants.

The second, and more subtle, difference is that Unicode \u escape sequences are processed before the other escape characters, and thus the two types of escape sequences can have very different semantics. A Unicode escape is simply an alternative way to represent a character that may not be displayable on certain (non-Unicode) systems. Some of the character escapes, however, represent special characters in a way that prevents the usual interpretation of those characters by the compiler. The following examples make this difference clear. Note that \u0022 and \u005c are the Unicode escapes for the double-quote character and the backslash character.

```
// \" represents a " character, and prevents the normal
// interpretation of that character by the compiler.
// This is a string consisting of a double-quote character.
String quote = "\"";

// We can't represent the same string with a single Unicode escape.
// \u0022 has exactly the same meaning to the compiler as ".
// The string below turns into """": an empty string followed
// by an unterminated string, which yields a compilation error.
String quote = "\u0022";
```

```
// Here we represent both characters of an \" escape as
// Unicode escapes. This turns into "\"", and is the same
// string as in our first example.
String quote = "\u005c\u0022";
```

Primitive Data Types

Java adds `byte` and `boolean` primitive types to the standard set of C types. In addition, it strictly defines the size and signedness of its types. In C, an `int` may be 16, 32, or 64 bits, and a `char` may act signed or unsigned depending on the platform. Not so in Java. In C, an uninitialized local variable usually has garbage as its value. In Java, all variables have guaranteed default values, though the compiler may warn you in places where you rely, accidentally or not, on these default values. Table 2-2 lists Java's primitive data types. The subsections below provide details about these types.

Table 2-2: Java Primitive Data Types

Type	Contains	Default	Size	Min Value	Max Value
boolean	true or false	false	1 bit	N.A.	N.A.
char	Unicode character	\u0000	16 bits	\u0000	\uFFFF
byte	signed integer	0	8 bits	-128	127
short	signed integer	0	16 bits	-32768	32767
int	signed integer	0	32 bits	-2147483648	2147483647
long	signed integer	0	64 bits	-9223372036854775808	9223372036854775807
float	IEEE 754 floating-point	0.0	32 bits	±3.40282347E+38	±1.40239846E-45
double	IEEE 754 floating-point	0.0	64 bits	±1.79769313486231570E+308	±4.94065645841246544E-324

The boolean Type

`boolean` values are not integers, may not be treated as integers, and may never be cast to or from any other type. To perform C-style conversions between a `boolean` value b and an `int` i, use the following code:

```
b = (i != 0);     // integer-to-boolean: non-0 -> true; 0 -> false;
i = (b)?1:0;      // boolean-to-integer: true -> 1; false -> 0;
```

The char Type

Values of type char do not have a sign. If a char is cast to a byte or a short, a negative value may result.

The char type in Java holds a two-byte Unicode character. While this may seem intimidating to those not familiar with Unicode and the techniques of program internationalization, it is in fact totally transparent. Java does not provide a way to compute the size of a variable, nor does it allow any sort of pointer arithmetic. What this means is that if you are only using ASCII or Latin-1 characters, there is no way to distinguish a Java char from a C char.

Integral Types

All integral types, other than char, are signed. There is no unsigned keyword as there is in C.

It is not legal to write long int or short int as it is in C.

A long constant may be distinguished from other integral constants by appending the character 1 or L to it.

Integer division by zero or modulo zero causes an ArithmeticException to be thrown.*

Floating-Point Types

Floating-point literals may be specified to be of type float by appending an f or F to the value; they may be specified to be of type double by appending a d or D.

float and double types have special values that may be the result of certain floating-point operations: positive infinity, negative infinity, negative zero and not-a-number. The java.lang.Float and java.lang.Double classes define some of these values as constants: POSITIVE_INFINITY, NEGATIVE_INFINITY, and NaN.

NaN is unordered—comparing it to any other number, including itself, yields false. Use Float.isNaN() or Double.isNaN() to test for NaN.

Negative zero compares equal to regular zero (positive zero), but the two zeros may be distinguished by division: one divided by negative zero yields negative infinity; one divided by positive zero yields positive infinity.

Floating-point arithmetic never causes exceptions, even in the case of division by zero.

Reference Data Types

The non-primitive data types in Java are objects and arrays. These non-primitive types are often called "reference types" because they are handled "by reference"—in other words, the address of the object or array is stored in a variable, passed to methods, and so on. By comparison, primitive types are handled "by value"—the actual primitive values are stored in variables and passed to methods.

---

*Exceptions signal errors in Java. Exception handling is described later in this chapter.

In C, you can manipulate a value by reference by taking its address with the & operator, and you can "dereference" an address with the * and -> operators. These operators do not exist in Java. Primitive types are always passed by value; arrays and objects are always passed by reference.

Because objects are passed by reference, two different variables may refer to the same object:

```
Button a, b;
p = new Button();          // p refers to a Button object
q = p;                     // q refers to the same Button.
p.setLabel("Ok");          // A change to the object through p...
String s = q.getLabel();   // ...is also visible through q.
                           // s now contains "Ok".
```

This is not true of primitive types, however:

```
int i = 3;                 // i contains the value 3.
int j = i;                 // j contains a copy of the value in i.
i = 2;                     // Changing i doesn't change j.
                           // Now, i == 2 and j == 3.
```

Copying Objects

Because reference types are not passed by value, assigning one object to another in Java does not copy the value of the object. It merely assigns a reference to the object. Consider the following code:

```
Button a = new Button("Okay");
Button b = new Button("Cancel");
a = b;
```

After these lines are executed, the variable a contains a reference to the object that b refers to. The object that a used to refer to is lost.

To copy the data of one object into another object, use the clone() method:

```
Vector b = new Vector;
c = b.clone();
```

After these lines run, the variable c refers to an object that is a duplicate of the object referred to by b. Note that not all types support the clone() method. Only classes that implement the Cloneable interface may be cloned. Look up java.lang.Cloneable and java.lang.Object.clone() in Section 23, *The java.lang Package*, for more information on cloning objects.

Arrays are also reference types, and assigning an array simply copies a reference to the array. To actually copy the values stored in an array, you must assign each of the values individually or use the System.arraycopy() method.

Checking Objects for Equality

Another implication of passing objects by reference is that the == operator tests whether two variables refer to the same object, not whether two objects contain the same values. To actually test whether two separate objects are the same, you must use a specially written method for that object type (just as you might use strcmp()

to compare C strings for equality). In Java, a number of classes define an `equals()` method that you can use to perform this test.

Java Has No Pointers

The referencing and dereferencing of objects is handled for you automatically by Java. Java does not allow you to manipulate pointers or memory addresses of any kind:

- It does not allow you to cast object or array references into integers or vice-versa.

- It does not allow you to do pointer arithmetic.

- It does not allow you to compute the size in bytes of any primitive type or object.

There are two reasons for these restrictions:

- Pointers are a notorious source of bugs. Eliminating them simplifies the language and eliminates many potential bugs.

- Pointers and pointer arithmetic could be used to sidestep Java's run-time checks and security mechanisms. Removing pointers allows Java to provide the security guarantees that it does.

To a C programmer, the lack of pointers and pointer arithmetic may seem an odious restriction in Java. But once you get used to the Java object-oriented programming model, it no longer seems like a serious restriction at all. The lack of pointers does mean that you probably can't do things like write UNIX device drivers in Java (at least not without using native methods written in C). But big deal—most of us never have to do this kind of low-level programming anyway.

null

The default value for variables of all reference types is `null`. `null` is a reserved value that indicates "an absence of reference"—i.e., that a variable does not refer to any object or array.

In Java, `null` is a reserved keyword, unlike NULL in C, where it is just a constant defined to be 0. `null` is an exception to the strong typing rules of Java—it may be assigned to any variable of reference type (i.e., any variable which has a class, interface, or array as its type).

`null` cannot be cast to any primitive type, including integral types and `boolean`. It should not be considered equal to zero (although it may well be implemented this way).

Reference Type Summary

The distinction between primitive types passed by value, and objects and arrays passed by reference is a crucial one in Java. Be sure you understand the following:

- All objects and arrays are handled by reference in Java.

- The = and == operators assign and test references to objects. Use `clone()` and `equals()` to actually copy or test the objects themselves.

- The necessary referencing and dereferencing of objects and arrays is handled automatically by Java.

- A reference type can never be cast to a primitive type.

- A primitive type can never be cast to a reference type.

- There is no pointer arithmetic in Java.

- There is no `sizeof` operator in Java.

- `null` is a special value that means "no object" or indicates an absence of reference.

Objects

Now that you know objects are passed by reference, we should discuss how they are created, used, and destroyed. The following subsections provide a very brief overview of objects. Section 3, *Classes and Objects in Java*, explains classes and objects in much greater detail.

Creating Objects

Declaring a variable to hold an object does not create the object itself; the variable only holds the reference to the object. To actually create an object, you must use the new keyword. This is followed by the object's class (i.e., its type) and an optional argument list in parentheses. These arguments are passed to the constructor method for the class, which serves to initialize internal fields in the new object. For example:

```
java.awt.Button b = new java.awt.Button();
ComplexNumber c = new ComplexNumber(1.0, 1.414);
```

There are actually two other ways to create an object. First, you can create a `String` object simply by enclosing characters in double quotes:

```
String s = "This is a test";
```

Because strings are used so frequently, the Java compiler provides this technique as a shortcut. The second alternative way to create objects is by calling the `newInstance()` method of a `Class` object. This technique is generally used only when dynamically loading classes, so we won't discuss it here.

The memory for newly created objects is dynamically allocated. Creating an object with new in Java is like calling `malloc()` in C to allocate memory for an instance of a `struct`. It is also, of course, a lot like using the new operator in C++. (Below, though, we'll see where this analogy to `malloc()` in C and new in C++ breaks down.)

Accessing Objects

As you've probably noticed in various example code fragments by now, the way you access the fields of an object is with a dot:

```
ComplexNumber c = new ComplexNumber();
c.x = 1.0;
c.y = -1.414;
```

This syntax is reminiscent of accessing the fields of a `struct` in C. Recall, though, that Java objects are always accessed by reference, and that Java performs any necessary dereferencing for you. Thus, the dot in Java is more like `->` in C. Java hides the fact that there is a reference here in an attempt to make your programming easier.

The other difference between C and Java when accessing objects is that in Java you refer to an object's methods as if they were fields in the object itself:

```
ComplexNumber c = new ComplexNumber(1.0, -1.414);
double magnitude = c.magnitude();
```

Garbage Collection

Objects in Java are created with the `new` keyword, but there is no corresponding `old` or `delete` keyword or `free()` method to get rid of them when they are no longer needed. If creating an object with `new` is like calling `malloc()` in C or using `new` in C++, then it would seem that Java is full of memory leaks, because we never call `free()` or use the `delete` operator.

In fact, this isn't the case. Java uses a technique called *garbage collection* to automatically detect objects that are no longer being used (an object is no longer in use when there are no more references to it) and to free them. This means that in our programs, we never need to worry about freeing memory or destroying objects—the garbage collector takes care of that.

If you are a C or C++ programmer, it may take some getting used to to just let allocated objects go without worrying about reclaiming their memory. Once you get used to it, however, you'll begin to appreciate what a nice feature this is. We'll discuss garbage collection in more detail in the next chapter.

Arrays

Most of what we learned in the previous sections about reference types and objects applies equally well to arrays in Java:

* Arrays are manipulated by reference.

* They are dynamically created with `new`.

* They are automatically garbage collected when no longer referred to.

The following subsections explain these and other details.

Creating and Destroying Arrays

There are two ways to create arrays in Java. The first uses `new`, and specifies how large the array should be:

```
byte octet_buffer[] = new byte[1024];
Button buttons[] = new Button[10];
```

Since creating an array does not create the objects that are stored in the array, there is no constructor to call, and the argument list is omitted with this form of the `new` keyword. The elements of an array created in this way are initialized to the default value for their type. The elements of an array of int are initialized to 0, for example, and the elements of an array of objects are initialized to null.

The second way to create an array is with a static initializer, which looks just like it does in C:

```
int lookup_table[] = {1, 2, 4, 8, 16, 32, 64, 128};
```

This syntax dynamically creates an array and initializes its elements to the specified values. The elements specified in an array initializer may be arbitrary expressions. This is different than in C, where they must be constant expressions.

Arrays are automatically garbage collected, just like objects are.

Multidimensional Arrays

Java also supports multidimensional arrays. These are implemented as arrays-of-arrays, as they are in C. You specify a variable as a multidimensional array type simply by appending the appropriate number of [ ] pairs after it. You allocate a multidimensional array with new by specifying the appropriate number of elements (between square brackets) for each dimension. For example:

```
byte TwoDimArray[][] = new byte[256][16];
```

This statement does three things:

- Declares a variable named TwoDimArray. This variable has type byte[][] (array-of-array-of-byte).

- Dynamically allocates an array with 256 elements. The type of this newly allocated array is byte[][], so it can be assigned to the variable we declared. Each element of this new array is of type byte[]—a single-dimensional array of byte.

- Dynamically allocates 256 arrays of bytes, each of which holds 16 bytes, and stores a reference to these 256 byte[] arrays into the 256 elements of the byte[][] array allocated in the second step. The 16 bytes in each of these 256 arrays are initialized to their default value of 0.

When allocating a multidimensional array, you do not have to specify the number of elements that are contained in each dimension. For example:

```
int threeD[][][] = new int[10][][];
```

This expression allocates an array that contains ten elements, each of type int[][]. It is a single-dimensional allocation, although when the array elements are properly initialized to meaningful values, the array will be multidimensional. The rule for this sort of array allocation is that the first *n* dimensions (where *n* is at least one) must have the number of elements specified, and these dimensions may be followed by *m* additional dimensions with no dimension size specified. The following is legal:

```
String lots_of_strings[][][][] = new String[5][3][][];
```

This is not:

```
double temperature_data[][][] = new double[100][][10];    // illegal
```

Multidimensional arrays can also be allocated and initialized with nested initializers. For example, you might declare the following multidimensional array of strings for use by the `getParameterInfo()` method of an applet:

```
String param_info[][] = {
    {"foreground",      "Color",     "foreground color"},
    {"background",      "Color",     "background color"},
    {"message",         "String",    "the banner to display"}
};
```

Note that since Java implements multidimensional arrays as arrays-of-arrays, multidimensional arrays need not be "rectangular." For example, this is how you could create and initialize a "triangular array":

```
short triangle[][] = new short[10][];       // a single-dimensional array
for(int i = 0; i < triangle.length; i++) {  // for each element of that array
    triangle[i] = new short[i+1];           // allocate a new array
    for(int j=0; j < i+1; j++)              // for each element of the new array
        triangle[i][j] = i + j;             // initialize it to a value.
}
```

You can also declare and initialize non-rectangular arrays with nested initializers:

```
static int[][] twodim = {{1, 2}, {3, 4, 5}, {5, 6, 7, 8}};
```

To simulate multiple dimensions within a single-dimensional array, you'd use code just as you would in C:

```
final int rows = 600;
final int columns = 800;
byte pixels[] = new byte[rows*columns];

// access element [i,j] like this:
byte b = pixels[i + j*columns];
```

Accessing Array Elements

Array access in Java is just like array access in C—you access an element of an array by putting an integer-valued expression between square brackets after the name of the array:

```
int a[] = new int[100];
a[0] = 0;
for(int i = 1; i < a.length; i++) a[i] = i + a[i-1];
```

Notice how we computed the number of elements of the array in this example—by accessing the `length` field of the array. This is the only field that arrays support. Note that it is a read-only field—any attempt to store a value into the `length` field of an array will fail.

In all Java array references, the index is checked to make sure it is not too small (less than zero) or too big (greater than or equal to the array length). If the index is out of bounds, an `ArrayIndexOutOfBoundsException` is thrown.* This is another way that Java works to prevent bugs (and security problems).

---

*The discussion of exceptions and exception handling is still to come.

Are Arrays Objects?

It is useful to consider arrays to be a separate kind of reference type from objects. In some ways, though, arrays behave just like objects. As we saw, arrays use the object syntax .length to refer to their length. Arrays may also be assigned to variables of type Object, and the methods of the Object class may be invoked for arrays. (Object is the root class in Java, which means that all objects can be assigned to a variable of type Object and all objects can invoke the methods of Object.)

The evidence suggests that arrays are, in fact, objects. Java defines enough special syntax for arrays, however, that it is still most useful to consider them a different kind of reference type than objects.

Declaring Array Variables and Arguments

In C, you declare an array variable or array function argument by placing square brackets next to the variable name:

```
void reverse(char strbuf[], int buffer_size) {
    char buffer[500];
    ...
}
```

In Java, you would have to declare buffer as an array variable, and then allocate the array itself with new, but otherwise you could use the same syntax, with the array brackets after the variable or argument name.

However, Java also allows you to put the array brackets after the type name instead. So you could rewrite this code fragment to look something like this:

```
void reverse(char[] strbuf, int buffer_size) {
    char[] buffer = new char[500];
    ...
}
```

In a lot of ways, this new array syntax is easier to read and easier to understand. (It doesn't work in C, by the way, because pointers make C's type declaration syntax a real mess.) The only problem with this new syntax is that if you get in the habit of using it, it will make it harder for you when you (hopefully only occasionally!) have to switch back and program in C.

Java even allows you to mix the declaration styles, which is something you may find occasionally useful (or frequently confusing!) for certain data structures or algorithms. For example:

```
// row and column are arrays of byte.
// matrix is an array of an array of bytes.
byte[] row, column, matrix[];

// This method takes an array of bytes and an
// array of arrays of bytes
public void dot_product(byte[] column, byte[] matrix[]) { ... }
```

A final point to note about array declarations is that (as we've seen throughout this section) the size of an array is not part of its type as it is in C. Thus, you can declare a variable to be of type String[], for example, and assign any array of String objects to it, regardless of the length of the array:

```
String[] strings;        // this variable can refer to any String array
strings = new String[10];  // one that contains 10 Strings
strings = new String[20];  // or one that contains 20.
```

Strings

Strings in Java are *not* null-terminated arrays of characters as they are in C. Instead, they are instances of the `java.lang.String` class. Java strings are unusual, in that the compiler treats them almost as if they were primitive types—for example, it automatically creates a `String` object when it encounters a double-quoted constant in the program. And, the language defines an operator that operates on `String` objects—the + operator for string concatenation.

An important feature of `String` objects is that they are immutable—i.e., there are no methods defined that allow you to change the contents of a `String`. If you need to modify the contents of a `String`, you have to create a `StringBuffer` object from the `String` object, modify the contents of the `StringBuffer`, and then create a new `String` from the contents of the `StringBuffer`.

Note that it is moot to ask whether Java strings are terminated with a NUL character (\u0000) or not. Java performs run-time bounds checking on all array and string accesses, so there is no way to examine the value of any internal terminator character that appears after the last character of the string.

Both the `String` and `StringBuffer` classes are documented in Section 23, *The java.lang Package*, and you'll find a complete set of methods for string handling and manipulation there. Some of the more important `String` methods are: `length()`, `charAt()`, `equals()`, `compareTo()`, `indexOf()`, `lastIndexOf()`, and `substring()`.

Operators

Java supports almost all of the standard C operators. These standard operators have the same precedence and associativity in Java as they do in C. They are listed in Table 2-3 and also in quick reference form in Section 10, *Java Syntax*.

Table 2-3: Java Operators

Prec.	Operator	Operand Type(s)	Assoc.	Operation Performed
1	++	arithmetic	R	pre-or-post increment (unary)
	--	arithmetic	R	pre-or-post decrement (unary)
	+, -	arithmetic	R	unary plus, unary minus
	~	integral	R	bitwise complement (unary)
	!	boolean	R	logical complement (unary)
	(*type*)	any	R	cast
2	*, /, %	arithmetic	L	multiplication, division, remainder
3	+, -	arithmetic	L	addition, subtraction
	+	String	L	string concatenation
4	<<	integral	L	left shift
	>>	integral	L	right shift with sign

Table 2-3: Java Operators (continued)

Prec.	Operator	Operand Type(s)	Assoc.	Operation Performed
				extension
	>>>	integral	L	right shift with zero extension
5	<, <=	arithmetic	L	less than, less than or equal
	>, >=	arithmetic	L	greater than, greater than or equal
	instanceof	object, type	L	type comparison
6	==	primitive	L	equal (have identical values)
	!=	primitive	L	not equal (have different values)
	==	object	L	equal (refer to same object)
	!=	object	L	not equal (refer to different objects)
7	&	integral	L	bitwise AND
	&	boolean	L	boolean AND
8	^	integral	L	bitwise XOR
	^	boolean	L	boolean XOR
9	|	integral	L	bitwise OR
	|	boolean	L	boolean OR
10	&&	boolean	L	conditional AND
11	||	boolean	L	conditional OR
12	?:	boolean, any, any	R	conditional (ternary) operator
13	=	variable, any	R	assignment
	*=, /=, %=, +=, -=, <<=, >>=, >>>=, &=, ^=, |=,	variable, any	R	assignment with operation

Note the following Java operator differences from C. Java does not support the comma operator for combining two expressions into one (although the for statement simulates this operator in a useful way). Since Java does not allow you to manipulate pointers directly, it does not support the reference and dereference operators * and &, nor the sizeof operator. Further, Java doesn't consider [] (array access) and . (field access) to be operators, as C does.

Java also adds some new operators:

+

The + operator applied to `String` values concatenates them.* If only one operand of + is a `String`, the other one is converted to a string. The conversion is done automatically for primitive types, and by calling the `toString()` method of non-primitive types. This `String` + operator has the same precedence as the arithmetic + operator. The += operator works as you would expect for `String` values.

instanceof

The `instanceof` operator returns `true` if the object on its left-hand side is an instance of the class (or implements the interface) specified on its right-hand side. `instanceof` returns `false` if the object is not an instance of the specified class or does not implement the specified interface. It also returns `false` if the specified object is `null`. The `instanceof` operator has the same precedence as the <, <=, >, and >= operators.

>>>

Because all integral types in Java are signed values, the Java >> operator is defined to do a right shift with sign extension. The >>> operator treats the value to be shifted as an unsigned number and shifts the bits right with zero extension. The >>>= operator works as you would expect.

& and |

When & and | are applied to integral types in Java, they perform the expected bitwise AND and OR operations. Java makes a strong distinction between integral types and the `boolean` type, however. Thus, if these operators are applied to `boolean` types, they perform logical AND and logical OR operations. These logical AND and logical OR operators always evaluate both of their operands, even when the result of the operation is determined after evaluating only the left operand. This is useful when the operands are expressions with side effects (such as method calls) and you always want the side effects to occur. However, when you do not want the right operand evaluated if it is not necessary, you can use the && and || operators, which perform "short-circuited" logical AND and logical OR operations just as in C. The &= and |= operators perform a bitwise or logical operation depending on the type of the operators, as you would expect.

Statements

Many of Java's control statements are similar or identical to C statements. This section lists and, where necessary, explains Java's statements. Note that the topic of exceptions and the `try`/`catch`/`finally` statement is substantial enough that it is covered later in a section of its own.

---

*To C++ programmers, this looks like operator overloading. In fact, Java does not support operator overloading—the language designers decided (after much debate) that overloaded operators were a neat idea, but that code that relied on them became hard to read and understand.

The if/else, while, and do/while Statements

The if, else, do, and while statements are exactly the same in Java as they are in C. The only substantial difference arises because the Java boolean type cannot be cast to other types. In Java, the values 0 and null are not the same as false, and non-zero and non-null values are not the same as true.

The conditional expression that is expected by the if, the while, and the do/while statements must be of boolean type in Java. Specifying an integer type or a reference type won't do. Thus, the following C code is not legal in Java:

```
int i = 10;
while(i--) {
  Object o = get_object();
  if (o) {
    do { ... } while(j);
  }
}
```

In Java, you must make the condition you are testing for clear by explictly testing your value against 0 or null. Use code like the following:

```
int i = 10;
while(i-- > 0) {
  Object o = get_object();
  if (o != null) {
    do { ... } while(j != 0);
  }
}
```

The switch Statement

The switch statement is the same in Java as it is in C. You may use byte, char, short, int, or long types as the values of the case labels, and you may also specify a default label just as you do in C.

The for Loop

The for statement is perhaps the most useful looping construct available in Java. There are only two differences between the Java for loop and the C for loop. The first difference is that although Java does not support the C comma operator (which allows multiple expressions to be joined into a single expression), the Java for loop simulates it by allowing multiple comma-separated expressions to appear in the initialization and increment sections, but not the test section, of the loop. For example:

```
int i;
String s;
for(i=0, s = "testing";          // initialize variables
    (i < 10) && (s.length() >= 1);   // test for continuation
    i++, s = s.substring(1))      // increment variables
{
    System.out.println(s);        // loop body
}
```

As you can see, this "difference" between the Java and C for loops is really a similarity.

The second difference is the addition of the C++ ability to declare local loop variables in the initialization section of the loop:

```
for(int i = 0; i < my_array.length; i++)
    System.out.println("a[" + i + "] = " + my_array[i]);
```

Variables declared in this way have the for loop as their scope. In other words, they are only valid within the body of the for loop and within the initialization, test, and increment expressions of the loop. Variables with the same name outside of the loop are not changed.

Note that because variable declaration syntax also uses the comma, the Java syntax allows you to either specify multiple comma-separated initialization expressions or to declare and initialize multiple comma-separated variables of the same type. You may not mix variable declarations with other expressions. For example, the following for loop declares and initializes two variables that are valid only within the for loop. Variables by the same name outside of the loop are not changed.

```
int j = -3;        // this j remains unchanged.
for(int i=0, j=10; i < j; i++, j--) System.out.println("k = " + i*j);
```

Labelled break and continue Statements

The break and continue statements, used alone, behave the same in Java as they do in C. However, in Java, they may optionally be followed by a label that specifies an enclosing loop (for continue) or any enclosing statement (for break). The labelled forms of these statements allow you to "break" and "continue" any specified statement or loop within a method definition, not only the nearest enclosing statements or loop.

The break statement, without a label, transfers control out of ("breaks out of" or terminates) the nearest enclosing for, while, do or switch statement, exactly as in C. If the break keyword is followed by an identifier that is the label of an arbitrary enclosing statement, execution transfers out of that enclosing statement. After the break statement is executed, any required finally clauses are executed, and control resumes at the statement following the terminated statement. (The finally clause and the try statement it is associated with are exception handling constructs and are explained in the next section.) For example:

```
test: if (check(i)) {
    try {
        for(int j=0; j < 10; j++) {
            if (j > i) break;          // terminate just this loop
            if (a[i][j] == null)
                break test;            // do the finally clause and
        }                              // terminate the if statement.
    }
    finally { cleanup(a, i, j); }
}
```

Without a label, the continue statement works exactly as in C: It stops the iteration in progress and causes execution to resume after the last statement in the while, do, or for loop, just before the loop iteration is to begin again. If the continue keyword is followed by an identifier that is the label of an enclosing loop, execution skips to the end of that loop instead. If there are any finally clauses between the continue statement and the end of the appropriate loop, these clauses are executed before control is transferred to the end of the loop.

The following code fragment illustrates how the `continue` statement works in its labelled and unlabelled forms.

```
big_loop: while(!done) {
    if (test(a,b) == 0) continue;       // control goes to point 2.
    try {
        for(int i=0; i < 10; i++) {
            if (a[i] == null)
                continue;                // control goes to point 1.
            else if (b[i] == null)
                continue big_loop;       // control goes to point 2,
                                         // after doing the finally block.

            doit(a[i],b[i]);
                                         // point 1.  Increment and start loop again with the test.

        }
    }
    finally { cleanup(a,b); }
                                         // point 2.  Start loop again with the (!done) test.

}
```

Note the non-intuitive feature of the labelled `continue` statement: The loop label must appear at the top of the loop, but `continue` causes execution to transfer to the very bottom of the loop.

No goto Statement

`goto` is a reserved word in Java, but the `goto` statement is not currently part of the language. Labelled `break` and `continue` statements replace some important and legitimate uses of `goto`, and the `try/catch/finally` statement replaces the others.

The synchronized Statement

Since Java is a multithreaded system, care must often be taken to prevent multiple threads from modifying objects simultaneously in a way that might leave the object's state corrupted. Sections of code that must not be executed simultaneously are known as "critical sections." Java provides the `synchronized` statement to protect these critical sections. The syntax is:

```
synchronized (expression) statement
```

expression is an expression that must resolve to an object or an array. The *statement* is the code of the critical section, which is usually a block of statements (within { and }). The `synchronized` statement attempts to acquire an exclusive lock for the object or array specified by *expression*. It does not execute the critical section of code until it can obtain this lock, and in this way, ensures that no other threads can be executing the section at the same time.

Note that you do not have to use the `synchronized` statement unless your program creates multiple threads that share data. If only one thread ever accesses a data structure, there is no need to protect it with `synchronized`. When you do have to use it, it might be in code like the following:

```
public static void SortIntArray(int[] a) {
        // Sort the array a. This is synchronized so that some other
        // thread can't change elements of the array while we're sorting it.
        // At least not other threads that protect their changes to the
        // array with synchronized.
    synchronized (a) {
            // do the array sort here.
    }
}
```

The `synchronized` keyword is more often used as a method modifier in Java. When applied to a method, it indicates that the entire method is a critical section. For a `synchronized` class method (a static method), Java obtains an exclusive lock on the class before executing the method. For a `synchronized` instance method, Java obtains an exclusive lock on the class instance. (Class methods and instance methods are discussed in the next chapter.)

The package and import Statements

The `package` statement, as we saw earlier in the chapter, specifies the package that the classes in a file of Java source code are part of. If it appears, it must be the first statement of a Java file. The `import` statement, which we also saw earlier, allows us to refer to classes by abbreviated names. `import` statements must appear after the `package` statement, if any, and before any other statements in a Java file. For example:

```
package games.tetris;

import java.applet.*;
import java.awt.*;
```

Exceptions and Exception Handling

Exception handing is a significant new feature of Java.* There are a number of new terms associated with exception handling. First, an *exception* is a signal that indicates that some sort of exceptional condition (such as an error) has occurred. To *throw* an exception is to signal an exceptional condition. To *catch* an exception is to handle it—to take whatever actions are necessary to recover from it.

Exceptions propagate up through the lexical block structure of a Java method, and then up the method call stack. If an exception is not caught by the block of code that throws it, it propagates to the next higher enclosing block of code. If it is not caught there, it propagates up again. If it is not caught anywhere in the method, it propagates to the invoking method, where it again propagates through the block structure. If an exception is never caught, it propagates all the way to the `main()` method from which the program started, and causes the Java interpreter to print an error message and a stack trace and exit.

As we'll see in the subsections below, exceptions make error handling (and "exceptional condition" handling) more regular and logical by allowing you to group all your exception handling code into one place. Instead of worrying about all of the things that can go wrong with each line of your code, you can concentrate on the

---

*It is similar to, but not quite the same as, exception handling in C++.

algorithm at hand and place all your error handling code (that is, your exception catching code) in a single place.

Exception Objects

An exception in Java is an object that is an instance of some subclass of `java.lang.Throwable`. Throwable has two standard subclasses: `java.lang.Error` and `java.lang.Exception`.* Exceptions that are subclasses of `Error` generally indicate linkage problems related to dynamic loading, or virtual machine problems such as running out of memory. They should almost always be considered unrecoverable, and should not be caught. While the distinction is not always clear, exceptions that are subclasses of `Exception` indicate conditions that may be caught and recovered from. They include such exceptions as `java.io.EOFException`, which signals the end of a file and `java.lang.ArrayAccessOutOfBounds`, which indicates that a program has tried to read past the end of an array.

Since exceptions are objects, they can contain data and define methods. The `Throwable` object, at the top of the exception class hierarchy, includes a `String` message in its definition and this field is inherited by all exception classes. This field is used to store a human-readable error message that describes the exceptional condition. It is set when the exception object is created by passing an argument to the constructor method. The message can be read from the exception with the `Throwable.getMessage()` method. Most exceptions contain only this single message, but a few add other data. The `java.io.InterruptedIOException`, for example, adds the following field:

```
public int bytesTransferred;
```

This field specifies how much of the I/O was complete before the exceptional condition occurred.

Exception Handling

The `try/catch/finally` statement is Java's exception handling mechanism. `try` establishes a block of code that is to have its exceptions and abnormal exits (through `break`, `continue`, `return`, or exception propagation) handled. The `try` block is followed by zero or more `catch` clauses that catch and handle specified types of exceptions. The `catch` clauses are optionally followed by a `finally` block that contains "clean-up" code. The statements of a `finally` block are guaranteed to be executed, regardless of how the code in the `try` block exits. A detailed example of the `try/catch/finally` syntax is shown in Example 2-2.

Example 2-2: The try/catch/finally statement

```
try {
        // Normally this code runs from the top of the block to the bottom
        // without problems. But it sometimes may raise exceptions or
        // exit the block via a break, continue, or return statement.
}
catch (SomeException e1) {
        // Handle an exception object e1 of type SomeException
        // or of a subclass of that type.
```

---

*We'll use the term "exception" to refer to any subclass of Throwable, whether it is actually an Exception or an Error.

Example 2-2: The try/catch/finally statement (continued)

```
}
catch (AnotherException e2) {
        // Handle an exception object e2 of type AnotherException
        // or of a subclass of that type.
}
finally {
        // Always execute this code, after we leave the try clause,
        // regardless of whether we leave it:
        //   1) Normally, after reaching the bottom of the block.
        //   2) With an exception that is handled by a catch.
        //   3) With an exception that is not handled.
        //   4) Because of a break, continue, or return statement.
}
```

try

The `try` clause simply establishes a block of code that is to have its exceptions and abnormal exits (through `break`, `continue`, `return`, or exception propagation) handled. The `try` clause by itself doesn't do anything interesting; it is the `catch` and `finally` clauses that do the exception handling and clean-up operations.

catch

A `try` block may be followed by zero or more `catch` clauses that specify code to handle various types of exceptions. `catch` clauses have an unusual syntax: each is declared with an argument, much like a method argument. This argument must be of type `Throwable` or a subclass. When an exception occurs, the first `catch` clause that has an argument of the appropriate type is invoked. The type of the argument must match the type of the exception object, or it must be a superclass of the exception. This `catch` argument is valid only within the `catch` block, and refers to the actual exception object that was thrown.

The code within a `catch` block should take whatever action is necessary to cope with the exceptional condition. If the exception was a `java.io.FileNotFoundException` exception, for example, you might handle it by asking the user to check his or her spelling and try again. Note that it is not required to have a `catch` clause for every possible exception—in some cases the correct response is to allow the exception to propagate up and be caught by the invoking method. In other cases, such as a programming error signaled by `NullPointerException`, the correct response is to not catch the exception at all, but to allow it to propagate and to have the Java interpreter exit with a stack trace and an error message.

finally

The `finally` clause is generally used to clean up (close files, release resources, etc.) after the `try` clause. What is useful about the `finally` clause is that the code in a `finally` block is guaranteed to be executed, if any portion of the `try` block is executed, regardless of how the code in the `try` block completes. In the normal case, control reaches the end of the `try` block and then proceeds to the `finally` block, which performs any necessary cleanup.

If control leaves the `try` block because of a `return`, `continue`, or `break` statement, the contents of the `finally` block are executed before control transfers to its new destination.

If an exception occurs in the `try` block and there is a local `catch` block to handle the exception, control transfers first to the `catch` block, and then to the `finally` block. If there is not a local `catch` block to handle the exception, control transfers first to the `finally` block, and then propagates up to the nearest `catch` clause that can handle the exception.

Note that if a `finally` block itself transfers control with a `return`, `continue`, or `break` statement, or by raising an exception, the pending control transfer is abandoned, and this new transfer is processed.

Also note that `try` and `finally` can be used together without exceptions or any `catch` clauses. In this case, the `finally` block is simply cleanup code that is guaranteed to be executed regardless of any `break`, `continue`, or `return` statements within the `try` clause.

Declaring Exceptions

Java requires that any method that can cause a "normal exception" to occur must either catch the exception or specify the type of the exception with a `throws` clause in the method declaration.* Such a `throws` clause might look like these:

```
public void open_file() throws IOException {
    // Statements here that might generate an uncaught java.io.IOException
}

public void myfunc(int arg) throws MyException1, MyException2 {
    ...
}
```

Note that the exception class specified in a `throws` clause may be a superclass of the exception type that is actually thrown. Thus if a method throws exceptions a, b, and c, all of which are subclasses of d, the `throws` clause may specify all of a, b, and c, or it may simply specify d.

We said above that the `throws` clause must be used to declare any "normal exceptions." This oxymoronic phrase refers to any subclass of `Throwable` that is not a subclass of `Error` or a subclass of `RuntimeException`. Java does not require these types of exceptions to be declared because practically any method can conceivably generate them, and it would quickly become tedious to properly declare them all. For example, every method running on a buggy Java interpreter can throw an `InternalError` exception (a subclass of `Error`) and it doesn't make sense to have to declare this in a `throws` clause for every method. Similarly, as far as the Java compiler is concerned, any method that accesses an array can generate an `ArrayIndexOutOfBoundsException` exception (a subclass of `RuntimeException`).

The standard exceptions that you often have to declare are `java.io.IOException` and a number of its more specific subclasses. `java.lang.InterruptedException` and several other less commonly used exceptions must also be declared. How

---

*C++ programmers note that Java uses throws where C++ uses throw.

do you know when you have to declare a `throws` clause? One way is to pay close attention to the documentation for the methods you call—if any "normal exceptions" can be thrown, either catch them or declare them. Another way to know what exceptions you've got to declare is to declare none and wait for the compilation errors—the compiler will tell you what to put in your `throws` clause!

Defining and Generating Exceptions

You can signal your own exceptions with the `throw` statement. The `throw` keyword must be followed by an object that is `Throwable` or a subclass. Often, exception objects are allocated in the same statement that they are thrown in:

```
throw new MyException("my exceptional condition occurred.");
```

When an exception is thrown, normal program execution stops and the interpreter looks for a `catch` clause that can handle the exception. Execution propagates up through enclosing statements and through invoking functions until such a handler is found. Any `finally` blocks that are passed during this propagation are executed.

Using exceptions is a good way to signal and handle errors in your own code. By grouping all your error handling and recover code together within the `try`/`catch`/`finally` structure, you will end up with cleaner code that is easier to understand. Sometimes, when you are throwing an exception, you can use one of the exception classes already defined by Java API. Often, though, you will want to define and throw your own exception types.

Example 2-3 shows how you can define your own exception types, throw them, and handle them. It also helps clarify how exceptions propagate. It is a long example, but worth studying in some detail. You'll know you understand exception handling if you can answer the following: What happens when this program is invoked with no argument; with a string argument; and with integer arguments 0, 1, 2, and 99?

Example 2-3: Defining, throwing, and handling exceptions

```
// Here we define some exception types of our own.
// Exception classes generally have constructors but no data or
// other methods.  All these do is call their superclass constructors.
class MyException extends Exception {
   public MyException() { super(); }
   public MyException(String s) { super(s); }
}
class MyOtherException extends Exception {
   public MyOtherException() { super(); }
   public MyOtherException(String s) { super(s); }
}
class MySubException extends MyException {
   public MySubException() { super(); }
   public MySubException(String s) { super(s); }
}

public class throwtest {
        // This is the main() method.  Note that it uses two
        // catch clauses to handle two standard Java exceptions.
      public static void main(String argv[]) {
        int i;
```

Example 2-3: Defining, throwing, and handling exceptions (continued)

```
        // First, convert our argument to an integer
        // Make sure we have an argument and that it is convertible.
    try {
      i = Integer.parseInt(argv[0]);
    }
    catch (ArrayIndexOutOfBoundsException e) { // argv is empty
      System.out.println("Must specify an argument");
      return;
    }
    catch (NumberFormatException e) { // argv[0] isn't an integer
      System.out.println("Must specify an integer argument.");
      return;
    }

        // Now, pass that integer to method a().
    a(i);
}

        // This method invokes b(), which is declared to throw
        // one type of exception.  We handle that one exception.
public static void a(int i) {
    try {
        b(i);
    }
    catch (MyException e) {                      // Point 1.
                // Here we handle MyException and
                // its subclass MyOtherException
        if (e instanceof MySubException)
            System.out.print("MySubException: ");
        else
            System.out.print("MyException: ");
        System.out.println(e.getMessage());
        System.out.println("Handled at point 1");
    }
}

        // This method invokes c(), and handles one of the
        // two exception types that that method can throw.  The other
        // exception type is not handled, and is propagated up
        // and declared in this method's throws clause.
        // This method also has a finally clause to finish up
        // the work of its try clause.  Note that the finally clause
        // is executed after a local catch clause, but before
        // a containing catch clause or one in an invoking procedure.
public static void b(int i) throws MyException {
    int result;
    try {
        System.out.print("i = " + i);
        result = c(i);
        System.out.print(" c(i) = " + result);
    }
    catch (MyOtherException e) {                 // Point 2
                // Handle MyOtherException exceptions:
        System.out.println("MyOtherException: " + e.getMessage());
        System.out.println("Handled at point 2");
    }
```

Example 2-3: Defining, throwing, and handling exceptions (continued)

```
        finally {
                // Terminate the output we printed above with a newline.
            System.out.print("\n");
        }
    }

        // This method computes a value or throws an exception.
        // The throws clause only lists two exceptions, because
        // one of the exceptions thrown is a subclass of another.
    public static int c(int i) throws MyException, MyOtherException {
        switch (i) {
            case 0: // processing resumes at point 1 above
                throw new MyException("input too low");
            case 1: // processing resumes at point 1 above
                throw new MySubException("input still too low");
            case 99:// processing resumes at point 2 above
                throw new MyOtherException("input too high");
            default:
                return i*i;
        }
    }
}
```

Miscellaneous Differences

A number of miscellaneous differences between Java and C are described in the sections that follow. Miscellaneous differences that were mentioned elsewhere, such as the lack of the `goto` statement and the `sizeof` operator, are not repeated here.

Local Variable Declarations

A feature that Java has borrowed from C++ is the ability to declare and initialize local variables anywhere in a method body or other block of code. Declarations and their initializers no longer have to be the first statements in any block—you can declare them where it is convenient and fits well with the structure of your code.

Don't let this freedom make you sloppy, however! For someone reading your program, it is nice to have variable declarations grouped together in one place. As a rule of thumb, put your declarations at the top of the block, unless you have some good organizational reason for putting them elsewhere.

Forward References

For compiler efficiency, C requires that variables and functions must be defined, or at least declared, before they can be used or called. That is, forward references are not allowed in C. Java does not make this restriction, and by lifting it, it also does away with the whole concept of a variable or function declaration that is separate from the definition.

Java allows very flexible forward references. A method may refer to a variable or another method of its class, regardless of where in the current class the variable or method are defined. Similarly, it may refer to any class, regardless of where in the current file (or outside of the file) that class is defined. The only place that forward

---

references are not allowed is in variable initialization. A variable initializer (for local variables, class variables, or instance variables) may not refer to other variables that have not yet been declared and initialized.

Method Overloading

A technique that Java borrows from C++ is called *method overloading*. Overloaded methods are methods that have the same name, but have different signatures. In other words, they return different values or they take different types of arguments, a different number of arguments, or the same type of arguments in different positions in the argument list. Method overloading is commonly used in Java to define a number of related functions with the same name, but different arguments. Overloaded methods usually perform the same basic operation, but allow the programmer to specify arguments in different ways depending on what is convenient in a given situation. Method overloading is discussed in more detail in the next chapter.

The void Keyword

The `void` keyword is used in Java, as in C, to indicate that a function returns no value. (As we will see in the next section, constructor methods are an exception to this rule.)

Java differs from C (and is similar to C++) in that methods that take no arguments are declared with empty parentheses, not with the `void` keyword. Also unlike C, Java does not have any `void *` type, nor does it require a `(void)` cast in order to correctly ignore the result returned by a call to a non-`void` method.

Modifiers

Java defines a number of modifier keywords that may be applied to variable and/or method declarations to provide additional information or place restrictions on the variable or method:

`final`
>   The `final` keyword is a modifier that may be applied to classes, methods, and variables. It has a similar, but not identical meaning in each case. A `final` class may never be subclassed. A `final` method may never be overridden. A `final` variable may never have its value set. This modifier is discussed in more detail in the next chapter.

`native`
>   `native` is a modifier that may be applied to method declarations. It indicates that the method is implemented elsewhere in C, or in some other platform-dependent fashion. A `native` method should have a semicolon in place of its body.

`synchronized`
>   We saw the `synchronized` keyword in a previous section where it was a statement that marked a critical section of code. The same keyword can also be used as a modifier for class or instance methods. It indicates that the method modifies the internal state of the class or the internal state of an instance of the class in a way that is not thread-safe. Before running a `synchronized` class method, Java obtains a lock on the class, to ensure that no

other threads can be modifiying the class concurrently. Before running a syn-chronized instance method, Java obtains a lock on the instance that invoked the method, ensuring that no other thread can be modifying the object at the same time.

transient
> The transient keyword is a modifier that may be applied to instance vari-ables in a class. It specifies that the variable is not part of the persistent state of the object. This modifier is not currently used by any part of Java. Eventu-ally it will be used to indicate things like scratch variables that are not part of an object's state, and thus never need to be saved to disk.

volatile
> The volatile keyword is a modifier that may be applied to variables. It specifies that the variable changes asynchronously (e.g., it may be a memory-mapped hardware register on a peripheral device), and that the compiler should not attempt to perform optimizations with it. For example, it should read the variable's value from memory every time and not attempt to save a copy of it in a register.

No Structures or Unions

Java does not support C struct or union types. Note, however that a class is essentially the same thing as a struct, but with more features. And you can simu-late the important features of a union by subclassing.

No Enumerated Types

Java does not support the C enum keyword for defining types that consist of one of a specified number of named values. This is somewhat surprising for a strongly-typed language like Java. Enumerated types can be partially simulated with the use of static final constant values.

No Bitfields

Java does not support the C ability to define variables that occupy particular bits within struct and union types. This feature of C is usually only used to interface directly to hardware devices, which is never necessary with Java's platform-indepen-dent programming model.

No typedef

Java does not support the C typedef keyword to define aliases for type names. Java has a much simpler type naming scheme than C does, however, and so there is no need for something like typedef.

No Variable-Length Argument Lists

Java does not allow you to define methods that take a variable number of arguments, as C does. This is because Java is a strongly typed language and there is no way to do appropriate type checking for a method with variable arguments. Method over-loading allows you to simulate C "varargs" functions for simple cases, but there is no general replacement for this C feature.

Classes and Objects in Java

Java is an *object-oriented* language. "Object-oriented" is a term that has become so commonly used as to have practically no concrete meaning. This section explains just what "object-oriented" means for Java. It covers:

- Classes and objects in Java

- Creating objects

- Garbage collection to free up unused objects

- The difference between class (or static) variables and instance variables, and the difference between class (or static) methods and instance methods

- Extending a class to create a subclass

- Overriding class methods and dynamic method lookup

- Abstract classes

- Interface types and their implementation by classes

If you are a C++ programmer, or have other object-oriented programming experience, many of the concepts in this list should be familiar to you. If you do not have object-oriented experiece, don't fear: This section assumes no knowledge of object-oriented concepts.

We saw in the last section that close analogies can be drawn between Java and C. Unfortunately for C++ programmers, the same is not true for Java and C++. Java uses object-oriented programming concepts that are familiar to C++ programmers, and it even borrows from C++ syntax in a number of places, but the analogies between

Java and C++ are not nearly as strong as those between Java and C.* C++ programmers should forget all they know about C++ and read this section carefully, as beginners, to learn Java without the preconceptions that might come with knowing C++.

Introduction to Classes and Objects

A *class* is a collection of data and methods that operate on that data.† The data and methods, taken together, usually serve to define the contents and capabilities of some kind of *object*.

For example, a circle can be described by the x, y position of its center and by its radius. There are a number of things we can do with circles: compute their circumference, compute their area, check whether points are inside them, and so on. Each circle is different (i.e., has a different center or radius), but as a *class*, circles have certain intrinsic properties that we can capture in a definition. Example 3-1 shows how we could partially define the class of circles in Java. Notice that the class definition contains data and methods (procedures) within the same pair of curly brackets.‡

Example 3-1: The class of circles, partially captured in Java code

```
public class Circle {
    public double x, y;        // the coordinates of the center
    public double r;           // the radius

    // Methods that return the circumference and area of the circle
    public double circumference() { return 2 * 3.14159 * r; }
    public double area() { return 3.14159 * r*r; }
}
```

Objects Are Instances of a Class

Now that we've defined (at least partially) the class `Circle`, we want to do something with it. We can't do anything with the class of circles itself—we need a particular circle to work with. We need an *instance* of the class, a single circle object.

By defining the `Circle` class in Java, we have created a new data type. We can declare variables of that type:

```
Circle c;
```

But this variable c is simply a name that *refers to* a circle object; it is not an object itself. In Java, all objects must be created dynamically. This is almost always done with the new keyword:

```
Circle c;
c = new Circle();
```

---

*As we'll see, Java supports garbage collection and dynamic method lookup. This actually makes it a closer relative, beneath its layer of C-like syntax, to languages like Smalltalk than to C++.

†A *method* is the object-oriented term for a procedure or a function. You'll see it used a lot in this book. Treat it as a synonym for "procedure."

‡C++ programmers should note that methods go inside the class definition in Java, not outside with the a : : operator as they usually do in C++.

Now we have created an instance of our `Circle` class—a circle object—and have assigned it to the variable c, which is of type `Circle`.

Accessing Object Data

Now that we've created an object, we can use its data fields. The syntax should be familiar to C programmers:

```
Circle c = new Circle();
// initialize our circle to have center (2, 2) and radius 1.0.
c.x = 2.0;
c.y = 2.0;
c.r = 1.0;
```

Using Object Methods

This is where things get interesting! To access the methods of an object, we use the same syntax as accessing the data of an object:

```
Circle c = new Circle();
double a;
c.r = 2.5;
a = c.area();
```

Take a look at that last line. We did not say:

```
a = area(c);
```

We said:

```
a = c.area();
```

This is why it is called "object-oriented" programming; the object is the focus here, not the function call. This is probably the single most important feature of the object-oriented paradigm.

Note that we don't have to pass an argument to `c.area()`. The object we are operating on, c, is implicit in the syntax. Take a look at Example 3-1 again: you'll notice the same thing in the definition of the `area()` method—it doesn't take an argument. It is implicit in the language that a method operates on an instance of the class within which it is defined. Thus our `area()` method can use the r field of the class freely—it is understood that it is referring to the radius of whatever `Circle` instance invokes the method.

How It Works

What's going on here? How can a method that takes no arguments know what data to operate on? In fact, the `area()` method does have an argument! `area()` is implemented with an implicit argument that is not shown in the method declaration. The implicit argument is named `this`, and refers to "this object"—the `Circle` object through which the method is invoked. `this` is often called the "this pointer."[*]

The implicit `this` argument is not shown in method signatures because it is usually not needed—whenever a Java method accesses the fields in its class, it is implied that it is accessing fields in the object referred to by the `this` argument. The same is

---

[*] "this pointer" is C++ terminology. Since Java does not support pointers, I prefer the term "this reference."

true, as we'll see, when a method in a class invokes other methods in the class—it is implicit that the methods are being invoked for the this object.

We can use the this keyword explicitly when we want to make explicit that a method is accessing its own variables and/or methods. For example, we could rewrite the area() method like this:

```
public double area() { return 3.14159 * this.r * this.r; }
```

In a method this simple, it is not necessary to be explicit. In more complicated cases, however, you may find that it increases the clarity of your code to use an explicit this where it is not strictly required.

An instance where the this keyword *is* required is when a method argument or a local variable in a method has the same name as one of the fields of the class. In this case, you must use this to access the field. If you used the field name alone, you would end up accessing the argument or local variable with the same name. We'll see examples of this in the next section.

Object Creation

Take another look at how we've been creating our circle object:

```
Circle c = new Circle();
```

What are those parentheses doing there? They make it look like we're calling a function! In fact, that is exactly what we're doing. Every class in Java has at least one *constructor* method, which has the same name as the class. The purpose of a constructor is to perform any necessary initialization for the new object. Since we didn't define one for our Circle class, Java gave us a default constructor that takes no arguments and performs no special initialization.

The way it works is this: The new keyword creates a new dynamic instance of the class—i.e., it allocates the new object. The constructor method is then called, passing the new object implicitly (a this reference, as we saw above), and passing the arguments specified between parentheses explicitly.

Defining a Constructor

There is some obvious initialization we could do for our circle objects, so let's define a constructor. Example 3-2 shows a constructor that lets us specify the initial values for the center and radius of our new Circle object. The example also shows a use of the this keyword, as described in the previous section.

Example 3-2: A constructor for the circle class

```
public class Circle {
public double x, y, r;    // the center and the radius

// Our constructor method.
public Circle(double x, double y, double r)
{
    this.x = x;
    this.y = y;
    this.r = r;
}
```

Example 3-2: A constructor for the circle class (continued)

```
    public double circumference() { return 2 * 3.14159 * r; }
    public double area() { return 3.14159 * r*r; }
}
```

With the old, default constructor, we had to write code like this:

```
Circle c = new Circle();
c.x = 1.414;
c.y = -1.0;
c.r = .25;
```

With this new constructor the initialization becomes part of the object creation step:

```
Circle c = new Circle(1.414, -1.0, .25);
```

There are two important notes about naming and declaring constructors:

- The constructor name is always the same as the class name.

- The return type is implicitly an instance of the class. No return type is specified in constructor declarations, nor is the void keyword used. The this object is implicitly returned; a constructor should not use a return statement to return a value.

Multiple Constructors

Sometimes you'll want to be able to initialize an object in a number of different ways, depending on what is most convenient in a particular circumstance. For example, we might want to be able to initialize the radius of a circle without initializing the center, or we might want to initialize a circle to have the same center and radius as another circle, or we might want to initialize all the fields to default values. Doing this is no problem: A class can have any number of constructor methods. Example 3-3 shows how.

Example 3-3: Multiple circle constructors

```
public class Circle {
    public double x, y, r;

    public Circle(double x, double y, double r) {
        this.x = x; this.y = y; this.r = r;
    }
    public Circle(double r) { x = 0.0; y = 0.0; this.r = r; }
    public Circle(Circle c) { x = c.x; y = c.y; r = c.r; }
    public Circle() { x = 0.0; y = 0.0; r = 1.0; }

    public double circumference() { return 2 * 3.14159 * r; }
    public double area() { return 3.14159 * r*r; }
}
```

Method Overloading

The surprising thing in this example (not so surprising if you're a C++ programmer) is that all the constructor methods have the same name! So how can the compiler tell them apart? The way that you and I tell them apart is that the four methods take different arguments and are useful in different circumstances. The compiler tells them apart in the same way. In Java, a method is distinguished by its name, return type, and by the number, type, and position of its arguments. This is not limited to constructor methods—any two methods are not the same unless they have the same name, the same return type, and the same number of arguments of the same type passed at the same position in the argument list. When you call a method and there is more than one method with the same name, the compiler automatically picks the one that matches the data types of the arguments you are passing.

Defining methods with the same name and different argument or return types is called *method overloading*. It can be a convenient technique, as long as you only give methods the same name when they perform similar functions on slightly different forms of input data, or when they return slightly different forms of output data. Don't confuse method overloading with *method overriding*, which we'll discuss later.

this Again

There is a specialized use of the `this` keyword that arises when a class has multiple constructors—it can be used from a constructor to invoke one of the other constructors of the same class. So we could rewrite the additional constructors from Example 3-3 in terms of the first one like this:

```
public Circle(double x, double y, double r) {
    this.x = x; this.y = y; this.r = r;
}
public Circle(double r) { this(0.0, 0.0, r); }
public Circle(Circle c) { this(c.x, c.y, c.r); }
public Circle() { this(0.0, 0.0, 1.0); }
```

Here, the `this()` call refers to whatever constructor of the class takes the specified type of arguments. This would be a more impressive example, of course, if the first constructor that we were invoking did a more significant amount of initialization, as it might, for example, if we were writing a more complicated class.

There is a very important restriction on this `this` syntax: it may only appear as the first statement in a constructor. It may, of course, be followed by any additional initialization that a particular version of the constructor needs to do. The reason for this restriction involves the automatic invocation of superclass constructor methods, which we'll explore later in this chapter.

Class Variables

In our `Circle` class definition, we declared three "instance" variables: `x`, `y`, and `r`. Each instance of the class—each circle—has its own copy of these three variables. These variables are like the fields of a `struct` in C—each instance of the `struct` has a copy of the fields. Sometimes, though, we want a variable of which there is only one copy—something like a global variable in C.

The problem is that Java doesn't allow global variables. (Actually, those in the know consider this is a feature!) Every variable in Java must be declared inside a class. So Java uses the `static` keyword to indicate that a particular variable is a *class variable* rather than an *instance variable*. That is, that there is only one copy of the variable, associated with the class, rather than many copies of the variable associated with each instance of the class. The one copy of the variable exists regardless of the number of instances of the class that are created—it exists and can be used even if the class is never actually instantiated.

This kind of variable, declared with the static keyword is often called a *static variable*. I prefer (and recommend) the name "class variable" because it is easily distinguished from its opposite, "instance variable." We'll use both terms in this book.

An Example

As an example (a somewhat contrived one), suppose that while developing the Circle class we wanted to do some testing on it and determine how much it gets used. One way to do this would be to count the number of Circle objects that are instantiated. To do this we obviously need a variable associated with the class, rather than with any particular instance. Example 3-4 shows how we can do it—we declare a static variable and increment it each time we create a Circle.

Example 3-4: Static variable example

```
public class Circle {
    static int num_circles = 0;          // class variable: how many circles created
    public double x, y, r;               // instance vars: the center and the radius

    public Circle(double x, double y, double r) {
        this.x = x; this.y = y; this.r = r;
        num_circles++;
    }
    public Circle(double r) { this(0.0, 0.0, r); }
    public Circle(Circle c) { this(c.x, c.y, c.r); }
    public Circle() { this(0.0, 0.0, 1.0); }

    public double circumference() { return 2 * 3.14159 * r; }
    public double area() { return 3.14159 * r*r; }
}
```

Accessing Class Variables

Now that we are keeping track of the number of Circle objects created, how can we access this information? Because static variables are associated with the class rather than with an instance, we access them through the class rather than through the instance. Thus, we might write:*

```
System.out.println("Number of circles created: " + Circle.num_circles);
```

Notice that in our definition of the constructor method in Example 3-4, we just used num_circles instead of Circle.num_circles. We're allowed to do this within the class definition of Circle itself. Anywhere else, though, we must use the class name as well.

---

*Recall that System.out.println() prints a line of text, and that the string concatenation operator, +, converts non-string types to strings as necessary.

Global Variables?

Earlier we said that Java does not support global variables. In a sense, though, `Circle.num_circles` behaves just like one. What is different from a global variable in C is that there is no possibility of name conflicts. If we use some other class with a class variable named `num_circles`, there won't be a "collision" between these two "global" variables, because they must both be referred to by their class names. Since each class variable must be part of a class and must be referred to with its class name, each has a unique name. Furthermore, each class has a unique name because, as we saw in Section 2, *How Java Differs from C*, it is part of a package with a unique name.

Constants: Another Class Variable Example

Let's try a less forced example of why you might want to use a class variable with the `Circle` class. When computing the area and circumference of circles, we use the value π. Since we use the value frequently, we don't want to keep typing out 3.14159, so we'll define it as a class variable that has a convenient name:

```
public class Circle {
    public static final double PI = 3.14159265358979323846;
    public double x, y, r;
    // ... etc....
}
```

Besides the `static` keyword that we've already seen, we use the `final` keyword, which means that this variable can never have its value changed. This prevents you from doing something stupid like:

```
Circle.PI = 4;
```

which would tend to give you some pretty square-looking circles.

The Java compiler is smart about variables declared `static` and `final`—it knows that they have constant values. So when you write code like this:

```
double circumference = 2 * Circle.PI * radius;
```

the compiler precomputes the value `2 * Circle.PI`, instead of leaving it for the interpreter.

Java does not have a preprocessor with a C-style `#define` directive. `static final` variables are Java's substitute for C's `#define`'d constants. Note that the C convention of capitalizing constants has been carried over into Java.

Class Methods

Let's define a new method in our `Circle` class. This one tests whether a specified point falls within the defined circle:

```
public class Circle {
    double x, y, r;

    // is point (a,b) inside this circle?
    public boolean isInside(double a, double b)
    {
        double dx = a - x;
        double dy = b - y;
```

```
        double distance = Math.sqrt(dx*dx + dy*dy);
        if (distance < r) return true;
        else return false;
    }

    .
    . // Other methods omitted
    .

}
```

What's this `Math.sqrt()` thing? It looks like a method call and, given its name and its context, we can guess that it is computing a square root. But the method calls we've discussed are done through an object. `Math` isn't the name of an object that we've declared, and there aren't any global objects in Java, so this must be a kind of method call that we haven't seen before.

static Methods

What's going on here is that `Math` is the name of a class. `sqrt()` is the name of a *class method* (or static method) defined in `Math`. It differs from the *instance methods*, such as `area()` in `Circle`, that we've seen so far.

Class methods are like class variables in a number of ways:

- Class methods are declared with the `static` keyword.

- Class methods are often referred to as "static methods."

- Class methods are invoked through the class rather than through an instance. (Although within the class they may be invoked by method name alone.)

- Class methods are the closest Java comes to "global" methods. Because they must be referred to by the class name, there is no danger of name conflicts.

No this

Class methods differ from instance methods in one important way: they are not passed an implicit `this` reference. Thus, these `this`-less methods are not associated with any instance of the class and may not refer to any instance variables or invoke instance methods.

Since class methods are not passed a `this` reference, and are not invoked through an object, they are the closest thing that Java offers to the "normal" C procedures that you may be accustomed to, and may therefore seem familiar and comforting. If you're sick and tired of this object-oriented business, it is perfectly possible to write complete Java programs using only class methods, although this does defeat an important purpose of using the language!

But don't think that class methods are somehow cheating—there are perfectly good reasons to declare a method `static`. And indeed, there are classes like `Math` that declare all their methods (and variables) `static`. Since `Math` is a collection of functions that operate on floating-point numbers, which are a primitive type, there are no objects involved, and no need for instance methods. `System` is another class that defines only class methods—it provides a varied collection of system functions for which there is no appropriate object framework.

A Class Method for Circles

Example 3-5 shows two (overloaded) definitions of a method for our `Circle` class. One is an instance method and one is a class method.

Example 3-5: A class method and an instance method

```
public class Circle {
    public double x, y, r;

    // an instance method.  Returns the bigger of two circles.
    public Circle bigger(Circle c) {
        if (c.r > r) return c; else return this;
    }
    // a class method.  Returns the bigger of two circles
    public static Circle bigger(Circle a, Circle b) {
        if (a.r > b.r) return a; else return b;
    }

    .
    . // other methods omitted here.
    .

}
```

You would invoke the instance method like this:

```
Circle a = new Circle(2.0);
Circle b = new Circle(3.0);
Circle c = a.bigger(b);           // or, b.bigger(a);
```

And you would invoke the class method like this:

```
Circle a = new Circle(2.0);
Circle b = new Circle(3.0);
Circle c = Circle.bigger(a,b);
```

Neither of these is the "correct" way to implement this method. One or the other will seem more natural, depending on circumstances.

A Mystery Explained

Now that we understand class variables, instance variables, class methods, and instance methods, we are in a position to explore that mysterious method call we saw in our very first Java "Hello World" example:

```
System.out.println("Hello world!");
```

One hypothesis is that `println()` is a class method in a class named `out`, which is in a package named `System`. Syntactically, this is perfectly reasonable (except perhaps that class names always seem to be capitalized by convention, and `out` isn't capitalized). But if you look at the API documentation, you'll find that `System` is not a package name; it is the name of a class (which is in the `java.lang` package, by the way). Can you figure it out?

Here's the story: `System` is a class. It has a class variable named `out`. `out` refers to an object of type `PrintStream`. The object `System.out` has an instance method named `println()`. Mystery solved!

Static Initializers

Both class and instance variables can have initializers attached to their declarations. For example:

```
static int num_circles = 0;
float r = 1.0;
```

Class variables are initialized when the class is first loaded. Instance variables are initialized when an object is created.

Sometimes we need more complex initialization than is possible with these simple variable initializers. For instance variables, there are constructor methods, which are run when a new instance of the class is created. Java also allows you to write an initialization method for class variables. Such a method is called a *static initializer.*

The syntax of static initializers gets kind of bizarre. Consider that a static initializer is invoked automatically by the system when the class is loaded. Thus there are no meaningful arguments that can be passed to it (unlike the arguments we can pass to a constructor method when creating a new instance). There is also no value to return. So a static initializer has no arguments and no return value. Furthermore, it is not really necessary to give it a name, since the system calls the method automatically for us. What part of a method declaration is left? Just the `static` keyword and the curly brackets!

Example 3-6 shows a class declaration with a static initializer. Notice that the class contains a regular static variable initializer of the kind we've seen before, and also a static initializer—an arbitrary block of code between { and }.

Example 3-6: A static initializer

```
// We can draw the outline of a circle using trigonometric functions.
// Trigonometry is slow though, so we pre-compute a bunch of values
public class Circle {
    // Here are our static lookup tables, and their own simple initializers.
    static private double sines[] = new double[1000];
    static private double cosines[] = new double[1000];

    // Here's a static initializer "method" that fills them in.
    // Notice the lack of any method declaration!
    static {
        double x, delta_x;
        int i;
        delta_x = (Circle.PI/2)/(1000-1);
        for(i = 0; x = 0.0; i < 1000; i++, x += deltax) {
            sines[i] = Math.sin(x);
            cosines[i] = Math.cos(x);
        }
    }
    .
    . // The rest of the class omitted.
    .
}
```

The syntax gets even a little stranger than this. Java allows any number of static initializer blocks of code to appear within a class definition. What the compiler actually does is to internally produce a single class initialization routine that combines all the

---

static variable initializers and all of the static initializer blocks of code, in the order that they appear in the class declaration. This single initialization procedure is run automatically, one time only, when the class is first loaded.

One common use of static initializers is for classes that implement `native` methods—i.e., methods written in C. The static initializer for such a class should call `System.load()` or `System.loadLibrary()` to read in the native library that implements these native methods.

Object Destruction

Now that we've seen how you can create and use objects, the next obvious question, a question that C and C++ programmers have been itching to have answered, is how do you destroy objects when they are no longer needed?

The answer is: You don't! Objects are not passed to any `free()` method, as allocated memory in C is. And there is no `delete` operator as there is in C++. Java takes care of object destruction for you, and lets you concentrate on other, more important things, like the algorithm you're working on.

Garbage Collection

The technique Java uses to get rid of objects once they are no longer needed is called *garbage collection*. It is a technique that has been around for years in languages such as Lisp. The Java interpreter knows what objects it has allocated. It can also figure out which variables refer to which objects, and which objects refer to which other objects. Thus, it can figure out when an allocated object is no longer referred to by any other object or variable. When it finds such an object, it knows that it can destroy it safely, and does so.

The Java garbage collector runs as a low-priority thread, and does most of its work when nothing else is going on. Generally, it runs during idle time while waiting for user input in the form of keystrokes or mouse events. The only time the garbage collector must run while something high-priority is going on (i.e., the only time it will actually slow down the system) is when the interpreter has run out of memory. This doesn't happen often because there is that low-priority thread cleaning things up in the background.

This scheme may sound extremely slow and wasteful of memory. Actually though, good garbage collectors can be surprisingly efficient. No, garbage collection will never be as efficient as explicit, well-written memory allocation and deallocation. But it does make programming a lot easier and less prone to bugs. And for most real-world programs, rapid development, lack of bugs, and easy maintenance are more important features than raw speed or memory efficiency.

Putting the Trash Out

What garbage collection means for your programs is that when you are done with an object, you can just forget about it—the garbage collector finds it and takes care of it. Example 3-7 shows an example.

Example 3-7: Leaving an object out for garbage collection

```
String processString(String s)
{
    // Create a StringBuffer object to process the string in
    StringBuffer b = new StringBuffer(s);

    // process it somehow

    // return it as a String.
    // Just forget about the StringBuffer object--
    //   it will be automatically garbage collected.
    return b.toString();
}
```

If you're a C or C++ programmer, conditioned to allocating and deallocating your own dynamic memory, you may at first feel a nagging sense of misgiving when you write procedures that allocate and then forget objects. You'll get used to it though, and even learn to love it!

There is an instance where you may want to take some action to help the garbage collection process along by "forgetting quickly." Example 3-8 explains.

Example 3-8: Forced forgetting of an object

```
public static void main(String argv[])
{
    int big_array[] = new int[100000];

    // do some computations with big_array and get a result
    int result = compute(big_array);

    // We no longer need big_array.  It will get garbage collected when
    // there are no more references.  Since big_array is a local variable,
    // it refers to the array until this method returns.  But this
    // method doesn't return.  So we've got to get rid of the reference
    // ourselves, just to help out the garbage collector.
    big_array = null;

    // loop forever, handling the user's input
    for(;;) handle_input();
}
```

Object Finalization

Just as a constructor method performs initialization for an object, a Java *finalizer* method performs finalization for an object.

Garbage collection automatically frees up the memory resources used by objects. But objects may hold other kinds of resources, such as file descriptors or sockets, as well. The garbage collector can't free these resources up for you, so you should write a finalizer method that takes care of things like closing open files, terminating network connections, and so on.

Example 3-9 shows the finalizer method from the Java `FileOutputStream` class. Note that a finalizer is an instance method (i.e., non-`static`), takes no arguments, returns no value (i.e., `void`), and must be named `finalize()`.*

Example 3-9: A finalizer method

```
/**
 * Closes the stream when garbage is collected.
 * Checks the file descriptor first to make sure it is not already closed.
 */
protected void finalize() throws IOException {
    if (fd != null) close();
}
```

There are some additional things to be aware of about finalizers:

- If an object has a finalizer, that method is invoked before the system garbage collects the object.

- The Java interpreter may exit without garbage collecting all outstanding objects, so some finalizers may never be invoked. In this case, though, any outstanding resources are usually freed by the operating system.

- Java makes no guarantees about when garbage collection will occur, or what order objects will be collected in. Therefore, Java can make no guarantees about when a finalizer will be invoked, or in what order finalizers will be invoked, or what thread will execute finalizers.

- After a finalizer is invoked, objects are not freed right away. This is because a finalizer method may "resurrect" an object by storing the `this` pointer somewhere, so that the object once again has references. Thus, after `finalize()` is called, an object must once again be determined to be unreferenced before it can actually be garbage collected. Even if an object is "resurrected," the finalizer method is never invoked more than once.

- The finalizer shown in Example 3-9 declares that it may throw an exception (exceptions are described in detail in Section 2). If an uncaught exception actually occurs in a finalizer method, however, the exception is ignored by the system.

Subclasses and Inheritance

The `Circle` class we've defined is good for abstract mathematical manipulation. For some applications this is exactly what we need. For other applications, we want to be able to manipulate circles *and* draw them on the screen. This means we need a new class, `GraphicCircle`, that has all the functionality of `Circle`, but also has the ability to be drawn.

We want to implement `GraphicCircle` so that it can make use of the code we've already written for `Circle`. One way to do that is the following:

---

*C++ programmers, take note! Although Java constructor methods are named like C++ constructors, Java finalization methods are not named like C++ destructor methods.

```
public class GraphicCircle {
    public Circle c; // here's the mathematical circle
    // Here are the old methods
    public double area() { return c.area(); }
    public double circumference() { return c.circumference(); }

    // The new graphic variables and methods go here
    public Color outline, fill;
    public void draw(DrawWindow dw) { /* code omitted */ }
}
```

This approach would work, but it is not particularly elegant. The problem is that we have to write stubs for methods like `area()` and `circumference()` that have nothing to do with drawing circles. It would be nice if we didn't have to do this.

Extending a Class

In fact, we don't have to do it this way. Java allows us to define `GraphicCircle` as an extension, or *subclass* of `Circle`. Example 3-10 shows how. Note that this example assumes we have two other classes of objects defined: `Color`, which represents a color, and `DrawWindow`, a class that has the window into which drawing is done and that defines the primitive methods to do the drawing.

Example 3-10: Subclassing a class

```
public class GraphicCircle extends Circle {
    // we automatically inherit the variables and methods of
    // Circle, so we only have to put the new stuff here.
    // We've omitted the GraphicCircle constructor, for now.
    Color outline, fill;
    public void draw(DrawWindow dw) {
        dw.drawCircle(x, y, r, outline, fill);
    }
}
```

The `extends` keyword tells Java that `GraphicCircle` is a subclass of `Circle`, and that it *inherits* the variables and methods of that class.* The definition of the `draw()` method shows variable inheritance—this method uses the `Circle` variables `x`, `y`, and `r` as if they were defined right in `GraphicCircle` itself.

`GraphicCircle` also inherits the methods of `Circle`. Thus, if we have a `GraphicCircle` object referred to by variable `gc`, we can say:

```
double area = gc.area();
```

This works just as if the `area()` method were defined in `GraphicCircle` itself.

Another feature of subclassing is that every `GraphicCircle` object is also a perfectly legal `Circle` object. Thus, if `gc` refers to a `GraphicCircle` object, we can assign it to a `Circle` variable and forget all about its extra graphic capabilities:

```
Circle c = gc;
```

---

*Except for the `private` variables and methods. We'll talk about `private` fields of a class later. C++ programmers should note that `extends` is the Java equivalent of the : operator in C++—both indicate the superclass of a class.

final classes

When a class is declared with the `final` modifier, it means that it cannot be extended or subclassed. `java.lang.System` is an example of a `final` class. Declaring a class `final` prevents unwanted extensions to the class. But it also allows the compiler to make some optimizations when invoking the methods of a class. We'll explore this in more detail when we talk about method overriding later in this section.

Superclasses, Object, and the Class Hierarchy

In our example, `GraphicCircle` is a subclass of `Circle`. We can also say that `Circle` is the *superclass* of `GraphicCircle`. The superclass of a class is specified in its `extends` clause:

```
public class GraphicCircle extends Circle { ... }
```

Every class you define has a superclass. If you do not specify the superclass with an `extends` clause, the superclass is the class `Object`. `Object` is a special class for a couple of reasons:

- It is the only class that does not have a superclass

- The methods defined by `Object` can be called by any Java object

Because every class has a superclass, classes in Java form a *class hierarchy*, which can be represented as a tree with `Object` at its root. Figure 3-1 shows a class hierarchy diagram which includes our `Circle` and `GraphicCircle` classes, as well as some of the standard classes from the Java API.

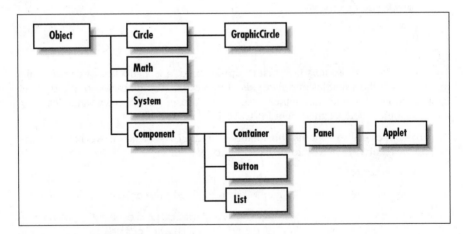

Figure 3-1: A class hierarchy diagram

The complete class hierarchy for the Java API is diagrammed in the figures of Part IV, *API Quick Reference.*

Subclass Constructors

In Example 3-10 we left out the constructor method for our new `GraphicCircle` class. Let's implement that now. Here's one way:

```
public GraphicCircle(double x, double y, double r,
               Color outline, Color fill)
{
    this.x = x;
    this.y = y;
    this.r = r;
    this.outline = outline;
    this.fill = fill;
}
```

This constructor relies on the fact that `GraphicCircle` inherits all of the variables of `Circle` and simply initializes those variables itself. But this duplicates the code of the `Circle` constructor, and if `Circle` did more elaborate initialization, it could become quite wasteful. What we want is a way of calling a `Circle` constructor from within our `GraphicCircle` constructor. Example 3-11 shows how we can do this.

Example 3-11: Invoking a superclass's constructor

```
public GraphicCircle(double x, double y, double r,
               Color outline, Color fill)
{
    super(x, y, r);
    this.outline = outline;
    this.fill = fill;
}
```

`super` is a reserved word in Java. One of its uses is that shown in the example—to invoke the constructor method of a superclass. Its use is analogous to the use of the `this` keyword to invoke one constructor method of a class from within another. Using `super` to invoke a constructor is subject to the same restrictions as using `this` to invoke a constructor:

- `super` may only be used in this way within a constructor method.

- The call to the superclass constructor must appear as the first statement within the constructor method. It must appear even before variable declarations.

Constructor Chaining

When you define a class, Java guarantees that the class's constructor method is called whenever an instance of that class is created. It also guarantees that the constructor is called when an instance of any subclass is created. In order to guarantee this second point, Java must ensure that every constructor method calls its superclass constructor method. If the first statement in a constructor is not an explicit call to a constructor of the superclass with the `super` keyword, then Java implicitly inserts the call `super()`—that is, it calls the superclass constructor with no arguments. If the superclass does not have a constructor that takes no arguments, this causes a compilation error.

There is one exception to the rule that Java invokes `super()` implicitly if you do not do so explicitly. If the first line of a constructor is a call to another constructor in the same class using the `this()` syntax that we saw earlier, Java does not implicitly call the superclass constructor. But note that if the constructor invoked with the `this()` syntax does not invoke `super()` (or invoke `this()` again) explicitly, Java does invoke `super()` implicitly. So while constructor methods within a class may invoke each other, eventually one of them must invoke (explicitly or implicitly) the superclass constructor method.

Consider what happens when we create a new instance of the `GraphicCircle` class. First, the `GraphicCircle` constructor shown in Example 3-11 is invoked. This constructor explicitly invokes a `Circle` constructor and that `Circle` constructor implicitly calls `super()` to invoke the constructor of its superclass, `Object`. The body of the `Object` constructor runs first, followed by the body of the `Circle` constructor, and finally followed by the body of the `GraphicCircle` constructor.

What this all means is that constructor calls are "chained"—any time an object is created, a sequence of constructor methods are invoked, from subclass to superclass on up to `Object` at the root of the class hierarchy. Because a superclass constructor is always invoked as the first statement of its subclass constructor, the body of the `Object` constructor always runs first, followed by the body of its subclass, and on down the class hierarchy to the class that is being instantiated.

The Default Constructor

There is one missing piece in the description of constructor chaining above. If a constructor does not invoke a superclass constructor, Java does so implicitly. But what if a class is declared without a constructor? In this case, Java implicitly adds a constructor to the class. This default constructor does nothing but invoke the superclass constructor.

For example, if we did not declare a constructor for the `GraphicCircle` class, Java would have implicitly inserted this constructor:

```
public GraphicCircle() { super(); }
```

It can be confusing when Java implicitly calls a constructor or inserts a constructor definition into a class—something is happening that does not appear in your code! Therefore, it is good coding style, whenever you rely on an implicit superclass constructor call or on a default constructor, to insert a comment noting this fact. Your comments might look like those in the following example:

```
class A {
    int i;
    public A() {
        // implicit call to super(); here.
        i = 3;
    }
}

class B extends A {
    // default constructor: public B() { super(); }
}
```

Finalizer Chaining?

You might assume that since Java chains constructor methods that it also automatically chains the finalizer methods for an object. In other words, you may think that the finalizer method of a class automatically invokes the finalizer of its superclass. In fact, Java does *not* do this. In practice, finalizer methods are relatively rare, and the need for finalizer chaining rarely arises. If a class B with a finalizer method is a subclass of a class A with its own finalizer method, then B's finalizer should be sure to invoke A's finalizer, explicitly creating a chain of finalizers. This is a little tricky, since finalizers always have the same name (`finalize()`), and we haven't yet learned how to invoke a method in the superclass when that method is also defined in the subclass. We'll return to the issue of finalizer chaining when we learn how.

Shadowed Variables

Suppose that our `GraphicCircle` class has a new variable that specifies the resolution, in dots per inch, of the `DrawWindow` object in which it is going to be drawn. And further, suppose that it names that new variable `r`:

```
public class GraphicCircle extends Circle {
    Color outline, fill;
    float r; // New variable. Resolution in dots-per-inch.
    public GraphicCircle(double x, double y, double radius, Color o, Color f) {
        super(x, y, radius); outline = o; fill = f;
    }
    public void setResolution(float resolution) { r = resolution; }
    public void draw(DrawWindow dw) { dw.drawCircle(x, y, r, outline, fill); }
}
```

Now, with this resolution variable declared, when we use the variable `r` in the `GraphicCircle` class, we are no longer referring to the radius of the circle. The resolution variable `r` in `GraphicCircle` *shadows* the radius variable `r` in `Circle`.*

So, how can we refer to the radius variable defined in the `Circle` class when we need it? Recall that using a variable, such as `r`, in the class in which it is defined is shorthand for:

```
this.r // refers to the GraphicCircle resolution variable
```

As you might guess, you can refer to a variable `r` defined in the superclass like this:

```
super.r // refers to the Circle radius variable.
```

Another way you can do this is to cast `this` to the appropriate class and then access the variable:

```
((Circle) this).r
```

This cast is exactly what the `super` keyword does when used like this. You can use this casting technique when you need to refer to a shadowed variable defined in a class that is not the immediate superclass. For example, if C is a subclass of B, which

---

*This is a contrived example, of course—we could simply rename the variable and avoid the issue.

is a subclass of A, and class C shadows a variable x that is also defined in classes A and B, then you can refer to these different variables from class C as follows:

x	// variable x in class C
this.x	// variable x in class C
super.x	// variable x in class B
((B)this).x	// variable x in class B
((A)this).x	// variable x in class A
super.super.x	// illegal; does not refer to x in class A.

Note that you cannot refer to a shadowed variable x in the superclass of a superclass with `super.super.x`. Java does not recognize this syntax.

Shadowed Methods?

Just as a variable .defined in one class can shadow a variable with the same name in a superclass, you might expect that a method in one class could shadow a method with the same name (and same arguments) in a superclass. In a sense, they do: "shadowed" methods are called overridden methods. But method overriding is significantly different than variable shadowing; it is discussed in the sections that follow.

Overriding Methods

When a class defines a method using the same name, return type, and arguments as a method in its superclass, the method in the class *overrides* the method in the superclass. When the method is invoked for an object of the class, it is the new definition of the method that is called, not the superclass' old definition.

Method overriding is an important and useful technique in object-oriented programming. Suppose we define a subclass `Ellipse` of our `Circle` class.* Then it would be important for `Ellipse` to override the `area()` and `circumference()` methods of `Circle`. `Ellipse` would have to implement new versions of these functions because the formulas that apply to circles don't work for ellipses.

Before we go any further with the discussion of method overriding, be sure that you understand the difference between method overriding and method overloading, which we discussed earlier. As you probably recall, method overloading refers to the practice of defining multiple methods (in the same class) with the same name but with differing argument lists or return types. This is very different from method overriding, and it is important not to get them confused!

Overriding Is Not Shadowing

Although Java treats the variables and methods of a class analogously in many ways, method overriding is not like variable shadowing at all: You can refer to shadowed variables simply by casting an object to the appropriate type. You cannot invoke overridden methods with this technique, however. Example 3-12 illustrates this crucial difference.

---

*This is admittedly a strange thing to do, since, mathematically, a circle is a kind of ellipse, and not the other way around. Nevertheless, it is a useful example here.

Example 3-12: Method overriding vs. variable shadowing

```
class A {
    int i = 1;
    int f() { return i; }
}

class B extends A {
    int i = 2;                       // shadows variable i in class A.
    int f() { return -i; }           // overrides method f in class A.
}

public class override_test {
    public static void main(String args[]) {
        B b = new B();
        System.out.println(b.i);     // refers to B.i; prints 2.
        System.out.println(b.f());   // refers to B.f(); prints -2

        A a = (A) b;                 // cast b to an instance of class A.
        System.out.println(a.i);     // now refers to A.i; prints 1;
        System.out.println(a.f());   // still refers to B.f(); prints -2;
    }
}
```

While this difference between method overriding and variable shadowing may seem surprising at first, a little thought makes the purpose clear. Suppose we have a bunch of `Circle` and `Ellipse` (a subclass of `Circle`) objects that we are manipulating. To keep track of the circles and ellipses, we store them in an array of type `Circle[]`, casting all the `Ellipse` objects to `Circle` objects before we store them. Then, when we loop through the elements of this array, we don't have to know or care whether the element is actually a `Circle` or an `Ellipse`. What we do care very much about, however, is that the correct value is computed when we invoke the `area()` method of any element of the array. That is, we don't want to use the formula for the area of a circle when the object is actually an ellipse!

Seen in this context, it is not surprising at all that method overriding is handled differently by Java than variable shadowing.

final Methods

If a method is declared `final`, it means that the method declaration is the "final" one—that it cannot be overridden. All `static` methods and `private` methods (which we haven't learned about yet) are implicitly final, as are all methods of a `final` class. If a method is explicitly or implicitly `final`, the compiler may perform certain optimizations on it, as we'll see below.

Dynamic Method Lookup

If we have an array of `Circle` and `Ellipse` objects, how does the compiler know to call the `Circle` `area()` method or the `Ellipse` `area()` method for any given item in the array? The compiler does not know this; it can't. The compiler knows that it does not know, however, and produces code that uses "dynamic method lookup" at run-time. The Java interpreter does know which objects in the array are of class `Circle` and which are of class `Ellipse`, so it is able to determine the appropriate `area()` method to call for each of the objects.*

Dynamic method lookup is fast, but it is not as fast as invoking a method directly. Fortunately, there are a number of cases in which Java does not need to use dynamic method lookup. `static` methods cannot be overridden, so they are always invoked directly. `private` methods (which we haven't learned about yet) are not inherited by subclasses and so cannot be overridden by subclasses; this means the Java compiler can safely invoke them without dynamic method lookup as well. Finally, `final` methods and methods in `final` classes are also invoked directly. These `static`, `final`, and `private` methods that can be invoked directly are also candidates for inlining—i.e., if the methods are short, the compiler may simply insert the method body into the code rather than inserting a call to the method.

Invoking an Overridden Method

We've seen the important differences between method overriding and variable shadowing. Nevertheless, the Java syntax for invoking an overridden method is very similar to the syntax for accessing a shadowed variable: both use the `super` keyword. Example 3-13 illustrates this.

Example 3-13: Invoking an overridden method

```
class A {
    int i = 1;
    int f() { return i; }          // A very simple method
}
class B extends A {
    int i;                         // This variable shadows i in A.
    int f() {                      // This method overrides f() in A.
        i = super.i + 1;           // It retrieves A.i this way.
        return super.f() + i;      // And it invokes A.f() this way.
    }
}
```

Recall that when you use `super` to refer to a shadowed variable, it is the same as casting `this` to the superclass type and accessing the variable through that. On the other hand, using `super` to invoke an overridden method is not the same as casting `this`. In this case, `super` has the special purpose of turning off dynamic method lookup and invoking the specific method that the superclass defines or inherits.

In Example 3-13 we use `super` to invoke an overridden method that is actually defined in the immediate superclass. `super` also works perfectly well to invoke overridden methods that are defined further up the class hierarchy. This is because the overridden method is inherited by the immediate superclass, and so the `super` syntax does in fact refer to the correct method. To make this more concrete, sup-

---

*C++ programmers should note that dynamic method lookup is what C++ does for `virtual` functions. A very important difference between Java and C++ is that Java does not have a `virtual` keyword; methods in Java are "virtual" by default.

pose class A defines method f, and that B is a subclass of A, and that C is a subclass of B that overrides method f. Then you can still use:

```
super.f()
```

to invoke the overridden method from within class C. This is because class B inherits method f from class A. If classes A, B, and C all define method f, however, then calling `super.f()` in class C invokes class B's definition of the method. In this case, there is no way to invoke `A.f()` from within class C. `super.super.f()` is not legal Java syntax!

It is important to note that `super` can only be used to invoke overridden methods from within the class that does the overriding. With our `Circle` and `ellipse` classes, for example, there is no way to write a program (with or without `super`) that invokes the `Circle area()` method on an object of type `Ellipse`. The only way to do this is to use `super` in a method within the `Ellipse` class.

Finally, note that this form of `super` does not have to occur in the first statement in a method, as it does when used to invoke a superclass constructor method.

Finalizer Chaining Revisited

Now that we've discussed method overriding and how to invoke an overridden method, we can return to the issue of the finalizer method that we left dangling earlier on.

In Java, constructor methods are automatically chained, but finalizer methods are not. If you define a `finalize()` method to free resources allocated by your class, you may be overriding a `finalize()` method in a superclass that frees resources allocated by that class. If your finalizer method does not invoke the superclass finalizer, the superclass finalizer never gets called, and resources are not deallocated when they should be.

To prevent this, you should be sure to invoke the superclass `finalize()` method. The best time to do this is usually after your `finalize()` method has done all of its deallocation. It is a good idea to add the following call:

```
super.finalize();
```

as the last line of all your finalizer methods. You should do this even if you know that none of your class's superclasses have finalizer methods, because future implementations of the class may include one.

Data Hiding and Encapsulation

We started this section by describing a class as "a collection of data and methods." One of the important object-oriented techniques that we haven't discussed so far is hiding the data within the class, and making it available only through the methods. This technique is often known as *encapsulation*, because it seals the class's data safely inside the "capsule" of the class, where it can be accessed only by trusted users—i.e., by the methods of the class.

Why would you want to do this? One reason is to protect your class against accidental or willful stupidity. A class often contains a number of variables that are interdependent and must be in a consistent state. If you allow a programmer (this may be you yourself) to manipulate those variables directly, he may change one variable without changing important related variables, thus leaving the class in an inconsistent state. If, instead, he had to call a method to change the variable, that method can be sure to do everything necessary to keep the state consistent.

Here's another way to think about encapsulation: When all of a class's variables are hidden, the class's methods define the only possible operations that can be performed on objects of that class. Once you have carefully tested and debugged your methods, you can be confident that the class will work as expected. On the other hand, if all the variables can be directly manipulated, the number of possibilities you have to test becomes unmanageable.

There are other reasons to hide data, too:

- Internal variables that are visible externally to the class just clutter up your class's API. Keeping visible variables to a minimum keeps your class tidy and elegant.

- If a variable is visible in your class, you have to document it. Save time by hiding it instead!

Visibility Modifiers

In most of our examples so far, you've probably noticed the `public` keyword being used. When applied to a class, it means that the class is visible everywhere. When applied to a method or variable, it means that the method or variable is visible everywhere.

To hide variables (or methods, for that matter) you just have to declare them `private`:

```
public class Laundromat {        // people can use this class
    private Laundry[] dirty;     // they can't see this internal variable
    public void wash();          // but they can use these public methods.
    public void dry();           // to manipulate the internal variable.
}
```

A `private` variable of a class is visible only in methods defined within that class. Similarly, a `private` method may only be invoked by methods within the class. Private methods and variables are not visible within subclasses, and are *not* inherited by subclasses as other methods and variables are. (Of course, non-`private` methods that invoke `private` methods internally are inherited and are visible in subclasses.)

Besides `public` and `private`, Java has three other visibility levels: `private protected`, `protected`, and the default visibility level, which applies if none of the `public`, `private`, and `protected` keywords are used.

A `private protected` method or variable is only visible within its own class and within subclasses. A `protected` method or variable is visible within the class where it is defined, of course, and within all subclasses of the class, and also within all classes that are in the same package as that class. A `protected` field is like a `private protected` field except that it is also visible throughout the package of the class in which it is defined. You should use `protected` or `private protected` visibility when you want to hide methods and variables from code that use your class, but want those methods and variables to be fully accessible to code that extends your class.

Somewhat counter-intuitively, the default visibility is *more* strict than `protected`. If a variable or method is not declared with any of the `public`, `private`, or `protected` keywords, it is visible only within the class that defines it, and within classes that are part of the same package. It is not visible to subclasses (unless they are subclasses in the same package).

A note about packages: A package is a group of related and possibly cooperating classes. All non-`private` variables and methods of all classes in the package are visible to all other classes in the package. This is okay because the classes are assumed to know about, and trust, each other.* The only time difficulty arises is when you write programs without a `package` statement. These classes are thrown into the default package with every other `package`-less class, and all their non-`private` fields are visible throughout the package.

There is an important point to make about subclass access to `private protected` and `protected` fields. Subclasses inherit `private protected` and `protected` fields, but they can't access those fields in instances of the superclass itself. For example, if class A has `private protected` fields, and B is a subclass of A, then B inherits those fields and can access them in instances of itself or in instances of subclasses of itself. B cannot access those `private protected` fields in instances of A, however. The same applies to `protected` fields when the subclass is not part of the same package as the superclass.

Table 3-1 shows the circumstances under which fields of the various visibility types are accessible and the circumstances under which they are inherited by subclasses.

Table 3-1: Java Field Visibility

Situation	public	default	protected	private protected	private
Accessible to non-subclass from same package?	yes	yes	yes	no	no
Accessible to subclass from same package?	yes	yes	yes	no	no
Accessible to non-subclass from different package?	yes	no	no	no	no
Accessible to subclass from different package?	yes	no	no	no	no
Inherited by subclass in same package?	yes	yes	yes	yes	no
Inherited by subclass in different package?	yes	no	yes	yes	no

All the details of field visibility in Java can become quite confusing. Here are some simple rules of thumb for using visibility modifiers:

- Use `private` for methods and variables that are only used inside the class and should be hidden everywhere else.

*If you are a C++ programmer, you might say that classes within the same package are `friend`-ly to each other.

- Use `public` for methods, constants, and other important variables that should be visible everywhere.

- Use `private protected` for methods and variables that aren't necessary to use the class, but that may be of interest to anyone extending the class. Use `protected` instead if you want classes in the same package to have access to those fields.

- Use the default visibility for methods and variables that you want to be hidden outside of the package, but which you want cooperating classes within the same package to have access to. Use `protected` instead, if you also want those fields to be visible to subclasses outside of the package.

- Use the `package` statement to group your classes into related packages.

Also see Section 10, *Java Syntax*, for a table that summarizes the Java visibility modifiers and other modifiers.

Data Access Methods

In the `Circle` example we've been using, we've declared the circle position and radius to be `public` fields. In fact, the `Circle` class is one where it may well make sense to keep those visible—it is a simple enough class, with no dependencies between the variables.

On the other hand, suppose we wanted to impose a maximum radius on objects of the `Circle` class. Then it would be better to hide the `r` variable so that it could not be set directly. Instead of a visible `r` variable, we'd implement a `setRadius()` method that verifies that the specified radius isn't too large and then sets the `r` variable internally. Example 3-14 shows how we might implement `Circle` with encapsulated data and a restriction on radius size. For convenience, we use `protected` fields for the radius and position variables. This means that subclasses of `Circle`, or cooperating classes within the `shapes` package are able to access these variables directly. To any other classes, however, the variables are hidden. Also, note the `private` constant and method used to check whether a specified radius is legal. And finally, notice the `public` methods that allow you to set and query the values of the class variables.

Example 3-14: Hiding variables in the Circle class

```
package shapes;                              // specify a package for the class.

public class Circle {                        // Note that the class is still public!
    protected double x, y;                   // position is hidden, but visible to subclasses
    protected double r;                      // radius is hidden, but visible to subclasses
    private static final double MAXR = 100.0;  // maximum radius
    private boolean check_radius(int r) { return (r <= MAXR); }

    // public constructors
    public Circle(double x, double y, double r) {
        this.x = x; this.y = y;
        if (check_radius(r)) this.r = r;
        else this.r = MAXR;
    }
    public Circle(double r) { this(0.0, 0.0, r); }
    public Circle() { this(0.0, 0.0, 1.0); }
```

Example 3-14: Hiding variables in the Circle class (continued)

```
    // public data access methods
    public void moveto(double x, double y) { this.x = x; this.y = y;}
    public void move(double dx, double dy) { x += dx;  y += dy; }
    public void setRadius(double r) { this.r = (check_radius(r))?r:MAXR; }

    // declare these trivial methods final so we don't get dynamic
    // method lookup and so that they can be inlined by the compiler.
    public final double getX() { return x; };
    public final double getY() { return y; };
    public final double getRadius() { return r; };
}
```

Abstract Classes and Interfaces

In Example 3-14, we declared our `Circle` class to be part of a package named `shapes`. Suppose we plan to implement a number of shape classes: `Rectangle`, `Square`, `Ellipse`, `Triangle`, and so on. We'll give all of these shape classes our two basic `area()` and `circumference()` methods. Now, to make it easy to work with an array of shapes, it would be helpful if all our shape classes have a common superclass, `Shape`. We want `Shape` to encapsulate whatever features all our shapes have in common. In this case, what they have in common is the `area()` and `circumference()` methods. But our generic `Shape` class can't actually implement these methods, since it doesn't represent any actual shape. Java handles this case with abstract methods.

Abstract Methods

Java lets us define a method without implementing it by making the method `abstract`. An `abstract` method has no body; it simply has a signature definition followed by a semicolon.* Here are the rules about `abstract` methods, and the `abstract` classes that contain them:

• Any class with an `abstract` method is automatically `abstract` itself; an `abstract` class must have at least one `abstract` method in it.

• An `abstract` class cannot be instantiated.

• A subclass of an `abstract` class can be instantiated if it overrides each of the `abstract` methods of its superclass and provides an implementation (i.e., a method body) for all of them.

• If a subclass of an `abstract` class does not implement all of the `abstract` methods it inherits, that subclass is itself `abstract`.

That description of the `abstract` keyword was pretty abstract! Example 3-15 is more concrete. It shows an `abstract` `Shape` class and two non-`abstract` subclasses of it.

---

*An `abstract` method in Java is something like a "pure virtual function" in C++ (i.e., a virtual function that is declared = 0). In C++, a class that contains a pure virtual function is called an "abstract class" and may not be instantiated. The same is true of Java classes that contain `abstract` methods.

Example 3-15: An abstract class and subclasses

```
public abstract class Shape {
    public abstract double area();
    public abstract double circumference();
}

public class Circle extends Shape {
    protected double r;
    protected static final double PI = 3.14159265358979323846;
    public Circle() { r = 1.0; }
    public Circle(double r) { this.r = r; }
    public double area() { return PI * r * r; }
    public double circumference() { return 2 * PI * r; }
    public double getRadius() { return r; }
}

public class Rectangle extends Shape {
    protected double w, h;
    public Rectangle() { w = 0.0; h = 0.0; }
    public Rectangle(double w, double h) { this.w = w;  this.h = h; }
    public double area() { return w * h; }
    public double circumference() { return 2 * (w + h); }
    public double getWidth() { return w; }
    public double getHeight() { return h; }
}
```

Note that the `abstract` methods in `Shape` have a semicolon right after their parentheses. There are no curly braces, and no method body is defined. Using the classes defined in Example 3-15, we can now write code like this:

```
Shape[] shapes = new Shape[3];          // create an array to hold shapes
shapes[0] = new Circle(2.0);            // fill in the array...
shapes[1] = new Rectangle(1.0, 3.0);
shapes[2] = new Rectangle(4.0, 2.0);

double total_area = 0;
for(int i = 0; i < shapes.length; i++)
    total_area += shapes[i].area();     // compute the area of the shapes
```

There are two important points to notice here:

- Subclasses of `Shape` can be assigned to elements of an array of `Shape`. No cast is necessary.

- You can invoke the `area()` and `circumference()` methods for `Shape` objects, even through `Shape` does not define a body for these methods, because `Shape` declared them `abstract`. If `Shape` did not declare them at all, the code would cause a compilation error.

Interfaces

Let's extend our `shapes` package further. Suppose we now want to implement a number of shapes that can be drawn on the screen. We could define an abstract `DrawableShape` class, and then implement various subclasses of it, such as `DrawableCircle`, `DrawableRectangle`, and so on. This would work fine.

But suppose we want our drawable shape types to support the `area()` and `circumference()` methods. We don't want to have to re-implement these methods, so we'd like to make `DrawableCircle` a subclass of `Circle`, for example, and `DrawableRectangle` a subclass of `Rectangle`. But classes in Java can only have one superclass. If `DrawableCircle` extends `Circle`, then it cannot also extend `DrawableShape`!*

Java's solution to this problem is called an *interface*. An interface looks a lot like an abstract class, except that it uses the keyword `interface` instead of the words `abstract` and `class`. Example 3-16 shows an interface named `Drawable`.

Example 3-16: An interface definition

```
public interface Drawable {
    public void setColor(Color c);
    public void setPosition(double x, double y);
    public void draw(DrawWindow dw);
}
```

While an `abstract` class may define some `abstract` methods and some non-abstract methods, all the methods defined within an interface are implicitly abstract. We've omitted the `abstract` keyword in this example, but it is perfectly legal to use it if you want to belabor the abstractness of interface methods. A further restriction on interfaces is that any variables declared in an interface must be `static` and `final`—that is, they must be constants.

So what can we do with an interface? Just as a class `extends` its superclass, it also optionally `implements` an interface. `implements` is a Java keyword that can appear in a class declaration following the `extends` clause. `implements` should be followed by the name of the interface that the class implements. In order to implement an interface, a class must first declare the interface in an `implements` clause, and then it must provide an implementation (i.e., a body) for all of the `abstract` methods of the interface.†

Example 3-17 shows how we can define a `DrawableRectangle` class that extends our `Rectangle` class and implements the `Drawable` interface we defined in Example 3-16. The example assumes that a `Color` class and a `DrawWindow` class are defined elsewhere, and that `DrawWindow` knows how to convert floating-point coordinates to pixel coordinates and knows how to draw primitive shapes.

Example 3-17: Implementing an interface

```
public class DrawableRectangle extends Rectangle implements Drawable {
    // new instance variables
    private Color c;
    private double x, y;
```

---

*C++ allows classes to have more than one superclass, using a technique known as "multiple inheritance." Multiple inheritance opens up a can of worms, so Java replaces it with what many believe is a more elegant solution.

†This is the real difference between multiple inheritance in C++ and interfaces in Java. In C++, a class can inherit method implementations from more than one superclass. In Java, a class can inherit actual implementations only from one superclass. It can inherit additional `abstract` methods from interfaces, but it must provide its own implementation of those methods. It is rare, however, to actually be able to use C++ multiple inheritance to inherit useful, nontrivial implementations from more than one class. The elegance and simplicity of Java's interface more than compensate for the inability to inherit implementations from more than one class.

Example 3-17: Implementing an interface (continued)

```
    // A constructor
    public DrawableRectangle(double w, double h) { super(w, h); }

    // Here are implementations of the Drawable methods
    // We also inherit all the public methods of Rectangle.
    public void setColor(Color c) { this.c = c; }
    public void setPosition(double x, double y) { this.x = x; this.y = y; }
    public void draw(DrawWindow dw) {
        dw.drawRect(x, y, w, h, c);
    }
}
```

Using Interfaces

Suppose we implement `DrawableCircle` and `DrawableSquare` just as we implemented `DrawableRectangle` in Example 3-17. As we saw earlier, instances of
these classes can be treated as instances of the abstract `Shape` class. They can also
be treated as instances of the `Drawable` interface. Example 3-18 demonstrates this.

Example 3-18: Casting objects to their interface type

```
    Shape[] shapes = new Shape[3];          // create an array to hold shapes
    Drawable[] drawables = new Drawable[3]; // and an array to hold drawables.

    // Create some drawable shapes
    DrawableCircle dc = new DrawableCircle(1.1);
    DrawableSquare ds = new DrawableSquare(2.5);
    DrawableRectangle dr = new DrawableRectangle(2.3, 4.5);

    // The shapes can be assigned to both arrays
    shapes[0] = dc;   drawables[0] = dc;
    shapes[1] = ds;   drawables[1] = ds;
    shapes[2] = dr;   drawables[2] = dr;

    // Compute total area and draw the shapes by invoking
    // the Shape and the Drawable abstract methods.
    double total_area = 0;
    for(int i = 0; i < shapes.length; i++) {
        total_area += shapes[i].area();        // compute the area of the shapes
        drawables[i].setPosition(i*10.0, i*10.0);
        drawables[i].draw(draw_window);        // assume draw_window defined somewhere
    }
```

What this example demonstrates is that interfaces are data types in Java, just as
classes are, and that when a class implements an interface, instances of that class can
be assigned to variables of the interface type. Don't interpret this example to imply
that you must assign a `DrawableRectangle` object to a `Drawable` variable before
you can invoke the `draw()` method or that you must assign it to a `Shape` variable
before you can invoke the `area()` method. `DrawableRectangle()` defines
`draw()` and inherits `area()` from its `Rectangle` superclass, and so you can always
invoke these methods.

Implementing Multiple Interfaces

Suppose we wanted shapes that could be scaled to be larger or smaller. One way we could do this is by defining a Scalable interface and implementing subclasses of DrawableRectangle and the other classes. To do this, though, the new subclass would have to implement both the Drawable interface and the Scalable interface. This is no problem. You may specify a list of comma-separated interfaces in the implements clause of any class:

```
public class DrawableScalableRectangle extends DrawableRectangle
        implements Drawable, Scalable {
    // The methods of the Scalable interface go here
}
```

Constants in Interfaces

As we noted above, constants may appear in interface definitions. What does it mean to implement an interface that contains constants? It simply means that the class that implements the interface "inherits" the constants (in a sense) and can use them as if they were defined directly in the class. There is no need to prefix them with the name of the interface:

```
class A { static final int CONSTANT1 = 3; }
interface B { static final int CONSTANT2 = 4; }
class C implements B {
    void f() {
        int i = A.CONSTANT1;      // have to use the class name here
        int j = CONSTANT2;        // No class name here, because we implement
    }                             // the interface that defines this constant.
}
```

When you have a lot of constants, used in classes throughout a package, one thing you might do is to define a class Constants that contains all the constants. Then in your code, you would refer to constants with names like Constants.PI and Constants.MAX_ARRAY_SIZE. Another way to handle the constants is to declare them in an interface Constants, and then declare all the classes that use constants to implement that interface. Then you can just use constant names like PI and MAX_ARRAY_SIZE.

Extending Interfaces

Interfaces can have sub-interfaces, just like classes can have subclasses. A sub-interface inherits all the abstract methods and constants of its super-interface, and may define new abstract methods and constants. Interfaces are different from classes in one very important way, however. An interface can extend more than one interface at a time:

```
public interface Transformable extends Scalable, Rotateable, Reflectable {}
public interface DrawingObject extends Drawable, Transformable {}
public class Shape implements DrawingObject { ... }
```

An interface that extends more than one interface inherits all the abstract methods and constants from each of those interfaces, and may define its own additional abstract methods and constants. A class that implements such an interface must implement the abstract methods defined in the interface itself as well as all the abstract methods inherited from all of the super-interfaces.

C++ Features Not Found in Java

Throughout this section, we've noted similarities and differences between Java and C++ in footnotes. Java shares enough concepts and features with C++ to make it an easy language for C++ programmers to pick up. There are several features of C++ that have no parallel in Java, however. In general, Java does not adopt those features of C++ that make the language significantly more complicated. These omissions from Java (or simplifications of C++) are described below.

C++ supports "multiple inheritance" of method implementations from more than one superclass at a time. While this seems like a very useful feature, adding it to the language actually turns out to introduce many complexities. The Java language designers chose to avoid the added complexity by using interfaces instead. Thus, a class in Java can only inherit method implementations from a single superclass, but it can inherit method declarations from any number of interfaces. In practice, this is not any particular hardship.

C++ supports (though not yet in a very standardized way) templates that allow you, for example, to implement a `Stack` class and then instantiate it as `Stack<int>` or `Stack<double>` to produce two separate types: a stack of integers and a stack of floating-point values. Java has no such facility. However, the fact that every class in Java is a subclass of `Object` means that every object can be cast to an instance of `Object`. Thus, in Java, it is often sufficient to define a data structure (such as a `Stack` class) that operates on `Object` values—the objects can be cast back to their actual type whenever necessary.

C++ allows you to define operators that perform arbitrary operations on instances of your classes. In effect, it allows you to extend the syntax of the language. This is a nifty feature, called operator overloading, that makes for very elegant examples. In practice however, it tends to make code hard to understand. After much debate, the Java language designers decided to omit such "operator overloading" from the language. Note, though, that the use of the + operator for string concatenation in Java is at least reminiscent of operator overloading.

C++ allows you to define "conversion functions" for a class that automatically invoke an appropriate constructor method when a value is assigned to a variable of that class. This is simply a syntactic shortcut (similar to overriding the assignment operator) and is not included in Java.

In C++, objects are by default manipulated by value; you must use & to specify a variable or function argument that is automatically manipulated by reference. In Java, all objects are manipulated by reference, so there is no need for this & syntax.

Section Summary

This has been a long and detailed section. The following list summarizes the most important points of the section. This summary is not intended to simplify the complex material we've covered, but it may allow you to test your comprehension of the material now, and to help jog your memory later:

- A class is a collection of data and methods that operate on that data.

- An object is a particular instance of a class.

- Object fields (variables and methods) are accessed with a dot between the object name and the field name.

- Instance (non-static) variables occur in each instance of a class.

- Class (static) variables are associated with the class. There is one copy of a class variable regardless of the number of instances of a class.

- Instance (non-static) methods of a class are passed an implicit `this` argument that identifies the object being operated on.

- Class (static) methods are not passed a `this` argument and therefore cannot use the instance methods or instance variables of the class.

- Objects are created with the `new` keyword, which invokes a class constructor method with a list of arguments.

- Objects are not explicitly freed or destroyed in any way. The Java garbage collector automatically reclaims objects that are no longer being used.

- If the first line of a constructor method does not invoke another constructor with a `this()` call, or a superclass constructor with a `super()` call, Java automatically inserts a call to the superclass constructor that takes no arguments. This enforces "constructor chaining."

- If a class does not define a constructor, Java provides a default constructor.

- A class may inherit the non-`private` methods and variables of another class by "subclassing"—i.e., by declaring that class in its `extends` clause.

- `java.lang.Object` is the default superclass for a class. It is the root of the Java class hierarchy and has no superclass itself. All Java classes inherit the methods defined by `Object`.

- Method overloading is the practice of defining multiple methods which have the same name but have different return types or argument lists.

- Method overriding occurs when a class redefines a method inherited from its superclass.

- Dynamic method lookup ensures that the correct method is invoked for an object, even when the object is an instance of a class that has overridden the method.

- `static`, `private`, and `final` methods cannot be overridden and are not subject to dynamic method lookup. This allows compiler optimizations such as inlining.

- You can explicitly invoke an overridden method with the `super` keyword.

- You can explictly refer to a shadowed variable with the `super` keyword.

- Data and methods may be hidden or encapsulated within a class by specifying the `private`, `private protected`, or `protected` visibility modifiers. Fields declared `public` are visible everywhere. Fields with no visibility modifiers are visible only within the package.

- An abstract method has no method body (i.e. no implementation).

- An abstract class contains abstract methods. The methods must be implemented in a subclass before the subclass can be instantiated.

- An interface is a collection of abstract methods and constants (static final variables). Declaring an interface creates a new data type.

- A class implements an interface by declaring the interface in its implements clause and by providing a method body for each of the abstract methods in the interface.

Part II

Programming with the Java API

The sections in Part II present real-world examples of programming with Java. You can study and learn from the examples, and you can adapt them for use in your own programs.

The example code in these chapters is available for downloading. See *http://www.ora.com/catalog/books/javanut.*

Section 4, *Applets*
Section 5, *Graphical User Interfaces*
Section 6, *Input and Output*
Section 7, *Networking*
Section 8, *Advanced Graphics and Images*
Section 9, *Advanced Threads*

Applets

This chapter demonstrates the techniques of applet writing. It proceeds from a trivial "Hello World" applet to quite sophisticated applets. Along the way, it shows you how to:

- Draw graphics and display images in your applet.

- Handle and respond to user input from the mouse or keyboard.

- Read and use values of applet parameters, allowing customization of an applet.

- Add push buttons to an applet.

- Create and manage a thread to display animation.

- Play audio clips.

Study the examples carefully. They are the important part of this chapter! You may find it useful to refer to the quick reference in Section 18, *The java.applet Package*, while reading these examples.

A First Applet

Figure 4-1 shows what is probably the simplest possible applet you can write in Java. Example 4-1 lists its code. This example introduces the paint() method, which is invoked by the applet viewer (or Web browser) when the applet needs to be drawn. This method should perform graphical output—such as drawing text or lines or displaying images—for your applet. The argument to paint() is a Graphics object that you use to do the drawing.

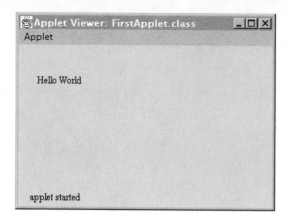

Figure 4-1: A simple applet

Example 4-1: The simplest applet

```
import java.applet.*;        // Don't forget this import statement!
import java.awt.*;           // Or this one for the graphics!

public class FirstApplet extends Applet {
    // This method displays the applet.
    // The Graphics class is how you do all drawing in Java.
    public void paint(Graphics g) {
        g.drawString("Hello World", 25, 50);
    }
}
```

To display an applet, you need an HTML file that references it. Here is an HTML fragment that can be used with our first applet:

```
<APPLET code="FirstApplet.class" width=150 height=100>
</APPLET>
```

With an HTML file that references the applet, you can now view the applet with an applet viewer or Web browser. For the rest of this chapter, we will generally not show the HTML files for our applets. See Section 15, *Java-Related HTML and HTTP Syntax*, for more details on the HTML <APPLET> tag.

Drawing Graphics

Example 4-2 shows an extension to our simple applet. As you can see from Figure 4-2, we've made the graphical display more interesting. This applet also does all of its drawing in the paint() method. It demonstrates the use of Font and Color objects. See Section 12, *Fonts, Colors, and Cursors*, for more information on fonts and colors in Java.

This example also introduces the init() method, which is used to perform any one-time initialization that is necessary when the applet is first created. The paint() method may be invoked many times in the life of an applet, so this example uses init() to create the Font object that paint() uses.

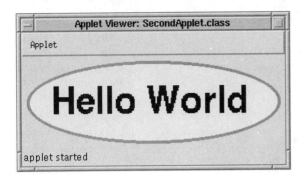

Figure 4-2: A fancier applet

Example 4-2: An applet with fancier graphics

```
import java.applet.*;
import java.awt.*;

public class SecondApplet extends Applet {
        static final String message = "Hello World";
        private Font font;

        // One-time initialization for the applet
        public void init() {
                font = new Font("Helvetica", Font.BOLD, 48);
        }

        // Draw the applet whenever necessary.  Do some fancy graphics.
        public void paint(Graphics g) {
                // The pink oval
                g.setColor(Color.pink);
                g.fillOval(10, 10, 330, 100);

                // The red outline.  java doesn't support wide lines, so we
                // try to simulate a 4-pixel wide line by drawing four ovals
                g.setColor(Color.red);
                g.drawOval(10,10, 330, 100);
                g.drawOval(9, 9, 332, 102);
                g.drawOval(8, 8, 334, 104);
                g.drawOval(7, 7, 336, 106);

                // The text
                g.setColor(Color.black);
                g.setFont(font);
                g.drawString(message, 40, 75);
        }
}
```

Applets

Handling Events

The previous two applets have only displayed output. If an applet is to be interactive in any way, it has to receive and respond to user input. Example 4-3 shows a simple applet that lets the user do a freehand sketch (or scribble) with the mouse. Figure 4-3 shows such a scribble.

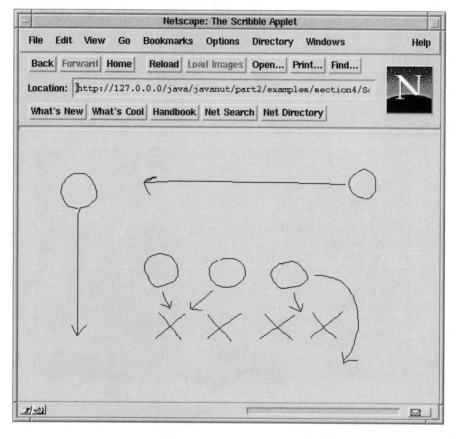

Figure 4-3: Scribbling with the Scribble applet

The mouseDown() and mouseDrag() methods are called by the system when the user presses a mouse button and moves the mouse with the button down, respectively. This applet draws lines directly in response to these events. It does not have a paint() method, which means that the user's scribble is lost any time that the applet is redrawn (for example, when a Web browser scrolls down a page and then scrolls back up again).

Note that both mouseDown() and mouseUp() return true. This is to tell the system that they've handled the Event object that was passed to them, and that the event should not be processed any further. The next section demonstrates event handling in more detail.

Section 4: Applets

Example 4-3: The Scribble applet

```
import java.applet.*;
import java.awt.*;

public class Scribble extends Applet {
    private int last_x = 0;
    private int last_y = 0;

    // called when the user clicks
    public boolean mouseDown(Event e, int x, int y)
    {
        last_x = x; last_y = y;
        return true;
    }

    // called when the mouse moves with the button down
    public boolean mouseDrag(Event e, int x, int y)
    {
        Graphics g = getGraphics();
        g.drawLine(last_x, last_y, x, y);
        last_x = x;
        last_y = y;
        return true;
    }
}
```

Events in Detail

Example 4-4 is an applet that displays simple instructions in an otherwise blank window; it is not pictured. Whenever user events (mouse and keyboard events, mainly) occur in the applet's window, it describes the event in the applet viewer's (or Web browser's) status line. This example uses the `Applet showStatus()` method to display the messages in the status line. More importantly, though, it defines a number of methods to handle events. These methods are invoked by the system when the events occur. When you define one of these methods, you should handle the specified event and return `true`. Or, if you determine that it is not an appropriate event for your code to handle, you should return `false` so that it is passed on to other event handling code.

The `keyDown()` and `keyUp()` methods are of particular interest. Notice how they distinguish regular keys from function keys, and how they determine which key has been pressed, with what keyboard modifiers.

Notice from the mouse event handling code that Java assumes a one-button mouse—the lowest-common denominator for all platforms. The `Event` class does not have any kind of `mouseButton` field to indicate which mouse button has been pressed. Instead, on systems with two or three-button mice, using the right mouse button generates mouse events that have the META keyboard modifier set. Similarly, on three-button mice, the middle mouse button generates mouse events that have the ALT modifier set. This technique allows platforms with one and two-button mice to simulate two and three-button mice by using them in conjunction with the keyboard. See Section 11, *Events*, for more details about events, modifiers, keys, and mouse buttons in Java.

Example 4-4: Handling applet events

```java
import java.applet.*;
import java.awt.*;

public class EventTester extends Applet {
    // display the instructions
    public void paint(Graphics g) {
        g.drawString("Click, drag, and type in this window.", 10, 20);
    }

    // Handle mouse events
    public boolean mouseDown(Event e, int x, int y) {
        showStatus(modifier_key_names(e.modifiers) +
            "Mouse Down: [" + x + "," + y + "]");
        return true;
    }
    public boolean mouseUp(Event e, int x, int y) {
        showStatus(modifier_key_names(e.modifiers) +
            "Mouse Up: [" + x + "," + y + "]");
        return true;
    }
    public boolean mouseDrag(Event e, int x, int y) {
        showStatus(modifier_key_names(e.modifiers) +
            "Mouse Drag: [" + x + "," + y + "]");
        return true;
    }
    public boolean mouseEnter(Event e, int x, int y) {
        showStatus("Mouse Enter: [" + x + "," + y + "]");
        return true;
    }
    public boolean mouseExit(Event e, int x, int y) {
        showStatus("Mouse Exit: [" + x + "," + y + "]");
        return true;
    }

    // Handle focus events
    public boolean gotFocus(Event e, Object what) {
        showStatus("Got Focus");
        return true;
    }
    public boolean lostFocus(Event e, Object what) {
        showStatus("Lost Focus");
        return true;
    }

    // Handle key down and key up events
    public boolean keyDown(Event e, int key) {
        int flags = e.modifiers;
        if (e.id == Event.KEY_PRESS)        // a regular key
            showStatus("Key Down: "
                + modifier_key_names(flags)
                + key_name(e));
        else if (e.id == Event.KEY_ACTION)  // a function key
            showStatus("Function Key Down: "
                + modifier_key_names(flags)
                + function_key_name(key));
        return true;
```

Example 4-4: Handling applet events (continued)

```
        }
        public boolean keyUp(Event e, int key) {
            int flags = e.modifiers;
            if (e.id == Event.KEY_PRESS)          // a regular key
                showStatus("Key Up: "
                            + modifier_key_names(flags)
                            + key_name(e));
            else if (e.id == Event.KEY_ACTION)    // a function key
                showStatus("Function Key Up: "
                            + modifier_key_names(flags)
                            + function_key_name(key));
            return true;
        }

        // The remaining methods help us sort out the various key events

        // Return the current list of modifier keys
        private String modifier_key_names(int flags) {
            String s = "[ ";
            if (flags == 0) return "";
            if ((flags & Event.SHIFT_MASK) != 0) s += "Shift ";
            if ((flags & Event.CTRL_MASK) != 0) s += "Control ";
            if ((flags & Event.META_MASK) != 0) s += "Meta ";
            if ((flags & Event.ALT_MASK) != 0) s += "Alt ";
            s += "] ";
            return s;
        }

        // Return the name of a regular (ASCII) key.
        private String key_name(Event e) {
            char c = (char) e.key;

            // If CTRL flag is set, handle ASCII control characters.
            if (e.controlDown()) {
                if (c < ' ') {
                    c += '@';
                    return "^" + c;
                }
            }
            else {
                // If CTRL flag is not set, then certain ASCII
                // control characters have special meaning.
                switch (c) {
                    case '\n': return "Return";
                    case '\t': return "Tab";
                    case '\033': return "Escape";
                    case '\010': return "Backspace";
                }
            }

            // Handle the remaining possibilities.
            if (c == '177') return "Delete";
            else if (c == ' ') return "Space";
            else return String.valueOf(c);
        }
```

Example 4-4: Handling applet events (continued)

```
// Return the name of a function key.
private String function_key_name(int key) {
    switch(key) {
        case Event.HOME: return "Home";
        case Event.END: return "End";
        case Event.PGUP: return "Page Up";
        case Event.PGDN: return "Page Down";
        case Event.UP: return "Up Arrow";
        case Event.DOWN: return "Down Arrow";
        case Event.LEFT: return "Left Arrow";
        case Event.RIGHT: return "Right Arrow";
        case Event.F1: return "F1";    case Event.F2: return "F2";
        case Event.F3: return "F3";    case Event.F4: return "F4";
        case Event.F5: return "F5";    case Event.F6: return "F6";
        case Event.F7: return "F7";    case Event.F8: return "F8";
        case Event.F9: return "F9";    case Event.F10: return "F10";
        case Event.F11: return "F11";  case Event.F12: return "F12";
    }
    return "Unknown Function Key";
}
}
```

Reading Applet Parameters

Example 4-5 shows an extension to our earlier Scribble applet. The ColorScribble class is a subclass of Scribble that adds the ability to scribble in a configurable foreground color over a configurable background color. (The ColorScribble applet looks a lot like the Scribble applet of Figure 4-3 and is not pictured here.)

ColorScribble has an init() method that reads the value of two "applet parameters" that can be optionally specified with the <PARAM> tag in the applet's HTML file. The returned string values are converted to colors and specified as the default foreground and background colors for the applet. Note that the init() method invokes its superclass's init() method, just in case a future version of Scribble defines that method to perform initialization.

This example also introduces the getAppletInfo() and getParameterInfo() methods. These methods provide textual information about the applet (its author, its version, its copyright, etc.) and the parameters that it can accept (the parameter names, their types, and their meanings). An applet should generally define these methods. Most Web browsers and applet viewers let the user examine the applet and parameter information, and some even let the user interactively specify parameter values for an applet.

Example 4-5: Reading applet parameters

```
import java.applet.*;
import java.awt.*;

public class ColorScribble extends Scribble {
    // Read in two color parameters and set the colors.
    public void init() {
        super.init();
```

Example 4-5: Reading applet parameters (continued)

```
        Color foreground = getColorParameter("foreground");
        Color background = getColorParameter("background");
        if (foreground != null) this.setForeground(foreground);
        if (background != null) this.setBackground(background);
    }

    // Read the specified parameter. Interpret it as a hexadecimal
    // number of the form RRGGBB and convert it to a color.
    protected Color getColorParameter(String name) {
        String value = this.getParameter(name);
        int intvalue;
        try { intvalue = Integer.parseInt(value, 16); }
        catch (NumberFormatException e) { return null; }
        return new Color(intvalue);
    }

    // Return info about the supported parameters. Web browsers and applet
    // viewers should display this information, and may also allow users to
    // set the parameter values.
    public String[][] getParameterInfo() {
        String[][] info = {
            // Array of arrays of strings describing each parameter.
            // Format: parameter name, parameter type, parameter description
            {"foreground", "hexadecimal color value", "foreground color"},
            {"background", "hexadecimal color value", "background color"}
        };
        return info;
    }

    // Return information suitable for display in an About dialog box.
    public String getAppletInfo() {
        return "Scribble v. 0.02.0ritten by David Flanagan.";
    }
}
```

The following HTML fragment references the applet, and demonstrates how parameter values can be set with the <PARAM> tag.

```
<APPLET code="ColorScribble.class" width=300 height=300>
<PARAM name="foreground" value="0000FF">
<PARAM name="background" value="FFCCCC">
</APPLET>
```

Adding a Button

Example 4-6 shows another extension to our `Scribble` applet. This one, pictured in Figure 4-4, adds a **Clear** button to the applet. Clicking on the button erases any scribbles that have been drawn.

The `ClearableScribble` applet is a subclass of the `ColorScribble` class we saw in Example 4-5. It creates the **Clear** button in its `init()` method, after first invoking the `ColorScribble init()` method. The button is created with `new` and added to the applet with the `add()` method. We set the foreground and background colors of the button so that they are distinct from the foreground and background scribble colors specified by parameters.

The `action()` method is invoked by the system when the user clicks on the button we've added to the applet. Note that we first check whether our button was the one clicked (this is useful when there is more than one button), and then proceed to clear the scribble area. If the event was not for our button, we pass it on to the `action()` method of the superclass. (The superclass, the `ColorScribble` applet, does not currently have buttons and does not define an `action()` method, but future versions of it might.)

We'll discuss adding user interface components and handling user interaction in much greater detail in Section 5, *Graphical User Interfaces.*

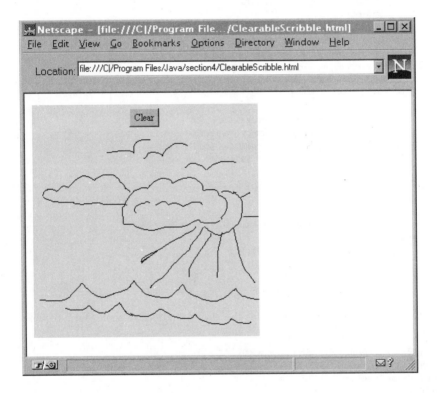

Figure 4-4: An applet with a button

Example 4-6: Adding a button to an applet

```
import java.applet.*;
import java.awt.*;

public class ClearableScribble extends ColorScribble {
        private Button clear_button;

        public void init() {
                // do ColorScribble initialization first
                super.init();
```

Section 4: Applets

Example 4-6: Adding a button to an applet (continued)

```
        // Create a button and add it to the applet.
        clear_button = new Button("Clear");
        clear_button.setForeground(Color.black);
        clear_button.setBackground(Color.lightGray);
        this.add(clear_button);
    }

    public boolean action(Event event, Object arg) {
        // If our button was clicked on, handle it.
        // Otherwise, let our superclass handle it if it wants to.
        if (event.target == clear_button) {
            Graphics g = this.getGraphics();
            Rectangle r = this.bounds();
            g.setColor(this.getBackground());
            g.fillRect(r.x, r.y, r.width, r.height);
            g.setColor(this.getForeground());
            return true;
        }
        else return super.action(event, arg);
    }
}
```

An Imagemap

Example 4-7 shows a Java applet that implements an imagemap, like that shown in Figure 4-5. That is, it displays a specified image and responds to mouse clicks on specified regions of the image. This provides an extremely flexible "client-side imagemap" capability in Web pages. (Conventional HTML supports "server-side" image maps, which require custom CGI programming and are much less convenient.)

The init() method of this applet looks up the parameter named "image" to find the name of the image to display. Then it reads in that image, using the Applet getImage() method and assuming that the image name is relative to the URL of the HTML document that references the applet.

The init() method also reads in properties that specify a number of rectangular regions and associated URLs for each region. It uses a helper function to parse the parameters, as well as an internal class and the java.util.Vector class to store these rectangle specifications. The following HTML fragment shows an example of the properties read by this applet:

```
<APPLET code="Imagemap.class" width=150 height=50>
<PARAM name="image" value="images/map.gif">
<PARAM name="rect0" value="0,0,50,50,Scribble.html">
<PARAM name="rect1" value="50,0,50,50,EventTester.html">
<PARAM name="rect2" value="100,0,50,50,NoSuchFile.html">
</APPLET>
```

The applet's paint() method displays the image. The update() method overrides the default applet update() method. The default method clears the applet background and then calls paint(). Our new definition doesn't clear the background, to reduce flickering. The destroy() method is automatically called by the system

---

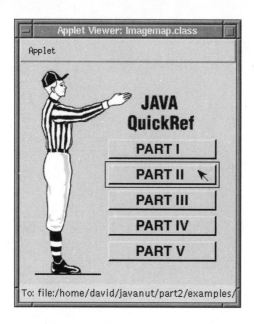

Figure 4-5: An imagemap applet

when the applet is being "unloaded" from the applet viewer or Web browser. Once destroy() has been called, the start() method will never be called again. destroy() is the complement of the init() method, but is less commonly used. In this case, it helps to free up memory used for the image (which might be quite large).

The mouseDown() method detects when the mouse button is pressed. If it is pressed within one of the defined rectangles, the method highlights that rectangle using XOR mode drawing (which can be erased by redrawing). The method also uses showStatus() to display the URL that the selected rectangle refers to in the applet viewer status line.

The mouseUp() method detects when the mouse button is released. If it is released in the same rectangle in which it was pressed, then this method calls showDocument() to ask the Web browser or applet viewer to display the document at the URL associated with the rectangle. This method also clears the status line and erases the highlighting drawn by mouseDown().

Example 4-7: An imagemap applet

```
import java.applet.*;
import java.awt.*;
import java.net.*;
import java.util.*;

public class Imagemap extends Applet {
    protected Image image;      // image to display.
    protected Vector rects;     // list of rectangles in it.

    public void init() {
        // load the image to be displayed.
        image = this.getImage(this.getDocumentBase(),
```

Example 4-7: An imagemap applet (continued)

```
                        this.getParameter("image"));
        // lookup a list of rectangular areas and the URLs they map to.
        rects = new Vector();
        ImagemapRectangle r;
        int i = 0;
        while((r = getRectangleParameter("rect" + i)) != null) {
                rects.addElement(r);
                i++;
        }
}


// Called when the applet is being unloaded from the system.
// We use it here to "flush" the image. This may result in memory
// and other resources being freed quicker than they otherwise would.
public void destroy() { image.flush(); }


// Display the image.
public void paint(Graphics g) {
        g.drawImage(image, 0, 0, this);
}


// We override this method so that it doesn't clear the background
// before calling paint().  Makes for less flickering in some situations.
public void update(Graphics g) { paint(g); }


// find the rectangle we're inside
private ImagemapRectangle findrect(int x, int y) {
        int i;
        ImagemapRectangle r = null;
        for(i = 0; i < rects.size(); i++)  {
                r = (ImagemapRectangle) rects.elementAt(i);
                if (r.inside(x, y)) break;
        }
        if (i < rects.size()) return r;
        else return null;
}


private ImagemapRectangle lastrect;


// On button down, highlight the rectangle, and display a message
public boolean mouseDown(Event e, int x, int y) {
        ImagemapRectangle r = findrect(x, y);
        if (r == null) return false;
        Graphics g = this.getGraphics();
        g.setXORMode(Color.red);
        g.drawRect(r.x, r.y, r.width, r.height);
        lastrect = r;
        this.showStatus("To: " + r.url);
        return true;
}


// On button up, unhighlight the rectangle.
// If still inside the rectangle go to the URL
public boolean mouseUp(Event e, int x, int y) {
        if (lastrect != null) {
                Graphics g = this.getGraphics();
```

Example 4-7: An imagemap applet (continued)

```
                        g.setXORMode(Color.red);
                        g.drawRect(lastrect.x, lastrect.y, lastrect.width, lastrect.height);
                        this.showStatus("");
                        ImagemapRectangle r = findrect(x,y);
                        if ((r != null) && (r == lastrect))
                                this.getAppletContext().showDocument(r.url);
                        lastrect = null;
                }
                return true;
        }

        // Parse a comma-separated list of rectangle coordinates and a URL.
        protected ImagemapRectangle getRectangleParameter(String name) {
                int x, y, w, h;
                URL url;
                String value = this.getParameter(name);
                if (value == null) return null;

                try {
                        StringTokenizer st = new StringTokenizer(value, ",");
                        x = Integer.parseInt(st.nextToken());
                        y = Integer.parseInt(st.nextToken());
                        w = Integer.parseInt(st.nextToken());
                        h = Integer.parseInt(st.nextToken());
                        url = new URL(this.getDocumentBase(), st.nextToken());
                }
                catch (NoSuchElementException e) return null;
                catch (NumberFormatException e) return null;
                catch (MalformedURLException e) return null;

                return new ImagemapRectangle(x, y, w, h, url);
        }
}

// A helper class.  Just like java.awt.Rectangle, but with a new URL field.
// The constructor lets us create them from parameter specifications.
class ImagemapRectangle extends Rectangle {
        URL url;
        public ImagemapRectangle(int x, int y, int w, int h, URL url) {
                super(x, y, w, h);
                this.url = url;
        }
}
```

Animation

Example 4-8 is an applet, `Animator`, that displays a simple animation. The `init()` method uses `getParameter()` to look up the number of images in the animation and the base name of each image. The base name is a file specification relative to the URL of the current document. `init()` forms the name of each image from the base name and the image number and reads in the images using `getImage()`.

The `start()` and `stop()` methods are called by the system to tell an applet to start and to stop whatever it does. They are like the `init()` and `destroy()` methods, but may be called multiple times throughout the applet's life. (For example, an applet might be stopped when it scrolls off the current page of a Web browser.) In this case, the `start()` method starts the animation and the `stop()` method stops it.

All the applets we've seen so far have been passive—they respond to user events and to methods called by the system, but take no action on their own. Animation is active; we need to draw something over and over again. We can't use `init()`, `paint()`, or any of the other standard applet methods to do this—those methods are supposed to do a simple job and then return to the system. So to perform our animation, we need to create a `Thread` object to create a separate thread of execution. The `start()` method creates this animation thread and starts it by calling the thread's `start()` method. The `stop()` method stops the thread by calling `stop()` on it.

Note how the thread is created. The `Applet` object (`this`) is passed to the thread constructor. This creates a thread that, when started, executes the code in the `run()` method of the applet. That method performs the actual animation—it draws an image, calls `Thread.sleep()` to wait 200 milliseconds, and then loops to draw the next image.

Example 4-8: The Animator applet

```
/**
 * This applet displays an animation. It doesn't handle errors while
 * loading images. It doesn't wait for all images to be loaded before
 * starting the animation. These problems will be addressed later.
 **/
import java.applet.*;
import java.awt.*;
import java.net.*;
import java.util.*;

public class Animator extends Applet implements Runnable {
    protected Image[] images;
    protected int current_image;

    // Read the basename and num_images parameters.
    // Then read in the images, using the specified base name.
    // For example, if basename is images/anim, read images/anim0,
    // images/anim1, etc. These are relative to the current document URL.
    public void init() {
        String basename = this.getParameter("basename");
        int num_images;
        try { num_images = Integer.parseInt(this.getParameter("num_images")); }
        catch (NumberFormatException e) { num_images = 0; }

        images = new Image[num_images];
        for(int i = 0; i < num_images; i++) {
            images[i] = this.getImage(this.getDocumentBase(), basename + i);
        }
    }

    // This is the thread that runs the animation, and the methods
    // that start it and stop it.
    private Thread animator_thread = null;
```

Example 4-8: The Animator applet (continued)

```
public void start() {
    if (animator_thread == null) {
        animator_thread = new Thread(this);
        animator_thread.start();
    }
}
public void stop() {
    if ((animator_thread != null) && animator_thread.isAlive())
        animator_thread.stop();
    // We do this so the garbage collector can reclaim the Thread object.
    // Otherwise it might sit around in the Web browser for a long time.
    animator_thread = null;
}

// This is the body of the thread--the method that does the animation.
public void run() {
    while(true) {
        if (++current_image >= images.length) current_image = 0;
        this.getGraphics().drawImage(images[current_image], 0, 0, this);
        try { Thread.sleep(200); } catch (InterruptedException e) ;
    }
}
}
```

Sound

Example 4-9 shows a subclass of our animator applet, `AudioAnimator`, that adds the ability to play an audio clip when the applet starts up. In this simple example, the sound is not synchronized with the animation in any way—it is simply played at some point not too long after the applet starts. It is a technique that could be used to add some sort of a "welcome" sound to a Web page, for example.

The `init()` method first calls the superclass initialize method, as we've seen in previous examples. Then it reads the "sound" property to find the name of the sound to download. Instead of downloading and playing the sound directly, however, it creates a thread to handle this, so that it does not delay the start of the animation. (On the other hand, if it is important that the sound begin before the animation starts, then creating this thread would not be a good technique.)

The `SoundPlayer` class is the thread that plays the sound. Its `run()` method uses the `Applet play()` method to download and play the specified sound. The constructor method for the `SoundPlayer` object calls `start()` to start the thread running. Note that this is an example of a thread created by subclassing `Thread` directly, rather than writing a class that implements `Runnable`, as we did in the `Animator` example.

Note that the `run()` method that performs the animation is not listed here. It is inherited from the `Animator` superclass.

Example 4-9: Playing a sound

```java
import java.applet.*;
import java.awt.*;

public class AudioAnimator extends Animator {
    public void init() {
        // do Animator initialization first
        super.init();

        // look up the name of a sound, and then
        // load and play it (just once), in a separate thread.
        String soundname = this.getParameter("sound");
        new SoundPlayer(this, soundname);
    }
}

// This is the thread class that loads and plays the sound
class SoundPlayer extends Thread {
    private Applet applet;
    private String sound_url;
    // Store the information the run() method needs, and start it.
    public SoundPlayer(Applet app, String url) {
        applet = app;
        sound_url = url;
        this.start();
    }
    // This is the code the thread runs to load and play the sound
    public void run() { applet.play(applet.getDocumentBase(), sound_url); }
}
```

Applets

Standalone Applets

Example 4-10, the final example of this chapter, begins a transition from Java applets to Java applications. It is a trivial subclass of the Scribble applet that adds a main() method that allows it to run as a standalone Java application. The main() method creates an instance of the applet and then creates a window to put it in. The window is an instance of the AppletFrame class, which is also shown here. The AppletFrame creates a menu bar with a **File** menu and a **Quit** button. (The next chapter contains examples of using these and other GUI components.) The Applet-Frame displays the applet and calls its init() and start() methods. The action() method calls System.exit() when the user selects **Quit** from the menu.

This AppletFrame object only works for very simple applets and is certainly no replacement for a real applet viewer. It has many restrictions: the applet cannot use getParameter(), showStatus(), showDocument(), getImage(), or other Applet methods that depend on the AppletContext. On the other hand, it is a useful example because it demystifies applets and shows how they can be manipulated.

Example 4-10: Running an applet as an application

```
import java.applet.*;
import java.awt.*;

// This is a simple example of allowing an applet to run as a standalone
// Java application.  The only problem is that when running standalone,
// it can't read applet parameters.
public class StandaloneScribble extends Scribble {
    public static void main(String args[]) {
        Applet applet = new StandaloneScribble();
        Frame frame = new AppletFrame("Scribble", applet, 300, 300);
    }
}


class AppletFrame extends Frame {
    public AppletFrame(String title, Applet applet, int width, int height) {
        // create the Frame with the specified title.
        super(title);

        // Add a menu bar, with a File menu, with a Quit button.
        MenuBar menubar = new MenuBar();
        Menu file = new Menu("File", true);
        menubar.add(file);
        file.add("Quit");
        this.setMenuBar(menubar);

        // Add the applet to the window.  Set the window size.  Pop it up.
        this.add("Center", applet);
        this.resize(width, height);
        this.show();

        // Start the applet.
        applet.init();
        applet.start();
    }

    // Handle the Quit menu button.
    public boolean action(Event e, Object arg)
    {
        if (e.target instanceof MenuItem) {
            String label = (String) arg;
            if (label.equals("Quit")) System.exit(0);
        }
        return false;
    }
}
```

Graphical User Interfaces

The examples in this section demonstrate how to build graphical user interfaces with Java. They show you how to:

- Create interface components and add them to containers.

- Arrange components within a container using various layout managers.

- Create simple dialog boxes.

- Receive and handle notification from user interface components that the user has interacted with them.

- Work with scrollbars.

- Create new components of your own.

The examples all use the classes of the `java.awt` package. Read the introduction to Section 19, *The java.awt Package*, for a useful overview of the classes in this package. You may also want to refer to the class descriptions in that section while reading these examples.

An Information Dialog

Example 5-1 shows how you can create a dialog box, like the one pictured in Figure 5-1, to display information to the user.

The constructor method creates a window with the specified title for the dialog box. It also creates a `MultiLineLabel` component to display the message and an **Okay** button that the user can use to dismiss the dialog. The `MultiLineLabel` class is a

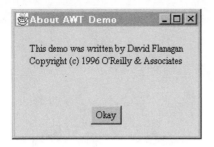

Figure 5-1: An information dialog

custom component that will be defined in a later example. It behaves much like the `java.awt.Label` object, but can display multiple lines of text.

This example shows the use of two different layout managers. A layout manager is an object that arranges Java components within their containers. Different subclasses of `LayoutManager` arrange components in a container in different ways. As you read through this example, pay particular attention to the use of the `BorderLayout` and `FlowLayout` objects.

Note that this example is a Java application, not an applet. The `main()` method tests and demonstrates the `InfoDialog` class, but this class could also be used within other, larger applications, or within applets.

Example 5-1: An information dialog

```
import java.awt.*;

public class InfoDialog extends Dialog {
    protected Button button;
    protected MultiLineLabel label;

    public InfoDialog(Frame parent, String title, String message)
    {
        // Create a dialog with the specified title
        super(parent, title, false);

        // Create and use a BorderLayout manager with specified margins
        this.setLayout(new BorderLayout(15, 15));

        // Create the message component and add it to the window
        label = new MultiLineLabel(message, 20, 20);
        this.add("Center", label);

        // Create an Okay button in a Panel; add the Panel to the window
        // Use a FlowLayout to center the button and give it margins.
        button = new Button("Okay");
        Panel p = new Panel();
        p.setLayout(new FlowLayout(FlowLayout.CENTER, 15, 15));
        p.add(button);
        this.add("South", p);

        // Resize the window to the preferred size of its components
        this.pack();
    }
```

Example 5-1: An information dialog (continued)

```
// Pop down the window when the button is clicked.
public boolean action(Event e, Object arg)
{
      if (e.target == button) {
            this.hide();
            this.dispose();
            return true;
      }
      else return false;
}

// When the window gets the keyboard focus, give it to the button.
// This allows keyboard shortcuts to pop down the dialog.
public boolean gotFocus(Event e, Object arg) {
      button.requestFocus();
      return true;
}

public static void main(String[] args) {
      Frame f = new Frame("InfoDialog Test");
      f.resize(100, 100);
      f.show();
      InfoDialog d = new InfoDialog(f, "About AWT Demo",
                      "This demo was written by David Flanagan\n" +
                      "Copyright (c) 1996 O'Reilly & Associates");
      d.show();
}
}
```

The constructor method creates a `BorderLayout` layout manager and uses the `setLayout()` method to tell the dialog to use it. The `BorderLayout` manager works by positioning four components against the four edges of the container and positioning another in the center, where it receives all the remaining space in the container. The position of components is specified to the `BorderLayout` by giving them specific names. In this case, we use the `BorderLayout` to position the button against the bottom edge by giving it the name "South," and we position the label in the center by giving it the name "Center." Note the use of the `add()` method to add a component to a container and to specify a name for it.

If you followed the code closely, you noticed that we do not add the button directly to the window. If we did that, the `BorderLayout` layout manager would force it to expand horizontally to fill the entire bottom of the dialog. Instead, we want it centered along the bottom of the dialog, with space on either side. To achieve this, we create a new container, a `Panel`, with a `FlowLayout` layout manager, and place the button in this new container. The `FlowLayout` layout manager arranges its components in rows. We create a `FlowLayout` that centers each row. Since there is only one component (the button) in this panel, the `FlowLayout` centers the button in the panel. Note that there is no need to specify a name for the button when calling the panel's `add()` method—the `FlowLayout` does not care about component names. With the button centered in the panel, it is the panel itself that we add to the dialog container, with the name "South" so that the `BorderLayout` positions it correctly.

The final call of interest in the constructor method is pack(). Dialog and Frame containers support this method. It sets the size of the window to the preferred size of all of the components of the window—i.e., it makes the window just big enough to display everything comfortably. You'll use this method frequently just before making a window visible.

The action() method handles the button click. When the **Okay** button is pressed, it first pops the window down with the hide() method and then "destroys" any window system resources associated with the dialog by calling dispose(). Once dispose() has been called, the window may never be used again.

The gotFocus() method is called by the system when the window gets the keyboard focus—i.e., when keystrokes are delivered to that window instead of any other window. Here, the method simply asks to pass the focus on to the **Okay** button. On many platforms, this allows the **Okay** button to be invoked by typing SPACE or RETURN at the keyboard.

Finally, the main() method demonstrates how this InfoDialog class might be used—a dialog is created with a specified title and message for a specified Frame, and is popped up with the show() method. One enhancement that we might add to this class is the ability to display an image along with the message (perhaps against the left side of the window, using a "West" layout of the BorderLayout). Another enhancement might be the ability to reuse the dialog by removing the dispose() call and defining methods to allow the title and message to be changed.

A Dialog with User Response

The InfoDialog class we saw in the previous example only displays information. The user can dismiss the dialog, but the program never has to respond when the user dismisses it. Many other dialogs, however, require the program to respond to the user's input. Example 5-2 shows the YesNoDialog class that can be used to create dialogs like that shown in Figure 5-2.

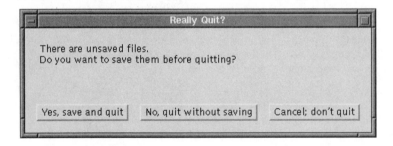

Figure 5-2: A yes-or-no dialog

As you can see, the YesNoDialog constructor method is much like that of the InfoDialog class, except that it creates three buttons, with specified labels, rather than a single **Okay** button. The difference between these two dialog types is in the action() method. In this case, the action() method checks which button the user clicked and passes that information to the answer() method, which calls the yes(), no(), or cancel() method, as appropriate.

Example 5-2: A yes-or-no dialog

```java
import java.awt.*;

public class YesNoDialog extends Dialog {
    public static final int NO = 0;
    public static final int YES = 1;
    public static final int CANCEL = -1;

    protected Button yes = null, no = null, cancel = null;
    protected MultiLineLabel label;

    public YesNoDialog(Frame parent, String title, String message,
                String yes_label, String no_label, String cancel_label)
    {
        // Create the window.
        super(parent, title, true);

        // Specify a LayoutManager for it
        this.setLayout(new BorderLayout(15, 15));

        // Put the message label in the middle of the window.
        label = new MultiLineLabel(message, 20, 20);
        this.add("Center", label);

        // Create a panel of buttons, center the row of buttons in
        // the panel, and put the pane at the bottom of the window.
        Panel p = new Panel();
        p.setLayout(new FlowLayout(FlowLayout.CENTER, 15, 15));
        if (yes_label != null) p.add(yes = new Button(yes_label));
        if (no_label != null)  p.add(no = new Button(no_label));
        if (cancel_label != null) p.add(cancel = new Button(cancel_label));
        this.add("South", p);

        // Set the window to its preferred size.
        this.pack();
    }

    // Handle button events by calling the answer() method.
    // Pass the appropriate constant value, depending on the button.
    public boolean action(Event e, Object arg)
    {
        if (e.target instanceof Button) {
            this.hide();
            this.dispose();
            if (e.target == yes) answer(YES);
            else if (e.target == no) answer(NO);
            else answer(CANCEL);
            return true;
        }
        else return false;
    }

    // Call yes(), no(), and cancel() methods depending on the button the
    // user clicked.  Subclasses define how the answer is processed by
    // overriding this method or the  yes(), no(), and cancel() methods.
    protected void answer(int answer) {
        switch(answer) {
```

Example 5-2: A yes-or-no dialog (continued)

```
                    case YES: yes(); break;
                    case NO:  no(); break;
                    case CANCEL: cancel(); break;
            }
    }
    protected void yes() {}
    protected void no() {}
    protected void cancel() {}
}
```

Notice that the constructor method for this class allows us to omit button labels for the **Yes**, **No**, and **Cancel** buttons. If a label is omitted, the button simply won't be created.

In the `YesNoDialog` class itself, the `yes()`, `no()`, and `cancel()` methods don't do anything. To actually respond to the user's input, the Java programming model requires us to subclass `YesNoDialog` and provide our own custom definitions of these three methods. Example 5-3 shows such a subclass. Notice that there is no `main()` method in this example that shows how the `ReallyQuitDialog` class is created and used. We'll see it used in an example later in this chapter.

Example 5-3: A subclass of the dialog

```
import java.awt.*;

public class ReallyQuitDialog extends YesNoDialog {
    TextComponent status;
    // Create the kind of YesNoDialog we want
    // And store away a piece of information we need later.
    public ReallyQuitDialog(Frame parent, TextComponent status) {
        super(parent, "Really Quit?", "Really Quit?", "Yes", "No", null);
        this.status = status;
    }
    // Define these methods to handle the user's answer
    public void yes() { System.exit(0); }
    public void no() {
        if (status != null) status.setText("Quit cancelled.");
    }
}
```

All Java GUI Components

Example 5-4 shows the code required to create each of the GUI components supported by Java. Figure 5-3 shows the resulting interface on a UNIX/Motif platform; Figure 5-4 shows the interface on a Windows platform.

This example introduces the `GridBagLayout` layout manager and shows how you can use it to arrange components into more complicated arrangements than we've seen before. This layout manager is a powerful and quite confusing one. It is explained following the example code. You may also want to refer to the API quick reference material for more information about `GridBagLayout` and `GridBagCon-straints`.

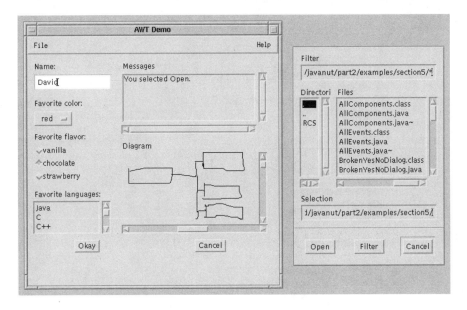

Figure 5-3: Java GUI components in Motif

Example 5-4: Creating all the Java GUI components

```
import java.awt.*;

public class AllComponents extends Frame {
    MenuBar menubar;                    // The menu bar
    Menu file, help;                    // Menu panes
    Button okay, cancel;                // Buttons
    List list;                          // A list of choices
    Choice choice;                      // A menu of choices
    CheckboxGroup checkbox_group;       // A group of button choices
    Checkbox[] checkboxes;              // The buttons to choose from
    TextField textfield;                // One line of text input
    TextArea textarea;                  // A text window
    ScrollableScribble scribble;        // An area to draw in
    FileDialog file_dialog;

    Panel panel1, panel2 ;              // Sub-containers for all this stuff.
    Panel buttonpanel;

    // The layout manager for each of the containers.
    GridBagLayout gridbag = new GridBagLayout();

    public AllComponents(String title) {
        super(title);

        // Create the menu bar.  Tell the frame about it.
        menubar = new MenuBar();
        this.setMenuBar(menubar);
        // Create the file menu.  Add two items to it. Add to menu bar.
        file = new Menu("File");
        file.add(new MenuItem("Open"));
        file.add(new MenuItem("Quit"));
        menubar.add(file);
```

Example 5-4: Creating all the Java GUI components (continued)

```
// Create Help menu; add an item; add to menu bar
help = new Menu("Help");
help.add(new MenuItem("About"));
menubar.add(help);
// Display the help menu in a special reserved place.
menubar.setHelpMenu(help);

// Create pushbuttons.
okay = new Button("Okay");
cancel = new Button("Cancel");

// Create a menu of choices.
choice = new Choice();
choice.addItem("red");
choice.addItem("green");
choice.addItem("blue");

// Create checkboxes, and group them.
checkbox_group = new CheckboxGroup();
checkboxes = new Checkbox[3];
checkboxes[0] = new Checkbox("vanilla", checkbox_group, false);
checkboxes[1] = new Checkbox("chocolate", checkbox_group, true);
checkboxes[2] = new Checkbox("strawberry", checkbox_group, false);

// Create a list of choices.
list = new List(4, true);
list.addItem("Java"); list.addItem("C"); list.addItem("C++");
list.addItem("Smalltalk"); list.addItem("Lisp");
list.addItem("Modula-3"); list.addItem("Forth");

// Create a one-line text field, and multiline text area.
textfield = new TextField(15);
textarea = new TextArea(6, 40);
textarea.setEditable(false);

// Create a scrolling canvas to scribble in.
scribble = new ScrollableScribble();

// Create a file selection dialog box.
file_dialog = new FileDialog(this, "Open File", FileDialog.LOAD);

// Create a Panel to contain all the components along the
// left-hand side of the window.  Use a GridBagLayout for it.
panel1 = new Panel();
panel1.setLayout(gridbag);

// Use several versions of the constrain() convenience method
// to add components to the panel and to specify their
// GridBagConstraints values.
constrain(panel1, new Label("Name:"), 0, 0, 1, 1);
constrain(panel1, textfield, 0, 1, 1, 1);
constrain(panel1, new Label("Favorite color:"), 0, 2, 1, 1,
        10, 0, 0, 0);
constrain(panel1, choice, 0, 3, 1, 1);
constrain(panel1, new Label("Favorite flavor:"), 0, 4, 1, 1,
        10, 0, 0, 0);
```

Example 5-4: Creating all the Java GUI components (continued)

```
        constrain(panel1, checkboxes[0], 0, 5, 1, 1);
        constrain(panel1, checkboxes[1], 0, 6, 1, 1);
        constrain(panel1, checkboxes[2], 0, 7, 1, 1);
        constrain(panel1, new Label("Favorite languages:"), 0, 8, 1, 1,
                10, 0, 0, 0);
        constrain(panel1, list, 0, 9, 1, 3, GridBagConstraints.VERTICAL,
                GridBagConstraints.NORTHWEST, 0.0, 1.0, 0, 0, 0, 0);

        // Create a panel for the items along the right side.
        // Use a GridBagLayout, and arrange items with constrain(), as above.
        panel2 = new Panel();
        panel2.setLayout(gridbag);

        constrain(panel2, new Label("Messages"), 0, 0, 1, 1);
        constrain(panel2, textarea, 0, 1, 1, 3, GridBagConstraints.HORIZONTAL,
                GridBagConstraints.NORTH, 1.0, 0.0, 0, 0, 0, 0);
        constrain(panel2, new Label("Diagram"), 0, 4, 1, 1, 10, 0, 0, 0);
        constrain(panel2, scribble, 0, 5, 1, 5, GridBagConstraints.BOTH,
                GridBagConstraints.CENTER, 1.0, 1.0, 0, 0, 0, 0);

        // Do the same for the buttons along the bottom.
        buttonpanel = new Panel();
        buttonpanel.setLayout(gridbag);
        constrain(buttonpanel, okay, 0, 0, 1, 1, GridBagConstraints.NONE,
                GridBagConstraints.CENTER, 0.3, 0.0, 0, 0, 0, 0);
        constrain(buttonpanel, cancel, 1, 0, 1, 1, GridBagConstraints.NONE,
                GridBagConstraints.CENTER, 0.3, 0.0, 0, 0, 0, 0);

        // Finally, use a GridBagLayout to arrange the panels themselves
        this.setLayout(gridbag);
        // And add the panels to the toplevel window
        constrain(this, panel1, 0, 0, 1, 1, GridBagConstraints.VERTICAL,
                GridBagConstraints.NORTHWEST, 0.0, 1.0, 10, 10, 5, 5);
        constrain(this, panel2, 1, 0, 1, 1, GridBagConstraints.BOTH,
                GridBagConstraints.CENTER, 1.0, 1.0, 10, 10, 5, 10);
        constrain(this, buttonpanel, 0, 1, 2, 1, GridBagConstraints.HORIZONTAL,
                GridBagConstraints.CENTER, 1.0, 0.0, 5, 0, 0, 0);
    }

    // This is the main constrain() method.
    // It has arguments for all constraints.
    public void constrain(Container container, Component component,
                    int grid_x, int grid_y, int grid_width, int grid_height,
                    int fill, int anchor, double weight_x, double weight_y,
                    int top, int left, int bottom, int right)
    {
        GridBagConstraints c = new GridBagConstraints();
        c.gridx = grid_x; c.gridy = grid_y;
        c.gridwidth = grid_width; c.gridheight = grid_height;
        c.fill = fill; c.anchor = anchor;
        c.weightx = weight_x; c.weighty = weight_y;
        if (top+bottom+left+right > 0)
                c.insets = new Insets(top, left, bottom, right);

        ((GridBagLayout)container.getLayout()).setConstraints(component, c);
```

Example 5-4: Creating all the Java GUI components (continued)

```
            container.add(component);
        }

        // This version of constrain() specifies the position of a component
        // that does not grow and does not have margins.
        public void constrain(Container container, Component component,
                        int grid_x, int grid_y, int grid_width, int grid_height) {
            constrain(container, component, grid_x, grid_y,
                    grid_width, grid_height, GridBagConstraints.NONE,
                    GridBagConstraints.NORTHWEST, 0.0, 0.0, 0, 0, 0, 0);
        }

        // This version of constrain() positions a component that does
        // not grow, but does have margins.
        public void constrain(Container container, Component component,
                        int grid_x, int grid_y, int grid_width, int grid_height,
                        int top, int left, int bottom, int right) {
            constrain(container, component, grid_x, grid_y,
                    grid_width, grid_height, GridBagConstraints.NONE,
                    GridBagConstraints.NORTHWEST,
                    0.0, 0.0, top, left, bottom, right);
        }

        public static void main(String[] args) {
            Frame f = new AllComponents("AWT Demo");
            f.pack();
            f.show();
        }
    }
```

The constructor method in this example is a long one—it does all the component
creation and layout. Creating the components is straightforward; study the example
to see how it is done. Arranging the components with the GridBagLayout layout
manager is more confusing. Before proceeding further, read about GridBagLayout
and GridBagConstraints in the quick reference section of this book.

The GridBagLayout arranges components as specified by the values in a Grid-
BagConstraints object associated with each component. In this example, the various constrain() methods simplify the use of the GridBagLayout. We use them
to combine the process of specifying constraints for a component and adding the
component to its container.

Note that the components in this example are arranged in three separate panels, and
that the panels are all arranged within a Frame; each of these containers is separately laid out by a GridBagLayout manager. Nesting the components within panels in this way is not strictly necessary, but greatly simplifies the layout—we specify
four relatively simple layouts instead of one very complicated one. Notice that a
single GridBagLayout object is used to lay out all of the containers—the layout
specifications are contained in the constraints, not in the layout manager itself, so a
single manager can be used for many containers.

Recall that the GridBagLayout manager divides the container into rows and columns, which may each be a different size. Each column is as wide as the widest
component it contains, and each row is as tall as the tallest component it contains.

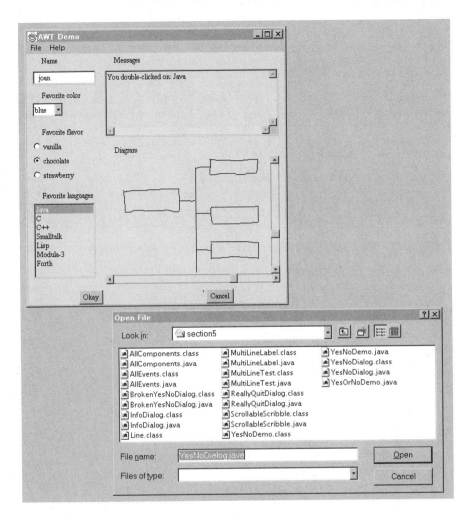

Figure 5-4: Java GUI components in Windows

Components are placed within the cells of this row/column grid, and they are allowed to span multiple rows or columns. Therefore, the four most important constraint values that specify a component's position in a GridBagLayout are the component's position in the grid, its width in columns, and its height in rows. All versions of the constrain() method require these four constraints to be specified.

Another important constraint is the fill value, which specifies whether the component should grow to fill any extra space available to it in the grid. Legal values are the GridBagConstraints constants HORIZONTAL (grow to fill horizontal space), VERTICAL (grow to fill vertical space), BOTH (grow in both directions) and NONE (never grow at all). For components that do not grow in both directions, the anchor constraint specifies how they should be positioned within their grid cells when there is extra space.

The weightx and weighty constraints specify how rows and columns in the grid should resize when the whole container is resized. When a container is made larger, the rows and columns of the grid receive the extra space in proportion to their relative weights. If all the items in a column have a `weightx` of 0.0, then that column will never become any wider when the container grows. If all the items in a row have a `weighty` of 0.0, then the row will never get any taller.

Finally, the optional `top`, `left`, `bottom`, and `right` arguments to `constrain()` specify margins for each side of each component. The `GridBagLayout` allocates the specified amount of extra space on each side of the component. Specifying margins is useful to prevent components from appearing squished together. The four optional margin arguments to `constrain()` are used to create an `Insets` object, which is specified as the `insets` constraint in the `GridBagConstraints` object.

The `GridBagLayout` is the most powerful and generally useful of the Java layout managers. It is difficult, but important to understand. Study the example; reread the explanation above; refer back to Figure 5-4; draw sketches if you need to. Whatever you do, it is important to take the time to be sure you understand exactly how each component is laid out in the window.

Handling GUI Events

In the previous example, we created lots of GUI components. None of the components actually did anything, however. When a user interacts with a Java GUI component (e.g., clicks on a button or selects an item in a list), the component generates an `Event` object. In order to respond to the user's interaction, we must handle the event. Example 5-5 shows how this can be done for each of the Java components that we created in the previous example.

Example 5-5: Handling GUI events

```java
import java.awt.*;

public class AllEvents extends AllComponents {
    public AllEvents(String title) {
        super(title);
    }
    // This method handles all the events generated by all the components.
    public boolean handleEvent(Event event) {
        switch(event.id) {
        // Most components generate ACTION_EVENT
        // We test the target field to find out which component.
        case Event.ACTION_EVENT:
            if (event.target == textfield) {
                textarea.setText("Your name is: " + (String)event.arg + "\n");
            }
            else if (event.target == choice) {
                textarea.setText("Your favorite color is: " +
                        (String) event.arg + "\n");
            }
            else if ((event.target == checkboxes[0]) ||
                    (event.target == checkboxes[1]) ||
                    (event.target == checkboxes[2])) {
                textarea.setText("Your favorite flavor is: " +
                        checkbox_group.getCurrent().getLabel() + "\n");
            }
            else if (event.target == list) {
                textarea.setText("You double-clicked on: " +
                        (String)event.arg + "\n");
            }
```

Example 5-5: Handling GUI events (continued)

```
            else if (event.target == okay) {
                textarea.setText("Okay button clicked.\n");
            }
            else if (event.target == cancel) {
                textarea.setText("Cancel button clicked.\n");
            }
            else if (event.target instanceof MenuItem) {
                // Since we didn't save references to each of the menu objects,
                // we check which one was pressed by comparing labels.
                // Note that we respond to these menu items by
                // popping up dialog boxes.
                if (((String)event.arg).equals("Quit")) {
                    YesNoDialog d = new ReallyQuitDialog(this, textarea);
                    d.show();
                }
                else if (((String)event.arg).equals("Open")) {
                    textarea.setText("You selected Open.\n");
                    // Use the dialog box created by our superclass.
                    file_dialog.pack();      // bug workaround
                    file_dialog.show();      // blocks until user selects a file
                    textarea.setText("You selected file: " +
                                  file_dialog.getFile());
                }
                else if (((String)event.arg).equals("About")) {
                    InfoDialog d;
                    d = new InfoDialog(this, "About AWT Demo",
                                 "This demo was written by David Flanagan\n" +
                                 "Copyright (c) 1996 O'Reilly & Associates");
                    d.show();
                    textarea.setText("You selected About.\n");
                }
            }
            else {
                textarea.setText("Unknown action event.");
            }
            break;

        // Double-clicking on a list generates an action event.
        // But list selection and deselection are separate event types.
        case Event.LIST_SELECT:
            textarea.setText("You selected: " +
                          list.getItem(((Integer)event.arg).intValue()) + "\n");
            break;
        case Event.LIST_DESELECT:
            textarea.setText("You deselected: " +
                          list.getItem(((Integer)event.arg).intValue()) + "\n");
            break;

        // These are some events pertaining to the window itself.
        case Event.WINDOW_DESTROY:
            textarea.setText("Window Destroy\n");
            break;
        case Event.WINDOW_ICONIFY:
            textarea.setText("Window iconify\n");
            break;
        case Event.WINDOW_DEICONIFY:
```

Graphical Interfaces

Example 5-5: Handling GUI events (continued)

```
                    textarea.setText("Window deiconify\n");
                    break;
            case Event.WINDOW_MOVED:
                    textarea.setText("Window moved\n");
                    break;

            // We print a message about each of these mouse and key events,
            // but return false after so that they can still
            // be properly handled by their correct recipient.
            case Event.MOUSE_DOWN:
                    textarea.setText("Mouse down: [" + event.x + "," + event.y + "]\n");
                    return false;
            case Event.MOUSE_UP:
                    textarea.setText("Mouse up: [" + event.x + "," + event.y + "]\n");
                    return false;
            case Event.MOUSE_DRAG:
                    textarea.setText("Mouse drag: [" + event.x + "," + event.y + "]\n");
                    return false;
            case Event.KEY_PRESS:
            case Event.KEY_ACTION:
                    textarea.setText("Key press\n");
                    return false;
            case Event.KEY_RELEASE:
            case Event.KEY_ACTION_RELEASE:
                    textarea.setText("Key release\n");
                    return false;

            // We ignore these event types.
            case Event.GOT_FOCUS:
            case Event.LOST_FOCUS:
            case Event.MOUSE_ENTER:
            case Event.MOUSE_EXIT:
            case Event.MOUSE_MOVE:
                    return false;

            // We shouldn't ever get this...
            default:
                    textarea.setText("Unexpected Event type: " + event + "\n");
                    break;
            }
            return true;
    }

    // Here's the method that lets us run and test this class.
    public static void main(String[] args) {
            Frame f = new AllEvents("AWT Demo");
            f.pack();
            f.show();
    }
}
```

The event-handling code in this example is a single long `switch` statement within the `handleEvent()` method. `handleEvent()` is invoked by the system when an event is generated. In this example, `handleEvent()` detects all of the possible events and displays an appropriate message in the text area of the window.

(Actually, scrollbar events are not handled here; scrollbars and scrolling events are the subject of the next example.) Study the code to find out what kinds of events are generated by what kinds of components and to learn how these events can be handled. You might also want to look at Section 11, *Events*, which contains a quick reference table of components and the event types they generate.

The id field of an Event specifies the type of the event. The Event. ACTION_EVENT type is generated by a GUI component (though components can generate other types of events as well) and means that the user has clicked a button, selected an item from a menu, entered text in a text field, and so on. The target field of an Event specifies the particular component that generated the event. The arg field often specifies additional useful information about the event. For example, when a button is clicked, the arg field contains the label of the button. arg is of type Object; you have to cast it to the appropriate type before using it. See Section 11 for full information about how the arg and other Event fields are used for each event type.

Note that you do not always have to override handleEvent() to handle events in Java. In the previous chapter, we saw examples that overrode action(), mouse-Down(), and other methods specific to a particular event type. The problem with this approach is that it does not work for all event types. For example, there is no special method you can override to handle the Event.LIST_SELECT event type. Thus, for fully general-purpose event handling, you need to override the handleEvent() method. If you also want the convenience of being able to override action() and other specific event handling methods, be sure to invoke the superclass handleEvent() method at the end of your own handleEvent() method:

```
if (event_handled) return true;
else return super.handleEvent(e);
```

You must do this because it is the default implementation of handleEvent() that invokes action() and the other specific event handling methods. If you override handleEvent() without invoking the superclass handleEvent() method, then action() and the other methods will never be invoked.

Remember that an event handling method should return true if it has fully handled the event and the event needs no more processing. The method should return false if it did not handle the event and the event should be passed on to some other container for handling.

Working with Scrollbars

Figure 5-4 above showed a scrollable area that a user could scribble in. Example 5-4 created that area as an instance of the ScrollableScribble class. Now, Example 5-6 shows the definition of that class and demonstrates how to use scrollbars in your Java programs.

Example 5-6: Working with scrollbars

```
import java.awt.*;

public class ScrollableScribble extends Panel {
    Canvas canvas;
    Scrollbar hbar, vbar;
    java.util.Vector lines = new java.util.Vector(100, 100);
```

Example 5-6: Working with scrollbars (continued)

```
        int last_x, last_y;
        int offset_x, offset_y;
        int canvas_width, canvas_height;


        // Create a canvas and two scrollbars and lay them out in the panel.
        // Use a BorderLayout to get the scrollbars flush against the
        // right and bottom sides of the canvas.  When the panel grows,
        // the canvas and scrollbars will also grow appropriately.
        public ScrollableScribble() {
                // implicit super() call here creates the panel
                canvas = new Canvas();
                hbar = new Scrollbar(Scrollbar.HORIZONTAL);
                vbar = new Scrollbar(Scrollbar.VERTICAL);
                this.setLayout(new BorderLayout(0, 0));
                this.add("Center", canvas);
                this.add("South", hbar);
                this.add("East", vbar);
        }


        // Draw the scribbles that we've saved in the Vector.
        // The offset_x and offset_y variables specify which portion of
        // the larger (1000x1000) scribble is to be displayed in the
        // relatively small canvas.  Moving the scrollbars changes these
        // variables, and thus scrolls the picture.  Note that the Canvas
        // component automatically does clipping; we can't accidentally
        // draw outside of its borders.
        public void paint(Graphics g) {
                Line l;
                Graphics canvas_g = canvas.getGraphics();
                for(int i = 0; i < lines.size(); i++) {
                        l = (Line)lines.elementAt(i);
                        canvas_g.drawLine(l.x1 - offset_x, l.y1 - offset_y,
                                        l.x2 - offset_x, l.y2 - offset_y);
                }
        }


        // Handle user's mouse scribbles.  Draw the scribbles
        // and save them in the vector for later redrawing.
        public boolean mouseDown(Event e, int x, int y)
        {
                last_x = x; last_y = y;
                return true;
        }
        public boolean mouseDrag(Event e, int x, int y)
        {
                Graphics g = canvas.getGraphics();
                g.drawLine(last_x, last_y, x, y);
                lines.addElement(new Line(last_x + offset_x, last_y + offset_y,
                                        x + offset_x, y + offset_y));
                last_x = x;
                last_y = y;
                return true;
        }
        // handle mouse up, too, just for symmetry.
        public boolean mouseUp(Event e, int x, int y) { return true; }
```

Example 5-6: Working with scrollbars (continued)

```
// This method handles the scrollbar events.  It updates the
// offset_x and offset_y variables that are used by the paint()
// method, and then calls update(), which clears the canvas and
// invokes the paint() method to redraw the scribbles.
public boolean handleEvent(Event e) {
    if (e.target == hbar) {
        switch(e.id) {
        case Event.SCROLL_LINE_UP:
        case Event.SCROLL_LINE_DOWN:
        case Event.SCROLL_PAGE_UP:
        case Event.SCROLL_PAGE_DOWN:
        case Event.SCROLL_ABSOLUTE:
                offset_x = ((Integer)e.arg).intValue(); break;
        }
        this.update(canvas.getGraphics());
        return true;
    }
    else if (e.target == vbar) {
        switch(e.id) {
        case Event.SCROLL_LINE_UP:
        case Event.SCROLL_PAGE_UP:
        case Event.SCROLL_LINE_DOWN:
        case Event.SCROLL_PAGE_DOWN:
        case Event.SCROLL_ABSOLUTE:
                offset_y = ((Integer)e.arg).intValue(); break;
        }
        this.update(canvas.getGraphics());
        return true;
    }

    // If we didn't handle it above, pass it on to the superclass
    // handleEvent routine, which will check its type and call
    // the mouseDown(), mouseDrag(), and other methods.
    return super.handleEvent(e);
}

// This method is called when our size is changed.  We need to
// know this so we can update the scrollbars
public synchronized void reshape(int x, int y, int width, int height) {
    // do the real stuff
    super.reshape(x, y, width, height);
    // Update our scrollbar page size
    Dimension hbar_size = hbar.size();
    Dimension vbar_size = vbar.size();
    canvas_width = width - vbar_size.width;
    canvas_height = height - hbar_size.height;
    hbar.setValues(offset_x, canvas_width, 0, 1000-canvas_width);
    vbar.setValues(offset_y, canvas_height, 0, 1000-canvas_height);
    hbar.setPageIncrement(canvas_width/2);
    vbar.setPageIncrement(canvas_height/2);
    this.update(canvas.getGraphics());

}
}

// This class stores the coordinates of one line of the scribble.
```

Example 5-6: Working with scrollbars (continued)

```
class Line {
    public int x1, y1, x2, y2;
    public Line(int x1, int y1, int x2, int y2) {
        this.x1 = x1; this.y1 = y1; this.x2 = x2; this.y2 = y2;
    }
}
```

`ScrollableScribble` is a subclass of `Panel`. The constructor method creates a `Canvas` component and horizontal and vertical scrollbars. These components are laid out within the panel with a `BorderLayout` layout manager, which is perfect for getting the scrollbars flush against the edges of the canvas.

In this example, the `mouseDown()` and `mouseDrag()` methods are used to detect the user's scribbles. When the user drags the mouse, `mouseDrag()` draws the appropriate line. It also saves the coordinates of the line so that it can be redrawn later. It creates a `Line` object to hold the coordinates and adds each `Line` to a `Vector` object. The `Vector` class implements an array that can grow to have an arbitrary number of elements. Elements are added in `mouseDrag()` with `addElement()`, and are extracted in `paint()` with `elementAt()`.

The `handleEvent()` method handles events from the scrollbars. As we described for the previous example, it invokes its superclass `handleEvent()` method so that non-scrollbar events are properly dispatched to the `mouseDown()` and `mouseDrag()` methods.

The scrollbars are used to display a large (1000 pixels by 1000 pixels) drawing (or scribble) within a much smaller canvas. The example is thoroughly commented. Study it, and you'll understand how the scrolling is done.

Defining a Custom Component

At the beginning of this chapter, our `InfoDialog` and `YesNoDialog` examples used a `MultiLineLabel` class to display their message, because the standard Java `Label` component can only display a single line of text. Example 5-7 shows the definition of the `MultiLineLabel` class. By studying it, you can learn how to create custom Java components of your own.

Example 5-7: A custom component

```
import java.awt.*;
import java.util.*;

public class MultiLineLabel extends Canvas {
    public static final int LEFT = 0;        // Alignment constants
    public static final int CENTER = 1;
    public static final int RIGHT = 2;
    protected String[] lines;                // The lines of text to display
    protected int num_lines;                 // The number of lines
    protected int margin_width;              // Left and right margins
    protected int margin_height;             // Top and bottom margins
    protected int line_height;               // Total height of the font
    protected int line_ascent;               // Font height above baseline
    protected int[] line_widths;             // How wide each line is
    protected int max_width;                 // The width of the widest line
```

Example 5-7: A custom component (continued)

```
    protected int alignment = LEFT;         // The alignment of the text.


    // This method breaks a specified label up into an array of lines.
    // It uses the StringTokenizer utility class.
    protected void newLabel(String label) {
        StringTokenizer t = new StringTokenizer(label, "\n");
        num_lines = t.countTokens();
        lines = new String[num_lines];
        line_widths = new int[num_lines];
        for(int i = 0; i < num_lines; i++) lines[i] = t.nextToken();
    }


    // This method figures out how large the font is, and how wide each
    // line of the label is, and how wide the widest line is.
    protected void measure() {
        FontMetrics fm = this.getFontMetrics(this.getFont());
        // If we don't have font metrics yet, just return.
        if (fm == null) return;

        line_height = fm.getHeight();
        line_ascent = fm.getAscent();
        max_width = 0;
        for(int i = 0; i < num_lines; i++) {
            line_widths[i] = fm.stringWidth(lines[i]);
            if (line_widths[i] > max_width) max_width = line_widths[i];
        }
    }


    // Here are four versions of the constructor.
    // Break the label up into separate lines, and save the other info.
    public MultiLineLabel(String label, int margin_width, int margin_height,
                    int alignment) {
        newLabel(label);
        this.margin_width = margin_width;
        this.margin_height = margin_height;
        this.alignment = alignment;
    }
    public MultiLineLabel(String label, int margin_width, int margin_height) {
        this(label, margin_width, margin_height, LEFT);
    }
    public MultiLineLabel(String label, int alignment) {
        this(label, 10, 10, alignment);
    }
    public MultiLineLabel(String label) {
        this(label, 10, 10, LEFT);
    }


    // Methods to set the various attributes of the component
    public void setLabel(String label) {
        newLabel(label);
        measure();
        repaint();
    }
    public void setFont(Font f) {
        super.setFont(f);
        measure();
```

Defining a Custom Component

Example 5-7: A custom component (continued)

```
                repaint();
        }
        public void setForeground(Color c) {
                super.setForeground(c);
                repaint();
        }
        public void setAlignment(int a) { alignment = a; repaint(); }
        public void setMarginWidth(int mw) { margin_width = mw; repaint(); }
        public void setMarginHeight(int mh) { margin_height = mh; repaint(); }
        public int getAlignment() { return alignment; }
        public int getMarginWidth() { return margin_width; }
        public int getMarginHeight() { return margin_height; }


        // This method is invoked after our Canvas is first created
        // but before it can actually be displayed.  After we've
        // invoked our superclass's addNotify() method, we have font
        // metrics and can successfully call measure() to figure out
        // how big the label is.
        public void addNotify() { super.addNotify(); measure(); }


        // This method is called by a layout manager when it wants to
        // know how big we'd like to be.
        public Dimension preferredSize() {
                return new Dimension(max_width + 2*margin_width,
                                num_lines * line_height + 2*margin_height);
        }


        // This method is called when the layout manager wants to know
        // the bare minimum amount of space we need to get by.
        public Dimension minimumSize() {
                return new Dimension(max_width, num_lines * line_height);
        }


        // This method draws the label (applets use the same method).
        // Note that it handles the margins and the alignment, but that
        // it doesn't have to worry about the color or font--the superclass
        // takes care of setting those in the Graphics object we're passed.
        public void paint(Graphics g) {
                int x, y;
                Dimension d = this.size();
                y = line_ascent + (d.height - num_lines * line_height)/2;
                for(int i = 0; i < num_lines; i++, y += line_height) {
                        switch(alignment) {
                        case LEFT:
                                x = margin_width; break;
                        case CENTER:
                        default:
                                x = (d.width - line_widths[i])/2; break;
                        case RIGHT:
                                x = d.width - margin_width - line_widths[i]; break;
                        }
                        g.drawString(lines[i], x, y);
                }
        }
}
```

Much of the code in this example is taken up with the mechanics of breaking the label up into separate lines, using the useful `java.util.StringTokenizer` class. And also with figuring out how wide the lines are using the `FontMetrics` class. But the most important code for this example is in several required methods that make this custom component work correctly.

The most important method of any custom component is the `paint()` method, which actually draws the component. (This is the same method you use to draw an applet, by the way). The `preferredSize()` and `minimumSize()` methods are also very important. These methods must be defined, or layout managers won't be able to arrange your custom component correctly.

The `addNotify()` method is also sometimes important. The system invokes this method when it wants a component to create the platform-dependent object (e.g., a Motif widget on a UNIX platform or a Windows control on a Windows platform) that actually implements the component. `addNotify()` is misleadingly named, and should probably be called `createPeer()`.

Our custom component is platform-independent; so we don't need to create a peer object. We use it, however, as a way to find out when our superclass's peer is created. The first thing our version of `addNotify()` does is to invoke the superclass version of the function. Once that call returns, we know that the peer has been created. What this means for the `MultiLineLabel` is that font metrics are now available and we can call the `measure()` method to figure out how big the lines of the label are. We need to ensure that the `measure()` method is called sometime before the `paint()` or `preferredSize()` methods are called, but not before font metrics are available. Our overridden `addNotify()` method does exactly this.

Input and Output

The examples in this chapter demonstrate how to use the Java input and output facilities. They show you how to:

- List directories.

- Read and write files.

- Use various Java stream classes.

- Define filter streams to process input data

The examples in this chapter use the classes in the `java.io` package. The introduction to Section 22, *The java.io Package*, gives a good overview of this package. You may also want to refer to the quick reference material of that section while studying the examples in this section.

Reading and Displaying Files

Example 6-1 combines the use of the `File` class with the GUI techniques we saw from the previous section. This `FileViewer` class reads in the contents of a file with the `read()` method of a `FileInputStream` and displays the file in a `TextArea` component. The `FileViewer` class is designed to be used by other classes. It also has its own `main()` method, however, so that it can be run as a standalone program. To do this, just invoke it with the name of the file specified, like this

%java FileViewer foo.java

Figure 6-1 shows a `FileViewer` window.

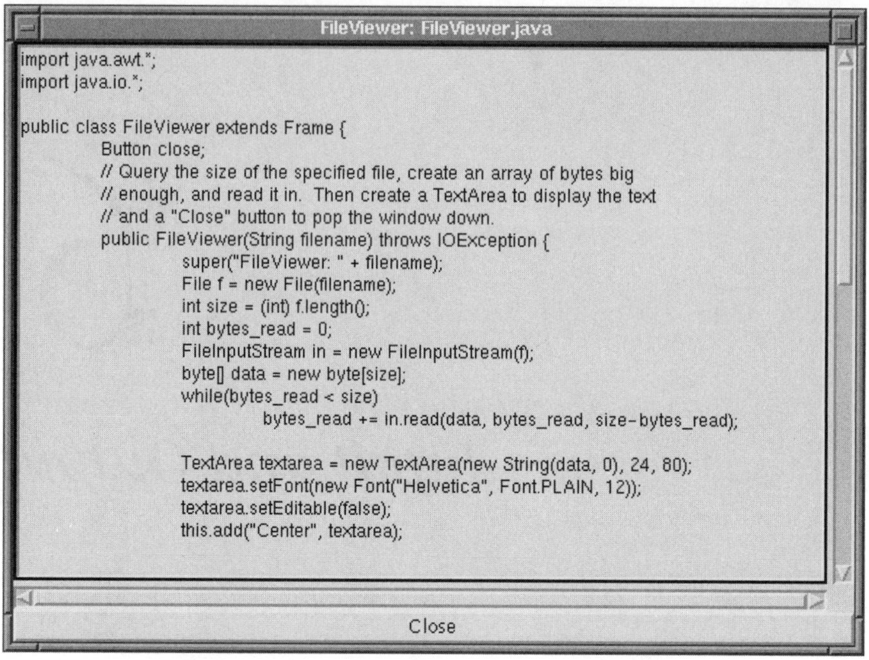

```
FileViewer: FileViewer.java

import java.awt.*;
import java.io.*;

public class FileViewer extends Frame {
        Button close;
        // Query the size of the specified file, create an array of bytes big
        // enough, and read it in.  Then create a TextArea to display the text
        // and a "Close" button to pop the window down.
        public FileViewer(String filename) throws IOException {
                super("FileViewer: " + filename);
                File f = new File(filename);
                int size = (int) f.length();
                int bytes_read = 0;
                FileInputStream in = new FileInputStream(f);
                byte[] data = new byte[size];
                while(bytes_read < size)
                        bytes_read += in.read(data, bytes_read, size-bytes_read);

                TextArea textarea = new TextArea(new String(data, 0), 24, 80);
                textarea.setFont(new Font("Helvetica", Font.PLAIN, 12));
                textarea.setEditable(false);
                this.add("Center", textarea);
```

                                            Close

Figure 6-1: A FileViewer window

Example 6-1: Displaying file contents

```
import java.awt.*;
import java.io.*;

public class FileViewer extends Frame {
        Button close;
        // Query the size of the specified file, create an array of bytes big
        // enough, and read it in.  Then create a TextArea to display the text
        // and a "Close" button to pop the window down.
        public FileViewer(String filename) throws IOException {
                super("FileViewer: " + filename);
                File f = new File(filename);
                int size = (int) f.length();
                int bytes_read = 0;
                FileInputStream in = new FileInputStream(f);
                byte[] data = new byte[size];
                while(bytes_read < size)
                        bytes_read += in.read(data, bytes_read, size-bytes_read);

                TextArea textarea = new TextArea(new String(data, 0), 24, 80);
                textarea.setFont(new Font("Helvetica", Font.PLAIN, 12));
                textarea.setEditable(false);
                this.add("Center", textarea);

                close = new Button("Close");
                this.add("South", close);
                this.pack();
                this.show();
        }
```

Example 6-1: Displaying file contents (continued)

```
// Handle the close button by popping this window down
public boolean action(Event e, Object what) {
    if (e.target == close) {
        this.hide();
        this.dispose();
        return true;
    }
    return false;
}

// The FileViewer can be used by other classes, or it can be
// used standalone with this main() method.
static public void main(String[] args) throws IOException {
    if (args.length != 1) {
        System.out.println("Usage: java FileViewer <filename>");
        System.exit(0);
    }
    try Frame f = new FileViewer(args[0]);
    catch (IOException e) System.out.println(e);
}
}
```

Getting Directory and File Information

Just as the `FileViewer` class displays the contents of a file in a `TextArea` component, the `FileLister` class, shown in Example 6-2, displays the contents of a directory in a `List` component. When you select a file or directory name from the list, it displays information (size, modification date, etc.) about the file or directory in a `TextField` component. When you double-click on a directory, it displays the contents of that directory. When you double-click on a file, it displays the contents of the file in a `FileViewer` object. Figure 6-2 shows a `FileLister` window.

This example also demonstrates the use of the `FilenameFilter` interface for specifying what files in a directory should be listed. And it shows how you can get the current directory by querying the `user.dir` property. Note the frequent use of `try` and `catch` to handle possibilities of exceptions.

Like the `FileViewer` class, the `FileLister` can be used by other classes, or it can be invoked as a standalone program. To use it standalone, invoke it with an optional directory name and an optional -e argument specifying a file extension.

Example 6-2: Directory listings and file information

```
import java.awt.*;
import java.io.*;

public class FileLister extends Frame {
    private List list;
    private TextField infoarea;
    private Panel buttons;
    private Button parent, quit;
    private FilenameFilter filter;
```

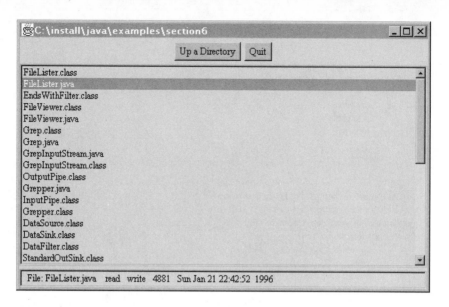

Figure 6-2: A FileLister window

Example 6-2: Directory listings and file information (continued)

```
private File cwd;
private String[] entries;

// Create the graphical user interface, and list the initial directory.
public FileLister(String directory, FilenameFilter filter) throws IOException
{
    super("File Lister");
    this.filter = filter;
    list = new List(12, false);
    infoarea = new TextField();
    infoarea.setEditable(false);
    buttons = new Panel();
    parent = new Button("Up a Directory");
    quit = new Button("Quit");
    buttons.add(parent);
    buttons.add(quit);
    this.add("Center", list);
    this.add("South", infoarea);
    this.add("North", buttons);
    this.resize(550, 350);
    this.show();

    // list the initial directory.
    list_directory(directory);
}

// This method uses the list() method to get all entries in a directory
// and then displays them in the List component.
public void list_directory(String directory) throws IOException {
    File dir = new File(directory);

    if (!dir.isDirectory())
```

Example 6-2: Directory listings and file information (continued)

```
                throw new IllegalArgumentException("FileLister: no such directory");
        list.clear();
        cwd = dir;
        this.setTitle(directory);

        entries = cwd.list(filter);
        for(int i = 0; i < entries.length; i++)
                list.addItem(entries[i]);
}

// This method uses various File methods to obtain information about
// a file or directory. Then it displays that info in a TextField.
public void show_info(String filename) throws IOException {
        File f = new File(cwd, filename);
        String info;

        if (!f.exists())
                throw new IllegalArgumentException("FileLister.show_info(): " +
                                        "no such file or directory");

        if (f.isDirectory()) info = "Directory: ";
        else info = "File: ";

        info += filename + "   ";

        info += (f.canRead()?"read   ":"     ") +
                (f.canWrite()?"write   ":"     ") +
                        f.length() + "   " +
                                new java.util.Date(f.lastModified());

        infoarea.setText(info);
}

// This method handles the buttons and list events.
public boolean handleEvent(Event e) {
        if (e.target == quit) System.exit(0);
        else if (e.target == parent) {
                String parent = cwd.getParent();
                if (parent == null) parent = "/";        // Bug workaround
                try list_directory(parent);
                catch (IllegalArgumentException ex)infoarea.setText("Already at top");
                catch (IOException ex) infoarea.setText("I/O Error");
                return true;
        }
        else if (e.target == list) {
                // when an item is selected, show its info.
                if (e.id == Event.LIST_SELECT) {
                        try show_info(entries[((Integer)e.arg).intValue()]);
                        catch (IOException ex) infoarea.setText("I/O Error");
                }
                // When the user double-clicks, change to the selected directory
                // or display the selected file.
                else if (e.id == Event.ACTION_EVENT) {
                        try {
                                String item = new File(cwd, (String)e.arg).getAbsolutePath();
                                try list_directory(item);
```

Input and Output

Example 6-2: Directory listings and file information (continued)

```
                            catch (IllegalArgumentException ex) new FileViewer(item);
                        }
                        catch (IOException ex) infoarea.setText("I/O Error");
                    }
                    return true;
                }
                return super.handleEvent(e);
            }

            public static void usage() {
                System.out.println("Usage: java FileLister [directory_name] " +
                                    "[-e file_extension]");
                System.exit(0);
            }
            // Parse command line arguments and create the FileLister object.
            // If an extension is specified, create a FilenameFilter for it.
            // If no directory is specified, use the current directory.
            public static void main(String args[]) throws IOException {
                FileLister f;
                FilenameFilter filter = null;
                String directory = null;

                for(int i = 0; i < args.length; i++) {
                    if (args[i].equals("-e")) {
                        i++;
                        if (i >= args.length) usage();
                        filter = new EndsWithFilter(args[i]);
                    }
                    else {
                        if (directory != null) usage();    // Already set
                        else directory = args[i];
                    }
                }

                // if no directory specified, use the current directoy
                if (directory == null) directory = System.getProperty("user.dir");
                // Create the FileLister object
                f = new FileLister(directory, filter);
            }
        }
        // This class is a simple FilenameFilter.  It defines the required accept()
        // method to determine whether a specified file should be listed.  A file
        // will be listed if its name ends with the specified extension, or if
        // it is a directory.
        class EndsWithFilter implements FilenameFilter {
            private String extension;
            public EndsWithFilter(String extension) {
                this.extension = extension;
            }
            public boolean accept(File dir, String name) {
                if (name.endsWith(extension)) return true;
                else return (new File(dir, name)).isDirectory();
            }
        }
```

Copying a File

Example 6-3 shows a `FileCopy` class that you can use to copy the contents of one file to another. This example uses a number of the classes from the `java.io` package. For example, it uses `File` to make sure that the source file exists and is readable. It also uses `File` to make sure either that the destination file exists and is writable or that the directory exists and is writable. It uses the `FileInputStream` and `FileOutputStream` classes to read bytes from the source file and write them to the destination file.

The example also shows how you can read lines of user input from `System.in` by creating a `DataInputStream`. Finally, it uses `System.out` and `System.err`, which are both instances of the `PrintStream` class.

The `copy()` method implements the functionality of the class. This method is heavily commented, so that you can follow the steps it takes. First it verifies that the source file exists and is readable. Then it checks on the destination file. If that file exists and is writable, the method asks if it is okay to overwrite the existing file. If everything checks out, the method copies the file. Note how the example throws exceptions and uses the `finally` statement to clean up.

The `FileCopy.copy()` method can be used directly by any program. `FileCopy` also provides a `main()` method so that it can be used as a standalone program. To use it this way, pass the source file name and the destination file name on the command line, like this:

```
%java FileCopy foo.java bar.java
```

Example 6-3: Copying a file

```java
import java.io.*;

public class FileCopy {
    public static void copy(String source_name, String dest_name)
        throws IOException
    {
        File source_file = new File(source_name);
        File destination_file = new File(dest_name);
        FileInputStream source = null;
        FileOutputStream destination = null;
        byte[] buffer;
        int bytes_read;

        try {
            // First make sure the specified source file
            // exists, is a file, and is readable.
            if (!source_file.exists() || !source_file.isFile())
                throw new FileCopyException("FileCopy: no such source file: " +
                                            source_name);
            if (!source_file.canRead())
                throw new FileCopyException("FileCopy: source file " +
                                            "is unreadable: " + source_name);

            // If the destination exists, make sure it is a writable file
            // and ask before overwriting it.  If the destination doesn't
            // exist, make sure the directory exists and is writable.
```

Example 6-3: Copying a file (continued)

```
if (destination_file.exists()) {
    if (destination_file.isFile()) {
        DataInputStream in = new DataInputStream(System.in);
        String response;

        if (!destination_file.canWrite())
            throw new FileCopyException("FileCopy: destination " +
                                        "file is unwritable: " + dest_name);

        // Tell the user the file already exists
        // and ask if it is okay to overwrite it.
        System.out.print("File " + dest_name +
                         " already exists.  Overwrite? (Y/N): ");
        System.out.flush();
        // Read the user's response.  Note that we use
        // a DataInputStream created from System.in
        // in order to read lines rather than characters.
        response = in.readLine();
        if (!response.equals("Y") && !response.equals("y"))
            throw new FileCopyException("FileCopy: copy cancelled.");
    }
    else
        throw new FileCopyException("FileCopy: destination "
                                    + "is not a file: " +  dest_name);
}
else {
    File parentdir = parent(destination_file);
    if (!parentdir.exists())
        throw new FileCopyException("FileCopy: destination "
                                    + "directory doesn't exist: " + dest_name);
    if (!parentdir.canWrite())
        throw new FileCopyException("FileCopy: destination "
                                    + "directory is unwritable: " + dest_name);

}

// If we've gotten this far, then everything is okay;
// we can go ahead and copy the file.
// Create an input stream from the source file and an ouput
// stream to the destination file.  Then read arrays of bytes
// from one and write them to the other.  When the read() method
// returns -1, we've reached the end of the file and can stop.
source = new FileInputStream(source_file);
destination = new FileOutputStream(destination_file);
buffer = new byte[1024];
while(true) {
    bytes_read = source.read(buffer);
    if (bytes_read == -1) break;
    destination.write(buffer, 0, bytes_read);
}
}
// No matter what happens, always close any streams we've opened.
finally {
    if (source != null)
        try source.close(); catch (IOException e) ;
    if (destination != null)
        try destination.close(); catch (IOException e) ;
```

Example 6-3: Copying a file (continued)

```
            }
      }

      // File.getParent() can return null when the file is specified without
      // a directory or is in the root directory.
      // This method handles those cases.
      private static File parent(File f) {
            String dirname = f.getParent();
            if (dirname == null) {
                  if (f.isAbsolute()) return new File(File.separator);
                  else return new File(System.getProperty("user.dir"));
            }
            return new File(dirname);
      }

      public static void main(String[] args) {
            if (args.length != 2)
                  System.err.println("Usage: java FileCopy " +
                              "<source file> <destination file>");
            else {
                  try copy(args[0], args[1]);
                  catch (IOException e) System.err.println(e.getMessage());
            }
      }
}

class FileCopyException extends IOException {
      public FileCopyException(String msg) { super(msg); }
}
```

Filtering Input

Example 6-4 demonstrates how you can define a subclass of `FilterInputStream` to do custom filtering of input data. The `GrepInputFilter` approximates the behavior of the UNIX *fgrep* command—it filters out all lines that do not contain a specified substring.

Note that this filter stream must be created with a `DataInputStream` specified, so that it has a stream from which to read lines of text. A regular `InputStream` will not work. The filter is extremely simple—the `readLine()` method reads lines from the specified `DataInputStream`, but only returns those that match the specified substring. Note that this filter only filters data read with the `readLine()` call. Data read through the `read()` call, for example, is not filtered.

Example 6-4: A grep-style filter stream

```
import java.io.*;

// This class is a FilterInputStream that filters out all lines that
// do not contain the specified substring.
public class GrepInputStream extends FilterInputStream {
      String substring;
      DataInputStream in;
```

Example 6-4: A grep-style filter stream (continued)

```
public GrepInputStream(DataInputStream in, String substring) {
    super(in);
    this.in = in;
    this.substring = substring;
}

// This is the filter:  read lines from the DataInputStream,
// but only return the lines that contain the substring.
// When the DataInputStream returns null, we return null.
public final String readLine() throws IOException {
    String line;
    do {
        line = in.readLine();
    }
    while ((line != null) && line.indexOf(substring) == -1);
    return line;
}
}
```

Example 6-5 shows how you might use the `GrepInputStream` class to implement a *grep*-like command with Java. You invoke this program by specifying the substring to search for and the name of the file to search on the command line, like this:

%java Grep needle haystack.txt

Example 6-5: Using the GrepInputStream

```
import java.io.*;

// This class demonstrates the use of the GrepInputStream class.
// It prints the lines of a file that contain a specified substring.
public class Grep {
    public static void main(String args[]) {
        if ((args.length == 0) || (args.length > 2)) {
            System.out.println("Usage: java Grep <substring> [<filename>]");
            System.exit(0);
        }

        try {
            DataInputStream d;
            if (args.length == 2)
                d = new DataInputStream(new FileInputStream(args[1]));
            else
                d = new DataInputStream(System.in);

            GrepInputStream g = new GrepInputStream(d, args[0]);

            String line;
            for(;;) {
                line = g.readLine();
                if (line == null) break;
                System.out.println(line);
            }
            g.close();
        }
```

Example 6-5: Using the GrepInputStream (continued)

```
                catch (IOException e) System.err.println(e);
        }
    }
```

Pipes

The Java `PipedInputStream` and `PipedOutputStream` classes allow separate threads to read and write data from and to each other. Example 6-6 shows how you might make use of this ability. It is a long and complicated example, but will repay detailed study.

The code in this example allows you to set up UNIX-style "pipes"—data flows from a "source," through any number of "filters," and then into a "sink." For example, the source might be a file, the filter might be one that performs a search-and-replace operation on the data, and the sink might be another file or the `System.out` stream. The source, filters, and sink of a pipe are all implemented as separate threads, which means that they work independently of each other, running when data is available to be read in the pipe, and blocking when there is no data available.

This example defines `PipeSource`, `PipeSink`, and `PipeFilter` interfaces that define the methods necessary for data sources, sinks, and filters. It defines two simple classes, `StreamPipeSource` and `StreamPipeSink`, that use input streams and output streams, respectively, as data sources and sinks. The example later uses these classes to set up a file as a data source and to set up `System.out` as a data sink.

The example also defines a `BasicPipeFilter` filter class that defines most of the functionality needed for a data filter. The only thing this `abstract` class leaves out is a `filter()` method. The example defines two subclasses of `BasicPipeFilter`, `GrepFilter`, and `Rot13Filter` to perform two different filtering operations on data.

The best place to start studying this example is at the end, where the class `Pipes` and its `main()` method show how all these other classes are used. `main()` shows the creation of a source, three filters, and a sink. It connects them to each other, and then starts the various threads on their tasks.

Example 6-6: Pipes in Java

```
import java.io.*;

// This interface defines the methods that the source of data for a pipe
// must define. These methods are used to allow the source to easily be
// connected to a sink.
// Note that a PipeSource is Runnable--it is a thread body.
interface PipeSource extends Runnable {
    abstract PipedOutputStream getPipedOutputStream();
    abstract void connectOutputTo(PipeSink sink) throws IOException;
    abstract PipeSink getSink();
    abstract void start();
}
// This interface defines the methods required for a sink of data from
// a pipe. The methods are used when connecting a source to the sink.
```

Example 6-6: Pipes in Java (continued)

```
// A PipeSink is also Runnable.
interface PipeSink extends Runnable {
      abstract PipedInputStream getPipedInputStream();
      abstract void connectInputTo(PipeSource source) throws IOException;
}
// A filter in a pipe behaves like both a source of data and a sink of data.
interface PipeFilter extends PipeSource, PipeSink {
};
// This is an implementation of the PipeSource interface that uses an
// InputStream as the source of data.  It creates a PipedOutputStream
// to write the data to.  The run() method copies data from the stream
// to the pipe.
class StreamPipeSource implements PipeSource {
      protected PipedOutputStream out = new PipedOutputStream();
      protected InputStream in;
      protected PipeSink sink;

      public StreamPipeSource(InputStream in) { this.in = in; }
      public PipedOutputStream getPipedOutputStream() { return out; }
      public PipeSink getSink() { return sink; }
      public void connectOutputTo(PipeSink sink) throws IOException {
            this.sink = sink;
            out.connect(sink.getPipedInputStream());
            sink.connectInputTo(this);
      }

      public void start() {
            // Start ourselves
            new Thread(this).start();

            // If our output is a filter, then call its start() method.
            // otherwise, just start our sink
            if (sink instanceof PipeFilter) ((PipeFilter)sink).start();
            else new Thread(sink).start();
      }

      public void run() {
            byte[] buffer = new byte[512];
            int bytes_read;
            try {
                  for(;;) {
                        bytes_read = in.read(buffer);
                        if (bytes_read == -1) { return; }
                        out.write(buffer, 0, bytes_read);
                  }
            }
            catch (IOException e) {
                  if (e instanceof EOFException) return;
                  else System.out.println(e);
            }
            finally { try out.close(); catch (IOException e); }
      }
}
// This is an implementation of the PipeSink interface that uses an output
// stream as the source of data.  It creates a PipedInputStream to read
// data from the pipe.  The run() method reads data from that pipe and
```

Example 6-6: Pipes in Java (continued)

```
// writes it to the output stream (which might be a file or System.out, e.g.)
class StreamPipeSink implements PipeSink {
      protected PipedInputStream in = new PipedInputStream();
      protected OutputStream out;

      public StreamPipeSink(OutputStream out) {
            this.out = out;
      }

      public PipedInputStream getPipedInputStream() { return in; }
      public void connectInputTo(PipeSource source) throws IOException {
            in.connect(source.getPipedOutputStream());
      }

      public void run() {
            byte[] buffer = new byte[512];
            int bytes_read;
            try {
                  for(;;) {
                        bytes_read = in.read(buffer);
                        if (bytes_read == -1) return;
                        out.write(buffer, 0, bytes_read);
                  }
            }
            catch (IOException e) {
                  if (e instanceof EOFException) return;
                  else System.out.println(e);
            }
            finally { try in.close(); catch (IOException e); }
      }
}
// This is an abstract implementation of the PipeFilter interface.
// It creates both a PipedInputStream to read from and a PipedOutputStream
// to write to.  The abstract method filter() needs to be defined by
// a subclass to read data from one pipe, filter it, and write the filtered
// data to the other pipe.
abstract class BasicPipeFilter implements PipeFilter {
      protected PipedInputStream in = new PipedInputStream();
      protected PipedOutputStream out = new PipedOutputStream();
      protected PipeSink sink;
      public PipedInputStream getPipedInputStream() { return in; }
      public PipedOutputStream getPipedOutputStream() { return out; }

      public void connectOutputTo(PipeSink sink) throws IOException {
            this.sink = sink;
            out.connect(sink.getPipedInputStream());
            sink.connectInputTo((PipeSource) this);
      }

      public void start() {
            // Start ourselves
            new Thread(this).start();

            // If our output is a filter, then call its start() method.
            // otherwise, just start our sink
            if (sink instanceof PipeFilter) ((PipeFilter)sink).start();
```

Example 6-6: Pipes in Java (continued)

```
                else new Thread(sink).start();
        }

        public PipeSink getSink() { return sink; }

        public void connectInputTo(PipeSource source) throws IOException {
                in.connect(source.getPipedOutputStream());
        }

        public void run() {
                try { filter(); }
                catch (IOException e) {
                        if (e instanceof EOFException) return;
                        else System.out.println(e);
                }
                finally {
                        try { out.close(); in.close(); }
                        catch (IOException e) ;
                }
        }

        abstract public void filter() throws IOException;
}
// This is a non-abstract implementation of the PipeFilter interface.
// It uses the GrepInputStream we defined elsewhere to do the filtering.
class GrepFilter extends BasicPipeFilter {
        protected GrepInputStream gis;
        protected PrintStream pout = new PrintStream(out);

        public GrepFilter(String pattern) {
                gis = new GrepInputStream(new DataInputStream(in), pattern);
        }

        public void filter() throws IOException {
                String line;
                for(;;) {
                        line = gis.readLine();
                        if (line == null) return;
                        pout.println(line);
                }
        }
}
// This is another implementation fo PipeFilter.  It implements the
// trival rot13 cypher on the letters A-Z and a-z.
class Rot13Filter extends BasicPipeFilter {
        public void filter() throws IOException {
                byte[] buffer = new byte[512];
                int bytes_read;

                for(;;) {
                        bytes_read = in.read(buffer);
                        if (bytes_read == -1) return;
                        for(int i = 0; i < bytes_read; i++) {
                                if ((buffer[i] >= 'a') && (buffer[i] <= 'z')) {
                                        buffer[i] = (byte) ('a' + ((buffer[i]-'a') + 13) % 26);
                                }
```

Example 6-6: Pipes in Java (continued)

```
                    if ((buffer[i] >= 'A') && (buffer[i] <= 'Z')) {
                        buffer[i] = (byte) ('A' + ((buffer[i]-'A') + 13) % 26);
                    }
                }
                out.write(buffer, 0, bytes_read);
            }
        }
    }
// This class demonstrates how you might use these pipe classes.
// It is another implementation of a UNIX-like grep command.
// Note that it frivolously passes the output of the grep pipe through two
// rot13 pipes (which, combined, leave the output unchanged).
// With the source, filter, and sink infrastructure defined above, it
// is easy to define new filters and create pipes to perform many useful
// operations.  Other filter possibilities include sorting lines, removing
// duplicate lines, and doing search-and-replace.
public class Pipes {
    public static void main(String[] args) throws IOException {
        if (args.length != 2) {
            System.out.println("Usage: java Pipes <pattern> <filename>");
            System.exit(0);
        }

        // Create a source, three filters, and a sink for the pipe.
        PipeSource source =
                new StreamPipeSource(new FileInputStream(args[1]));
        PipeFilter filter = new GrepFilter(args[0]);
        PipeFilter filter2 = new Rot13Filter();
        PipeFilter filter3 = new Rot13Filter();
        PipeSink sink = new StreamPipeSink(System.out);

        // Connect them all up.
        source.connectOutputTo(filter);
        filter.connectOutputTo(filter2);
        filter2.connectOutputTo(filter3);
        filter3.connectOutputTo(sink);

        // And start their threads running.
        source.start();
    }
}
```

Input and Output

Networking

The examples in this section demonstrate Java's networking capabilities at a number of different levels of abstraction. They show you how to:

- Use the URL class.

- Use the URLConnection class to gain more control over the downloading of network resources.

- Write servers and clients that communicate over the Net.

- Send and receive low-overhead datagram packets.

The introduction to Section 24, *The java.net Package*, gives a good overview of the classes in the java.net package; the quick reference material in that section may be useful while you study the examples in this section.

Downloading the Contents of a URL

Example 7-1 shows the simplest possible use of the URL class. It creates a URL from a specified WWW address and then downloads the contents of the URL with the getContent() method. This technique relies on resident "content handlers" that know how to parse the incoming data and convert it to an appropriate object. The standard Java distribution does not have many of these content handlers installed. Thus, the fetch() method shown here only works for URLs with content type of "text/plain" and the fetchimage() method only works for image URLs of type "image/gif," "image/jpeg," and a few other standard types.

Note that it is possible to define your own content handler to parse any kind of data you want. This capability is usually used by Web browsers, like Sun's HotJava browser, that need the ability to download and display many different types of data. Most applications do not need to define content handlers—if they need to parse a

---

particular type of data, they can simply write the code that does that. In the next example, we'll see how you can use a URLConnection to download arbitrary data from a URL.

Example 7-1: Fetching a URL

```
import java.awt.*;
import java.io.*;
import java.net.*;

// The fetch() method in this class only works for fetching text/plain
// data, and a few standard image types.  The standard Java distribution
// doesn't contain content handlers for other types (such as text/html),
// so this code exits with an exception.
public class Fetch {
    // Get the contents of a URL and return it as a string.
    public static String fetch(String address)
        throws MalformedURLException, IOException
    {
        URL url = new URL(address);
        return (String) url.getContent();
    }

    // Get the contents of a URL and return it as an image
    public static String fetchimage(String address)
        throws MalformedURLException, IOException
    {
        URL url = new URL(address);
        return (Image) url.getContent();
    }

    // Test out the fetch() method.
    public static void main(String[] args)
        throws MalformedURLException, IOException
    {
        System.out.println(fetch(args[0]));
    }
}
```

Using a URLConnection

You can gain a lot more control over downloading the contents of a URL by using that object's associated URLConnection object. Example 7-2 shows how to use a URLConnection to obtain the content type, size, last-modified date, and other information about the resource referred to by a URL. It also shows how you can use a stream to download the contents of a URL, regardless of its type. Note the use of the DataInputStream to read lines of text from the URLConnection, and the use of the java.util.Date class to convert a long timestamp to a textual form.

Example 7-2: Getting information about a URL

```
import java.net.*;
import java.io.*;
import java.util.*;
```

Example 7-2: Getting information about a URL (continued)

```
public class GetURLInfo {
    public static void printinfo(URLConnection u) throws IOException {
        // Display the URL address, and information about it.
        System.out.println(u.getURL().toExternalForm() + ":");
        System.out.println("  Content Type: " + u.getContentType());
        System.out.println("  Content Length: " + u.getContentLength());
        System.out.println("  Last Modified: " + new Date(u.getLastModified()));
        System.out.println("  Expiration: " + u.getExpiration());
        System.out.println("  Content Encoding: " + u.getContentEncoding());

        // Read and print out the first five lines of the URL.
        System.out.println("First five lines:");
        DataInputStream in = new DataInputStream(u.getInputStream());
        for(int i = 0; i < 5; i++) {
            String line = in.readLine();
            if (line == null) break;
            System.out.println("  " + line);
        }
    }

    // Create a URL from the specified address, open a connection to it,
    // and then display information about the URL.
    public static void main(String[] args)
        throws MalformedURLException, IOException {
        URL url = new URL(args[0]);
        URLConnection connection = url.openConnection();
        printinfo(connection);
    }
}
```

Networking

Sending and Receiving Datagrams

Example 7-3 and Example 7-4 show how you can implement simple network communication using datagrams. Datagram communication is sometimes called "UDP"—unreliable datagram protocol. Sending datagrams is fast, but the tradeoff is that that they are not guaranteed to reach their destination, and separate datagrams are not even guaranteed to reach their destination in the order in which they were sent. Communication with datagrams is useful when you want low-overhead communication of non-critical data and when a stream model of communication is not necessary.

To send and receive datagrams, you use the `DatagramPacket` and `Datagram-Socket` classes. These objects are created and initialized differently depending on whether they are to be used to send or receive. Example 7-3 shows how to send a datagram. Example 7-4 shows how to receive a datagram, and to find out who sent it.

To send a datagram, you first create a `DatagramPacket`, specifying the data to be sent, the length of the data, the host that the packet is to be sent to, and the port on the host that it is to be sent to. You then use the `send()` method of a `Datagram-Socket` to send the packet. The `DatagramSocket` is a generic one, created with no arguments. It can be reused to send any packet to any address and port.

Example 7-3: Sending a datagram

```
import java.io.*;
import java.net.*;

// This class sends the specified text as a datagram to port 6010 of the
// specified host.
public class UDPSend {
    static final int port = 6010;
    public static void main(String args[]) throws Exception {
        if (args.length != 2) {
            System.out.println("Usage: java UDPSend <hostname> <message>");
            System.exit(0);
        }

        // Get the internet address of the specified host
        InetAddress address = InetAddress.getByName(args[0]);
        // Convert the message to an array of bytes
        int msglen = args[1].length();
        byte[] message = new byte[msglen];
        args[1].getBytes(0, msglen, message, 0);
        // Initilize the packet with data and address
        DatagramPacket packet = new DatagramPacket(message, msglen,
                                    address, port);
        // Create a socket, and send the packet through it.
        DatagramSocket socket = new DatagramSocket();
        socket.send(packet);
    }
}
```

To receive a datagram, you must first create a `DatagramSocket` that listens on a particular port of the local host. This socket can only be used to receive packets sent to that particular port. Then, you must create a `DatagramPacket` with a buffer specified to receive the data. Finally, the `DatagramSocket receive()` method blocks until data is received and stores the data into the packet's buffer. The Internet address and port of the sender are also stored in the `DatagramPacket`.

Example 7-4: Receiving a datagram

```
import java.io.*;
import java.net.*;

// This program waits to receive datagrams sent to port 6010.
// When it receives one, it displays the sending host and port,
// and prints the contents of the datagram as a string.
public class UDPReceive {
    static final int port = 6010;
    public static void main(String args[]) throws Exception
    {
        byte[] buffer = new byte[1024];
        String s;
        // Create a packet with an empty buffer to receive data
        DatagramPacket packet = new DatagramPacket(buffer, buffer.length);
        // Create a socket to listen on the port.
        DatagramSocket socket = new DatagramSocket(port);
```

Section 7: Networking

Example 7-4: Receiving a datagram (continued)

```
for(;;) {
    // Wait to receive a datagram
    socket.receive(packet);
    // Convert the contents to a string
    s = new String(buffer, 0, 0, packet.getLength());
    // And display them
    System.out.println("UDPReceive: received from " +
                packet.getAddress().getHostName() + ":" +
                packet.getPort() + ": " + s);
        }
    }
}
```

Implementing a Server

For more reliable communication than is possible with datagrams, you need to use the Socket class, which implements a reliable stream network connection. A common model for network communication is for one or more clients to send requests to a single server program. Example 7-5 shows how you might implement such a server.

The server uses the ServerSocket class to accept connections from clients. When a client connects to the port that a ServerSocket is listening on, the Server-Socket allocates a new Socket object (connected to some new port) for the client to communicate through. The server can then go back to listening on the Server-Socket for additional client connections.

Note that this server is multithreaded. The Server object itself is a thread. Its run() method loops forever, listening for connections from clients. Each time a client connects, the ServerSocket creates a new Socket and the server creates a new thread (in this example, a new Connection object) to handle communication over the Socket. This new Connection object handles all communication with the client. The constructor method for the Connection object initializes streams for communication through the Socket object and starts the thread running. The run() method of the Connection object does all the communication with the client, and performs the "service" that this server provides. In this case, it simply reads a line of text from the client, reverses it, and sends it back.

Example 7-5: A server

```
import java.io.*;
import java.net.*;

public class Server extends Thread {
    public final static int DEFAULT_PORT = 6789;
    protected int port;
    protected ServerSocket listen_socket;

    // Exit with an error message, when an exception occurs.
    public static void fail(Exception e, String msg) {
        System.err.println(msg + ": " + e);
        System.exit(1);
    }
```

Example 7-5: A server (continued)

```
// Create a ServerSocket to listen for connections on; start the thread.
public Server(int port) {
    if (port == 0) port = DEFAULT_PORT;
    this.port = port;
    try { listen_socket = new ServerSocket(port); }
    catch (IOException e) fail(e, "Exception creating server socket");
    System.out.println("Server: listening on port " + port);
    this.start();
}

// The body of the server thread.  Loop forever, listening for and
// accepting connections from clients.  For each connection,
// create a Connection object to handle communication through the
// new Socket.
public void run() {
    try {
        while(true) {
            Socket client_socket = listen_socket.accept();
            Connection c = new Connection(client_socket);
        }
    }
    catch (IOException e) fail(e, "Exception while listening for connections");
}

// Start the server up, listening on an optionally specified port
public static void main(String[] args) {
    int port = 0;
    if (args.length == 1) {
        try port = Integer.parseInt(args[0]);
        catch (NumberFormatException e) port = 0;
    }
    new Server(port);
}
}

// This class is the thread that handles all communication with a client
class Connection extends Thread {
    protected Socket client;
    protected DataInputStream in;
    protected PrintStream out;

    // Initialize the streams and start the thread
    public Connection(Socket client_socket) {
        client = client_socket;
        try {
            in = new DataInputStream(client.getInputStream());
            out = new PrintStream(client.getOutputStream());
        }
        catch (IOException e) {
            try client.close(); catch (IOException e2) ;
            System.err.println("Exception while getting socket streams: " + e);
            return;
        }
        this.start();
    }
```

Example 7-5: A server (continued)

```
        // Provide the service.
        // Read a line, reverse it, send it back.
        public void run() {
                String line;
                StringBuffer revline;
                int len;
                try {
                        for(;;) {
                                // read in a line
                                line = in.readLine();
                                if (line == null) break;
                                // reverse it
                                len = line.length();
                                revline = new StringBuffer(len);
                                for(int i = len-1; i >= 0; i--)
                                        revline.insert(len-1-i, line.charAt(i));
                                // and write out the reversed line
                                out.println(revline);
                        }
                }
                catch (IOException e) ;
                finally try client.close(); catch (IOException e2) ;
        }
}
```

Implementing a Client

Example 7-6 shows a client that communicates with the server of Example 7-5. The client creates a `Socket` object to establish the connection to the server. Then, it creates a `DataInputStream` to read lines of text from the socket's `InputStream` and a `PrintStream` to write lines of text to the socket's `OutputStream`. Finally, it reads lines from the standard input, writes them to the server, reads the reply from the server, and writes that reply to the standard output. The client exits when it detects the end-of-file on either the socket input stream or on the standard input stream.

To use this client program, run it with the name of the server host specified on the command line. You may also optionally specify the port to use as the second argument:

%java Client oxymoron.ora.com 5001

Example 7-6: A client

```
import java.io.*;
import java.net.*;

public class Client {
        public static final int DEFAULT_PORT = 6789;
        public static void usage() {
                System.out.println("Usage: java Client <hostname> [<port>]");
                System.exit(0);
        }
```

Example 7-6: A client (continued)

```java
public static void main(String[] args) {
    int port = DEFAULT_PORT;
    Socket s = null;

    // Parse the port specification
    if ((args.length != 1) && (args.length != 2)) usage();
    if (args.length == 1) port = DEFAULT_PORT;
    else {
        try port = Integer.parseInt(args[1]);
        catch (NumberFormatException e) usage();
    }

    try {
        // Create a socket to communicate to the specified host and port
        s = new Socket(args[0], port);
        // Create streams for reading and writing lines of text
        // from and to this socket.
        DataInputStream sin = new DataInputStream(s.getInputStream());
        PrintStream sout = new PrintStream(s.getOutputStream());
        // Create a stream for reading lines of text from the console
        DataInputStream in = new DataInputStream(System.in);

        // Tell the user that we've connected
        System.out.println("Connected to " + s.getInetAddress()
                    + ":"+ s.getPort());

        String line;
        while(true) {
            // print a prompt
            System.out.print("> ");
            System.out.flush();
            // read a line from the console; check for EOF
            line = in.readLine();
            if (line == null) break;
            // Send it to the server
            sout.println(line);
            // Read a line from the server.
            line = sin.readLine();
            // Check if connection is closed (i.e. for EOF)
            if (line == null) {
                System.out.println("Connection closed by server.");
                break;
            }
            // And write the line to the console.
            System.out.println(line);
        }
    }
    catch (IOException e) System.err.println(e);
    // Always be sure to close the socket
    finally {
        try if (s != null) s.close(); catch (IOException e2) ;
    }
}
```

An Applet Client

Example 7-7 shows another client for the server we developed. This one has a graphical user interface that sends input from a `TextField` component to the server and displays results from the server in a `TextArea` component. If you provide some kind of service from your host, you might want to include a simple client applet like this one on your home page so that people can try out the service. (Remember, though, that applets can only open network connections to the host that they came from—so don't try to create applet clients that connect to other machines.) Note that this applet uses a separate thread to read (and wait for) data from the server and display it in the text area.

Example 7-7: Another client

```
import java.applet.*;
import java.awt.*;
import java.io.*;
import java.net.*;

public class AppletClient extends Applet {
    public static final int PORT = 6789;
    Socket s;
    DataInputStream in;
    PrintStream out;
    TextField inputfield;
    TextArea outputarea;
    StreamListener listener;

    // Create a socket to communicate with a server on port 6789 of the
    // host that the applet's code is on.  Create streams to use with
    // the socket. Then create a TextField for user input and a TextArea
    // for server output.  Finally, create a thread to wait for and
    // display server output.
    public void init() {
        try {
            s = new Socket(this.getCodeBase().getHost(), PORT);
            in = new DataInputStream(s.getInputStream());
            out = new PrintStream(s.getOutputStream());

            inputfield = new TextField();
            outputarea = new TextArea();
            outputarea.setEditable(false);
            this.setLayout(new BorderLayout());
            this.add("North", inputfield);
            this.add("Center", outputarea);

            listener = new StreamListener(in, outputarea);

            this.showStatus("Connected to "
                    + s.getInetAddress().getHostName()
                    + ":" + s.getPort());
        }
        catch (IOException e) this.showStatus(e.toString());
    }
```

Networking

Example 7-7: Another client (continued)

```
        // When the user types a line, send it to the server.
        public boolean action(Event e, Object what) {
            if (e.target == inputfield) {
                out.println((String)e.arg);
                inputfield.setText("");
                return true;
            }
            return false;
        }
    }


    // Wait for output from the server on the specified stream, and display
    // it in the specified TextArea.
    class StreamListener extends Thread {
        DataInputStream in;
        TextArea output;
        public StreamListener(DataInputStream in, TextArea output) {
            this.in = in;
            this.output = output;
            this.start();
        }
        public void run() {
            String line;
            try {
                for(;;) {
                    line = in.readLine();
                    if (line == null) break;
                    output.setText(line);
                }
            }
            catch (IOException e) output.setText(e.toString());
            finally output.setText("Connection closed by server.");
        }
    }
```

Advanced Graphics and Images

The examples in this section demonstrate several important techniques for animation and image processing. They show you how to:

- Use double-buffering to produce smoother animation.

- Use clipping to produce smoother animation.

- Use the `MediaTracker` class to force images to be loaded and verify that there were no errors while loading.

- Modify the colors of an image using the `FilteredImageSource` and `RGBImageFilter` classes.

The examples in this section use classes in the `java.awt` and `java.awt.image` packages. The introductions to Section 19, *The java.awt Package*, and Section 20, *The java.awt.image Package*, describe these packages in more detail. You may find it useful to refer to the quick reference class descriptions in those sections while reading through the examples here.

Smooth Animation

Example 8-1 animates a line of text by moving it smoothly over a complex background. Figure 8-1 shows a snapshot of the animation. This example demonstrates two very important techniques for smooth animation: double-buffering and clipping. Some animation is automatically smooth—when it is done in one place, over a blank background, there is no need for these techniques. But when the object being animated moves across a non-blank background, special care is needed to prevent bad flickering.

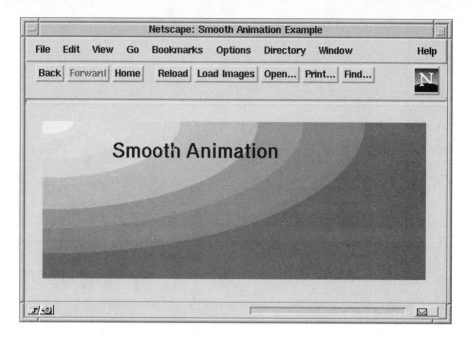

Figure 8-1: An animation in progress

Double-buffering is the practice of doing all your drawing into an offscreen "buffer," and then copying the contents of the buffer to the screen all at once. This prevents flicker that would otherwise result from erasing and redrawing the figure. In Java, our "buffer" is an offscreen Image, created with one of the Component createImage() methods. To draw into an offscreen image, you simply use its Graphics object, which is obtained with the Image getGraphics() method. In our example applet, we pass this Graphics object to the paint() method to fool the applet into drawing in the offscreen image, rather than on the screen.

Once the drawing is complete in the offscreen image, we use the Component getGraphics() method to get the Graphics object for the applet, and use that Graphics object to copy the offscreen image onto the screen. Note that we create the offscreen image the first time it is needed, and that we are careful to make sure that it is always the same size as the applet.

Clipping is the second important technique for making animations smooth and speedy. Animation often involves erasing and redrawing only a small region of a larger area. Unfortunately, typical paint() methods only know how to redraw the entire applet, not small regions of it. What we can do, though, is to set a rectangular "clipping region" in the Graphics objects we use. Such a clip region tells the system that it only needs to draw within a specified rectangle and that it can ignore any drawing requested outside of that rectangle. When we know the area of an applet that needs to be redrawn, we can specify a clip rectangle that surrounds that area and do a full redraw, knowing that the applet will only be redrawn inside the clip rectangle. This is usually quite efficient and much faster than doing the full redraw without clipping.

Our example applet uses this technique. Note that it is careful in the `init()` method to measure the text it animates. This way it can know exactly what region of the picture needs to be redrawn. In the `run()` method, it creates two `Rectangle` objects, which represent the area of the screen to be erased (where text currently is) and the new area where the text will be drawn. It uses the `Rectangle union()` method to find the smallest rectangle that contains both these rectangles, and uses this combined rectangle as the clipping region. It uses the rectangle both when drawing to the offscreen image and when copying the offscreen image to the screen.

A final interesting point about this example is that clicking the mouse button stops and restarts the animation. The animation is not stopped by actually calling `stop()` for the `animator` thread. Doing that might leave the screen in a partially drawn state, so instead we simply set a `please_stop` variable that the `animator` thread checks after each complete redraw.

Example 8-1: Implementing smooth animation

```
import java.applet.*;
import java.awt.*;


public class Smooth extends Applet implements Runnable {
    static final int deltax = 4;
    static final int deltay = 2;
    static final String message = "Smooth Animation";
    int x = 0;
    int y = 0;
    Color c1 = new Color(0x0000ff);
    Color c2 = new Color(0xffffff);
    Font font = new Font("Helvetica", Font.BOLD, 24);
    Image offscreen;
    int imagewidth, imageheight;
    int stringwidth, stringheight, stringascent;
    Thread animator = null;
    boolean please_stop = false;

    // Measure the size of the text we'll be animating.  We need this
    // information later to do clipping.
    public void init() {
        FontMetrics fm = this.getFontMetrics(font);
        stringwidth = fm.stringWidth(message);
        stringheight = fm.getHeight();
        stringascent = fm.getAscent();
    }

    // Start the animation
    public void start() {
        animator = new Thread(this);
        animator.start();
    }
    // Stop it.
    public void stop() {
        if (animator != null) animator.stop();
        animator = null;
    }
    // Stop and start animating on mouse clicks.
    public boolean mouseDown(Event e, int x, int y) {
        // if running, stop it.  Otherwise, start it.
        if (animator != null) please_stop = true;
```

Example 8-1: Implementing smooth animation (continued)

```
            else { please_stop = false; start(); }
            return true;
    }


    // Draw a fancy background.  Because this background is time-consuming
    // to draw, our animation techniques must be efficient to avoid bad
    // flickering.
    void drawBackground(Graphics gr, Color c1, Color c2, int numsteps) {
        int r, g, b;
        int dr = (c2.getRed() - c1.getRed())/numsteps;
        int dg = (c2.getGreen() - c1.getGreen())/numsteps;
        int db = (c2.getBlue() - c1.getBlue())/numsteps;
        Dimension size = this.size();
        int w = size.width, h = size.height;
        int dw = size.width/numsteps;
        int dh = size.height/numsteps;

        gr.setColor(c1);
        gr.fillRect(0, 0, w, h);

        for(r = c1.getRed(), g = c1.getGreen(), b = c1.getBlue();
            h > 0;
            h -= dh, w -= dw, r += dr, g += dg, b += db) {
                gr.setColor(new Color(r, g, b));
                gr.fillArc(-w, -h, 2*w, 2*h, 0, -90);
        }
    }


    // This method draws the background and  text at its current position.
    public void paint(Graphics g) {
                drawBackground(g, c1, c2, 25);
                g.setColor(Color.black);
                g.setFont(font);
                g.drawString(message, x, y);
    }


    // The body of the animator thread.
    public void run() {
        while(!please_stop) {
            Dimension d = this.size();

                // Make sure the offscreen image is created and is the right size.
                if ((offscreen == null) ||
                    ((imagewidth != d.width) || (imageheight != d.height))) {
                        // if (offscreen != null) offscreen.flush();
                        offscreen = this.createImage(d.width, d.height);
                        imagewidth = d.width;
                        imageheight = d.height;
                }

                // Set up clipping. We only need to draw within the
                // old rectangle that needs to be cleared and the new
                // one that is being drawn.

                // the old rectangle
                Rectangle oldrect = new Rectangle(x, y-stringascent,
```

Example 8-1: Implementing smooth animation (continued)

```
                              stringwidth, stringheight);
              // Update the coordinates for animation.
              x = ((x + deltax)%d.width);
              y = ((y + deltay)%d.height);

              // the new rectangle
              Rectangle newrect = new Rectangle(x, y-stringascent,
                                     stringwidth, stringheight);
              // Compute the union of the rectangles
              Rectangle r = newrect.union(oldrect);

              // Use this rectangle as the clipping region when
              // drawing to the offscreen image, and when copying
              // from the offscreen image to the screen.
              Graphics g = offscreen.getGraphics();
              g.clipRect(r.x, r.y, r.width, r.height);
              // Draw into the offscreen image.
              paint(g);
              // Copy it all at once to the screen, using clipping.
              g = this.getGraphics();
              g.clipRect(r.x, r.y, r.width, r.height);
              g.drawImage(offscreen, 0, 0, this);

              // wait a tenth of a second, then draw it again!
              try Thread.sleep(100); catch (InterruptedException e);
       }
       animator = null;
   }
}
```

Keeping Track of Images

In Section 4, *Applets*, we saw a simple animator applet that displayed a sequence of images one after the other. (This is the kind of simple animation that does not require the double-buffering or clipping techniques described above.) There were some problems with that simple animator applet, however. It would start animating before the images were all loaded, which meant that the first cycle of animations went very slowly. Also, it had no provisions for handling errors while loading images. Example 8-2 is a new animator applet that addresses these problems.

The secret is to use a `MediaTracker` object. This class lets you register images and then call a method that blocks until they have completed loading. It also allows you to check for errors in the loading process. The `init()` method creates all the `Image` objects and stores them in an array. The method also registers the images with the `MediaTracker` object. Then the `run()` method uses the `MediaTracker` to force each image to be loaded, and to check whether it loaded sucessfully. This method displays image loading results in the status line.

Note that instead of registering and loading images individually, we could instead have registered all the images with the same integer identifier. In this case, a single call to the `MediaTracker waitForID()` method would have loaded all the images, and a single call to `isErrorID()` would have specified whether there were errors with any of the images. The drawback to this approach is that you can't

---

provide feedback in the status line for each individual image. The potentially important advantage, however, is that the `MediaTracker` can attempt to download the images in parallel. This could be useful, for example, over a slow network connection.

Example 8-2: Tracking image loading

```java
// This applet displays an animation.  It uses the MediaTracker class to
// load the images and verify that there are no errors.
import java.applet.*;
import java.awt.*;
import java.net.*;
import java.util.*;

public class Animator2 extends Applet implements Runnable {
    protected Image[] images;
    protected int num_images;
    protected int current_image;
    protected MediaTracker tracker;

    // Read the basename and num_images parameters.
    // Then read in the images, using the specified base name.
    // For example, if basename is images/anim, read images/anim0,
    // images/anim1, etc.  These are relative to the current document URL.
    public void init() {
        String basename = this.getParameter("basename");
        try { num_images = Integer.parseInt(this.getParameter("num_images")); }
        catch (NumberFormatException e) { num_images = 0; }

        // getImage() creates an Image object from a URL specification,
        // but it doesn't actually load the images; that is done
        // asynchronously.  Store all the images in a MediaTracker
        // so we can wait until they have all loaded (in run()).
        tracker = new MediaTracker(this);
        images = new Image[num_images];
        for(int i = 0; i < num_images; i++) {
            images[i] = this.getImage(this.getDocumentBase(), basename + i);
            tracker.addImage(images[i], i);
        }
    }

    // This is the thread that runs the animation, and the methods
    // that start it and stop it.
    private Thread animator_thread = null;
    public void start() {
        if (animator_thread == null) {
            animator_thread = new Thread(this);
            animator_thread.start();
        }
    }
    public void stop() {
        if ((animator_thread != null) && animator_thread.isAlive())
            animator_thread.stop();
        animator_thread = null;
    }

    // This is the body of the thread--the method that does the animation.
    public void run() {
```

Example 8-2: Tracking image loading (continued)

```
// First, force all the images to be loaded, and wait until
// they have all loaded completely.
for (int i = 0; i < num_images; i++) {
        this.showStatus("Loading image: " + i);
        // The argument is the same one we passed to addImage()
        try tracker.waitForID(i); catch (InterruptedException e) ;
        // Check for errors loading it.
        if (tracker.isErrorID(i)) {
                this.showStatus("Error loading image " + i + "; quitting.");
                return;
        }
}
this.showStatus("Loading images: done.");

// Now do the animation
while(true) {
        if (++current_image >= images.length) current_image = 0;
        this.getGraphics().drawImage(images[current_image], 0, 0, this);
        try { Thread.sleep(200); } catch (InterruptedException e) ;
}
    }
}
```

Filtering Images

A common way to specify that a button in a graphical interface is currently inactive is to "gray it out." When a button displays an image, this means that we need a "grayed out" version of the image. Example 8-3 is an applet that demonstrates a simple way to created grayed-out images. Figure 8-2 shows an image and the grayed-out version created by this applet.

Figure 8-2: Filtered image colors

The init() method of this example demonstrates how you can use a source image, a FilteredImageSource object, and an ImageFilter object to produce a new, filtered image. The contents of this new image depend, of course, on the image filter. In this example, we define a GrayFilter as a subclass of RGBImageFilter. The body of this filter is the filterRGB() method which takes an RGB color value as input, averages it with white, and returns the result. This makes all the colors in the image more gray. Note that we are careful in this example not to modify the alpha transparency value stored in the top eight bits of the color value.

Note that the `filterRGB()` method does not use its **x** and **y** arguments. The filtering it performs is position independent, which means that the filter can be used more efficiently on the entries of a colormap instead of on each pixel of the image. To indicate that our `GrayFilter` is position independent, we set the `canFilterIndexColorModel` variable to `true` in the constructor method. On the other hand, if we were implementing an `RGBImageFilter` that produced a blurring effect, for example, the filter would be position dependent, and we would have to set `canFilterIndexColorModel` to `false`.

Finally, note that the `CropImageFilter` is another useful kind of image filter. It allows you to extract a rectangular region from a larger image.

Example 8-3: Producing a grayed out image

```
import java.applet.*;
import java.awt.*;
import java.awt.image.*;

public class GrayButton extends Applet {
    Image i, gray;

    // Load an image from a file.  Create a new image that is a grayer
    // version of it, using a FilteredImageSource ImageProducer and a
    // GrayFilter ImageFilter.
    public void init() {
        i = this.getImage(this.getDocumentBase(), "images/button.gif");
        ImageFilter f = new GrayFilter();
        ImageProducer producer = new FilteredImageSource(i.getSource(), f);
        gray = this.createImage(producer);
    }

    // Display the image
    public void update(Graphics g) {
        g.drawImage(i, 0, 0, this);
    }

    // When the user clicks, display the gray image
    public boolean mouseDown(Event e, int x, int y) {
        Graphics g = this.getGraphics();
        Dimension d = this.size();
        g.clearRect(0, 0, d.width, d.height);
        g.drawImage(gray, 0, 0, this);
        return true;
    }
    // And restore the normal one when the mouse goes up.
    public boolean mouseUp(Event e, int x, int y) {
        update(this.getGraphics());
        return true;
    }
}

// Filter an image by averaging all of its colors with white.
// This washes it out and makes it grayer.
class GrayFilter extends RGBImageFilter {
    public GrayFilter() { canFilterIndexColorModel = true; }
    public int filterRGB(int x, int y, int rgb) {
        int a = rgb & 0xff000000;
        int r = ((rgb & 0xff0000) + 0xff0000)/2;
```

Example 8-3: Producing a grayed out image (continued)

```
        int g = ((rgb & 0x00ff00) + 0x00ff00)/2;
        int b = ((rgb & 0x0000ff) + 0x0000ff)/2;
        return a | r | g | b;
    }
}
```

9

Advanced Threads

The use of threads is basic to the Java programming model. We've used them in applets to perform animations and in network servers to serve more than one client at once. The examples in this section demonstrate some advanced uses of threads:

- Obtaining information about threads and thread groups

- Specifying the name, group, and priority of a thread

- Using synchronized to prevent simultaneous access by multiple threads to critical data structures

- Using wait() to make a thread wait until some condition occurs

- Using notify() to tell a waiting thread that a condition has occurred

You may want to refer to the quick reference descriptions of the Thread, Thread-Group, and Object classes, in Section 23, *The java.lang Package*, while studying these examples.

Threads and Thread Groups

Example 9-1 is a ThreadLister class, with a public listAllThreads() method that does just that—lists all threads (and all of their thread groups) that are running on the Java interpreter. Recall that every Java Thread belongs to some Thread-Group, and that every ThreadGroup is also contained in some "parent" Thread-Group. Figure 9-1 shows the output of the listAllThreads() method displayed in an applet.

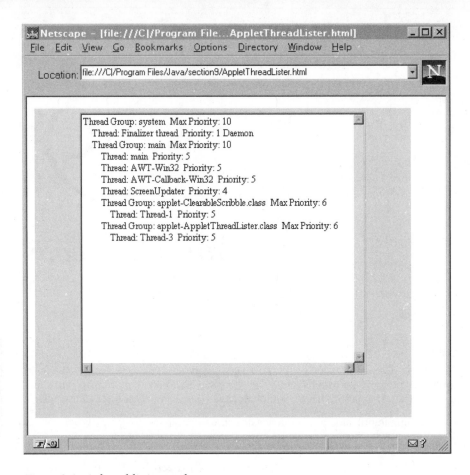

```
Thread Group: system  Max Priority: 10
  Thread: Finalizer thread  Priority: 1 Daemon
  Thread Group: main  Max Priority: 10
      Thread: main  Priority: 5
      Thread: AWT-Win32  Priority: 5
      Thread: AWT-Callback-Win32  Priority: 5
      Thread: ScreenUpdater  Priority: 4
      Thread Group: applet-ClearableScribble.class  Max Priority: 6
          Thread: Thread-1  Priority: 5
      Thread Group: applet-AppletThreadLister.class  Max Priority: 6
          Thread: Thread-3  Priority: 5
```

Figure 9-1: A thread-listing applet

Example 9-1: Listing all threads and thread groups

```java
import java.io.*;

public class ThreadLister {
    // Display info about a thread.
    private static void print_thread_info(PrintStream out, Thread t,
                                String indent) {
        if (t == null) return;
        out.println(indent + "Thread: " + t.getName() +
            " Priority: " + t.getPriority() +
            (t.isDaemon()?" Daemon":"") +
            (t.isAlive()?"":" Not Alive"));
    }

    // Display info about a thread group and its threads and groups
    private static void list_group(PrintStream out, ThreadGroup g,
                           String indent) {
        if (g == null) return;
        int num_threads = g.activeCount();
        int num_groups = g.activeGroupCount();
```

Example 9-1: Listing all threads and thread groups (continued)

```
        Thread[] threads = new Thread[num_threads];
        ThreadGroup[] groups = new ThreadGroup[num_groups];

        g.enumerate(threads, false);
        g.enumerate(groups, false);

        out.println(indent + "Thread Group: " + g.getName() +
            " Max Priority: " + g.getMaxPriority() +
            (g.isDaemon()?" Daemon":""));

        for(int i = 0; i < num_threads; i++)
            print_thread_info(out, threads[i], indent + "   ");
        for(int i = 0; i < num_groups; i++)
            list_group(out, groups[i], indent + "   ");
    }

    // Find the root thread group and list it recursively
    public static void listAllThreads(PrintStream out) {
        ThreadGroup current_thread_group;
        ThreadGroup root_thread_group;
        ThreadGroup parent;

        // Get the current thread group
        current_thread_group = Thread.currentThread().getThreadGroup();

        // Now go find the root thread group
        root_thread_group = current_thread_group;
        parent = root_thread_group.getParent();
        while(parent != null) {
            root_thread_group = parent;
            parent = parent.getParent();
        }

        // And list it, recursively
        list_group(out, root_thread_group, "");
    }


    public static void main(String[] args) {
        ThreadLister.listAllThreads(System.out);
    }
}
```

The `listAllThreads()` method uses the `Thread` static method `currentThread()` to obtain the current thread, and uses `getThreadGroup()` to find the thread group of that thread. It then uses the `ThreadGroup getParent()` method to move through the thread group hierarchy until it finds the "root" thread group, the thread group that contains all other threads and thread groups.

`listAllThreads()` then calls the private `ThreadLister list_group()` method to display the contents of the root thread group, and to recursively display the contents of all thread groups it contains. `list_group()`, and the `print_thread_info()` method it calls, use various `Thread` and `ThreadGroup` methods to obtain information about the threads and their groups. Note that the `isDaemon()` method returns whether a thread is a "daemon thread" or not. Daemon threads are expected to run in the background and are not expected to exit. The Java interpreter exits when all non-daemon threads have quit.

The `ThreadLister` class has a `main()` method so that it can be run alone. It is more interesting, of course, to invoke the `listAllThreads()` method from within another program or applet—it can help you to figure out problems you are having with threads.

Example 9-2 is a short listing that shows how the `ThreadLister` output can be displayed in an applet window, as we saw in Figure 9-1. Note the use of a `ByteArrayOutputStream` to capture the `ThreadLister` output and convert it to a string for display.

Example 9-2: Listing threads in an applet

```
import java.applet.*;
import java.awt.*;
import java.io.*;

public class AppletThreadLister extends Applet {
    TextArea textarea;

    // Create a text area to put our listing in
    public void init() {
        textarea = new TextArea(20, 60);
        this.add(textarea);
        Dimension prefsize = textarea.preferredSize();
        this.resize(prefsize.width, prefsize.height);
    }

    // Do the listing.  Note the cool use of ByteArrayOutputStream.
    public void start() {
        ByteArrayOutputStream os = new ByteArrayOutputStream();
        PrintStream ps = new PrintStream(os);
        ThreadLister.listAllThreads(ps);
        textarea.setText(os.toString());
    }
}
```

synchronized, wait(), and notify()

Example 9-3 is an extended version of the `Server` class we saw in Section 7, *Networking*. As you may recall, that class creates a new thread to handle each connection to a client. We've made the following changes to the server:

- It creates a `ThreadGroup` to contain all of the client connection threads it creates.

- It gives a descriptive name to each of the threads it creates.

- It assigns each client connection thread a priority that is lower than the default, so that they cannot end up overloading the system and preventing other threads from running.

- It displays a list of all current connections in a window.

- It creates a new thread, which it calls a "vulture," that waits for the connection threads to die (i.e., to exit), and then removes them from the list of current connections.

Creating the new thread group and giving the threads names and priorities is straightforward. You can see how it is done in the code. The last two changes are a little more tricky. First, the server has to ensure that it is not adding a new thread to the list while the "vulture" thread is removing one. The way to provide "mutual exclusion" (i.e., to prevent simultaneous access to a resource) is with synchronized methods or synchronized blocks of code. The example demonstrates this technique.

The second tricky change is having the "vulture" thread wait for the other threads to exit. We do this by having the vulture call its own wait() method, (wait() is a method of the Object class) and having each of the connection threads invoke the vulture's notify() method just before they exit. The notify() call "wakes up" the vulture thread, which can then check the list for threads that are no longer alive and remove them. Note that the code acquires a lock on the vulture thread (i.e., is in a synchronized method or block) before calling the wait() and notify() methods. This is required for them to work correctly.

Example 9-3: Using synchronized, wait(), and notify()

```java
import java.net.*;
import java.io.*;
import java.awt.*;
import java.util.*;

public class Server extends Thread {
    public final static int DEFAULT_PORT = 6789;
    protected int port;
    protected ServerSocket listen_socket;
    protected ThreadGroup threadgroup;
    protected List connection_list;
    protected Vector connections;
    protected Vulture vulture;

    // Exit with an error message, when an exception occurs.
    public static void fail(Exception e, String msg) {
        System.err.println(msg + ": " + e);
        System.exit(1);
    }

    // Create a ServerSocket to listen for connections on;  start the thread.
    public Server(int port) {
        // Create our server thread with a name.
        super("Server");
        if (port == 0) port = DEFAULT_PORT;
        this.port = port;
        try { listen_socket = new ServerSocket(port); }
        catch (IOException e) fail(e, "Exception creating server socket");
        // Create a thread group for our connections
         threadgroup = new ThreadGroup("Server Connections");
```

Example 9-3: Using synchronized, wait(), and notify() (continued)

```
            // Create a window to display our connections in
            Frame f = new Frame("Server Status");
            connection_list = new List();
            f.add("Center", connection_list);
            f.resize(400, 200);
            f.show();

            // Initialize a vector to store our connections in
            connections = new Vector();

            // Create a Vulture thread to wait for other threads to die.
            // It starts itself automatically.
            vulture = new Vulture(this);

            // Start the server listening for connections
            this.start();
    }

    // The body of the server thread.  Loop forever, listening for and
    // accepting connections from clients.  For each connection,
    // create a Connection object to handle communication through the
    // new Socket.  When we create a new connection, add it to the
    // Vector of connections, and display it in the List.  Note that we
    // use synchronized to lock the Vector of connections.  The Vulture
    // class does the same, so the vulture won't be removing dead
    // connections while we're adding fresh ones.
    public void run() {
        try {
            while(true) {
                Socket client_socket = listen_socket.accept();
                Connection c = new Connection(client_socket, threadgroup,
                                              3, vulture);
                // prevent simultaneous access.
                synchronized (connections) {
                    connections.addElement(c);
                    connection_list.addItem(c.toString());
                }
            }
        }
        catch (IOException e) fail(e, "Exception while listening for connections");
    }

    // Start the server up, listening on an optionally specified port
    public static void main(String[] args) {
        int port = 0;
        if (args.length == 1) {
            try port = Integer.parseInt(args[0]);
            catch (NumberFormatException e) port = 0;
        }
        new Server(port);
    }
}
```

Example 9-3: Using synchronized, wait(), and notify() (continued)

```
// This class is the thread that handles all communication with a client
// It also notifies the Vulture when the connection is dropped.
class Connection extends Thread {
    static int connection_number = 0;
    protected Socket client;
    protected Vulture vulture;
    protected DataInputStream in;
    protected PrintStream out;

    // Initialize the streams and start the thread
    public Connection(Socket client_socket, ThreadGroup threadgroup,
                int priority, Vulture vulture)
    {
        // Give the thread a group, a name, and a priority.
        super(threadgroup, "Connection-" + connection_number++);
        this.setPriority(priority);
        // Save our other arguments away
        client = client_socket;
        this.vulture = vulture;
        // Create the streams
        try {
            in = new DataInputStream(client.getInputStream());
            out = new PrintStream(client.getOutputStream());
        }
        catch (IOException e) {
            try client.close(); catch (IOException e2) ;
            System.err.println("Exception while getting socket streams: " + e);
            return;
        }
        // And start the thread up
        this.start();
    }

    // Provide the service.
    // Read a line, reverse it, send it back.
    public void run() {
        String line;
        StringBuffer revline;
        int len;

        // Send a welcome message to the client
        out.println("Line Reversal Server version 1.0");
        out.println("A service of O'Reilly & Associates");

        try {
            for(;;) {
                // read in a line
                line = in.readLine();
                if (line == null) break;
                // reverse it
                len = line.length();
                revline = new StringBuffer(len);
                for(int i = len-1; i >= 0; i--)
                    revline.insert(len-1-i, line.charAt(i));
```

Example 9-3: Using synchronized, wait(), and notify() (continued)

```
                    // and write out the reversed line
                    out.println(revline);
                }
            }
            catch (IOException e) ;
            // When we're done, for whatever reason, be sure to close
            // the socket, and to notify the Vulture object.  Note that
            // we have to use synchronized first to lock the vulture
            // object before we can call notify() for it.
            finally {
                try client.close(); catch (IOException e2) ;
                synchronized (vulture) vulture.notify();
            }
        }


        // This method returns the string representation of the Connection.
        // This is the string that will appear in the GUI List.
        public String toString() {
            return this.getName() + " connected to: "
                + client.getInetAddress().getHostName()
                + ":" + client.getPort();
        }
    }


    // This class waits to be notified that a thread is dying (exiting)
    // and then cleans up the list of threads and the graphical list.
    class Vulture extends Thread {
        protected Server server;

        protected Vulture(Server s) {
            super(s.threadgroup, "Connection Vulture");
            server = s;
            this.start();
        }


        // This is the method that waits for notification of exiting threads
        // and cleans up the lists.  It is a synchronized method, so it
        // acquires a lock on the 'this' object before running.  This is
        // necessary so that it can call wait() on 'this'.  Even if the
        // the Connection objects never call notify(), this method wakes up
        // every five seconds and checks all the connections, just in case.
        // Note also that all access to the Vector of connections and to
        // the GUI List component are within a synchronized block as well.
        // This prevents the Server class from adding a new connection while
        // we're removing an old one.
        public synchronized void run() {
            for(;;) {
                try this.wait(5000); catch (InterruptedException e) ;
                // prevent simultaneous access
                synchronized(server.connections) {
                    // loop through the connections
                    for(int i = 0; i < server.connections.size(); i++) {
                        Connection c;
                        c = (Connection)server.connections.elementAt(i);
```

Example 9-3: Using synchronized, wait(), and notify() (continued)

```
                        // if the connection thread isn't alive anymore,
                        // remove it from the Vector and List.
                        if (!c.isAlive()) {
                            server.connections.removeElementAt(i);
                            server.connection_list.delItem(i);
                            i--;
                        }
                    }
                }
            }
        }
    }
```

A Multithreaded Client

Example 9-4 shows a new version of our `Client` program from Section 7. The old version used a single thread, expected the server to always send a single-line response to the client's input, and to never send any other text. Our new `Server` class, however, sends two lines of identifying text when it first connects with a client. Our old `Client` would not handle that text correctly.

The new client creates two threads when it starts up. One, the `Reader` thread, is responsible for reading data from the server and printing it to the console. The other, the `Writer` thread, reads user input from the console and writes it to the server. This way, any text the server sends is displayed at the appropriate time.

Note that there is apparently some problem with shared access by these threads to the console. To work around the problem, it is necessary to give the `Reader` thread a higher priority than the `Writer` thread. This is done right after the threads are created in the `Client` constructor method.

Example 9-4: A multithreaded client

```
import java.io.*;
import java.net.*;

public class Client {
    public static final int DEFAULT_PORT = 6789;
    Socket socket;
    Thread reader, writer;

    // Create the client by creating its reader and writer threads
    // and starting them.
    public Client(String host, int port) {
        try {
            socket = new Socket(host, port);
            // Create reader and writer sockets
            reader = new Reader(this);
            writer = new Writer(this);
            // Give the reader a higher priority to work around
            // a problem with shared access to the console.
            reader.setPriority(6);
            writer.setPriority(5);
```

Advanced
Threads

Example 9-4: A multithreaded client (continued)

```
                    // Start the threads
                    reader.start();
                    writer.start();
             }
             catch (IOException e) System.err.println(e);
    }

    public static void usage() {
             System.out.println("Usage: java Client <hostname> [<port>]");
             System.exit(0);
    }
    public static void main(String[] args) {
             int port = DEFAULT_PORT;
             Socket s = null;

             // Parse the port specification
             if ((args.length != 1) && (args.length != 2)) usage();
             if (args.length == 1) port = DEFAULT_PORT;
             else {
                    try port = Integer.parseInt(args[1]);
                    catch (NumberFormatException e) usage();
             }

             new Client(args[0], port);
    }
}


// This thread reads data from the server and prints it on the console
// As usual, the run() method does the interesting stuff.
class Reader extends Thread {
    Client client;
    public Reader(Client c) {
             super("Client Reader");
             this.client = c;
    }
    public void run() {
             DataInputStream in = null;
             String line;
             try {
                    in = new DataInputStream(client.socket.getInputStream());
                    while(true) {
                          line = in.readLine();
                          if (line == null) {
                                 System.out.println("Server closed connection.");
                                 break;
                          }
                          System.out.println(line);
                    }
             }
             catch (IOException e) System.out.println("Reader: " + e);
             finally try if (in != null) in.close(); catch (IOException e) ;
             System.exit(0);
    }
}
```

Example 9-4: A multithreaded client (continued)

```java
// This thread reads user input from the console and sends it to the server.
class Writer extends Thread {
    Client client;
    public Writer(Client c) {
        super("Client Writer");
        client = c;
    }
    public void run() {
        DataInputStream in = null;
        PrintStream out = null;
        try {
            String line;
            in = new DataInputStream(System.in);
            out = new PrintStream(client.socket.getOutputStream());
            while(true) {
                line = in.readLine();
                if (line == null) break;
                out.println(line);
            }
        }
        catch (IOException e) System.err.println("Writer: " + e);
        finally if (out != null) out.close();
        System.exit(0);
    }
}
```

Part III

Java Language Reference

Part III contains a variety of reference material on the Java language and closely related topics. The *How to Use This Book* section at the beginning of the book explains what material is presented in each of these sections.

Java Syntax

Primitive Data Types

Java supports a complete set of primitive data types, listed in Table 10-1. In Java, the size of each type is defined by the language, and is *not* implementation dependent, as it is in C.

Table 10-1: Java Primitive Data Types

Type	Contains	Default	Size	Min Value Max Value
boolean	true or false	false	1 bit	N.A. N.A.
char	Unicode character	\u0000	16 bits	\u0000 \uFFFF
byte	signed integer	0	8 bits	-128 127
short	signed integer	0	16 bits	-32768 32767
int	signed integer	0	32 bits	-2147483648 2147483647
long	signed integer	0	64 bits	-9223372036854775808 9223372036854775807
float	IEEE 754 floating-point	0.0	32 bits	±3.40282347E+38 ±1.40239846E-45
double	IEEE 754 floating-point	0.0	64 bits	±1.79769313486231570E+308 ±4.94065645841246544E-324

Java Syntax

Character Escape Sequences

Java uses the escape sequences listed in Table 10-2 to represent certain special character values. These escape sequences may appear in any Java char or String literal.

Table 10-2: Java Escape Characters

Escape Sequence	Character Value
\b	Backspace
\t	Horizontal tab
\n	Newline
\f	Form feed
\r	Carriage return
\"	Double quote
\'	Single quote
\\	Backslash
\xxx	The character corresponding to the octal value *xxx*, where *xxx* is between 000 and 0377.
\uxxxx	The Unicode character with encoding *xxxx*, where *xxxx* is one to four hexidecimal digits. Unicode escapes are distinct from the other escape types listed here; they are described below in more detail.

Java characters, strings, and identifiers (e.g., variable, method, and class names) are composed of 16-bit Unicode characters. The Unicode \u escape sequence may be used anywhere in a Java program (not only in char and String literals) to represent a Unicode character.

Unicode \u escape sequences are processed before the other escape sequences described in Table 10-2, and thus the two types of escape sequences can have very different semantics. A Unicode escape is simply an alternative way to represent a character which may not be displayable on non-Unicode systems. The character escapes, however, can represent special characters in a way that prevents the usual interpretation of those characters by the compiler.

Operators

Table 10-3 lists the operators of the Java language, along with their precedence, operand types, and associativity.

Table 10-3: Java Operators

Prec.	Operator	Operand Type(s)	Assoc.	Operation Performed
1	++	arithmetic	R	pre-or-post increment (unary)
	--	arithmetic	R	pre-or-post decrement (unary)
	+, -	arithmetic	R	unary plus, unary minus
	~	integral	R	bitwise complement (unary)
	!	boolean	R	logical complement (unary)

Table 10-3: Java Operators (continued)

Prec.	Operator	Operand Type(s)	Assoc.	Operation Performed
	(*type*)	any	R	cast
2	`*`, `/`, `%`	arithmetic	L	multiplication, division, remainder
3	`+`, `-`	arithmetic	L	addition, subtraction
	`+`	String	L	string concatenation
4	`<<`	integral	L	left shift
	`>>`	integral	L	right shift with sign extension
	`>>>`	integral	L	right shift with zero extension
5	`<`, `<=`	arithmetic	L	less than, less than or equal
	`>`, `>=`	arithmetic	L	greater than, greater than or equal
	`instanceof`	object, type	L	type comparison
6	`==`	primitive	L	equal (have identical values)
	`!=`	primitive	L	not equal (have different values)
	`==`	object	L	equal (refer to same object)
	`!=`	object	L	not equal (refer to different objects)
7	`&`	integral	L	bitwise AND
	`&`	boolean	L	boolean AND
8	`^`	integral	L	bitwise XOR
	`^`	boolean	L	boolean XOR
9	`|`	integral	L	bitwise OR
	`|`	boolean	L	boolean OR
10	`&&`	boolean	L	conditional AND
11	`||`	boolean	L	conditional OR
12	`? :`	boolean, any, any	R	conditional (ternary) operator
13	`=`	variable, any	R	assignment
	`*=`, `/=`, `%=`, `+=`, `-=`, `<<=`, `>>=`, `>>>=`, `&=`, `^=`, `|=`,	variable, any	R	assignment with operation

Java Syntax

Operator precedence controls the order in which operations are performed. Consider the following example:

```
w = x + y * z;
```

The multiplication operator `*` has a higher precedence than the addition operator `+`, so the multiplication is performed before the addition. Furthermore, the assignment operator `=` has the lowest precedence of any operators, so the assignment is done after all the operations on the right-hand side are performed. Operators with the same precedence (like addition and subtraction) are performed in order according to their associativity (usually left-to-right). Operator precedence can be overridden with the explicit use of parentheses. For example:

```
w = (x + y) * z;
```

The associativity of an operator specifies the order that operations of the same precedence are performed in. In Table 10-3, a value of L specifies left-to-right associativity, and a value of R specifies right-to-left associativity. Left-to-right associativity means that operations are performed left-to-right. For example:

```
w = x + y + z;
```

Is the same as:

```
w = ((x + y) + z);
```

because the addition operator has left-to-right associativity. On the other hand, the following expressions:

```
x = ~-~y;
q = a?b:c?d:e?f:g;
```

Are equivalent to:

```
x = ~(-(~y));
q = a?b:(c?d:(e?f:g));
```

because the unary operators and the ternary conditional ?: operator have right-to-left associativity.

Java operators are basically identical to C operators, except for the following differences:

- The + operator applied to String values concatenates them. If only one operand of + is a String, the other one is converted to a string. The conversion is done automatically for primitive types and by calling the toString method of non-primitive types.

- Java does not have the comma operator like C does. It does, however, simulate this operator in the limited context of the for loop initialization and increment expressions.

- Since all Java integral types are signed, the >> operator always does a signed right shift, filling in high bits with the sign bit of the operand. The new >>> operator performs an unsigned right shift, filling in high bits of the shifted value with zero bits.

- The & and | operators perform bitwise AND and OR operations on integral operands, and perform logical AND and OR operators on boolean operands. && and || also perform logical AND and OR on boolean operands, but do not evaluate the right-hand operand, if the result of the operation is fully determined by the left-hand operand.

- The instanceof operator returns true if the object on the left-hand side is an instance of the class or implements the interface on the right-hand side. Otherwise it returns false. If the left-hand side is null, it returns false.

Section 10: Java Syntax

Modifiers

The visibility modifiers in Java specify the accessibility of classes, methods, and variables from other packages, classes, and methods. They are described in Table 10-4.

Table 10-4: Class, Method, and Variable Visibility Modifiers

Modifier	Meaning
public	A public class or interface is visible anywhere. A public method or variable is visible anywhere its class is visible.
protected	A protected method or variable is visible throughout the package of its class, and in any subclass of its class. Classes may not be protected. A subclass in a different package than its superclass can access the protected fields inherited by its instances, but it cannot access those fields in instances of the superclass.
default (no modifiers)	If no modifiers are specified, a class, interface, method, or variable is visible only within its package.
private protected	A private protected method or variable is only visible within its own class and within any subclasses. Classes may not be private protected. A subclass can access the private protected fields inherited by its instances, but it cannot access those fields in instances of the superclass.
private	A private method or variable is only visible within its own class. Classes may not be private.

Table 10-5 summarizes the visibility modifiers; it shows the circumstances under which fields of the various visibility types are accessible and the circumstances under which they are inherited by subclasses.

Table 10-5: Java Field Visibility

Situation	public	default	protected	private protected	private
Accessible to non-subclass from same package?	yes	yes	yes	no	no
Accessible to subclass from same package?	yes	yes	yes	no	no
Accessible to non-subclass from different package?	yes	no	no	no	no
Accessible to subclass from different package?	yes	no	no	no	no
Inherited by subclass in same package?	yes	yes	yes	yes	no
Inherited by subclass in different package?	yes	no	yes	yes	no

The other Java modifiers specify a number of attributes of classes, methods, and variables. They are described in Table 10-6.

Table 10-6: Other Modifiers

Modifier	Used On	Meaning
abstract	class	The class contains unimplemented methods and cannot be instantiated.
	interface	All interfaces are abstract. The modifier is optional in interface declarations.
	method	No body is provided for the method (it is provided by a subclass). The signature is followed by a semicolon. The enclosing class must also be abstract.
final	class	The class may not be subclassed.
	method	The method may not be overridden (compiler may optimize).
	variable	The variable may not have its value changed (compiler may precompute expressions).
native	method	The method is implemented in C, or in some other platform-dependent way. No body is provided; the signature is followed by a semicolon.
static	method	The method is a "class method." It is not passed as an implicit this object reference, and so it cannot refer to non-static variables or methods of the class. It is implictly final. It may be invoked through the class name.
	variable	The variable is a "class variable." There is only one instance of the variable, regardless of the number of class instances created. It may be accessed through the class name.
synchronized	method	The method makes non-atomic modifications to the class or instance, and care must be taken to ensure that two threads cannot modify the class or instance at the same time. For a static method, a lock for the class is acquired before executing the method. For a non-static method, a lock for the specific object instance is acquired.
transient	variable	The variable is not part of the persistant state of the object. (This modifier currently has no effect).
volatile	variable	The variable changes asynchronously (e.g., it may be a hardware register on a peripheral device). The compiler should not try to save its value in registers.

Reserved Words

Table 10-7 lists reserved words in Java. These are keywords or boolean literal values. Note that byvalue, cast, const, future, generic, goto, inner, operator, outer, rest, and var are reserved by Java but currently unused.

Table 10-7: Java Reserved Words

abstract	default	goto	operator	synchronized
boolean	do	if	outer	this
break	double	implements	package	throw
byte	else	import	private	throws
byvalue	extends	inner	protected	transient
case	false	instanceof	public	true
cast	final	int	rest	try
catch	finally	interface	return	var
char	float	long	short	void
class	for	native	static	volatile
const	future	new	super	while
continue	generic	null	switch	

Reserved Method Names

Table 10-8 lists the method names of the Object class. Strictly speaking, these method names are not reserved, but since the methods are inherited by every class, they should not be used as the name of a method, except when intentionally overriding an Object method.

Table 10-8: Reserved Method Names

clone	getClass	notifyAll
equals	hashCode	toString
finalize	notify	wait

Java Documentation Comment Syntax

The Java language supports special "doc comments," which begin with /** and end with */. These comments are not actually treated specially by the compiler, but can be extracted and automatically turned into HTML documentation by the *javadoc* program.

A doc comment may contain HTML markup tags, such as <PRE> and <TT> for code usage examples, but should not contain HTML structural tags such as <H2> or <HR>. Doc comments are associated with the declaration of the class, variable, or method that they precede.

Doc comments may also use special tags, which all begin with the @ character and allow *javadoc* to provide additional formatting for the documentation. When you use a special *javadoc* tag, it must be the first thing on its line within the doc comment. Also, if you use more than one tag of the same type, they should be on subsequent lines. For example, a class with multiple authors, or a method with multiple arguments would use multiple @author or @param tags. The available tags are listed below:

@see *classname*
> This tag adds a "See Also:" entry to the documentation that contains a hyperlink to the specified class. It may be used before classes, methods, or variables.

@see *full-classname*
> This tag adds a "See Also:" entry to the documentation that contains a hyperlink to the specified class. It may be used before classes, methods, or variables.

@see *full-classname#method-name*
> This tag adds a "See Also:" entry to the documentation that contains a hyperlink to the specified method of the specified class. It may be used before classes, methods, or variables.

@version *text*
> This tag adds a "Version:" entry containing the specified text to the documentation. May only be used before a class definition.

@author *text*
> This tag adds an "Author:" entry containing the specified text to the documentation. May only be used before a class definition.

@param *parameter-name description*
> This tag adds the specified parameter and its specified description to the "Parameters:" section of the current method. If the description is longer than one line, it may be continued on the next. May only be used before a method definition.

@return *description*
> Adds a "Returns:" section containing the specified description to the documentation. May only be used before a method definition.

@exception *full-classname description*
> Adds a "Throws:" entry to the documentation. The entry contains the specified class name of the exception and the description specified, which should explain the significance of the exception. May only be used before a method definition.

Events

Event Types

Table 11-1 lists the events that can be generated by each `Component` type in the `java.awt` package. The first column of the table specifies both the type of the component and the type of the event. The event type values are constants defined by the `java.awt.Event` class and are stored in the `id` field of the `Event` object.

The second through sixth columns indicate whether the `when` (timestamp), `x` (mouse X coordinate), `y` (mouse y coordinate), `key` (the key that was pressed), and `modifiers` (modifier keys that were down) fields are set for a given event. If a dot appears in this column, the event sets a value for the corresponding field. The seventh column explains what occurred to trigger the event, and what the value of the `arg` field of the `Event` object is.

Events listed for the `Component` component type apply to all `java.awt` Component subclasses. The events listed for the `Window` component type also apply to the Window subclasses, `Dialog` and `Frame`.

Table 11-1: Events

Component Event Type (id)	w h e n	x	y	k e y	m o d s	Event Meaning arg (Type: value)
Button ACTION_EVENT						User clicked on the button String: the button label
Checkbox ACTION_EVENT						User clicked on checkbox Boolean: new checkbox state

Table 11-1: Events (continued)

Component Event Type (id)	when	x	y	key	mods	Event Meaning arg (Type: value)
Choice ACTION_EVENT						User selected an item String: label of selected item
Component GOT_FOCUS						Got input focus *unused*
Component KEY_ACTION	•	•	•	•	•	User pressed a function key *unused*—key contains key constant
Component KEY_ACTION_RELEASE	•	•	•	•	•	User released a function key *unused*—key contains key constant
Component KEY_PRESS	•	•	•	•	•	User pressed a key *unused*—key contains ASCII key value
Component KEY_RELEASE	•	•	•	•	•	User released a key *unused*—key contains ASCII key value
Component LOST_FOCUS						Lost input focus *unused*
Component MOUSE_ENTER	•	•	•			Mouse entered the Component *unused*
Component MOUSE_EXIT	•	•	•			Mouse left the Component *unused*
Component MOUSE_DOWN	•	•	•		•	User pressed mouse button *unused*
Component MOUSE_UP	•	•	•		•	User released mouse button *unused*
Component MOUSE_MOVE	•	•	•		•	User moved mouse *unused*
Component MOUSE_DRAG	•	•	•		•	User dragged mouse *unused*
List ACTION_EVENT						User double-clicked on an item String: label of activated item
List LIST_SELECT						User selected an item Integer: index of selected item
List LIST_DESELECT						User deselected an item Integer: index of deselected item
MenuItem ACTION_EVENT						User selected an item String: label of selected item
Scrollbar SCROLL_LINE_UP						User requested scroll Integer: position to scroll to
Scrollbar SCROLL_LINE_DOWN						User requested scroll Integer: position to scroll to

· Table 11-1: Events (continued)

Component Event Type (`id`)	w h e n	x	y	k e y	m o d s	Event Meaning `arg` (Type: value)
Scrollbar SCROLL_PAGE_UP						User requested scroll Integer: position to scroll to
Scrollbar SCROLL_PAGE_DOWN						User requested scroll Integer: position to scroll to
Scrollbar SCROLL_ABSOLUTE						User requested scroll Integer: position to scroll to
TextField ACTION_EVENT						User struck <Return> String: user's input text
Window WINDOW_DESTROY						Window was destroyed *unused*
Window WINDOW_ICONIFY						Window was iconified *unused*
Window WINDOW_DEICONIFY						Window was deiconified *unused*
Window WINDOW_MOVED		•	•			Window was moved *unused*

Key and Modifier Constants

The `java.awt.Event` class contains the field `key`, which is filled in when a keyboard event has occurred, and the field `modifiers`, which list the keyboard modifier keys currently in effect for key and mouse events.

Four modifier constants are defined by the `java.awt.Event` class; they are listed in Table 11-2. They are mask values that are OR'ed into the `modifiers` field. You can test for them using AND. You can also check a given event for the first three of the modifiers with the `Event` methods `shiftDown()`, `controlDown()`, and `metaDown()`.

Table 11-2: Java Keyboard Modifiers

Modifier Constant	Meaning
`Event.SHIFT_MASK`	SHIFT key is held down (or CAPS LOCK on)
`Event.CTRL_MASK`	CONTROL key is held down
`Event.META_MASK`	META key is held down
`Event.ALT_MASK`	ALT key is held down

When a KEY_PRESS or KEY_RELEASE event occurs, it means that the user pressed a key which is a normal printing character, a control character, or a non-printing character with a standard ASCII value—one of RETURN (ASCII 10 or '\n'), TAB (ASCII 9 or '\t'), ESCAPE (ASCII 27), BACKSPACE (ASCII 8), and DELETE (ASCII 127). In this case,

Events

the value of the key field in the event is simply the ASCII value of the key that was pressed or released.

When a KEY_ACTION or KEY_ACTION_RELEASE event occurs, it means that the user pressed some sort of function key, one which does not have an ASCII representation. java.awt.Event defines constants for each of these function keys, which are listed in Table 11-3.

Table 11-3: Java Function Key Constants

Key Constant	Meaning
Event.HOME	HOME key
Event.END	END key
Event.PGUP	PAGE UP key
Event.PGDOWN	PAGE DOWN key
Event.UP	UP arrow key
Event.DOWN	DOWN arrow key
Event.LEFT	LEFT arrow key
Event.RIGHT	RIGHT arrow key
Event.F1, ..., Event.F12	Function keys 1 through 12

Mouse Buttons

In order to maintain platform independence, Java only recognizes a single mouse button—the Event class does not have any kind of mouseButton field to indicate which button has been pressed on a multibutton mouse. On platforms that support two- or three-button mouses, the right and center buttons generate mouse down, mouse drag, and mouse up events as if the user was holding down modifier keys (as shown in Table 11-4).

Table 11-4: Mouse Button Modifiers

Mouse Button	Flags set in Event.modifiers field
Left button	*none*
Right button	Event.META_MASK
Middle button	Event.ALT_MASK

Using keyboard modifiers to indicate which mouse button is pressed maintains compatibility with platforms that only have one-button mouses, but still allows programs to use the right and middle buttons on platforms that support them. Suppose, for example, you want to write a program that allows the user to draw lines with the mouse using two different colors. You might draw in the primary color if there are no modifier flags set, and draw in the secondary color when the META modifier is set. In this way, users with a two- or three-button mouse can simply use the left and right mouse buttons to draw in the two colors; and users with a one-button mouse can use the META key, in conjunction with the mouse, to draw in the secondary color.

12

Fonts, Colors, and Cursors

Fonts

Java defines platform-independent standard names for five common fonts that should reasonably be available on any platform. These names, and their corresponding platform-specific fonts, for Solaris and other UNIX/X platforms and for Microsoft Windows platforms, are listed in Table 12-1. Note that the table lists six font names. The last, "ZapfDingbats," is not commonly available on UNIX platforms running the X Window System, and so should not be considered portable. Finally, notice that the table specifies a default that is used when a requested font is undefined or cannot be found.

Table 12-1: Java Font Names

Java Font Name	Corresponding X Font	Corresponding Windows Font
Helvetica	adobe-helvetica	Arial
TimesRoman	adobe-times	Times New Roman
Courier	adobe-courier	Courier New
Dialog	b&h-lucida	MS Sans Serif
DialogInput	b&h-lucidatypewriter	MS Sans Serif
ZapfDingbats	itc-zapfdingbats	WingDings
default	misc-fixed	Arial

Font Styles

Java specifies font styles with integer constants defined in the Font class. Table 12-2 lists the available styles and Figure 12-1 shows each of the standard fonts in each of the standard styles.

Table 12-2: Java Font Styles

Constant	Style
Font.PLAIN	Plain or roman
Font.ITALIC	Italic
Font.BOLD	Bold
Font.BOLD + Font.ITALIC	Bolditalic

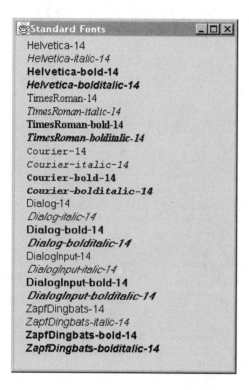

Figure 12-1: Standard Java Fonts and Font Styles

Java Font Properties

To allow customization, programs often call the static method Font.getFont() to look up fonts by name from the system properties list. In order to specify fonts on the system properties list, you must specify the font name, style, and point size in a single string. The syntax for doing this is:

fontname-style-size

The `style` specification should be plain, italic, bold, or bolditalic. The `size` specification should be an integer that specifies the desired point size for the font. The `style` specification may optionally be omitted. Or both the `style` and `size` may be omitted to obtain a plain, 12-point font. Here are some example property specifications:

```
mypackage.myprogram.big_font=Dialog-bolditalic-48
mypackage.myprogram.main_font=Helvetica-14
mypackage.myprogram.heading_font=TimesRoman-bold-20
mypackage.myprogram.listing_font=Courier
```

See Section 13, *System Properties and Applet Parameters*, for more information on specifying properties in the system properties list.

Creating Font Name Aliases

You can make one font name an alias for another by setting a property like:

awt.font.*fontalias*=*fontname*

fontname should be one of the standard Java font names described above. *fontalias* should be the alias you want to define, converted to all lowercase letters.

For example, if we wanted to give the illusion that our program supported the New Century Schoolbook font, we might alias it to TimesRoman, by having the program insert a property definition like this:

awt.font.schoolbook=TimesRoman

into the system properties before we fetch any fonts with Font.getFont(). With this done, we can document "Schoolbook" as a supported font name, and users can select fonts with properties like the following:

mypackage.myprogram.main_text_font=Schoolbook-14

Colors

The java.awt.Color class defines a number of constant Color values. Table 12-3 lists them.

Table 12-3: Java Color Constants

Color.black	Color.green	Color.red
Color.blue	Color.lightGray	Color.white
Color.cyan	Color.magenta	Color.yellow
Color.darkGray	Color.orange	
Color.gray	Color.pink	

The Java Color Model

To create a `Color` object, you must specify the red, green, and blue components of the desired color. Java allows you to specify these values as `float` values between 0.0 and 1.0, and even lets you create a color using the HSB (hue, saturation, brightness) color model. But internally, the red, green, and blue values are stored as 8-bit values between 0 and 255. The internal representation of color components is in a single integer, in the form:

```
0xAARRGGBB
```

RR represents the red component, GG the green component, and BB the blue component. AA is the "alpha" component, which is used to represent transparency in image processing. When you create a `Color` object, the alpha component is always set to 0xFF (fully opaque) internally. Transparency can be used for image manipulation, but it is not used by any of Java's drawing operations.

Color Properties

To allow customization, Java programs and applets often call `Color.getColor()` to look up and return a color specified as the value of a named property. To specify a color as the value of a property, convert it to the default 0x*RRGGBB* form and specify it as an integer. Specifying the integer in hexadecimal form is usually the easiest. Here are some example properties:

```
mypackage.myprogram.foreground=0              0 is black
mypackage.myprogram.highlight=0xFFFF00        yellow
mypackage.myprogram.background=0xE0E0E0       light gray
```

See Section 13 for more information on specifying properties in the system properties list.

Cursors

Java defines a number of standard platform-independent cursors that can be specified as the mouse pointer for a `Frame`. Table 12-4 lists the constants and describes the cursors they represent. Figure 12-2 shows what the cursors look like on a UNIX platform running the X Window System.

Table 12-4: Standard Java Cursors

Cursor Constant	Cursor Description
Frame.CROSSHAIR_CURSOR	A simple crosshair.
Frame.DEFAULT_CURSOR	The platform-dependent default cursor. Usually an arrow.
Frame.E_RESIZE_CURSOR	A cursor useful to indicate that the right edge of something is to be dragged.
Frame.HAND_CURSOR	A hand; can be used to indicate that a selection is to be made.
Frame.MOVE_CURSOR	A cursor that indicates that something is to be moved.
Frame.NE_RESIZE_CURSOR	A cursor useful to indicate that the upper-right corner of something is to be dragged.

Table 12-4: Standard Java Cursors (continued)

Cursor Constant	Cursor Description
Frame.NW_RESIZE_CURSOR	A cursor useful to indicate that the upper-left corner of something is to be dragged.
Frame.N_RESIZE_CURSOR	A cursor useful to indicate that the top edge of something is to be dragged.
Frame.SE_RESIZE_CURSOR	A cursor useful to indicate that the lower-right corner of something is to be dragged.
Frame.SW_RESIZE_CURSOR	A cursor useful to indicate that the lower-left corner of something is to be dragged.
Frame.S_RESIZE_CURSOR	A cursor useful to indicate that the bottom edge of something is to be dragged.
Frame.TEXT_CURSOR	A cursor used to indicate editable text. Often an I-bar of some kind.
Frame.WAIT_CURSOR	A cursor used to indicate that the program is busy and that the user should wait. Often a wristwatch or an hourglass.
Frame.W_RESIZE_CURSOR	A cursor useful to indicate that the left edge of something is to be dragged.

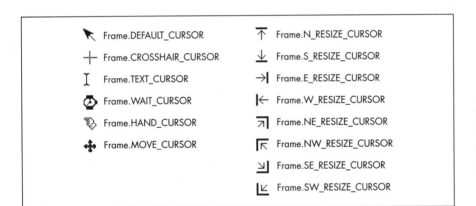

Figure 12-2: Standard Java Cursors

13

System Properties and Applet Parameters

Java programs and applets cannot read environment variables the way that C programs can. Similar mechanisms exist, however, that allow applications and applets to read the value of a named resource. These resource values allow customization of an application's or applet's behavior based on site-specific parameters, such as the type of host, or based on user preferences.

Named resource values are specified for applications in the "system properties" list. Applications (and applets as well, though this is less common) can read these "system properties" with the `System.getProperties()` method and other methods based on that one, such as `Font.getFont()`, `Color.getColor()`, `Integer.getInteger()`, and `Boolean.getBoolean()`.

The customization mechanism for applets does not use the system properties list. Instead it relies on a very similar list of "applet parameters." An applet can look up a named parameter value with the `Applet.getParameter()` method. Unfortunately, there are no convenient methods for reading color and font specifications from the applet parameters list.

Standard System Properties

When the Java interpreter starts, it inserts fifteen standard properties into the system properties list. These properties, and the meaning of their values, are listed in Table 13-1. The table also specifies whether applets are allowed (at least by default) to read the value of these properties. Certain sensitive values are hidden from "untrusted" applets.

Sys Properties and Applets

Table 13-1: Standard System Properties

Name	Value	Applet Can Read
java.version	Version of the Java interpreter	yes
java.vendor	Vendor-specific identifier string	yes
java.vendor.url	Vendor's URL	yes
java.home	The directory Java is installed in	no
java.class.version	The version of the Java API	yes
java.class.path	The classpath value	no
os.name	The name of the operating system	yes
os.arch	The host hardware architecture	yes
os.version	Version of the host operating system	yes
file.separator	Platform-dependent file separator (e.g., / or \)	yes
path.separator	Platform-dependent path separator (e.g., : or ;)	yes
line.separator	Platform-dependent line separator (e.g., \n or \r\n)	yes
user.name	The username of the current user	no
user.home	The home directory of the current user	no
user.dir	The current working directory	no

Other Important Properties

There are several other important properties that various portions of the Java API read. These are not standard properties that the interpreter sets to default values, but instead resources that you can set to customize the behavior of some of the standard Java classes. The properties are:

awt.toolkit

> This property specifies the name of the class that implements the abstract java.awt.Toolkit class to be used as the default Toolkit for all user interface components. The specified class essentially defines the look and feel of all Java user interfaces. The default value for this property is "sun.awt.motif.MToolkit" on UNIX platforms.

awt.appletWarning

> This property specifies a warning string that is to appear in a prominent place in all windows created by an applet. The purpose of the warning is to prevent applets from creating windows that masquerade as trusted windows. The default value of this property is "Warning: Applet Window".

awt.font.*fontname*

> When a Java program or applet creates a new font, the system converts the font name to lower case, appends it to the string "awt.font." and looks up the resulting property name. If the property is defined, the system uses the property value instead of the font name when creating the

font. This allows programs or users to create aliases for font names, or to modify the fonts used by an application.

In addition to these properties read by portions of the Java API, the JDK *appletviewer* program from Sun reads a number of properties that affect its security policies for untrusted applets. See the *appletviewer* reference pages in Section 17, *JDK Development Tools*, for details, and see Section 14, *Applet Security*, for more information on applet security.

Specifying Property Values

If a Java application reads properties to allow user customization, then you can specify values for those properties to perform that customization. To specify properties that the Java interpreter should insert into the system properties list, use the –D option. For example:

```
%java -Dgames.tetris.level=9 -Dgames.tetris.sound=off games.tetris
```

Specifying Properties in a File

A program may support user customization by reading in a file of property specifications when it starts up. Similarly, a Web browser might read a file of properties in order to support customization of the applets it runs. The *appletviewer* application, for example, reads (on UNIX systems) the properties in the file ˜*/.hotjava/properties* when it starts. To specify properties that are applicable to the *appletviewer*, you simply need to specify them, one to a line, in the form *name=value*. For example:

```
# These are resources from ˜/.hotjava/properties
package.restrict.access.netscape=true
package.restrict.access.sun=true
appletviewer.security.mode=host
```

Note that lines beginning with # are comments, and that no –D is needed to specify these resources

Applet Parameters

Applet parameters are much like system properties. There are a few important differences, however:

- There is no standard list of applet parameters that is set for all applets. An applet may read the system properties to determine things such as the version of the Java interpreter and the type of platform it is being run on.

- Applet parameters are implicitly specified for a particular applet. Therefore there is no need for hierarchical names such as the property name "games.tetris.level." For a corresponding parameter, the name "level" would be sufficient.

- While an application may modify the system properties list, an applet may only read the parameters. An applet cannot set parameter values or add new parameters to the list.

Specifying Parameters for an Applet

To specify parameter values for an applet, you use the HTML <PARAM> tag in the file that references the applet. For example:

```
<APPLET code="games/tetris.class" width=200 height=400>
<PARAM name="level" value="9">
<PARAM name="sound" value="off">
</APPLET>
```

Web browsers and applet viewers may in the future provide a way in which users can interactively modify the parameter settings for a given applet. They may even allow such parameter settings to be saved.

14

Applet Security

Applets loaded over the network are untrusted. The only way to be sure that an untrusted applet cannot perform any malicious actions (e.g., deleting your files, sending out fake email that looks like it came from you, using your computer as a remote file server) is to run it in a very limited environment. For this reason, Web browsers and applet viewers carefully restrict what an applet is allowed to do.

Applet Security Restrictions

When designing an applet, you must bear in mind the list of things that an applet is not allowed to do. Different Web browsers and applet viewers may place slightly different restrictions on applets, and some may even allow the user to relax some of these restrictions, but, in general, applets are not allowed to:

- Read files on the local system.

- Write files to the local system.

- Delete files on the local system, either by calling the `File.delete()` method, or by invoking the system's *rm* or *del* command.

- Rename files on the local system, either by calling the `File.renameTo()` method or by invoking the system's *mv* or *rename* command.

- Create a directory on the local system, either by calling the `File.mkdir()` or `File.mkdirs()` methods, or by invoking the system's *mkdir* command.

- List directory contents.

- Check for the existence of a file.

- Obtain the type, size, or modification time of a file.

- Create a network connection to any computer other than the one from which the applet was itself loaded.

- Listen for or accept network connections on any port of the local system.

- Create a top-level window without a visible warning indicator that the window is "untrusted." This prevents applets from spoofing other, trusted programs into which users may type sensitive data.

- Obtain the user's username or home directory name, or in general, read any of the following system properties: `user.name`, `user.home`, `user.dir`, `java.home`, `java.class.path`.

- Define any system properties.

- Invoke any program on the local system. In other words, an applet cannot call any of the `Runtime.exec()` methods.

- Make the Java interpreter quit; an applet cannot call `System.exit()` or `Runtime.exit()`.

- Load dynamic libraries on the local system. In other words, an applet cannot call the `load()` or `loadLibrary()` methods of the `Runtime` or `System` classes.

- Create or manipulate any thread that is not part of the same `ThreadGroup` as the applet.

- Manipulate any `ThreadGroup` other than its own.

- Create a `ClassLoader` object.

- Create a `SecurityManager` object.

- Specify a `ContentHandlerFactory`, `SocketImplFactory`, or `URLStreamHandlerFactory` for the system. (These classes control how Java handles networking.)

- Access or load classes in any package other than the standard eight of the Java API: `java.applet`, `java.awt`, `java.awt.image`, `java.awt.peer`, `java.io`, `java.lang`, `java.net`, `java.util`.

- Define classes that are part of packages on the local system.

Local Applet Restrictions

When an applet is loaded from the local file system, instead of through a network protocol, Web browsers and applet viewers may relax some, or even many, of the above restrictions. The reason for this is that local applets are assumed to be more trustworthy than anonymous applets from the network.

Intermediate applet security policies are also possible. For example, an applet viewer could be written that would place fewer restrictions on applets loaded from an internal corporate network than on those loaded from the Internet.

Applet Security Implementation

Implementing the security restrictions described above is the responsibility of the `java.lang.SecurityManager` class. This class defines a number of methods that the system calls to check whether a certain operation (such as reading a file) is permitted in the current environment. Applet viewers create a subclass of `SecurityManager` to implement a particular security policy. A security policy is put in place by instantiating a `SecurityManager` object and registering it with `System.setSecurityManager()`. (One of the obvious security restrictions that must be enforced is that untrusted code may not register its own `SecurityManager` object!)

Loading Classes Securely

Another component of Java security is the way Java classes are loaded over the network. The `java.lang.ClassLoader` class defines how this is done. Applet viewers and Web browsers create subclasses of this class that implement security policies and define how class files are loaded via various protocols.

One important function of the class loader is to ensure that loaded classes reside in a separate namespace than classes loaded from the local system. This prevents naming conflicts, and also prevents a malicious applet from replacing standard Java classes with its own versions.

Byte-Code Verification

Another important function of the class loader is to ensure that all untrusted Java code (generally code loaded over the network) is passed through the Java byte-code verification process. This process ensures that the loaded code does not violate Java namespace restrictions or type conversion restrictions. It also checks that the code:

- Is valid Java Virtual Machine code.

- Does not overflow or underflow the stack.

- Does not use registers incorrectly.

- Does not convert data types illegally.

The purpose of these checks is to verify that the loaded code cannot forge pointers or do memory arithmetic, which could give it access to the underlying machine. The checks also ensure that the code cannot crash the Java interpreter or leave it in an undefined state, which might allow malicious code to take advantage of security flaws that could exist in some interpreter implementations. Essentially, the byte-code verification process protects against code from an "untrusted" Java compiler.

Denial of Service Attacks

The one "security hole" that remains when running an untrusted applet is that the applet can perform a "denial of service attack" on your computer. For example, it could frivolously allocate lots of memory, run many threads, or download lots of data. This sort of attack consumes system resources and can slow your computer (or your network connection) considerably. While this sort of attack by an applet is inconvenient, fortunately it cannot do any real damage. (Except to your patience and your deadlines.)

Future Directions: Applet Certification

A possibility being seriously explored for future releases of Java is the ability for applets to carry an attached digital signature and cryptologic checksum. Using public key encryption technology, this would enable a Web browser or applet viewer to verify that an applet is from the source it claims to be from, and that it has not been modified in transmission. With these guarantees, it is possible to load a trusted applet (one that can run without severe security restrictions) over an untrusted network as long as you trust the source of the applet (i.e., whatever individual, corporation, or certification agency has attached their digital signature to the applet).

Java-Related HTML and HTTP Syntax

This section explains what you need to know about HTML and HTTP to work with Java applets.

The <APPLET> Tag

A Java applet is included in a Web page with the <APPLET> tag, which has the following syntax:

```
<APPLET
        [CODEBASE = applet-url]
        CODE = applet-filename
        WIDTH = pixel-width
        HEIGHT = pixel-height
        [ALT = alternate-text]
        [NAME = applet-name]
        [ALIGN = alignment]
        [VSPACE = vertical-pixel-space]
        [HSPACE = horizontal-pixel-space]
    >
    [<PARAM NAME = parameter VALUE = value>]
    [<PARAM NAME = parameter VALUE = value>]
       ...
    [alternate-html]
    </APPLET>
```

APPLET   The <APPLET> tag specifies an applet to be run within a Web document. A Web browser that does not support Java and does not understand the <APPLET> tag ignores this tag and any related <PARAM> tags, and simply displays any *alternate-html* that appears between

<APLET> and </APPLET>. A browser that does support Java runs the specified applet, and does *not* display the `alternate-html`.

CODEBASE

This optional attribute specifies the base URL (absolute or relative) of the applet to be displayed. This should be a directory, not the applet file itself. If this attribute is unspecified, then the URL of the current document is used.

CODE   This required attribute specifies the file that contains the compiled Java code for the applet. It must be relative to the CODEBASE if that attribute is specified, or relative to the current document's URL. It must not be an absolute URL.

WIDTH   This attribute specifies the initial width, in pixels, that the applet needs in the browser's window. It is required.

HEIGHT   This attribute specifies the initial height, in pixels, that the applet needs in the browser's window. It is required.

ALT   This optional attribute specifies text that should be displayed by browsers that understand the <APPLET> tag but do not support Java.

NAME   This optional attribute gives a name to the applet instance. Applets that are running at the same time can look each other up by name and communicate with each other.

ALIGN   This optional attribute specifies the applet's alignment on the page. It behaves just like the ALIGN attribute of the <IMG> tag, and should support at least the same alignment values that the <IMG> tag does. These values include: top, middle, and bottom.

VSPACE   This optional attribute specifies the margin, in pixels, that the browser should put above and below the applet. It behaves just like the VSPACE attribute of the <IMG> tag.

HSPACE   This optional attribute specifies the margin, in pixels, that the browser should put on either side of the applet. It behaves just like the HSPACE attribute of the <IMG> tag.

PARAM   The <PARAM> tag, with its NAME and VALUE attributes, specifies a named parameter and a string value that are passed to the applet. These parameters function like environment variables or command-line arguments do for a regular application. An applet can look up the value of a parameter specified in a <PARAM> tag with the `Applet.getParameter()` method.

Any number of <PARAM> tags may appear between <APPLET> and </APPLET>.

Example 15-1 shows an HTML fragment that displays Sun's "Steaming cup of Java" animation applet.

Example 15-1: Example HTML page containing an applet

```
<APPLET codebase="betaclasses" code="Animator.class" width=66 height=100>
    <PARAM name="imagesource" value="graphics/100pixel">
    <PARAM name="pause" value="100">
    <PARAM name="repeat" value="true">
    <PARAM name="images" value="1|2|3|1|2|3|1|2|3|4|5|6|7|8|9">
</APPLET>
```

The <EMBED> Tag

It is unlikely that Java will be the only form of "executable content" available on the Web. And it is inconceivable that Java programs will be the only type of content that providers will want to "embed" in their Web pages, as opposed to displaying them in a separate window. The problem is that we don't want to have to invent (and support) a new tag like <APPLET> for each new kind of executable or embeddable content.

Thus, there is a proposal underway to standardize on a new <EMBED> tag. This tag specifies some network resource that is to be downloaded and displayed in the current page. It seems likely that this proposal will be well received, and as it is adopted, that <EMBED> will become a preferred alternative to <APPLET>. To switch from the <APPLET> to the <EMBED> tag, all you need to do is change the NAME attribute to ID and combine the CODEBASE and CODE attributes into a single SRC attribute.

Example 15-2 shows how the HTML fragment of Example 15-1 would appear using the <EMBED> tag.

Example 15-2: A Java applet using <EMBED>

```
<EMBED src="betaclasses/Animator.class" width=66 height=100>
    <PARAM name="imagesource" value="graphics/100pixel">
    <PARAM name="pause" value="100">
    <PARAM name="repeat" value="true">
    <PARAM name="images" value="1|2|3|1|2|3|1|2|3|4|5|6|7|8|9">
</EMBED>
```

Java-Related HTTP

The HTTP protocol specifies the MIME type of each Net resource that it delivers. For example, HTML documents are delivered with a MIME type of "text/html." This type lets the browser know that it should interpret the data as an HTML file (as opposed, for example, to a plain text file, a PostScript file, or a JPEG image).

The same is true of Java applets. Sun's de facto standard has been to send Java applet code with the MIME type "application/octet-stream." If you plan on serving Java applets over the Net, you will probably have to configure your Web server to supply this MIME type. You'll have to edit a file (probably named something like *mime.types*) that maps between filename extensions and MIME types. In this case, you want to serve all files ending in *.class* as type "application/octet-stream."

Currently, the MIME type of applets seems to be something of a moot point. When a Web browser sees an <APPLET> tag in HTML, it assumes that the specified resource is a Java program, and ignores the MIME type supplied by the server. Since the MIME tag is generally ignored, most sites have apparently not customized their Web servers to use the "application/octet-stream" tag, and are serving Java applets as type "text/plain."

When the <EMBED> tag comes into common use, the MIME type specified for Java code will no longer be ignored, and sites will have to make their Web servers aware of Java applications. Furthermore, as other types of binary executable content (i.e., other Java-like interpreters) become available on the Web, the MIME tag "application/octet-stream" may no longer seem specific enough. Thus, it seems likely that some Java-specific MIME type will come into use.

The Unicode Standard

Unicode is a 16-bit character encoding established by the Unicode Consortium, which describes the standard this way:

> The Unicode Worldwide Character Standard is a character coding system designed to support the interchange, processing, and display of the written texts of the diverse languages of the modern world. In addition, it supports classical and historical texts of many written languages.

> In its current version, the Unicode standard contains 34,168 distinct coded characters derived from 24 supported scripts. These characters cover the principal written languages of the Americas, Europe, the Middle East, Africa, India, Asia, and Pacifica.

> Some modern written languages are not yet supported or only partially supported due to a need for further research into the encoding needs of certain scripts.

Unicode is related to, but not the same as ISO 10646, the UCS (Universal Character Set) encoding. The UCS encoding is a four-byte encoding that simply lumps together all known character encodings. For example, it includes the separate Chinese, Japanese, and Korean national encodings for Han ideographic characters. Unicode, by contrast (since it only has two bytes to work with), "unifies" these disparate national encodings into a single set of Han characters that works for all three countries. Unicode is one of the encodings that is adopted as part of UCS—the Unicode character '\u*xxxx*' is equivalent to the UCS character '0000 *xxxx*'.

In the canonical form of the Unicode encoding, which is what Java `char` and `String` types use, every character occupies two bytes. The Unicode characters \u0020 to \u007E are equivalent to the ASCII and ISO8859-1 (Latin-1) characters 0x20 through 0x7E. The Unicode characters \u00A0 to \u00FF are identical to the ISO8859-1 characters 0xA0 to 0xFF. Thus there is a trivial mapping between Latin-1 and Unicode characters. A number of other portions of the Unicode encoding are based on pre-existing standards, such as ISO8859-5 (Cyrillic) and ISO8859-8 (Hebrew), though the mappings between these standards and Unicode may not be as trivial as the Latin-1 mapping.

Unicode is a trademark of the Unicode Consortium. Version 1.0 of the standard (the current version is 1.1) is fully defined in two volumes: *The Unicode Standard, Worldwide Character Encoding, Version 1.0, Volume 1* (Addison-Wesley, 1990. ISBN 0-201-56788-1) and *The Unicode Standard, Worldwide Character Encoding, Version 1.0, Volume 2* (Addison-Wesley, 1992. ISBN 0-201-60845-6). Further information about the Unicode standard and the Unicode Consortium can be obtained at *http://unicode.org/*.

Although Java uses Unicode characters internally, note that Unicode support on many platforms is likely to be limited to the use of the \u*xxxx* escape sequence in input and output text. One of the difficulties with the use of Unicode is the poor availability of fonts that can display all of the Unicode characters. Windows 95 platforms provide partial support for Unicode, including a partial Unicode font (which omits the Han Chinese/Japanese/Korean characters, and others). Also note that the `java.io.PrintStream` class (of which `System.out` is an instance) discards the top 8 bits of 16-bit Unicode characters. Thus, at least in current implementations, "standard output" supports only ASCII and Latin-1 characters.

Table 16-1 provides an overview of the Unicode 1.1 encoding.

Table 16-1: Outline of the Unicode 1.1 Encoding

Start	End	Description
0000	1FFF	**Alphabets**
0020	007E	Basic Latin (US-ASCII printing characters)
00A0	00FF	Latin-1 Supplement (right half of ISO8859-1)
0100	017F	Latin Extended-A
0180	024F	Latin Extended-B
0250	02AF	IPA Extensions
02B0	02FF	Spacing Modifier Letters
0300	036F	Combining Diacritical marks
0370	03CF	Basic Greek (based on ISO8859-7)
03D0	03FF	Greek Symbols and Coptic
0400	04FF	Cyrillic (based on ISO8859-5)
0500	052F	unassigned
0530	058F	Armenian
0590	05CF	Hebrew Extended-A
05D0	05EA	Basic Hebrew (based on ISO8859-8)
05EB	05FF	Hebrew Extended-B
0600	0652	Basic Arabic (based on ISO8859-6)
0653	06FF	Arabic Extended
0700	08FF	Ethiopic (not finalized)
0900	097F	Devanagari (based on ISCII 1988)
0980	09FF	Bengali (based on ISCII 1988)
0A00	0A7F	Gurmukhi (based on ISCII 1988)
0A80	0AFF	Gujarati (based on ISCII 1988)
0B00	0B7F	Oriya (based on ISCII 1988)
0B80	0BFF	Tamil (based on ISCII 1988)

Table 16-1: Outline of the Unicode 1.1 Encoding (continued)

Start	End	Description
0C00	0C7F	Telugu (based on ISCII 1988)
0C80	0CFF	Kannada (based on ISCII 1988)
0D00	0D7F	Malayalam (based on ISCII 1988)
0D80	0DFF	Sinhala (not finalized)
0E00	0E7F	Thai (based on TIS 620-2529)
0E80	0EFF	Lao (based on TIS 620-2529)
0F00	0F7F	Burmese (not finalized)
0F80	0FDF	Khmer (not finalized)
1000	105F	Tibetan (not finalized)
1060	109F	Mongolian (not finalized)
10A0	10CF	Georgian Extended
10D0	10FF	Basic Georgian
1100	11FF	Hangul Jamo
1200	125F	Ethiopian (not finalized)
1E00	1EFF	Latin Extended Additional
1F00	1FFF	Greek Extended
2000	2FFF	**Symbols and Punctuation**
2000	206F	General Punctuation
2070	209F	Superscripts and Subscripts
20A0	20CF	Currency Symbols
20D0	20FF	Combining Diacritical Marks for Symbols
2100	214F	Letterlike Symbols
2150	218F	Number Forms
2190	21FF	Arrows
2200	22FF	Mathematical Operators
2300	23FF	Miscellaneous Technical
2400	243F	Control Pictures
2440	245F	Optical Character Recognition
2460	24FF	Enclosed Alphanumerics
2500	257F	Box Drawing
2580	259F	Block Elements
25A0	25FF	Geometric Shapes
2600	26FF	Miscellaneous Symbols
2700	27BF	Dingbats
3000	4DFF	**CJK Auxiliary**
3000	303F	CJK Symbols and Punctuation
3040	309F	Hiragana (based on JIS X0208-1990)
30A0	30FF	Katakana (based on JIS X0208-1990)
3100	312F	Bopomofo (based on GB 2312-80)
3190	319F	CJK Miscellaneous (Kaeriten)
3200	32FF	Enclosed CJK Letters and Months
3300	33FF	CJK Compatibility
3400	3D2D	Hangul (based on KSC 5601-1987)
3D2E	44B7	Hangul Supplementary-A
44B8	4DFF	Hangul Supplementary-B
4E00	9FFF	**CJK Unified Ideographs** Han characters used in China, Japan, Korea, Taiwan, and Vietnam

Unicode

Table 16-1: Outline of the Unicode 1.1 Encoding (continued)

Start	End	Description
A000	DFFF	**Reserved for future assignment**
E000	FFFD	**Restricted use**
E000	F8FF	Private Use Area
F900	FAFF	CJK Compatibility Ideographs
FB00	FB4F	Alphabetic Presentation Forms
FB50	FDFF	Arabic Presentation Forms-A
FE20	FE2F	Combining Half Marks
FE30	FE4F	CJK Compatibility Forms (verticals and overlines)
FE50	FE6F	Small Form Variants
FE70	FEFE	Arabic Presentation Forms-B
FEFF	FEFF	Zero-width no-break space (Byte Order Mark)
FF00	FFEF	Halfwidth and Fullwidth Forms
FFF0	FFFC	Specials
FFFD	FFFD	Replacement Character
FFFE	FFFF	**Excluded from standard**

The UTF-8 Encoding

The canonical two-bytes per character encoding is useful for the manipulation of character data, and is the internal representation used throughout Java. Because a large amount of text used by Java programs is 8-bit text, and because there are so many existing computer systems that support only 8-bit characters, the 16-bit canonical form is not usually the most efficient way to store Unicode text nor the most portable way to transmit it.

Because of this, other encodings called "transformation formats" have been developed. Java provides simple support for the UTF-8 encoding with the `DataInputStream.readUTF()` and `DataOutputStream.writeUTF()` methods. UTF-8 is a variable-width or "multi-byte" encoding format; this means that different characters require different numbers of bytes. In UTF-8, the standard ASCII characters occupy only one byte, and remain untouched by the encoding (i.e., a string of ASCII characters is a legal UTF-8 string). As a tradeoff, however, other Unicode characters occupy two or three bytes.

In UTF-8, Unicode characters between \u0000 and \u007F occupy a single byte, which has a value of between 0x00 and 0x7F, and which always has its high-order bit set to 0. Characters between \u0080 and \u07FF occupy two bytes, and characters between \u0800 and \uFFFF occupy three bytes. The first byte of a two-byte character always has high-order bits 110, and the first byte of a three-byte character always has high-order bits 1110. Since single-byte characters always have 0 as their high-order bit, the one-, two-, and three-byte characters can easily be distinguished from each other.

The second and third bytes of two- and three-byte characters always have high-order bits 10, which distinguishes them from one-byte characters, and also distinguishes them from the first byte of a two- or three-byte sequence. This is important because it allows a program to locate the start of a character in a multibyte sequence.

The remaining bits in each character (i.e., the bits that are not part of one of the required high-order bit sequences) are used to encode the actual Unicode character data. In the single-byte form, there are seven bits available, suitable for encoding characters up to \u007F. In the two-byte form, there are 11 data bits available, which are enough to encode values to \u07FF, and in the three-byte form there are 16 available data bits, which are enough to encode all 16-bit Unicode characters.

Table 16-2 summarizes the encoding.

Table 16-2: The UTF-8 Encoding

Start Charcter	End Character	Required Data Bits	Binary Byte Sequence (x = data bits)
\u0000	\u007F	7	0xxxxxxx
\u0080	\u07FF	11	110xxxxx 10xxxxxx
\u0800	\uFFFF	16	1110xxxx 10xxxxxx 10xxxxxx

The UTF-8 has the following desirable features:

- All ASCII characters are one-byte UTF-8 characters. A legal ASCII string is a legal UTF-8 string.

- Any non-ASCII characters (i.e., any character with the high-order bit set) is part of a multibyte character.

- The first byte of any UTF-8 character indicates the number of additional bytes in the character.

- The first byte of a multibyte character is easily distinguished from the subsequent bytes. Thus, it is easy to locate the start of a character from an arbitrary position in a data stream.

- It is easy to convert between UTF-8 and Unicode.

- The UTF-8 encoding is relatively compact. For text with a large percentage of ASCII characters, it is more compact than Unicode. In the worst case, a UTF-8 string is only 50% larger than the corresponding Unicode string.

Unicode

17

JDK Development Tools

appletviewer — The Java Applet Viewer

SYNOPSIS

appletviewer [-debug] *urls*

DESCRIPTION

appletviewer downloads one or more HTML documents specified by URL on the command line. It downloads all the applets referenced in each document and displays them, each in their own window. If none of the named documents has an <APPLET> tag, *appletviewer* does nothing.

OPTIONS

−debug

If this option is specified, the *appletviewer* is started within *jdb* (the Java debugger). This allows you to debug the applets referenced by the document or documents.

PROPERTIES

When it starts up, *appletviewer* reads property definitions from the file *˜/.botjava/properties* (UNIX) or *\.botjava\properties* (Windows). It reads the value of the following

○ *Man Pages*

properties to determine what security restrictions should be placed on untrusted applets:

acl.read
> This is a list of files and directories that an untrusted applet is allowed to read. The elements of the list should be separated with colons on UNIX systems and semicolons on Windows systems. On UNIX systems, the ~ character is replaced with the home directory of the current user. If the plus character appears as an element in the list, it is replaced by the value of the acl.read.default property. This provides an easy way to enable read access—by simply setting acl.read to "+". By default, untrusted applets are not allowed to read any files or directories.

acl.read.default
> This is a list of files and directories that are readable by untrusted applets if the acl.read property contains a plus character.

acl.write
> This is a list of files and directories that an untrusted applet is allowed to write to. The elements of the list should be separated with colons on UNIX systems and semicolons on Windows systems. On UNIX systems, the ~ character is replaced with the home directory of the current user. If the plus character appears as an element in the list, it is replaced by the value of the acl.write.default property. This provides an easy way to enable write access—by simply setting acl.write to "+". By default, untrusted applets are not allowed to write to any files or directories.

acl.write.default
> This is a list of files and directories that are writable by untrusted applets if the acl.write property contains a plus character.

appletviewer.security.model
> This property specifies the types of network access an untrusted applet is allowed to perform. The none value specifies that the applet can perform no networking at all. The value host is the default, and it specifies that the applet can connect only to the host from which it was loaded. The value unrestricted specifies that an applet may connect to any host without restrictions.

firewallHost
> This is the firewall proxy host to connect to if the firewallSet property is true.

firewallPort
> This is the port of the firewall proxy host to connect to if the firewallSet property is true.

firewallSet
> This tells you whether the applet viewer should use a firewall proxy. Values are true or false.

`package.restrict.access.`*`package-prefix`*

Properties of this form may be set to `true` to prevent untrusted applets from using classes in any package that has the specified package name prefix as the first component of its name. For example, to prevent applets from using any of the Sun classes (such as the Java compiler and the appletviewer itself) that are shipped with the JDK, you could specify the following property:

package.restrict.access.sun=true

appletviewer sets this property to `true` by default.

`package.restrict.definition.`*`package-prefix`*

Properties of this form may be set to `true` to prevent untrusted applets from defining classes in a package that has the specified package name prefix as the first component of its name. For example, to prevent an applet from defining classes in any of the standard Java packages, you could specify the following property:

package.restrict.definition.java=true

appletviewer sets this property to `true` by default.

`proxyHost`

This is the caching proxy host to connect to if the `proxySet` property is `true`.

`proxyPort`

This is the port of the caching proxy host to connect to if the `proxySet` property is `true`.

`proxySet`

This tells you whether the applet viewer should use a caching proxy. Values are `true` or `false`.

ENVIRONMENT

`CLASSPATH`

Specifies an ordered list (colon-separated on UNIX, semicolon-separated on Windows systems) of directories and zip files in which *appletviewer* should look for class definitions. When a path is specified with this environment variable, *appletviewer* always implictly appends the location of the system classes to the end of the path. If this environment variable is not specified, the default path is the current directory and the system classes. Note that *appletviewer* does not support the -classpath option that other JDK tools do.

SEE ALSO

java, javac, jdb

java — The Java Interpreter
SYNOPSIS

java [*interpreter options*] *classname* [*program arguments*]

DESCRIPTION

java is the Java byte-code interpreter—it runs Java programs.

The program to be run is the class specified by `classname`. This must be a fully qualified name, it must include the package name of the class, but not the *.class* file extension. Note that you specify the package and class name, with components separated by '.', not the directory and filename of the class, which has its components separated by '/' or '\'. If a Java class has no `package` statement, then it is not in any package, and the class name is specified alone. Examples:

%java david.games.Checkers
%java test

See the description of the −classpath option and the CLASSPATH environment variable below for information on specifying where *java* should look for classes.

The class specified by `classname` must contain a method `main()` with exactly the following signature:

public static void main(String argv[])

Any arguments following the `classname` on the *java* command line are placed into an array and passed to the `main()` method when *java* starts up.

If `main()` creates any threads, *java* runs until the last thread exits. Otherwise, the interpreter executes the body of `main()` and exits.

Although only a single class name is specified when invoking *java*, the interpreter automatically loads any additional classes required by the program. These class files must reside in the current directory, with the standard system classes, or in a location specified by the −classpath option or the CLASSPATH environment variable. Classes are looked up in a file which has the same name as the class with a *.class* extension added. Each such class file is expected to be within a directory hierarchy that corresponds to the package name. Thus, the class `java.lang.String` would be found in *java/lang/String.class*.

`java` can also look up classes within zip files. For UNIX users not familiar with this file format, zip is an archive format, much like tar—a zip file is a single file that contains many other files, which may be individually extracted. The contents of a zip file may be compressed or uncompressed; *java* expects uncompressed zip files. Using zip files is an especially useful way to store classes on systems that do not support long filenames.

By default, *java* runs a byte-code verifier on all dynamically loaded classes (i.e., classes loaded from untrusted sources, such as the network). This verifier performs a number of tests on the byte-code of the loaded class to ensure, for example, that it does not corrupt the internal operand stack and that it performs appropriate run-time checks on such things as array references. The −verify, −noverify, and -verifyremote options control the byte-code verification process.

`-classpath` *path*

> The path that *java* uses to look up the specified *classname* and all other classes that it loads. Specifying this option overrides the default path and the CLASSPATH environment variable.
>
> The class path is an ordered list of directories and zip files within and below which *java* searches for named classes. On UNIX systems, a path is specified as a colon-separated list of directories and zip files. On Windows systems, directories and zip files (which may have drive specifiers that use colons) are separated from each other with semicolons. For example, a UNIX `-classpath` specification might look like this:
>
> > -classpath /usr/lib/java/classes:.:˜/java/classes
>
> On a Windows system, the specification might be:
>
> > -classpath C:\tools\java\classes.zip;.;D:\users\david\classes
>
> A period by itself in the path indicates that the current working directory is searched. Directories and zip files are searched in the order they appear. Place the standard Java classes first in the path if you do not want them to be accidentally or maliciously overridden by classes with the same name in other directories.
>
> *java* expects to find class files in a directory hierarchy (or with a directory name within a zip file) that maps to the fully qualified name; of the class. Thus, on a UNIX system, Java would load the class `java.lang.String` by looking for the file *java/lang/String.class* beneath one of the directories specified in the class path. Similarly, on a Windows 95 or Windows NT system (which support long filenames), *java* would look for the file *java\lang\String.class* beneath a specified directory or within a specified zip file.
>
> If you do not specify `-classpath` or the CLASSPATH environment variable, the default class path is:
>
> > .:$JAVA/classes:$JAVA/classes.zip   *UNIX systems*
> > .;$JAVA\classes;$JAVA\classes.zip   *Windows systems*
>
> Where $JAVA is the main Java directory.

`-cs`, `-checksource`

> This options tells *java* to check the modification times on the specified class file and its corresponding source file. If the object file is out of date, it is automatically recompiled from the source.

`-D`*propertyname*`=`*value*

> Defines *propertyname* to equal *value* in the system properties list. Your Java program can then look up the specified value by its property name. You may specify any number of `-D` options. For example:
>
> > **%java -Dawt.button.color=gray -Dmy.class.pointsize=14 my.class**

Man Pages

`-debug`

> Causes *java* to display a password as it starts up. This password can be used to allow the *jdb* debugger to attach itself to this interpreter session. Note that this password should not be considered cryptologically secure.

`-ms initmem[k|m]`

> Specifies how much memory is allocated for the heap when the interpreter starts up. By default, *initmem* is specified in bytes. You can specify it in kilobytes by appending the letter k or in megabytes by appending the letter m. The default initial allocation is 1 MB. For large or memory intensive applications (such as the Java compiler), you can improve run-time performance by starting the interpreter with a larger amount of memory. You must specify an initial heap size of at least 1000 bytes.

`-mx maxmem[k|m]`

> Specifies the maximum heap size the interpreter will use for dynamically allocated objects and arrays. *maxmem* is specified in bytes by default. You can specify *maxmem* in kilobytes by appending the letter k and in megabytes by appending the letter m. The default maximum heap size is 16 MB. You must not specify a heap size less than 1000 bytes.

`-noasyncgc`

> Do not do garbage collection asynchronously. With this option specified, *java* only performs garbage collection when it runs out of memory or when the garbage collector is explicitly invoked. Without this option, *java* runs the garbage collector as a separate, low-priority thread.

`-noverify`

> Never run the byte-code verifier.

`-oss stacksize[k|m]`

> Sets the size of each thread's Java code stack. By default, *stacksize* is specified in bytes. You can specify it in kilobytes by appending the letter k or in megabytes by appending the letter m. The default value is 400 KB. You must specify at least 1000 bytes.

`-ss stacksize[k|m]`

> Sets the size of each thread's native code stack. By default, *stacksize* is specified in bytes. You can specify it in kilobytes by appending the letter k or in megabytes by appending the letter m. The default value is 128 KB. You must specify at least 1000 bytes.

`-v, -verbose`

> Print a terminal message each time *java* loads a class.

`-verbosegc`

> Print a message whenever the garbage collector frees memory.

`-verify`

> Run the byte-code verifier on all classes that are loaded.

```
-verifyremote
```
Run the byte-code verifier on all classes that are loaded through a class loader. (This generally means classes that are dynamically loaded from an untrusted location.) This is the default behavior for *java*.

ENVIRONMENT

CLASSPATH

Specifies an ordered list (colon-separated on UNIX, semicolon-separated on Windows systems) of directories and zip files in which *java* should look for class definitions. When a path is specified with this environment variable, *java* always implicitly appends the location of the system classes to the end of the path. If this environment variable is not specified, the default path is the current directory and the system classes. This variable is overridden by the `-classpath` option. See `-classpath` above for more information on specifying paths.

SEE ALSO

javac, jdb

Man Pages

javac — *The Java Compiler*

SYNOPSIS

javac [*options*] *files*

DESCRIPTION

javac is the Java compiler—it compiles Java source code (in *.java* files) into Java byte-codes (in *.class* files). The Java compiler is itself written in Java.

javac may be passed any number of Java source files, whose names must all end with the *.java* extension. *javac* produces a separate *.class* class file for each class defined in the source files, regardless of how many source files there are. In other words, there need not be a one-to-one mapping between Java source files and Java class files. Note also that the compiler requires that there be only a single public class defined in any one source file, and that the name of the file (minus the *.java* extension) be the same as the name of the class (minus its package name, of course).

By default, *javac* places the class files it generates in the same directory as the corresponding source file. You can override this behavior with the -d option.

When a source file references a class that is not defined in another source file on the command line, *javac* searches for the definition of that class using the class path. The default class path contains only the system classes. You may specify additional classes and packages to be searched with the -classpath option or the CLASSPATH environment variable.

OPTIONS

-classpath *path*

> The path that *javac* uses to look up classes referenced in the specified source code. This option overrides the default path and any path specified by the CLASSPATH environment variable. The *path* specified is an ordered list of directories and zip files, separated by colons on UNIX systems or semicolons on Windows systems.

> To specify additional directories or zip files to be searched, without overriding the default system class path, use the CLASSPATH environment variable. See the *java* reference page for more information on specifying paths.

-d *directory*

> The directory in which (or beneath which) class files should be stored. By default, *javac* stores the *.class* files it generates in the same directory as the *.java* file that those classes were defined in. If the -d flag is specified, however, the specified *directory* is treated as the root of the class hierarchy and *.class* files are placed in this directory, or in the appropriate subdirectory below it, depending on the package name of the class. Thus, the following command:

> **%javac -d java/classes java/src/Checkers.java**

> places the file *Checkers.class* in the directory *java/classes* if the *Check-*

ers.java file has no `package` statement. On the other hand, if the source file specifies that it is in a package:

```
package david.games;
```

then the *.class* file is stored in *java/classes/david/games*.

When the **-d** option is specified, *javac* automatically creates any directories it needs to store its class files in the appropriate place.

-g   This option tells *javac* to add line numbers and local variable information to the output class files, for use by debuggers. By default, *javac* only generates the line numbers. With the **-O** option, *javac* does not generate even that information.

-nowarn
     Tells *javac* not to print warning messages. Errors are still reported as usual.

-O   Enable optimization of class files. This option may cause *javac* to compile `static`, `final`, and `private` methods inline, so that they execute faster. The trade-off is that the class files will be larger. This option also prevents *javac* from adding line number debugging information to the class files.

-verbose
     Tells the compiler to display messages about what it is doing.

ENVIRONMENT

CLASSPATH
     Specifies an ordered list (colon-separated on UNIX, semicolon-separated on Windows systems) of directories and zip files in which *javac* should look for class definitions. When a path is specified with this environment variable, *javac* always implictly appends the location of the system classes to the end of the path. If this environment variable is not specified, the default path is the current directory and the system classes. This variable is overridden by the **-classpath** option.

SEE ALSO

java, jdb

Man Pages

javadoc — The Java Documentation Generator

SYNOPSIS

javadoc [*options*] *packagename*
javadoc [*options*] *filenames*

DESCRIPTION

javadoc generates API documentation, in HTML format, for the specified package, or for the individual Java source files specified on the command line.

When a package name is specified on the command line, *javadoc* looks for a corresponding package directory relative to the class path. It then parses all of the *.java* source files in that directory and generates an HTML documentation file for each class and an HTML index of the classes in the package. By default, the HTML files are placed in the current directory. The **-d** option allows you to override this default.

Note that the *packagename* argument to *javadoc* is the name of the package (components separated by periods) and not the name of the package directory. You may need to specify the **-classpath** option or the CLASSPATH environment variable so that Java can find your package source code correctly, if it is not stored in the same location as the package class files.

javadoc may also be invoked with any number of Java source files specified on the command line. Note that these are filenames, not class names, and are specified with any necessary directory components, and with the *.java* extension. When *javadoc* is invoked in this way, it reads the specified source files and generates HTML files (in the current directory, by default) that describe each public class defined in the specified source files.

The class documentation files that *javadoc* generates describe the class (or interface) and its inheritance hierarchy, and index and describe each of the non-private fields in the class. The generated file also contains any "doc comments" that are associated with the class and with its methods, constructors, and variables. A "doc comment," or documentation comment, is a Java comment that begins with /** and ends with */. A doc comment may include any HTML markup tags (although it should not include structuring tags like <H1> or <HR>), and may also include tag values that are treated specially by *javadoc*. These special tags and their syntax are documented fully in Section 10, *Java Syntax.*

OPTIONS

-classpath *path*

The path that *javadoc* uses to look up the specified *packagename*. This option overrides the default path and any path specified by the CLASSPATH environment variable. The *path* specified is an ordered list of directories and zip files, separated by colons on UNIX systems or semicolons on Windows systems.

To specify additional directories or zip files to search without overriding the default system class path, use the CLASSPATH environment variable. See the *java* reference page for more information on specifying paths.

-d *directory*

    The directory in which *javadoc* should store the HTML files it generates. The default is the current directory.

-verbose

    Tells *javadoc* to print messages about what it is doing.

ENVIRONMENT

CLASSPATH

    Specifies an ordered list (colon-separated on UNIX, semicolon-separated on Windows systems) of directories and zip files in which *javadoc* should look for class definitions. When a path is specified with this environment variable, *javadoc* always implictly appends the location of the system classes to the end of the path. If this environment variable is not specified, then the default path is the current directory and the system classes. This variable is overridden by the **-classpath** option.

BUGS

When *javadoc* cannot find a specified package, it produces a stub HTML file and does not warn you that the package was not found.

SEE ALSO

java, javac

Man Pages

javah — *Native Method C File Generator*

SYNOPSIS

javah [*options*] *classnames*

DESCRIPTION

javah generates C header and source files (*.h* and *.c* files) that describe the specified classes. These C files provide the information necessary for implementing `native` methods for the specified classes in C.

By default, *javah* generates a header file for the specified class or classes. This header file declares a C `struct` that contains fields that correspond to the instance fields of the Java class. The header also declares a procedure that you must implement for each of the native methods that the Java class contains. (A full description of how to implement Java `native` methods in C is beyond the scope of this reference page.)

If *javah* is run with the `-stubs` option, it generates a *.c* file that contains additional stub procedures necessary for linking the native method into the Java environment. Note that you should not put your native method implementation in this generated stub file.

By default, *javah* creates C files in the current directory and bases their name on the name of the class. If the name of the class includes a package name, then the C files include all the components of the fully qualified class name, with periods replaced by underscores. You can override this default behavior with the `-d` and `-o` options.

OPTIONS

`-classpath` *path*

> The path that *javah* uses to look up the classes named on the command line. This option overrides the default path, and any path specified by the `CLASSPATH` environment variable. The *path* specified is an ordered list of directories and zip files, separated by colons on UNIX systems or semicolons on Windows systems.

> To specify additional directories or zip files for *javah* to search without overriding the default system class path, use the `CLASSPATH` environment variable. See the *java* reference page for more information on specifying paths.

`-d` *directory*

> Specifies a directory where *javah* should store the files it generates. By default it stores them in the current directory. This option does not work with `-o`—you must specify any desired directory within the `-o` filename.

`-o` *outputfile*

> Combine all *.h* or *.c* file output into a single file, *outputfile*. This is a convenience when you want to implement native methods for a number of classes in a single package. It allows you to avoid having many short *.h* and *.c* files that must be manipulated separately.

`-stubs`

> Generate *.c* stub files for the class or classes, and do not generate the *.h* header files. Without this option, *javah* generates header files.

`-td directory`

> The directory where *javah* should store temporary files. The default is */tmp.*

`-v`   Verbose. Causes *javah* to print messages about what it is doing.

ENVIRONMENT

CLASSPATH

> Specifies an ordered list (colon-separated on UNIX, semicolon-separated on Windows systems) of directories and zip files in which *javah* should look for class definitions. When a path is specified with this environment variable, *javah* always implictly appends the location of the system classes to the end of the path. If this environment variable is not specified, the default path is the current directory and the system classes. This variable is overridden by the `-classpath` option.

SEE ALSO

java, javac

Man Pages

javap — The Java Class Disassembler

SYNOPSIS

javap [*options*] *classnames*

DESCRIPTION

javap disassembles the class files specified by the class names on the command line and prints a human-readable version of those classes.

By default, *javap* prints declarations of the non-`private` and non-`protected` fields (i.e., fields with `public` or default visibility), methods, constructors (even implicit constructors), and static initializers in each of the classes specified on the command line. The `-l`, `-p`, and `-c` options specify additional information to be printed.

OPTIONS

-c   Print the Java Virtual Machine instructions for each of the methods in each of the specified classes. This option disassembles all methods, including `private` and `protected` methods.

-classpath *path*

The path that *javap* uses to look up the classes named on the command line. This option overrides the default path and any path specified by the CLASSPATH environment variable. The *path* specified is an ordered list of directories and zip files, separated by colons on UNIX systems or semicolons on Windows systems.

To specify additional directories or zip files for *javap* to search without overriding the default system class path, use the CLASSPATH environment variable. See the *java* reference page for more information on specifying paths.

-l   Prints line numbers and local variable tables in addition to the public fields of the class. Note that line numbers and local variable information is included for use with debuggers. Local variable information is available only if a class was compiled with the -g option to *javac*; line number information is available only if a class was compiled *without* the -O option.

-p   Prints `private` and `protected` methods and variables of the specified class in addition to the `public` ones. Note that some compilers (though not *javac*) may allow this `private` field information to be "obfuscated" in such a way that `private` fields and method arguments no longer have meaningful names. This makes Java classes harder to disassemble or reverse engineer.

ENVIRONMENT

CLASSPATH

Specifies an ordered list (colon-separated on UNIX, semicolon-separated on Windows systems) of directories and zip files in which *javap* should look for class definitions. When a path is specified with this environment variable, *javap* always implictly appends the location of the system classes to the end of the path. If this environment variable is not specified, the default path is the current directory and the system classes. This variable is overridden by the -classpath option.

SEE ALSO

java, javac

Man Pages

jdb — The Java Debugger

SYNOPSIS

jdb [*java options*] *class*
jdb [-host hostname] -password *password*

DESCRIPTION

jdb is a debugger for Java classes. It is text-based, command-line oriented, and has a command syntax like that of the UNIX *dbx* or *gdb* debuggers.

When *jdb* is invoked with the name of a Java class, it starts another copy of the *java* interpreter, passing any specified *java* options to the interpreter. *jdb* is itself a Java program, running in its own copy of the interpreter. This new interpreter loads the specified class file and stops for debugging before executing the first Java byte-code.

jdb may also be started with the -password and optional -host arguments. Invoked in this way, *jdb* "attaches itself" to an already running copy of the interpreter. In order for this to work, the Java interpreter running the program to be debugged must have been started with the -debug option. When the interpreter is started with this option, it prints a password that must be used with the *jdb* -password option.

Once a debugging session is started, you may issue any of the commands described below.

OPTIONS

When invoking *jdb* with a specified class file, any of the *java* interpreter options may be specified. See the *java* reference page for an explanation of these options.

When attaching *jdb* to an already running Java interpreter, the following options are available:

-host *hostname*
> Specifies the name of the host upon which the desired interpreter session is running.

-password *password*
> This option is required to attach to a running interpreter. The interpreter must have been started with the -debug option, and this -password option specifies the password that the interpreter generated. Only a debugger that knows this password is allowed to attach to the interpreter. Note that the passwords generated by *java* should not be considered cryptologically secure.

COMMANDS

jdb understands the following debugging commands:

! !
> This is a shorthand command that is replaced with the text of the last command entered. It may be followed with additional text that is appended to that previous command.

---

catch [*exception class*]
> Cause a breakpoint whenever the specified exception is thrown. If no exception is specified, the command lists the exceptions currently being caught. Use `ignore` to stop these breakpoints from occurring.

classes
> List all classes that have been loaded.

clear [*class:line*]
> Remove the breakpoint set at the specified line of the specified class. Typing `clear` or `stop` with no arguments displays a list of current breakpoints and the line numbers that they are set at.

cont
> Resume execution. This command should be used when the current thread is stopped at a breakpoint.

down [*n*]
> Move down *n* frames in the call stack of the current thread. If *n* is not specified, move down one frame.

dump *id(s)*
> Print the value of all fields of the specified object or objects. If you specify the name of a class, `dump` displays all class (static) methods and variables of the class, and also displays the superclass and list of implemented interfaces. Objects and classes may be specified by name or by their eight-digit hexadecimal ID number. Threads may also be specified with the shorthand t@*thread-number*.

exit (or quit)
> Quit *jdb*.

gc
> Run the garbage collector to force unused objects to be reclaimed.

help (or ?)
> Display a list of all *jdb* commands.

ignore *exception class*
> Do not treat the specified exception as a breakpoint. This command turns off a `catch` command.

list [*line number*]
> List the specified line of source code as well as several lines that appear before and after it. If no line number is specified, use the line number of the current stack frame of the current thread. The lines listed are from the source file of the current stack frame of the current thread. Use the `use` command to tell *jdb* where to find source files.

load *classname*
> Load the specified class into *jdb*.

locals
> Display a list of local variables for the current stack frame. Java code must be compiled with the -g option in order to contain local variable information.

memory Display a summary of memory usage for the Java program being debugged.

methods *class*

List all methods of the specified class. Use dump to list the instance variables or an object or the class (static) variables of a class.

print *id(s)*

Print the value of the specified item or items. Each item may be a class, object, field, or local variable, and may be specified by name or by eight-digit hexadecimal ID number. You may also refer to threads with the special syntax t@*thread-number*. The print command displays an object's value by invoking its toString() method.

resume [*thread(s)*]

Resume execution of the specified thread or threads. If no threads are specified, all suspended threads are resumed. See also suspend.

run [*class*] [*args*]

Run the main() method of the specified class, passing the specified arguments to it. If no class or arguments are specified, use the class and arguments specified on the *jdb* command line.

step Run the current line of the current thread and stop again.

stop [at *class:line*]
stop [in *class.method*]

Set a breakpoint at the specified line of the specified class or at the beginning of the specified method of the specified class. Program execution stops when it reaches this line or enters the method. If stop is executed with no arguments, then it lists the current breakpoints.

suspend [*thread(s)*]

Suspend the specified thread or threads. If no threads are specified, suspend all running threads. Use resume to restart them.

thread *thread*

Set the current thread to the specified thread. This thread is used implicitly by a number of other *jdb* commands. The thread may be specified by name or number.

threadgroup *name*

Set the current thread group to the named thread group.

threadgroups

List all thread groups running in the Java interpreter session being debugged.

threads [*threadgroups*]

List all threads in the named thread group. If no thread group is specified, list all threads in the current thread group (specified by thread-group).

up [*n*]

Move up *n* frames in the call stack of the current thread. If *n* is not specified, move up one frame.

use [*source-file-path*]

      Set the path used by *jdb* to look up source files for the classes being debugged. If no path is specified, display the current source path being used.

where [*thread*] [all]

      Display a stack trace for the specified thread. If no thread is specified, display a stack trace for the current thread. If all is specified, display a stack trace for all threads.

ENVIRONMENT

CLASSPATH

      Specifies an ordered list (colon-separated on UNIX, semicolon-separated on Windows systems) of directories and zip files in which *jdb* should look for class definitions. When a path is specified with this environment variable, *jdb* always implictly appends the location of the system classes to the end of the path. If this environment variable is not specified, the default path is the current directory and the system classes. This variable is overridden by the -classpath option.

SEE ALSO

java

Man Pages

Part IV

API Quick Reference

Part IV is the real heart of this book. It is a *complete* quick reference to the Java API. The *How to Use This Book* section at the beginning of the book contains important information about using this quick reference, and getting the most out of it.

18

The java.applet Package

The `java.applet` package is a small one. It contains the `Applet` class, which is the superclass of all applets, and three related interfaces. An *applet* is a small, embeddable Java program. Figure 18-1 shows the class hierarchy of this package.

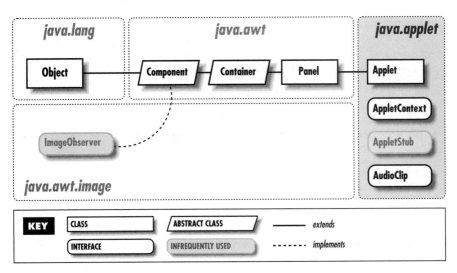

Figure 18-1: The java.applet package

See Section 4, *Applets*, for more information about this package.

java.applet.Applet

This class implements an applet. To create your own applet, you should create a subclass of this class and override some or all of the following methods. Note that you never need to call these methods—they are called when appropriate by a Web browser or other applet viewer.

getAppletInfo()
> Return text explaining who wrote the applet, what version it is, what the copyright is, and so on.

getParameterInfo()
> Return an arbitrary-length array of 3-element arrays of strings. Each element of this array has three elements and describes one of the parameters that this applet understands. The three elements of each parameter description are strings specifying, respectively, the parameter's name, type, and description.

init()
> Perform any initialization for the applet.

start()
> This is the method that makes the applet do its thing. Often, it starts a thread that runs the main applet code.

stop()
> Stop the applet from executing.

destroy()
> Free up any resources that the applet is holding.

In addition to these methods that your applet must define, the Applet class also defines some useful methods that your applet may call. resize() asks the Web browser or applet viewer to give your applet the amount of space it wants. A number of the other Applet methods are simple wrappers around AppletContext methods.

```
public class Applet extends Panel {
    // Default Constructor: public Applet()
    // Public Instance Methods
        public void destroy(); // Empty
        public AppletContext getAppletContext();
        public String getAppletInfo();
        public AudioClip getAudioClip(URL url);
        public AudioClip getAudioClip(URL url, String name);
        public URL getCodeBase();
        public URL getDocumentBase();
        public Image getImage(URL url);
        public Image getImage(URL url, String name);
        public String getParameter(String name);
        public String[][] getParameterInfo();
        public void init(); // Empty
```

```
        public boolean isActive();
        public void play(URL url);
        public void play(URL url, String name);
        public void resize(int width, int height); // Overrides Component.resize()
        public void resize(Dimension d); // Overrides Component.resize()
        public final void setStub(AppletStub stub);
        public void showStatus(String msg);
        public void start(); // Empty
        public void stop(); // Empty

}
```

java.applet.AppletContext

This interface defines the methods that allow an applet to interact with the context in which it runs (which is usually a Web browser or an applet viewer). The object that implements the `AppletContext` interface is returned by `Applet.getApplet-Context()`. You can use it to take advantage of a Web browser's cache, or to display a message to the user in the Web browser's or applet viewer's message area.

The `getAudioClip()` and `getImage()` methods may make use of a Web browser's caching mechanism. `showDocument()` and `showStatus()` give an applet a small measure of control over the appearance of the browser or applet viewer. The `getApplet()` and `getApplets()` methods allow an applet to find out what other applets are running at the same time.

```
public abstract interface AppletContext {
    // Public Instance Methods
        public abstract Applet getApplet(String name);
        public abstract Enumeration getApplets();
        public abstract AudioClip getAudioClip(URL url);
        public abstract Image getImage(URL url);
        public abstract void showDocument(URL url);
        public abstract void showDocument(URL url, String target);
        public abstract void showStatus(String status);

}
```

java.applet.AppletStub

This is an internal interface used when implementing an applet viewer.

```
public abstract interface AppletStub {
    // Public Instance Methods
        public abstract void appletResize(int width, int height);
        public abstract AppletContext getAppletContext();
        public abstract URL getCodeBase();
        public abstract URL getDocumentBase();
```

→

java.applet

```
        public abstract String getParameter(String name);
        public abstract boolean isActive();

}
```

java.applet.AudioClip

This interface describes the essential methods that an audio clip must have. `Applet-Context.getAudioClip()` and `Applet.getAudioClip()` both return an object that implements this interface. The `AudioClip` interface is in the `java.applet` package only because there is not a better place for it.

```
public abstract interface AudioClip {
    // Public Instance Methods
        public abstract void loop();
        public abstract void play();
        public abstract void stop();

}
```

The java.awt Package

The `java.awt` package is the Abstract Windowing Toolkit. The classes of this package may be roughly divided into three categories (see Figure 19-1 and Figure 19-2).

- Graphics: These classes define colors, fonts, images, polygons, and so forth.

- Components: These classes are GUI (graphical user interface) components such as buttons, menus, lists, and dialog boxes.

- Layout Managers: These classes control the layout of components within their container objects.

Note that a separate package, `java.awt.image`, contains classes for image manipulation.

In the first category of classes, `Graphics` is probably the most important. This class defines methods for doing line and text drawing and image painting. It relies on other classes such as `Color`, `Font`, `Image`, and `Polygon`. `Image` is itself an important class, used in many places in `java.awt` and throughout the related package `java.awt.image`. `Event` is another important class that describes a user or window system event that has occurred.

`Component` and `MenuComponent` are root classes in the second category of `java.awt` classes. Their subclasses are GUI components that can appear in interfaces and menus. The `Container` class is one that contains components and arranges them visually. You add components to a container with the `add()` method and specify a layout manager for the container with the `setLayout()` method. Typically, you subclass a container class to provide a definition of the methods that handle `Event` objects generated by the components it contains. These event-handling methods define the dynamic behavior of your interface.

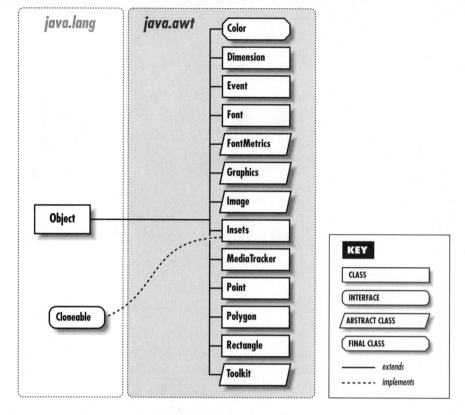

Figure 19-1: Graphics classes of the java.awt package

There are three commonly used `Container` subclasses. `Frame` is a toplevel window that can contain a menu bar and have a custom cursor and an icon. `Dialog` is a dialog window. `Panel` is a container that does not have its own window—it is contained within some other container.

The third category of `java.awt` classes is the layout managers. The subclasses of `LayoutManager` are responsible for arranging the `Component` objects contained within a specified `Container`. `GridBagLayout`, `BorderLayout`, and `GridLayout` are probably the most useful of these layout managers.

See Section 5, *Graphical User Interfaces*, for more detailed information on the `java.awt` package and for examples of using these classes.

java.awt.BorderLayout

This class implements the `LayoutManager` interface to lay out `Component` objects in a `Container`. The `BorderLayout` arranges components that have been added to their `Container` (using the `Container.add()` method) with the names "North," "South," "East," "West," and "Center." These named components are arranged along

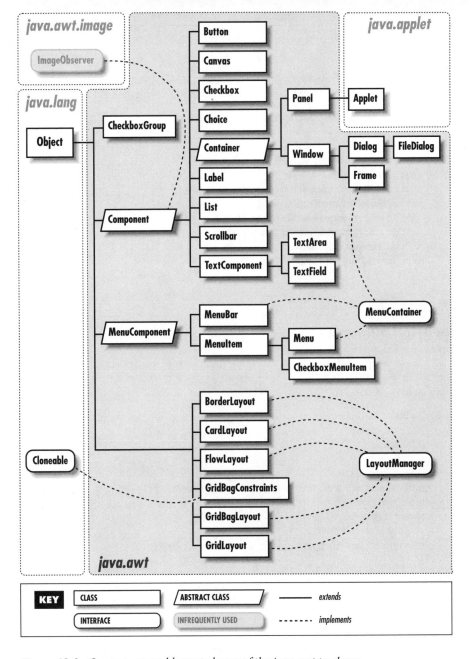

KEY

| CLASS | ABSTRACT CLASS | ———— extends |
| INTERFACE | INFREQUENTLY USED | - - - - - implements |

Figure 19-2: Component and layout classes of the java.awt package

java.awt.BorderLayout
←

the edges and in the center of the container. The *hgap* and *vgap* arguments to the BorderLayout constructor specify the desired horizontal and vertical spacing between adjacent components.

→

Note that applications should never call the `LayoutManager` methods of this class directly; the `Container` for which the `BorderLayout` is registered does this.

```
public class BorderLayout extends Object implements LayoutManager {
    // Public Constructors
        public BorderLayout( );  // Empty
        public BorderLayout(int hgap, int vgap);
    // Public Instance Methods
        public void addLayoutComponent(String name, Component comp);
        public void layoutContainer(Container target);
        public Dimension minimumLayoutSize(Container target);
        public Dimension preferredLayoutSize(Container target);
        public void removeLayoutComponent(Component comp);
        public String toString( );  // Overrides Object.toString( )
}
```

java.awt.Button

This class encapsulates a GUI pushbutton that displays a specified textual label. When the button is clicked, it generates an `ACTION_EVENT` event with the button label as its argument.

```
public class Button extends Component {
    // Public Constructors
        public Button( );
        public Button(String label);
    // Public Instance Methods
        public synchronized void addNotify( );  // Overrides Component.addNotify( )
        public String getLabel( );
        public void setLabel(String label);
    // Protected Instance Methods
        protected String paramString( );  // Overrides Component.paramString( )
}
```

java.awt.Canvas

This class is a `Component` that does no default drawing or event-handling on its own. You can subclass it to display any kind of drawing or image, and to handle any kind of user input event. `Canvas` generates `KEY_ACTION`, `KEY_ACTION_RELEASE`, `KEY_PRESS`, `KEY_RELEASE`, `MOUSE_ENTER`, `MOUSE_EXIT`, `MOUSE_DOWN`, `MOUSE_UP`, `MOUSE_MOVE`, and `MOUSE_DRAG` events.

```
public class Canvas extends Component {
    // Default Constructor: public Canvas( )
    // Public Instance Methods
```

```
    public synchronized void addNotify( ); // Overrides Component.addNotify( )
    public void paint(Graphics g); // Overrides Component.paint( )

}
```

java.awt.CardLayout

This class is a LayoutManager that ensures that only one of the components it manages is visible at a time. The standard LayoutManager methods are called by the Container object, and should not be called directly by applet or application code. first(), last(), next(), previous(), and show() make a particular Component in the Container visible. The names with which the components are added to the container are used only by the show() method.

```
public class CardLayout extends Object implements LayoutManager {
    // Public Constructors
        public CardLayout( );
        public CardLayout(int hgap, int vgap);
    // Public Instance Methods
        public void addLayoutComponent(String name, Component comp);
        public void first(Container parent);
        public void last(Container parent);
        public void layoutContainer(Container parent);
        public Dimension minimumLayoutSize(Container parent);
        public void next(Container parent);
        public Dimension preferredLayoutSize(Container parent);
        public void previous(Container parent);
        public void removeLayoutComponent(Component comp);
        public void show(Container parent, String name);
        public String toString( ); // Overrides Object.toString( )

}
```

java.awt.Checkbox

This class encapsulates a GUI checkbox with a textual label. The Checkbox maintains a boolean state—whether it is checked or not. The checkbox may optionally be part of a CheckboxGroup. When a Checkbox is selected, it generates an ACTION_EVENT event with a boolean containing the new checkbox state as its argument.

See also CheckboxGroup.

```
public class Checkbox extends Component {
    // Public Constructors
        public Checkbox( ); // Empty
        public Checkbox(String label);
        public Checkbox(String label, CheckboxGroup group, boolean state);
    // Public Instance Methods
```

→

java.awt

```
        public synchronized void addNotify( );  // Overrides Component.addNotify( )
        public CheckboxGroup getCheckboxGroup( );
        public String getLabel( );
        public boolean getState( );
        public void setCheckboxGroup(CheckboxGroup g);
        public void setLabel(String label);
        public void setState(boolean state);
    // Protected Instance Methods
        protected String paramString( );  // Overrides Component.paramString( )

}
```

java.awt.CheckboxGroup

A CheckboxGroup object enforces mutual exclusion (also known as "radio button" behavior) among any number of Checkbox buttons. A Checkbox component can specify a CheckboxGroup object with Checkbox.setCheckboxGroup(). If a Checkbox with a given CheckboxGroup object is selected, then the Checkbox-Group ensures that the previously selected Checkbox becomes unselected.

See also Checkbox.

```
public class CheckboxGroup extends Object {
    // Public Constructor
        public CheckboxGroup( );  // Empty
    // Public Instance Methods
        public Checkbox getCurrent( );
        public synchronized void setCurrent(Checkbox box);
        public String toString( );  // Overrides Object.toString( )

}
```

java.awt.CheckboxMenuItem

This class encapsulates a checkbox with a textual label in a GUI menu. It maintains a boolean state—whether it is checked or not.

See also MenuItem.

```
public class CheckboxMenuItem extends MenuItem {
    // Public Constructor
        public CheckboxMenuItem(String label);
    // Public Instance Methods
        public synchronized void addNotify( );  // Overrides MenuItem.addNotify( )
        public boolean getState( );
        public String paramString( );  // Overrides MenuItem.paramString( )
        public void setState(boolean t);

}
```

java.awt.Choice

This class encapsulates an "option menu"—a menu of options that drops down from a button. The currently selected option is displayed as the label of the button. The button displays a special icon to indicate that a menu is available from it.

The addItem() method adds an item with the specified label to a Choice menu. getSelectedIndex() returns the numerical position of the selected item in the menu, and getSelectedItem() returns the label of the selected item.

When an item is selected from the menu, Choice generates an ACTION_EVENT event with the label of the selected item as its argument.

```
public class Choice extends Component {
    // Public Constructor
        public Choice();
    // Public Instance Methods
        public synchronized void addItem(String item) throws NullPointerException;
        public synchronized void addNotify(); // Overrides Component.addNotify()
        public int countItems();
        public String getItem(int index);
        public int getSelectedIndex();
        public String getSelectedItem();
        public synchronized void select(int pos) throws IllegalArgumentException;
        public void select(String str);
    // Protected Instance Methods
        protected String paramString(); // Overrides Component.paramString()
}
```

java.awt.Color

The Color object describes a color. The Color() constructors describe a color as red, green, and blue components between 0 and 255, or as floating-point values between 0.0 and 1.0. The class method Color.getHSBColor() creates a color using the hue/saturation/brightness color model.

brighter() and darker() are useful methods when creating a palette of related colors. The getColor() methods look up a color name in the properties database and convert the resulting integer color value into a Color object. Two of these methods provide a default value to be used in case the specified color name is not found.

```
public final class Color extends Object {
    // Public Constructors
        public Color(int r, int g, int b);
        public Color(int rgb);
        public Color(float r, float g, float b);
    // Constants
        public final static Color black;
        public final static Color blue;
        public final static Color cyan;
```

$\rightarrow$

```
            public final static Color darkGray;
            public final static Color gray;
            public final static Color green;
            public final static Color lightGray;
            public final static Color magenta;
            public final static Color orange;
            public final static Color pink;
            public final static Color red;
            public final static Color white;
            public final static Color yellow;
       // Class Methods
            public static int HSBtoRGB(float hue, float saturation, float brightness);
            public static float[] RGBtoHSB(int r, int g, int b, float[] hsbvals);
            public static Color getColor(String nm);
            public static Color getColor(String nm, Color v);
            public static Color getColor(String nm, int v);
            public static Color getHSBColor(float h, float s, float b);
       // Public Instance Methods
            public Color brighter();
            public Color darker();
            public boolean equals(Object obj);  // Overrides Object.equals()
            public int getBlue();
            public int getGreen();
            public int getRGB();
            public int getRed();
            public int hashCode();  // Overrides Object.hashCode()
            public String toString();  // Overrides Object.toString()

}
```

java.awt.Component

Component is the superclass of all GUI components (except menu components) in the java.awt package. You may not instantiate a Component directly; only one of its subclasses.

Component defines many methods. Some of these are intended to be implemented by subclasses. Some are used internally. Some are to be implemented to handle events. And many are useful utility methods for working with GUI components. getParent() returns the Container that a Component is contained in. set-Background(), setForeground() and setFont() set the specified display attributes of a component. hide(), show(), enable(), and disable() perform the specified actions for a component. createImage() creates an Image object from a specified ImageProducer, or creates an offscreen image that can be draw into and used for double-buffering during animation.

Component generates GOT_FOCUS and LOST_FOCUS events when it gains and loses the input focus.

```
public abstract class Component extends Object implements ImageObserver {
    // No Constructor
    // Public Instance Methods
        public boolean action(Event evt, Object what);
        public void addNotify();
        public Rectangle bounds();
        public int checkImage(Image image, ImageObserver observer);
        public int checkImage(Image image, int width, int height, ImageObserver observer);
        public Image createImage(ImageProducer producer);
        public Image createImage(int width, int height);
        public void deliverEvent(Event e);
        public synchronized void disable();
        public synchronized void enable();
        public void enable(boolean cond);
        public Color getBackground();
        public synchronized ColorModel getColorModel();
        public Font getFont();
        public FontMetrics getFontMetrics(Font font);
        public Color getForeground();
        public Graphics getGraphics();
        public Container getParent();
        public ComponentPeer getPeer();
        public Toolkit getToolkit();
        public boolean gotFocus(Event evt, Object what);
        public boolean handleEvent(Event evt);
        public synchronized void hide();
        public boolean imageUpdate(Image img, int flags, int x, int y, int w, int h);
        public synchronized boolean inside(int x, int y);
        public void invalidate();
        public boolean isEnabled();
        public boolean isShowing();
        public boolean isValid();
        public boolean isVisible();
        public boolean keyDown(Event evt, int key);
        public boolean keyUp(Event evt, int key);
        public void layout();  // Empty
        public void list();
        public void list(PrintStream out);
        public void list(PrintStream out, int indent);
        public Component locate(int x, int y);
        public Point location();
        public boolean lostFocus(Event evt, Object what);
        public Dimension minimumSize();
        public boolean mouseDown(Event evt, int x, int y);
        public boolean mouseDrag(Event evt, int x, int y);
        public boolean mouseEnter(Event evt, int x, int y);
        public boolean mouseExit(Event evt, int x, int y);
        public boolean mouseMove(Event evt, int x, int y);
        public boolean mouseUp(Event evt, int x, int y);
        public void move(int x, int y);
        public void nextFocus();
        public void paint(Graphics g);  // Empty
        public void paintAll(Graphics g);
```

java.awt

```
    public boolean postEvent(Event e);
    public Dimension preferredSize();
    public boolean prepareImage(Image image, ImageObserver observer);
    public boolean prepareImage(Image image, int width, int height, ImageObserver observer);
    public void print(Graphics g);
    public void printAll(Graphics g);
    public synchronized void removeNotify();
    public void repaint();
    public void repaint(long tm);
    public void repaint(int x, int y, int width, int height);
    public void repaint(long tm, int x, int y, int width, int height);
    public void requestFocus();
    public synchronized void reshape(int x, int y, int width, int height);
    public void resize(int width, int height);
    public void resize(Dimension d);
    public synchronized void setBackground(Color c);
    public synchronized void setFont(Font f);
    public synchronized void setForeground(Color c);
    public synchronized void show();
    public void show(boolean cond);
    public Dimension size();
    public String toString();  // Overrides Object.toString()
    public void update(Graphics g);
    public void validate();
// Protected Instance Methods
    protected String paramString();

}
```

---

java.awt.Container

This class implements a component that can contain other components. You cannot instantiate `Container` directly, but must use one of its subclasses, such as `Panel` or `Frame`, or `Dialog`. Once a `Container` is created, you may set its `LayoutManager` with `setLayout()`, add components to it with `add()`, and remove them with `remove()`. `getComponents()` returns an array of the components contained in a `Container`. `locate()` determines within which contained component a specified point falls. `list()` produces helpful debugging output.

```
public abstract class Container extends Component {
    // No Constructor
    // Public Instance Methods
    public Component add(Component comp);
    public synchronized Component add(Component comp, int pos);
    public synchronized Component add(String name, Component comp);
    public synchronized void addNotify();  // Overrides Component.addNotify()
    public int countComponents();
    public void deliverEvent(Event e);  // Overrides Component.deliverEvent()
    public synchronized Component getComponent(int n) throws ArrayIndexOutOfBoundsException;
    public synchronized Component[] getComponents();
    public LayoutManager getLayout();
    public Insets insets();
```

```
        public synchronized void layout( );  // Overrides Component.layout( )
        public void list(PrintStream out, int indent);  // Overrides Component.list( )
        public Component locate(int x, int y);  // Overrides Component.locate( )
        public synchronized Dimension minimumSize( );  // Overrides Component.minimumSize( )
        public void paintComponents(Graphics g);
        public synchronized Dimension preferredSize( );  // Overrides Component.preferredSize( )
        public void printComponents(Graphics g);
        public synchronized void remove(Component comp);
        public synchronized void removeAll( );
        public synchronized void removeNotify( );  // Overrides Component.removeNotify( )
        public void setLayout(LayoutManager mgr);
        public synchronized void validate( );  // Overrides Component.validate( )
    // Protected Instance Methods
        protected String paramString( );  // Overrides Component.paramString( )

}
```

java.awt.Dialog

This class encapsulates a dialog box window. A `Dialog` may be modal so that it blocks user input to all other windows until dismissed, may optionally have a title, and may be resizable. A `Dialog` object is a `Container` and `Component` objects can be added to it in the normal way with the `add()` method. The default `Layout-Manager` for `Dialog` is `BorderLayout`. You may specify a different `Layout-Manager` object with `setLayout()`. Call the `Window.dispose()` method when the `Dialog` is no longer needed so that its window system resources may be reused.

Java programs typically subclass `Dialog` and provide customized event handling for the dialog and the components it contains by overriding the event-handling methods such as `Component.action()`, `Component.mouseDown()`, and `Component.-keyDown()`. The `Dialog` class itself generates `WINDOW_DESTROY`, `WINDOW_ICONIFY`, `WINDOW_DEICONIFY`, and `WINDOW_MOVED` events.

```
public class Dialog extends Window {
    // Public Constructors
        public Dialog(Frame parent, boolean modal);
        public Dialog(Frame parent, String title, boolean modal);
    // Public Instance Methods
        public synchronized void addNotify( );  // Overrides Window.addNotify( )
        public String getTitle( );
        public boolean isModal( );
        public boolean isResizable( );
        public void setResizable(boolean resizable);
        public void setTitle(String title);
```

java.awt

→

```
    // Protected Instance Methods
        protected String paramString( );  // Overrides Container.paramString( )
}
```

java.awt.Dimension

This class has two public instance variables that describe the width and height of something. The width and height fields are public and may be manipulated directly.

```
public class Dimension extends Object {
    // Public Constructors
        public Dimension( );
        public Dimension(Dimension d );
        public Dimension(int width, int height );
    // Public Instance Variables
        public int height;
        public int width;
    // Public Instance Methods
        public String toString( );  // Overrides Object.toString( )
}
```

java.awt.Event

This class contains public instance variables that describe some kind of GUI event. The class contains a large number of constants. Some of the constants specify the event type and are values for the id variable. Other constants are values for keys, like the function keys, that do not have ASCII (or Latin-1) values, and are set on the key field. Other constants are mask values that are ORed into the modifiers field to describe the state of the modifier keys on the keyboard. The target field is very important—it is the object for which the event occurred. The when field specifies when the event occurred. The x and y fields specify the mouse coordinates at which it occurred. Finally, the arg field is a value specific to the type of the event. Not all fields have valid values for all types of events.

```
public class Event extends Object {
    // Public Constructors
        public Event(Object target, long when, int id, int x, int y, int key, int modifiers, Object arg );
        public Event(Object target, long when, int id, int x, int y, int key, int modifiers );
        public Event(Object target, int id, Object arg );
    // Constants
    // Event Type Constants
        public final static int ACTION_EVENT;
        public final static int GOT_FOCUS, LOST_FOCUS;
        public final static int KEY_ACTION, KEY_ACTION_RELEASE;
        public final static int KEY_PRESS, KEY_RELEASE;
```

```
    public final static int LIST_SELECT, LIST_DESELECT;
    public final static int LOAD_FILE, SAVE_FILE;
    public final static int MOUSE_DOWN, MOUSE_UP;
    public final static int MOUSE_DRAG;
    public final static int MOUSE_MOVE;
    public final static int MOUSE_ENTER, MOUSE_EXIT;
    public final static int SCROLL_ABSOLUTE;
    public final static int SCROLL_LINE_UP, SCROLL_LINE_DOWN;
    public final static int SCROLL_PAGE_UP, SCROLL_PAGE_DOWN;
    public final static int WINDOW_EXPOSE;
    public final static int WINDOW_ICONIFY, WINDOW_DEICONIFY;
    public final static int WINDOW_DESTROY;
    public final static int WINDOW_MOVED;
// Keyboard Modifier Constants
    public final static int ALT_MASK;
    public final static int CTRL_MASK;
    public final static int META_MASK;
    public final static int SHIFT_MASK;
// Function Key Constants
    public final static int F1, F2, F3, F4, F5, F6;
    public final static int F7, F8, F9, F10, F11, F12;
    public final static int LEFT, RIGHT;
    public final static int UP, DOWN;
    public final static int HOME, END;
    public final static int PGUP, PGDN;
// Public Instance Variables
    public Object arg;
    public int clickCount;
    public Event evt;
    public int id;
    public int key;
    public int modifiers;
    public Object target;
    public long when;
    public int x;
    public int y;
// Public Instance Methods
    public boolean controlDown();
    public boolean metaDown();
    public boolean shiftDown();
    public String toString();  // Overrides Object.toString()
    public void translate(int x, int y);
// Protected Instance Methods
    protected String paramString();

}
```

java.awt

java.awt.FileDialog

This class encapsulates a file selection dialog box. The constants LOAD and SAVE are values of an optional constructor argument that specifies whether the dialog should be an "Open File" dialog or a "Save As" dialog. You may specify a Filename-Filter object to control which files are displayed in the dialog.

```
public class FileDialog extends Dialog {
    // Public Constructors
        public FileDialog(Frame parent, String title);
        public FileDialog(Frame parent, String title, int mode);
    // Constants
        public final static int LOAD;
        public final static int SAVE;
    // Public Instance Methods
        public synchronized void addNotify();   // Overrides Dialog.addNotify()
        public String getDirectory();
        public String getFile();
        public FilenameFilter getFilenameFilter();
        public int getMode();
        public void setDirectory(String dir);
        public void setFile(String file);
        public void setFilenameFilter(FilenameFilter filter);
    // Protected Instance Methods
        protected String paramString();   // Overrides Dialog.paramString()
}
```

java.awt.FlowLayout

This class implements the LayoutManager interface to lay out Component objects in a Container. FlowLayout arranges components from left to right in rows. It fits as many components as it can in a row before moving on to the next row. The constructor allows you to specify one of three constants as an alignment value for the rows, and also allows you to specify horizontal spacing between components and vertical spacing between rows.

Note that applications should never call the LayoutManager methods of this class directly; the Container for which the FlowLayout is registered does this.

```
public class FlowLayout extends Object implements LayoutManager {
    // Public Constructors
        public FlowLayout();
        public FlowLayout(int align);
        public FlowLayout(int align, int hgap, int vgap);
    // Constants
        public final static int CENTER;
        public final static int LEFT;
        public final static int RIGHT;
    // Public Instance Methods
        public void addLayoutComponent(String name, Component comp);   // Empty
```

```
        public void layoutContainer(Container target);
        public Dimension minimumLayoutSize(Container target);
        public Dimension preferredLayoutSize(Container target);
        public void removeLayoutComponent(Component comp); // Empty
        public String toString(); // Overrides Object.toString()

}
```

java.awt.Font

This class represents a font in a platform-independent way. The constructor accepts a font name, style, and point size. The style may be one of the constants PLAIN, BOLD, or ITALIC, or the sum BOLD+ITALIC. The class method getFont() looks up the specified name in the system properties list and returns the font specified as the value of that property. It takes an optional Font default to use if the named font property is not found. This allows user customizability.

```
public class Font extends Object {
        // Public Constructor
        public Font(String name, int style, int size);
        // Constants
        public final static int BOLD;
        public final static int ITALIC;
        public final static int PLAIN;
        // Protected Instance Variables
        protected String name;
        protected int size;
        protected int style;
        // Class Methods
        public static Font getFont(String nm);
        public static Font getFont(String nm, Font font);
        // Public Instance Methods
        public boolean equals(Object obj); // Overrides Object.equals()
        public String getFamily();
        public String getName();
        public int getSize();
        public int getStyle();
        public int hashCode(); // Overrides Object.hashCode()
        public boolean isBold();
        public boolean isItalic();
        public boolean isPlain();
        public String toString(); // Overrides Object.toString()

}
```

java.awt

java.awt.FontMetrics

This class represents font metrics for a specified Font. The methods allow you to determine the overall metrics for the font (ascent, descent, etc.), and also to compute the width of strings that are to be displayed in a particular font.

```
public abstract class FontMetrics extends Object {
    // Protected Constructor
    protected FontMetrics(Font font);
    // Protected Instance Variables
    protected Font font;
    // Public Instance Methods
    public int bytesWidth(byte[] data, int off, int len);
    public int charWidth(int ch);
    public int charWidth(char ch);
    public int charsWidth(char[] data, int off, int len);
    public int getAscent();
    public int getDescent();
    public Font getFont();
    public int getHeight();
    public int getLeading();
    public int getMaxAdvance();
    public int getMaxAscent();
    public int getMaxDecent();
    public int getMaxDescent();
    public int[] getWidths();
    public int stringWidth(String str);
    public String toString();  // Overrides Object.toString()
}
```

java.awt.Frame

This class encapsulates an optionally resizable top-level application window. This window may have a specified title, a menu bar, an icon, and a cursor. setTitle() specifies a title, setMenuBar() specifies a menu bar, setCursor() specifies a cursor, and setIconImage() specifies an icon. The constants defined by this class specify various cursor types. The dispose() method must be called when the Frame is no longer needed so that it can release its window system resources for reuse.

Java programs typically subclass Frame and provide customized event handling for the window and the components it contains by overriding the event-handling methods such as Component.action(), Component.mouseDown(), and Component.keyDown(). The Frame class itself generates WINDOW_DESTROY, WIN-DOW_ICONIFY, WINDOW_DEICONIFY, and WINDOW_MOVED events.

```
public class Frame extends Window implements MenuContainer {
    // Public Constructors
    public Frame();
    public Frame(String title);
```

```
// Constants
    public final static int CROSSHAIR_CURSOR;
    public final static int DEFAULT_CURSOR;
    public final static int E_RESIZE_CURSOR;
    public final static int HAND_CURSOR;
    public final static int MOVE_CURSOR;
    public final static int NE_RESIZE_CURSOR;
    public final static int NW_RESIZE_CURSOR;
    public final static int N_RESIZE_CURSOR;
    public final static int SE_RESIZE_CURSOR;
    public final static int SW_RESIZE_CURSOR;
    public final static int S_RESIZE_CURSOR;
    public final static int TEXT_CURSOR;
    public final static int WAIT_CURSOR;
    public final static int W_RESIZE_CURSOR;
// Public Instance Methods
    public synchronized void addNotify(); // Overrides Window.addNotify()
    public synchronized void dispose();  // Overrides Window.dispose()
    public int getCursorType();
    public Image getIconImage();
    public MenuBar getMenuBar();
    public String getTitle();
    public boolean isResizable();
    public synchronized void remove(MenuComponent m);
    public void setCursor(int cursorType);
    public void setIconImage(Image image);
    public synchronized void setMenuBar(MenuBar mb);
    public void setResizable(boolean resizable);
    public void setTitle(String title);
// Protected Instance Methods
    protected String paramString(); // Overrides Container.paramString()
}
```

java.awt.Graphics

This abstract class defines a device-independent interface to graphics. It specifies methods for doing line drawing, image painting, area copying, and graphics output clipping. Specific subclasses of Graphics are implemented for different platforms and different graphics output devices. A Graphics object cannot be created directly through a constructor—it must be obtained with the getGraphics() method of a Component or an Image, or copied from an existing Graphics object with create(). When a Graphics object is no longer needed, you should call dispose() to free up window system resources.

```
public abstract class Graphics extends Object {
    // Protected Constructor
        protected Graphics(); // Empty
    // Public Instance Methods
```

→

java.awt

```
public abstract void clearRect(int x, int y, int width, int height);
public abstract void clipRect(int x, int y, int width, int height);
public abstract void copyArea(int x, int y, int width, int height, int dx, int dy);
public abstract Graphics create();
public Graphics create(int x, int y, int width, int height);
public abstract void dispose();
public void draw3DRect(int x, int y, int width, int height, boolean raised);
public abstract void drawArc(int x, int y, int width, int height, int startAngle, int arcAngle);
public void drawBytes(byte[] data, int offset, int length, int x, int y);
public void drawChars(char[] data, int offset, int length, int x, int y);
public abstract boolean drawImage(Image img, int x, int y, ImageObserver observer);
public abstract boolean drawImage(Image img, int x, int y, int width, int height, ImageObserver observer);
public abstract boolean drawImage(Image img, int x, int y, Color bgcolor, ImageObserver observer);
public abstract boolean drawImage(Image img, int x, int y, int width, int height,
                                       Color bgcolor, ImageObserver observer);
public abstract void drawLine(int x1, int y1, int x2, int y2);
public abstract void drawOval(int x, int y, int width, int height);
public abstract void drawPolygon(int[] xPoints, int[] yPoints, int nPoints);
public void drawPolygon(Polygon p);
public void drawRect(int x, int y, int width, int height);
public abstract void drawRoundRect(int x, int y, int width, int height, int arcWidth, int arcHeight);
public abstract void drawString(String str, int x, int y);
public void fill3DRect(int x, int y, int width, int height, boolean raised);
public abstract void fillArc(int x, int y, int width, int height, int startAngle, int arcAngle);
public abstract void fillOval(int x, int y, int width, int height);
public abstract void fillPolygon(int[] xPoints, int[] yPoints, int nPoints);
public void fillPolygon(Polygon p);
public abstract void fillRect(int x, int y, int width, int height);
public abstract void fillRoundRect(int x, int y, int width, int height, int arcWidth, int arcHeight);
public void finalize();
public abstract Rectangle getClipRect();
public abstract Color getColor();
public abstract Font getFont();
public FontMetrics getFontMetrics();
public abstract FontMetrics getFontMetrics(Font f);
public abstract void setColor(Color c);
public abstract void setFont(Font font);
public abstract void setPaintMode();
public abstract void setXORMode(Color c1);
public String toString();  // Overrides Object.toString()
public abstract void translate(int x, int y);

}
```

java.awt.GridBagConstraints

This class encapsulates the instance variables that tell a `GridBagLayout` how to position a given `Component` within its `Container`.

gridx, gridy
These fields specify the grid position of the component. The `RELATIVE` constant specifies a position to the right or below the previous component.

gridwidth, gridheight
These fields specify the height and width of the component in grid cells. The constant `REMAINDER` specifies that the component is the last one and should get all remaining cells.

fill
This field specifies which dimensions of a component should grow when the space available for it is larger than its default size. Legal values are the constants `NONE`, `BOTH`, `HORIZONTAL`, and `VERTICAL`.

ipadx, ipady
These fields specify internal padding to add on each side of the component in each dimension. They increase the size of the component beyond its default minimum size.

insets
This `Insets` object specifies margins to appear on all sides of the component.

anchor
This field specifies how the component should be displayed within its grid cells when it is smaller than those cells. The `CENTER` constant and the compass-point constants are legal values.

weightx, weighty
These fields specify how extra space in the container should be distributed among its components in the X and Y dimensions. Larger weights specify that a component should receive a proportionally larger amount of extra space. A zero weight specifies that the component should not receive any extra space. These weights specify the resizing behavior of the component and its container.

See also `GridBagLayout`.

```
public class GridBagConstraints extends Object implements Cloneable {
    // Public Constructor
        public GridBagConstraints();
    // Constants
    // anchor Constants
        public final static int CENTER;
        public final static int EAST;
        public final static int NORTH;
        public final static int NORTHEAST;
```

$\rightarrow$

java.awt

```
        public final static int NORTHWEST;
        public final static int SOUTH;
        public final static int SOUTHEAST;
        public final static int SOUTHWEST;
        public final static int WEST;
    // fill Constants
        public final static int HORIZONTAL;
        public final static int VERTICAL;
        public final static int BOTH;
        public final static int NONE;
    // Position and Size Constants
        public final static int RELATIVE;
        public final static int REMAINDER;
    // Public Instance Variables
        public int anchor;
        public int fill;
        public int gridheight;
        public int gridwidth;
        public int gridx;
        public int gridy;
        public Insets insets;
        public int ipadx;
        public int ipady;
        public double weightx;
        public double weighty;
    // Public Instance Methods
        public Object clone();  // Overrides Object.clone()

}
```

---

java.awt.GridBagLayout

This class implements the LayoutManager interface to lay out Component objects in a Container. It is the most complicated and most powerful LayoutManager in the java.awt package. It divides the container into a grid of rows and columns (which need not have the same width and height) and places the components into this grid, adjusting the size of the grid cells as necessary to ensure that components do not overlap. Each component controls how it is positioned within this grid by specifying a number of variables (or "constraints") in a GridBagConstraints object.

Use setConstraints() to specify a GridBagConstraints object for each of the components in the container. The variables in this object specify the position of the component in the grid, the number of horizontal and vertical grid cells that the component occupies, and also control other important aspects of component layout. See GridBagConstraints for more information on these "constraint" variables. setConstraints() makes a copy of the constraints object, so you may reuse a single object in your code.

Note that applications should never call the LayoutManager methods of this class directly; the Container for which the GridBagLayout is registered does this.

Do not confuse this class with the much simpler GridLayout which arranges components in a grid of equally sized cells.

```
public class GridBagLayout extends Object implements LayoutManager {
    // Public Constructor
        public GridBagLayout();
    // Constants
        protected final static int MAXGRIDSIZE;
        protected final static int MINSIZE;
        protected final static int PREFERREDSIZE;
    // Public Instance Variables
        public double[] columnWeights;
        public int[] columnWidths;
        public int[] rowHeights;
        public double[] rowWeights;
    // Protected Instance Variables
        protected Hashtable comptable;
        protected GridBagConstraints defaultConstraints;
        protected GridBagLayoutInfo layoutInfo;
    // Public Instance Methods
        public void addLayoutComponent(String name, Component comp);  // Empty
        public GridBagConstraints getConstraints(Component comp);
        public int[][] getLayoutDimensions();
        public Point getLayoutOrigin();
        public double[][] getLayoutWeights();
        public void layoutContainer(Container parent);
        public Point location(int x, int y);
        public Dimension minimumLayoutSize(Container parent);
        public Dimension preferredLayoutSize(Container parent);
        public void removeLayoutComponent(Component comp);  // Empty
        public void setConstraints(Component comp, GridBagConstraints constraints);
        public String toString();  // Overrides Object.toString()
    // Protected Instance Methods
        protected void AdjustForGravity(GridBagConstraints constraints, Rectangle r);
        protected void ArrangeGrid(Container parent);
        protected void DumpConstraints(GridBagConstraints constraints);
        protected void DumpLayoutInfo(GridBagLayoutInfo s);
        protected GridBagLayoutInfo GetLayoutInfo(Container parent, int sizeflag);
        protected Dimension GetMinSize(Container parent, GridBagLayoutInfo info);
        protected GridBagConstraints lookupConstraints(Component comp);
}
```

java.awt

java.awt.GridLayout

This class implements the LayoutManager interface to lay out Component objects in a Container. It divides the Container into a specified number of rows and columns and arranges the components in those rows and columns, left-to-right and top-to-bottom. If either the number of rows or the number of columns is

$\rightarrow$

unspecified, it is computed from the other dimension and the total number of components. Do not confuse this class with the more flexible and complicated GridBagLayout.

Note that applications should never call the LayoutManager methods of this class directly; the Container for which the GridLayout is registered does this.

```
public class GridLayout extends Object implements LayoutManager {
    // Public Constructors
        public GridLayout(int rows, int cols);
        public GridLayout(int rows, int cols, int hgap, int vgap) throws IllegalArgumentException;
    // Public Instance Methods
        public void addLayoutComponent(String name, Component comp); // Empty
        public void layoutContainer(Container parent);
        public Dimension minimumLayoutSize(Container parent);
        public Dimension preferredLayoutSize(Container parent);
        public void removeLayoutComponent(Component comp); // Empty
        public String toString(); // Overrides Object.toString()
}
```

java.awt.Image

This abstract class represents a displayable image in a platform-independent way. An Image object may not be instantiated directly through a constructor; it must be obtained through a call like Applet.getImage() or Component.createImage(). getSource() method returns the ImageProducer object that produces the image data. getGraphics() returns a Graphics object that can be used for drawing into offscreen images (but not images that are downloaded or generated by an ImageProducer). getProperty() returns the value of a specified property for the image, or the UndefinedProperty constant if the property is not defined.

```
public abstract class Image extends Object {
    // Default Constructor: public Image()
    // Constants
        public final static Object UndefinedProperty;
    // Public Instance Methods
        public abstract void flush();
        public abstract Graphics getGraphics();
        public abstract int getHeight(ImageObserver observer);
        public abstract Object getProperty(String name, ImageObserver observer);
        public abstract ImageProducer getSource();
        public abstract int getWidth(ImageObserver observer);
}
```

java.awt.Insets

This class holds four values that represent the top, left, bottom, and right margins, in pixels, of a Container or other Component. Objects of this type may be specified in a `GridBagConstraints` layout object, and are returned by `Container.-insets()`, which queries the margins of a container.

```
public class Insets extends Object implements Cloneable {
    // Public Constructor
        public Insets(int top, int left, int bottom, int right);
    // Public Instance Variables
        public int bottom;
        public int left;
        public int right;
        public int top;
    // Public Instance Methods
        public Object clone();   // Overrides Object.clone()
        public String toString();   // Overrides Object.toString()
}
```

java.awt.Label

This class is a `Component` that displays a single specified line of read-only text. The constant values specify the text alignment within the component and may be specified to the constructor or to `setAlignment()`.

```
public class Label extends Component {
    // Public Constructors
        public Label();
        public Label(String label);
        public Label(String label, int alignment);
    // Constants
        public final static int CENTER;
        public final static int LEFT;
        public final static int RIGHT;
    // Public Instance Methods
        public synchronized void addNotify();   // Overrides Component.addNotify()
        public int getAlignment();
        public String getText();
        public void setAlignment(int alignment) throws IllegalArgumentException;
        public void setText(String label);
    // Protected Instance Methods
        protected String paramString();   // Overrides Component.paramString()
}
```

java.awt.LayoutManager

This interface defines the methods necessary for a class to be able to arrange `Component` objects within a `Container` object. Most programs use one of the existing classes that implements this interface: `BorderLayout`, `CardLayout`, `FlowLayout`, `GridBagConstraints`, `GridBagLayout`, or `GridLayout`.

→

java.awt

To define a new class that lays out components, you must implement each of the methods defined by this interface. addLayoutComponent() should add the specified component (with the specified name) to the Layout. removeLayout-Component() should remove it. layoutContainer() should perform the actual positioning of components in the container. minimumLayoutSize() should return the absolute minimum container width and height that the LayoutManager needs to lay out its components. preferredLayoutSize() should return the optimal container width and height for the LayoutManager to lay out its components.

Note that a Java applet or application never directly calls any of these Layout-Manager methods—the Container object for which the LayoutManager is registered does that.

```
public abstract interface LayoutManager {
    // Public Instance Methods
        public abstract void addLayoutComponent(String name, Component comp);
        public abstract void layoutContainer(Container parent);
        public abstract Dimension minimumLayoutSize(Container parent);
        public abstract Dimension preferredLayoutSize(Container parent);
        public abstract void removeLayoutComponent(Component comp);

}
```

java.awt.List

This class is a Component that displays a list of strings. The list is scrollable if necessary. The constructor takes optional arguments that specify the number of visible rows in the list and whether selection of more than one item is allowed. The various instance methods allow strings to be added and removed from the List, and allow the selected item or items to be queried.

When the user double-clicks on an item, a List generates an ACTION_EVENT event. When an item is selected, the List generates a LIST_SELECT event, and when an item is deselected, it generates a LIST_DESELECT event. In each of these cases the event argument is the label of the affected item in the List.

```
public class List extends Component {
    // Public Constructors
        public List();
        public List(int rows, boolean multipleSelections);
    // Public Instance Methods
        public synchronized void addItem(String item);
        public synchronized void addItem(String item, int index);
        public synchronized void addNotify(); // Overrides Component.addNotify()
        public boolean allowsMultipleSelections();
        public synchronized void clear();
        public int countItems();
        public synchronized void delItem(int position);
        public synchronized void delItems(int start, int end);
        public synchronized void deselect(int index);
        public String getItem(int index);
        public int getRows();
        public synchronized int getSelectedIndex();
```

```
        public synchronized int[] getSelectedIndexes();
        public synchronized String getSelectedItem();
        public synchronized String[] getSelectedItems();
        public int getVisibleIndex();
        public synchronized boolean isSelected(int index);
        public void makeVisible(int index);
        public Dimension minimumSize(int rows);
        public Dimension minimumSize();  // Overrides Component.minimumSize()
        public Dimension preferredSize(int rows);
        public Dimension preferredSize();  // Overrides Component.preferredSize()
        public synchronized void removeNotify();  // Overrides Component.removeNotify()
        public synchronized void replaceItem(String newValue, int index);
        public synchronized void select(int index);
        public void setMultipleSelections(boolean v);
    // Protected Instance Methods
        protected String paramString();  // Overrides Component.paramString()

}
```

java.awt.MediaTracker

This class provides a very convenient way to asynchronously load and keep track of
the status of any number of `Image` objects. You can use it to load one or more
images and to wait until those images have been completely loaded are are ready to
be used.

The `addImage()` method registers an image to be loaded and tracked and assigns it
a specified identifier value. `waitForID()` loads all images that have been assigned
the specified identifier and returns when they have all finished loading or received
an error. `isErrorAny()` and `isErrorID()` check whether any errors have
occurred while loading images. `statusAll()` and `statusID()` return the status of
all images or of all images with the specified identifier. The return value of these
two methods is one of the defined constants.

```
public class MediaTracker extends Object {
    // Public Constructor
        public MediaTracker(Component comp);
    // Constants
        public final static int ABORTED;
        public final static int COMPLETE;
        public final static int ERRORED;
        public final static int LOADING;
    // Public Instance Methods
        public void addImage(Image image, int id);
        public synchronized void addImage(Image image, int id, int w, int h);
        public boolean checkAll();
        public synchronized boolean checkAll(boolean load);
        public boolean checkID(int id);
        public synchronized boolean checkID(int id, boolean load);
        public synchronized Object[] getErrorsAny();
```

→

```
        public synchronized Object[] getErrorsID(int id);
        public synchronized boolean isErrorAny();
        public synchronized boolean isErrorID(int id);
        public int statusAll(boolean load);
        public int statusID(int id, boolean load);
        public void waitForAll() throws InterruptedException;
        public synchronized boolean waitForAll(long ms) throws InterruptedException;
        public void waitForID(int id) throws InterruptedException;
        public synchronized boolean waitForID(int id, long ms) throws InterruptedException;
}
```

java.awt.Menu

This class encapsulates a pulldown menu pane that appears within a `MenuBar`. Each `Menu` has a label that appears in the `MenuBar` and may optionally be a tear-off menu. The `add()` and `addSeparator()` methods add individual items to a `Menu`.

```
public class Menu extends MenuItem implements MenuContainer {
    // Public Constructors
        public Menu(String label);
        public Menu(String label, boolean tearOff);
    // Public Instance Methods
        public synchronized MenuItem add(MenuItem mi);
        public void add(String label);
        public synchronized void addNotify();  // Overrides MenuItem.addNotify()
        public void addSeparator();
        public int countItems();
        public MenuItem getItem(int index);
        public boolean isTearOff();
        public synchronized void remove(int index);
        public synchronized void remove(MenuComponent item);
        public synchronized void removeNotify();  // Overrides MenuComponent.removeNotify()
}
```

java.awt.MenuBar

This class encapsulates a menu bar. `add()` adds `Menu` objects to the menu bar, and `setHelpMenu()` adds a `Help` menu in a reserved location of the menu bar. A `MenuBar` object may be displayed within a `Frame` by passing it to `Frame.set-MenuBar()`.

```
public class MenuBar extends MenuComponent implements MenuContainer {
    // Public Constructor
        public MenuBar();  // Empty
    // Public Instance Methods
        public synchronized Menu add(Menu m);
```

```
    public synchronized void addNotify( );
    public int countMenus( );
    public Menu getHelpMenu( );
    public Menu getMenu(int i );
    public synchronized void remove(int index );
    public synchronized void remove(MenuComponent m );
    public void removeNotify( );  // Overrides MenuComponent.removeNotify( )
    public synchronized void setHelpMenu(Menu m );
}
```

java.awt.MenuComponent

This class is the superclass of all menu-related classes: MenuItem, Menu, and Menu-Bar. You never need to instantiate a MenuComponent directly. setFont() specifies the font to be used for all text within the menu component.

```
public abstract class MenuComponent extends Object {
    // Public Constructor
    public MenuComponent( );  // Empty
    // Public Instance Methods
    public Font getFont( );
    public MenuContainer getParent( );
    public MenuComponentPeer getPeer( );
    public boolean postEvent(Event evt );
    public void removeNotify( );
    public void setFont(Font f );
    public String toString( );  // Overrides Object.toString( )
    // Protected Instance Methods
    protected String paramString( );
}
```

java.awt.MenuContainer

This interface defines the methods necessary for MenuContainer types such as the Menu, Frame, and MenuBar objects. Unless you are implementing new menu-like components, you will never need to use it.

```
public abstract interface MenuContainer {
    // Public Instance Methods
    public abstract Font getFont( );
    public abstract boolean postEvent(Event evt );
    public abstract void remove(MenuComponent comp );
}
```

java.awt.MenuItem

This class encapsulates a menu item with a specified textual label. A MenuItem can be added to a menu pane with the Menu.add() method. The disable() method makes an item non-selectable; you might use it to "gray-out" a menu item when the command it represents is not valid in the current context. The enable() method makes an item selectable again.

When a menu item is selected, MenuItem generates an ACTION_EVENT event, with the label of the selected item as its argument.

```
public class MenuItem extends MenuComponent {
    // Public Constructor
        public MenuItem(String label);
    // Public Instance Methods
        public synchronized void addNotify();
        public void disable();
        public void enable();
        public void enable(boolean cond);
        public String getLabel();
        public boolean isEnabled();
        public String paramString();  // Overrides MenuComponent.paramString()
        public void setLabel(String label);
}
```

java.awt.Panel

This class is a Container that is itself contained within a container. Unlike Frame and Dialog, Panel is a container that does not create a separate window of its own. Panel is suitable for holding portions of a larger interface within a parent Frame or Dialog or within another Panel. (Note that Applet is a subclass of Panel, and thus applets are displayed in a Panel that is contained within a Web browser or applet viewer.) The default LayoutManager for a Panel is Flow-Layout.

```
public class Panel extends Container {
    // Public Constructor
        public Panel();
    // Public Instance Methods
        public synchronized void addNotify();  // Overrides Container.addNotify()
}
```

java.awt.Point

This class encapsulates the X and Y coordinates of a two-dimensional point. The move() method sets the coordinates, and the translate() method adds the specified values to the coordinates. The x and y fields are public and may be manipulated directly. `Point` objects are returned by and passed to several `java.awt` methods.

```
public class Point extends Object {
    // Public Constructor
        public Point(int x, int y);
    // Public Instance Variables
        public int x;
        public int y;
    // Public Instance Methods
        public boolean equals(Object obj);  // Overrides Object.equals( )
        public int hashCode();  // Overrides Object.hashCode( )
        public void move(int x, int y);
        public String toString();  // Overrides Object.toString( )
        public void translate(int x, int y);

}
```

java.awt.Polygon

This class encapsulates a polygon defined as an array of points. The points of the polygon may be specified by the constructor, or with the `addPoint()` method. `getBoundingBox()` returns the smallest `Rectangle` that contains the polygon, and `inside()` tests whether a specified point is within the `Polygon`. Note that the arrays of X and Y points and the number of points in the polygon (not necessarily the same as the array size) are defined as public variables. `Polygon` objects are used when drawing polygons with the `Graphics.drawPolygon()` and `Graphics.fillPolygon()` methods.

```
public class Polygon extends Object {
    // Public Constructors
        public Polygon();  // Empty
        public Polygon(int[] xpoints, int[] ypoints, int npoints);
    // Public Instance Variables
        public int npoints;
        public int[] xpoints;
        public int[] ypoints;
    // Public Instance Methods
        public void addPoint(int x, int y);
        public Rectangle getBoundingBox();
        public boolean inside(int x, int y);

}
```

java.awt.Rectangle

This class encapsulates a rectangle defined by the X and Y coordinate of its upper-left corner and a width and height. The instance methods perform various tests and transformations on the rectangle. The `x`, `y`, `width`, and `height` methods are public

$\rightarrow$

and may thus be manipulated directly. `Rectangle` objects are used in several places in the `java.awt` package to specify clipping rectangles and bounding boxes.

```
public class Rectangle extends Object {
    // Public Constructors
        public Rectangle();  // Empty
        public Rectangle(int x, int y, int width, int height);
        public Rectangle(int width, int height);
        public Rectangle(Point p, Dimension d);
        public Rectangle(Point p);
        public Rectangle(Dimension d);
    // Public Instance Variables
        public int height;
        public int width;
        public int x;
        public int y;
    // Public Instance Methods
        public void add(int newx, int newy);
        public void add(Point pt);
        public void add(Rectangle r);
        public boolean equals(Object obj);  // Overrides Object.equals()
        public void grow(int h, int v);
        public int hashCode();  // Overrides Object.hashCode()
        public boolean inside(int x, int y);
        public Rectangle intersection(Rectangle r);
        public boolean intersects(Rectangle r);
        public boolean isEmpty();
        public void move(int x, int y);
        public void reshape(int x, int y, int width, int height);
        public void resize(int width, int height);
        public String toString();  // Overrides Object.toString()
        public void translate(int x, int y);
        public Rectangle union(Rectangle r);
}
```

java.awt.Scrollbar

This `Component` encapsulates a scrollbar. `setValue()` sets the displayed value of the scrollbar. `setValues()` sets the displayed value, the page size, and the minimum and maximum values. The constants `HORIZONTAL` and `VERTICAL` are legal values for the scrollbar orientation.

When the user interacts with a `Scrollbar`, it generates one of these events: `SCROLL_LINE_UP`, `SCROLL_LINE_DOWN`, `SCROLL_PAGE_UP`, `SCROLL_PAGE_DOWN`, `SCROLL_ABSOLUTE`. The event argument is an `Integer` object that specifies the number of lines or pages to scroll, or the absolute position to scroll to.

```
public class Scrollbar extends Component {
    // Public Constructors
        public Scrollbar();
        public Scrollbar(int orientation) throws IllegalArgumentException;
        public Scrollbar(int orientation, int value, int visible, int minimum, int maximum);
```

```
    // Constants
        public final static int HORIZONTAL;
        public final static int VERTICAL;
    // Public Instance Methods
        public synchronized void addNotify();  // Overrides Component.addNotify()
        public int getLineIncrement();
        public int getMaximum();
        public int getMinimum();
        public int getOrientation();
        public int getPageIncrement();
        public int getValue();
        public int getVisible();
        public void setLineIncrement(int l);
        public void setPageIncrement(int l);
        public void setValue(int value);
        public void setValues(int value, int visible, int minimum, int maximum);
    // Protected Instance Methods
        protected String paramString();  // Overrides Component.paramString()
}
```

java.awt.TextArea

This class encapsulates a GUI component that allows viewing and optional editing of multiline text. The appendText(), insertText(), and replaceText() provide various techniques for specifying text to appear in the TextArea. Many important TextArea methods are defined by the TextComponent superclass.

See also TextComponent and TextField.

```
public class TextArea extends TextComponent {
    // Public Constructors
        public TextArea();
        public TextArea(int rows, int cols);
        public TextArea(String text);
        public TextArea(String text, int rows, int cols);
    // Public Instance Methods
        public synchronized void addNotify();  // Overrides Component.addNotify()
        public void appendText(String str);
        public int getColumns();
        public int getRows();
        public void insertText(String str, int pos);
        public Dimension minimumSize(int rows, int cols);
        public Dimension minimumSize();  // Overrides Component.minimumSize()
        public Dimension preferredSize(int rows, int cols);
        public Dimension preferredSize();  // Overrides Component.preferredSize()
        public void replaceText(String str, int start, int end);
    // Protected Instance Methods
        protected String paramString();  // Overrides TextComponent.paramString()
}
```

java.awt

java.awt.TextComponent

This class is the superclass of the `TextArea` and `TextField` components. It cannot be instantiated itself, but provides methods that are common to these two Component types. `setEditable()` specifies whether the text in the text component is editable or not. `getText()` returns the text in the component, and `setText()` specifies text to be displayed. `getSelectedText()` returns the currently selected text in the text component, and `getSelectionStart()` and `getSelection-End()` return the extents of the selected region of text. `select()` and `select-All()` select some or all of the text displayed in the text component.

See also `TextField`, and `TextArea`.

```
public class TextComponent extends Component {
    // No Constructor
    // Public Instance Methods
        public String getSelectedText();
        public int getSelectionEnd();
        public int getSelectionStart();
        public String getText();
        public boolean isEditable();
        public synchronized void removeNotify(); // Overrides Component.removeNotify()
        public void select(int selStart, int selEnd);
        public void selectAll();
        public void setEditable(boolean t);
        public void setText(String t);
    // Protected Instance Methods
        protected String paramString(); // Overrides Component.paramString()

}
```

java.awt.TextField

This `Component` encapsulates a line of optionally editable text. Most of its interesting methods are defined by the `TextComponent` superclass. Use `setEcho-Character()` to specify a character to be echoed when requesting sensitive input such as a password.

See also `TextComponent` and `TextArea`.

```
public class TextField extends TextComponent {
    // Public Constructors
        public TextField();
        public TextField(int cols);
        public TextField(String text);
        public TextField(String text, int cols);
    // Public Instance Methods
        public synchronized void addNotify(); // Overrides Component.addNotify()
        public boolean echoCharIsSet();
        public int getColumns();
        public char getEchoChar();
        public Dimension minimumSize(int cols);
```

```
        public Dimension minimumSize( );  // Overrides Component.minimumSize( )
        public Dimension preferredSize(int cols);
        public Dimension preferredSize( );  // Overrides Component.preferredSize( )
        public void setEchoCharacter(char c);
    // Protected Instance Methods
        protected String paramString( );  // Overrides TextComponent.paramString( )

}
```

java.awt.Toolkit

This abstract class defines methods that, when implemented, create platform-dependent "peers" for each of the java.awt Component types. Java supports its platform-independent GUI interface by implementing a subclass of Toolkit for each platform. Portable programs should never use these methods to create peers directly—they should use the Component classes themselves. A Toolkit object cannot be instantiated directly. Window.getToolkit() returns the Toolkit being used for a particular Frame or Dialog.

The Toolkit class defines a few methods that you can use directly: the static method getDefaultToolkit() returns the default Toolkit that is in use. getScreenSize() returns the screen size in pixels, and getScreenResolution() returns the resolution in dots-per-inch. getFontList() returns the names of supported fonts on this platform. sync() flushes all pending graphics output, which can be useful for animation.

```
public abstract class Toolkit extends Object {
    // Default Constructor: public Toolkit( )
    // Class Methods
        public static synchronized Toolkit getDefaultToolkit( ) throws AWTError;
    // Public Instance Methods
        public abstract int checkImage(Image image, int width, int height, ImageObserver observer);
        public abstract Image createImage(ImageProducer producer);
        public abstract ColorModel getColorModel( );
        public abstract String[] getFontList( );
        public abstract FontMetrics getFontMetrics(Font font);
        public abstract Image getImage(String filename);
        public abstract Image getImage(URL url);
        public abstract int getScreenResolution( );
        public abstract Dimension getScreenSize( );
        public abstract boolean prepareImage(Image image, int width, int height, ImageObserver observer);
        public abstract void sync( );
    // Protected Instance Methods
        protected abstract ButtonPeer createButton(Button target);
        protected abstract CanvasPeer createCanvas(Canvas target);
        protected abstract CheckboxPeer createCheckbox(Checkbox target);
        protected abstract CheckboxMenuItemPeer createCheckboxMenuItem(CheckboxMenuItem target);
        protected abstract ChoicePeer createChoice(Choice target);
        protected abstract DialogPeer createDialog(Dialog target);
        protected abstract FileDialogPeer createFileDialog(FileDialog target);
```

java.awt

→

```
        protected abstract FramePeer createFrame(Frame target);
        protected abstract LabelPeer createLabel(Label target);
        protected abstract ListPeer createList(List target);
        protected abstract MenuPeer createMenu(Menu target);
        protected abstract MenuBarPeer createMenuBar(MenuBar target);
        protected abstract MenuItemPeer createMenuItem(MenuItem target);
        protected abstract PanelPeer createPanel(Panel target);
        protected abstract ScrollbarPeer createScrollbar(Scrollbar target);
        protected abstract TextAreaPeer createTextArea(TextArea target);
        protected abstract TextFieldPeer createTextField(TextField target);
        protected abstract WindowPeer createWindow(Window target);

}
```

java.awt.Window

This class encapsulates a top level window with no borders or menu bar. `Window` is a `Container` with `BorderLayout` as its default layout manager. `Window` is rarely used directly; its subclasses `Frame` and `Dialog` are more commonly useful.

`show()` (which overrides `Component.show()`) makes a `Window` visible and brings it to the front of other windows. `toFront()` brings a window to the front, and `toBack()` buries a window beneath others. `pack()` is an important method that sets the window size to match the preferred size of the components contained within the window. `getToolkit()` returns the `Toolkit()` in use for this window. Call `dispose()` when a `Window` is no longer needed to free its window system resources.

The `Window` class generates `WINDOW_DESTROY`, `WINDOW_ICONIFY`, `WINDOW_DEICON-IFY`, and `WINDOW_MOVED` events.

```
public class Window extends Container {
    // Public Constructor
        public Window(Frame parent);
    // Public Instance Methods
        public synchronized void addNotify(); // Overrides Container.addNotify()
        public synchronized void dispose();
        public Toolkit getToolkit(); // Overrides Component.getToolkit()
        public final String getWarningString();
        public synchronized void pack();
        public synchronized void show(); // Overrides Component.show()
        public void toBack();
        public void toFront();

}
```

The java.awt.image Package

The java.awt.image package is, by any standard, a confusing one. The purpose of the package is to support image processing, and the classes in the package provide a powerful infrastructure for that purpose. (See Figure 20-1.) Most of the classes are part of the infrastructure, however, and are not normally used by ordinary applications that have only simple image manipulation requirements.

To understand this package, it is first important to note that that Image class itself is part of the java.awt package, not the java.awt.image package. Furthermore, the java.awt.image classes are not the source of images; they simply serve to manipulate images that come from somewhere else. The Applet.getImage() method is perhaps the most common method for obtaining an image in Java—it downloads the image from a specified URL.

The ImageProducer interface is one you'll encounter frequently in java.awt.image. It represents an image source. If you've created an Image object with Applet.getImage(), you can obtain the ImageProducer for that Image (which has not been downloaded yet) with Image.getSource(). Conversely, given an ImageProducer object, you can create an Image from it with the createImage() method of any Component (such as an Applet). Once you have an ImageProducer object, you can manipulate it with the other java.awt.image classes.

FilteredImageSource is the most important class for image manipulation. It is itself a type of ImageProducer that, when created, applies a specified Image-Filter object to some other specified ImageProducer object. The Filtered-ImageSource thus configured can be used as an ImageProducer to display a filtered image. CropImageFilter is a predefined type of ImageFilter that you can use to extract a specified rectangle out of a larger image.

java.awt.image

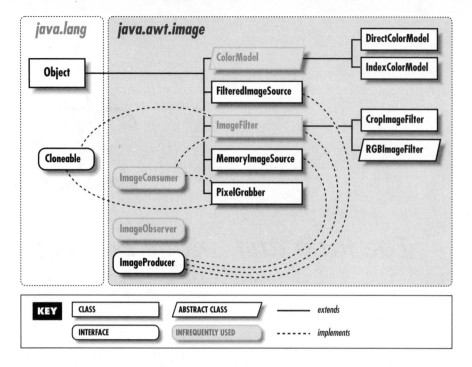

Figure 20-1: The java.awt.image package

RGBImageFilter is another subclass of ImageFilter that makes it easy to filter the colors of an image. To do so, you must subclass RGBImageFilter and provide the definition of a single simple method that manipulates the image colors. In order to manipulate image colors, you will probably need to be familiar with the Color-Model class and its two subclasses, DirectColorModel and IndexColorModel. An instance of ColorModel or of one of its subclasses converts a pixel value to the red, green, and blue components of the color it represents.

Finally, two other classes in the java.awt.image package are worth noting. MemoryImageSource is a type of ImageProducer that generates an image from an array of bytes or integers in memory. PixelGrabber does the reverse—it captures pixels from an ImageProducer and stores them into an array. You can use these classes separately or together to perform your own custom image manipulation.

See Section 8, *Advanced Graphics and Images*, for some examples of image manipulation.

java.awt.image.ColorModel

This abstract class defines a color model—i.e., a scheme for representing a color. Subclasses implement the methods of this interface to convert their particular representation of a pixel value into the default RGB color model. The static method get-RGBDefault() returns a ColorModel object that implements the default color model—RGB plus alpha transparency. You generally never need to call the instance methods of a ColorModel—they are called internally by other image manipulation classes.

See also DirectColorModel, and IndexColorModel.

```
public abstract class ColorModel extends Object {
    // Public Constructor
        public ColorModel(int bits);
    // Protected Instance Variables
        protected int pixel_bits;
    // Class Methods
        public static ColorModel getRGBdefault();
    // Public Instance Methods
        public abstract int getAlpha(int pixel);
        public abstract int getBlue(int pixel);
        public abstract int getGreen(int pixel);
        public int getPixelSize();
        public int getRGB(int pixel);
        public abstract int getRed(int pixel);
}
```

java.awt.image.CropImageFilter

This class implements an ImageFilter that crops an image to a specified rectangle. The methods defined by this class are used for communication between the filter and its FilteredImageSource, and should never be called directly.

```
public class CropImageFilter extends ImageFilter {
    // Public Constructor
        public CropImageFilter(int x, int y, int w, int h);
    // Public Instance Methods
        public void setDimensions(int w, int h);  // Overrides ImageFilter.setDimensions()
        public void setPixels(int x, int y, int w, int h, ColorModel model, byte[] pixels, int off, int scansize);
                // Overrides ImageFilter.setPixels()
        public void setPixels(int x, int y, int w, int h, ColorModel model, int[] pixels, int off, int scansize);
                // Overrides ImageFilter.setPixels()
        public void setProperties(Hashtable props);  // Overrides ImageFilter.setProperties()
}
```

java.awt.image

java.awt.image.DirectColorModel

This class is a ColorModel that extracts the red, green, blue, and alpha values directly from the bits of the pixel. The arguments to the constructor methods specify the number of significant bits in the pixel and the mask used to extract each of the color components from the pixel. The default RGB color model is a DirectColor-Model.

→

You should not need to instantiate any kind of `ColorModel` object unless you are processing image data, and that data does not use the standard RGB color format.

```
public class DirectColorModel extends ColorModel {
    // Public Constructors
        public DirectColorModel(int bits, int rmask, int gmask, int bmask);
        public DirectColorModel(int bits, int rmask, int gmask, int bmask, int amask);
    // Public Instance Methods
        public final int getAlpha(int pixel);   // Defines ColorModel.getAlpha()
        public final int getAlphaMask();
        public final int getBlue(int pixel);   // Defines ColorModel.getBlue()
        public final int getBlueMask();
        public final int getGreen(int pixel);   // Defines ColorModel.getGreen()
        public final int getGreenMask();
        public final int getRGB(int pixel);   // Overrides ColorModel.getRGB()
        public final int getRed(int pixel);   // Defines ColorModel.getRed()
        public final int getRedMask();
}
```

java.awt.image.FilteredImageSource

This class is an `ImageProducer` that produces image data filtered from some other `ImageProducer`. A `FilteredImageSource` is created with a specified `Image-Producer` and a specified `ImageFilter`. For example, an applet might use the following code to download and crop an image:

```
Image full_image = getImage(getDocumentBase(), "images/1.gif");
ImageFilter cropper = new CropImageFilter(10, 10, 100, 100);
ImageProducer prod = new FilteredImageSource(full_image.getSource(), cropper);
Image cropped_image = createImage(prod);
```

The methods of this class are the standard `ImageProducer` methods that you can invoke to add and remove `ImageConsumer` objects.

```
public class FilteredImageSource extends Object implements ImageProducer {
    // Public Constructor
        public FilteredImageSource(ImageProducer orig, ImageFilter imgf);
    // Public Instance Methods
        public synchronized void addConsumer(ImageConsumer ic);
        public synchronized boolean isConsumer(ImageConsumer ic);
        public synchronized void removeConsumer(ImageConsumer ic);
        public void requestTopDownLeftRightResend(ImageConsumer ic);
        public void startProduction(ImageConsumer ic);
}
```

java.awt.image.ImageConsumer

This interface defines the methods necessary for a class that consumes image data to communicate with a class that produces image data. The methods defined by this interface should never be called by a program directly; instead, they are invoked by an `ImageProducer` to pass the image data and other information about the image to the `ImageConsumer`. The constants defined by this interface are values passed to the `setHints()` and `imageComplete()` methods.

Unless you want to do low-level manipulation of image data, you never need to use or implement an `ImageConsumer`.

```
public abstract interface ImageConsumer {
    // Constants
        public final static int COMPLETESCANLINES;
        public final static int IMAGEABORTED;
        public final static int IMAGEERROR;
        public final static int RANDOMPIXELORDER;
        public final static int SINGLEFRAME;
        public final static int SINGLEFRAMEDONE;
        public final static int SINGLEPASS;
        public final static int STATICIMAGEDONE;
        public final static int TOPDOWNLEFTRIGHT;
    // Public Instance Methods
        public abstract void imageComplete(int status);
        public abstract void setColorModel(ColorModel model);
        public abstract void setDimensions(int width, int height);
        public abstract void setHints(int hintflags);
        public abstract void setPixels(int x, int y, int w, int h, ColorModel model, byte[] pixels, int off, int scansize);
        public abstract void setPixels(int x, int y, int w, int h, ColorModel model, int[] pixels, int off, int scansize);
        public abstract void setProperties(Hashtable props);

}
```

java.awt.image.ImageFilter

This class is used in conjunction with a `FilteredImageSource`. It accepts image data through the `ImageConsumer` interface and passes it on to an `ImageConsumer` specified by the controlling `FilteredImageSource`. `ImageFilter` is the superclass of all image filters, and performs no filtering itself. You must subclass it to perform the desired filtering. See `CropImageFilter` and `RGBImageFilter`. The `ImageFilter` methods are the `ImageConsumer` methods invoked by an `Image-Producer`. You should not call them directly.

See `FilteredImageSource` for an example of using an `ImageFilter`.

```
public class ImageFilter extends Object implements ImageConsumer, Cloneable {
    // Public Constructor
        public ImageFilter(); // Empty
    // Protected Instance Variables
        protected ImageConsumer consumer;
    // Public Instance Methods
        public Object clone(); // Overrides Object.clone()
        public ImageFilter getFilterInstance(ImageConsumer ic);
        public void imageComplete(int status);
        public void resendTopDownLeftRight(ImageProducer ip);
        public void setColorModel(ColorModel model);
        public void setDimensions(int width, int height);
```

$\rightarrow$

```
     public void setHints(int hints);
     public void setPixels(int x, int y, int w, int h, ColorModel model, byte[] pixels, int off, int scansize);
     public void setPixels(int x, int y, int w, int h, ColorModel model, int[] pixels, int off, int scansize);
     public void setProperties(Hashtable props);

}
```

---

java.awt.image.ImageObserver

This interface defines a method and associated constants used by classes that want to receive information asynchronously about the status of an image. Many methods that query information about an image take an `ImageObserver` as an argument. If the specified information is not available when requested, it is passed to the `Image-Observer` (by invoking the `imageUpdate()` method) when it becomes available.

Most applications will never need to use or implement this interface.

```
public abstract interface ImageObserver {
     // Constants
          public final static int ABORT;
          public final static int ALLBITS;
          public final static int ERROR;
          public final static int FRAMEBITS;
          public final static int HEIGHT;
          public final static int PROPERTIES;
          public final static int SOMEBITS;
          public final static int WIDTH;
     // Public Instance Methods
          public abstract boolean imageUpdate(Image img, int infoflags, int x, int y, int width, int height);

}
```

---

java.awt.image.ImageProducer

This interface defines the methods that any class that produces image data must define to enable communication with `ImageConsumer` classes. An `ImageConsumer` registers itself as interested in a producer's image by calling the `addConsumer()` method.

Most applications will never need to use or implement this interface.

```
public abstract interface ImageProducer {
     // Public Instance Methods
          public abstract void addConsumer(ImageConsumer ic);
          public abstract boolean isConsumer(ImageConsumer ic);
          public abstract void removeConsumer(ImageConsumer ic);
          public abstract void requestTopDownLeftRightResend(ImageConsumer ic);
          public abstract void startProduction(ImageConsumer ic);

}
```

java.awt.image.IndexColorModel

This class is a `ColorModel` that determines the red, green, blue, and alpha values for a pixel by using the pixel value as an index into colormap arrays. If no array of alpha values is specified, then all pixels are considered fully opaque, except for one optionally specified reserved value that is fully transparent. This color model is useful when working with image data that is defined in terms of a color map.

You should not need to instantiate any kind of `ColorModel` object unless you are processing image data, and that data does not use the standard RGB color format.

```
public class IndexColorModel extends ColorModel {
    // Public Constructors
        public IndexColorModel(int bits, int size, byte[] r, byte[] g, byte[] b);
        public IndexColorModel(int bits, int size, byte[] r, byte[] g, byte[] b, int trans);
        public IndexColorModel(int bits, int size, byte[] r, byte[] g, byte[] b, byte[] a);
        public IndexColorModel(int bits, int size, byte[] cmap, int start, boolean hasalpha);
        public IndexColorModel(int bits, int size, byte[] cmap, int start, boolean hasalpha, int trans);
    // Public Instance Methods
        public final int getAlpha(int pixel);   // Defines ColorModel.getAlpha()
        public final void getAlphas(byte[] a);
        public final int getBlue(int pixel);   // Defines ColorModel.getBlue()
        public final void getBlues(byte[] b);
        public final int getGreen(int pixel);   // Defines ColorModel.getGreen()
        public final void getGreens(byte[] g);
        public final int getMapSize();
        public final int getRGB(int pixel);   // Overrides ColorModel.getRGB()
        public final int getRed(int pixel);   // Defines ColorModel.getRed()
        public final void getReds(byte[] r);
        public final int getTransparentPixel();
}
```

java.awt.image.MemoryImageSource

This class is an `ImageProducer` that produces an image from data stored in memory. The various constructors specify image data, color model, array offset, scan line length, and properties in slightly different ways. The instance methods implement the standard `ImageProducer` interface that allows an `ImageConsumer` object to register interest in the image.

```
public class MemoryImageSource extends Object implements ImageProducer {
    // Public Constructors
        public MemoryImageSource(int w, int h, ColorModel cm, byte[] pix, int off, int scan);
        public MemoryImageSource(int w, int h, ColorModel cm, byte[] pix, int off, int scan, Hashtable props);
        public MemoryImageSource(int w, int h, ColorModel cm, int[] pix, int off, int scan);
        public MemoryImageSource(int w, int h, ColorModel cm, int[] pix, int off, int scan, Hashtable props);
        public MemoryImageSource(int w, int h, int[] pix, int off, int scan);
        public MemoryImageSource(int w, int h, int[] pix, int off, int scan, Hashtable props);
    // Public Instance Methods
        public synchronized void addConsumer(ImageConsumer ic);
```

$\rightarrow$

java.awt.image

```
        public synchronized boolean isConsumer(ImageConsumer ic);
        public synchronized void removeConsumer(ImageConsumer ic);
        public void requestTopDownLeftRightResend(ImageConsumer ic);  // Empty
        public void startProduction(ImageConsumer ic);

}
```

java.awt.image.PixelGrabber

This class is an `ImageConsumer` that extracts a specified rectangular array of pixels (in the default RGB color model) from a specified `Image` or `ImageProducer` and stores them into a specified array (using the specified offset into the array and specified scanline size). You would use this class when you wanted to inspect or manipulate the data of an image or some rectangular portion of an image.

The method `grabPixels()` makes the `PixelGrabber` start grabbing pixels. `status()` returns the status of the pixel-grabbing process. The return value uses the same flag value constants as the `ImageObserver` class does. The remaining methods are the standard `ImageConsumer` methods and should not be called directly.

```
public class PixelGrabber extends Object implements ImageConsumer {
    // Public Constructors
        public PixelGrabber(Image img, int x, int y, int w, int h, int[] pix, int off, int scansize);
        public PixelGrabber(ImageProducer ip, int x, int y, int w, int h, int[] pix, int off, int scansize);
    // Public Instance Methods
        public boolean grabPixels() throws InterruptedException;
        public synchronized boolean grabPixels(long ms) throws InterruptedException;
        public synchronized void imageComplete(int status);
        public void setColorModel(ColorModel model);
        public void setDimensions(int width, int height);
        public void setHints(int hints);
        public void setPixels(int srcX, int srcY, int srcW, int srcH, ColorModel model,
                        byte[] pixels, int srcOff, int srcScan);
        public void setPixels(int srcX, int srcY, int srcW, int srcH, ColorModel model,
                        int[] pixels, int srcOff, int srcScan);
        public void setProperties(Hashtable props);
        public synchronized int status();

}
```

java.awt.image.RGBImageFilter

This abstract class is an `ImageFilter` that provides an easy way to implement filters that modify the colors of an image. To create a color filter that modifies the colors of an image, you should subclass `RGBImageFilter` and provide a definition of `filterRGB()` that converts the input pixel value (in the default RGB color model) to an output value. If the conversion does not depend on the location of the pixel, set the `canFilterIndexColorModel` variable to true so that the

RGBImageFilter can save time by filtering the colormap of an image that uses an IndexColorModel instead of filtering each pixel of the image.

```
public abstract class RGBImageFilter extends ImageFilter {
    // Default Constructor: public RGBImageFilter( )
    // Protected Instance Variables
        protected boolean canFilterIndexColorModel;
        protected ColorModel newmodel;
        protected ColorModel origmodel;
    // Public Instance Methods
        public IndexColorModel filterIndexColorModel(IndexColorModel icm);
        public abstract int filterRGB(int x, int y, int rgb);
        public void filterRGBPixels(int x, int y, int w, int h, int[] pixels, int off, int scansize);
        public void setColorModel(ColorModel model);  // Overrides ImageFilter.setColorModel( )
        public void setPixels(int x, int y, int w, int h, ColorModel model, byte[] pixels, int off, int scansize);
                        // Overrides ImageFilter.setPixels( )
        public void setPixels(int x, int y, int w, int h, ColorModel model, int[] pixels, int off, int scansize);
                        // Overrides ImageFilter.setPixels( )
        public void substituteColorModel(ColorModel oldcm, ColorModel newcm);

}
```

java.awt.image

The java.awt.peer Package

The `java.awt.peer` package consists entirely of interface definitions. The hierarchy of these interfaces is shown in Figure 21-1. Each `java.awt.peer` interface corresponds to one of the `java.awt` Component or MenuComponent classes, and as you can see from the figure, the hierarchy of this package is identical to the hierarchy of those portions of the `java.awt` package.

The interfaces in this package define the methods that must be supported by the GUI components on a specific platform. Porting the `java.awt` GUI components to a new platform is a matter of implementing each of the methods in each of the interfaces in this package on top of the native GUI components of that platform. The `Toolkit` object in the `java.awt` package collects the implementations of these peer interfaces for a given platform. `Toolkit` contains methods that create instances of each of the interfaces in this package. Normal applications never need to instantiate these peers directly; instead they use the `java.awt` Component classes, which create peers as needed.

Because these peer interfaces are rarely used, and because the methods are quite similar to those of the corresponding `java.awt` component, there is no additional commentary for the individual interface definitions below.

java.awt.peer

java.awt.peer.ButtonPeer

```
public abstract interface ButtonPeer extends ComponentPeer {
    // Public Instance Methods
        public abstract void setLabel(String label);

}
```

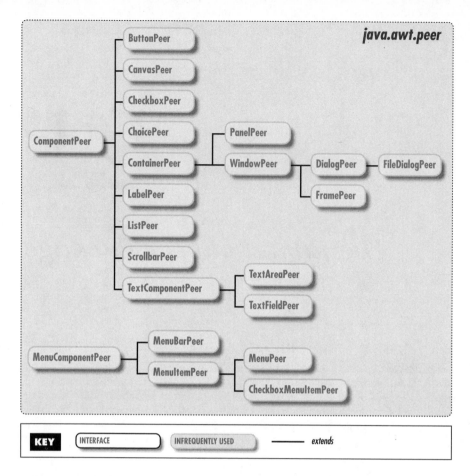

KEY   INTERFACE   INFREQUENTLY USED   ——— *extends*

Figure 21-1: The java.awt.peer package

java.awt.peer.CanvasPeer

public interface **CanvasPeer** extends ComponentPeer {

}

java.awt.peer.CheckboxMenuItemPeer

public abstract interface **CheckboxMenuItemPeer** extends MenuItemPeer {
    // *Public Instance Methods*
        public abstract void **setState**(boolean *t*);

}

java.awt.peer.CheckboxPeer

```
public abstract interface CheckboxPeer extends ComponentPeer {
    // Public Instance Methods
        public abstract void setCheckboxGroup(CheckboxGroup g);
        public abstract void setLabel(String label);
        public abstract void setState(boolean state);

}
```

java.awt.peer.ChoicePeer

```
public abstract interface ChoicePeer extends ComponentPeer {
    // Public Instance Methods
        public abstract void addItem(String item, int index);
        public abstract void select(int index);

}
```

java.awt.peer.ComponentPeer

```
public abstract interface ComponentPeer {
    // Public Instance Methods
        public abstract int checkImage(Image img, int w, int h, ImageObserver o);
        public abstract Image createImage(ImageProducer producer);
        public abstract Image createImage(int width, int height);
        public abstract void disable();
        public abstract void dispose();
        public abstract void enable();
        public abstract ColorModel getColorModel();
        public abstract FontMetrics getFontMetrics(Font font);
        public abstract Graphics getGraphics();
        public abstract Toolkit getToolkit();
        public abstract boolean handleEvent(Event e);
        public abstract void hide();
        public abstract Dimension minimumSize();
        public abstract void nextFocus();
        public abstract void paint(Graphics g);
        public abstract Dimension preferredSize();
        public abstract boolean prepareImage(Image img, int w, int h, ImageObserver o);
        public abstract void print(Graphics g);
        public abstract void repaint(long tm, int x, int y, int width, int height);
        public abstract void requestFocus();
        public abstract void reshape(int x, int y, int width, int height);
        public abstract void setBackground(Color c);
        public abstract void setFont(Font f);
```

$\rightarrow$

```
        public abstract void setForeground(Color c);
        public abstract void show( );
}
```

java.awt.peer.ContainerPeer

```
public abstract interface ContainerPeer extends ComponentPeer {
    // Public Instance Methods
        public abstract Insets insets( );
}
```

java.awt.peer.DialogPeer

```
public abstract interface DialogPeer extends WindowPeer {
    // Public Instance Methods
        public abstract void setResizable(boolean resizable);
        public abstract void setTitle(String title);
}
```

java.awt.peer.FileDialogPeer

```
public abstract interface FileDialogPeer extends DialogPeer {
    // Public Instance Methods
        public abstract void setDirectory(String dir);
        public abstract void setFile(String file);
        public abstract void setFilenameFilter(FilenameFilter filter);
}
```

java.awt.peer.FramePeer

```
public abstract interface FramePeer extends WindowPeer {
    // Public Instance Methods
        public abstract void setCursor(int cursorType);
        public abstract void setIconImage(Image im);
        public abstract void setMenuBar(MenuBar mb);
        public abstract void setResizable(boolean resizeable);
        public abstract void setTitle(String title);
}
```

java.awt.peer.LabelPeer

```
public abstract interface LabelPeer extends ComponentPeer {
    // Public Instance Methods
        public abstract void setAlignment(int alignment);
        public abstract void setText(String label);

}
```

java.awt.peer.ListPeer

```
public abstract interface ListPeer extends ComponentPeer {
    // Public Instance Methods
        public abstract void addItem(String item, int index);
        public abstract void clear();
        public abstract void delItems(int start, int end);
        public abstract void deselect(int index);
        public abstract int[] getSelectedIndexes();
        public abstract void makeVisible(int index);
        public abstract Dimension minimumSize(int v);
        public abstract Dimension preferredSize(int v);
        public abstract void select(int index);
        public abstract void setMultipleSelections(boolean v);

}
```

java.awt.peer.MenuBarPeer

```
public abstract interface MenuBarPeer extends MenuComponentPeer {
    // Public Instance Methods
        public abstract void addHelpMenu(Menu m);
        public abstract void addMenu(Menu m);
        public abstract void delMenu(int index);

}
```

java.awt.peer.MenuComponentPeer

```
public abstract interface MenuComponentPeer {
    // Public Instance Methods
        public abstract void dispose();

}
```

java.awt.peer.MenuItemPeer

```
public abstract interface MenuItemPeer extends MenuComponentPeer {
    // Public Instance Methods
        public abstract void disable( );
        public abstract void enable( );
        public abstract void setLabel(String label);
}
```

java.awt.peer.MenuPeer

```
public abstract interface MenuPeer extends MenuItemPeer {
    // Public Instance Methods
        public abstract void addItem(MenuItem item);
        public abstract void addSeparator( );
        public abstract void delItem(int index);
}
```

java.awt.peer.PanelPeer

```
public interface PanelPeer extends ContainerPeer {
}
```

java.awt.peer.ScrollbarPeer

```
public abstract interface ScrollbarPeer extends ComponentPeer {
    // Public Instance Methods
        public abstract void setLineIncrement(int l);
        public abstract void setPageIncrement(int l);
        public abstract void setValue(int value);
        public abstract void setValues(int value, int visible, int minimum, int maximum);
}
```

java.awt.peer.TextAreaPeer

```
public abstract interface TextAreaPeer extends TextComponentPeer {
    // Public Instance Methods
        public abstract void insertText(String txt, int pos);
        public abstract Dimension minimumSize(int rows, int cols);
```

```
        public abstract Dimension preferredSize(int rows, int cols);
        public abstract void replaceText(String txt, int start, int end);

}
```

---

java.awt.peer.TextComponentPeer

```
public abstract interface TextComponentPeer extends ComponentPeer {
    // Public Instance Methods
        public abstract int getSelectionEnd();
        public abstract int getSelectionStart();
        public abstract String getText();
        public abstract void select(int selStart, int selEnd);
        public abstract void setEditable(boolean editable);
        public abstract void setText(String l);

}
```

---

java.awt.peer.TextFieldPeer

```
public abstract interface TextFieldPeer extends TextComponentPeer {
    // Public Instance Methods
        public abstract Dimension minimumSize(int cols);
        public abstract Dimension preferredSize(int cols);
        public abstract void setEchoCharacter(char c);

}
```

---

java.awt.peer.WindowPeer

```
public abstract interface WindowPeer extends ContainerPeer {
    // Public Instance Methods
        public abstract void toBack();
        public abstract void toFront();

}
```

java.awt.peer

22

The java.io Package

The `java.io` package contains a relatively large number of classes, but, as you can see from Figure 22-1, the classes form a fairly structured hierarchy—most of them are subclasses of `InputStream` or `OutputStream`. Each of these stream types has a very specific purpose, and despite its size, `java.io` is a straightforward package to understand and to use.

Before we consider the stream classes in the package, we'll consider the important non-stream classes. `File` represents a file or directory name in a system independent way, and provides methods for listing directories, querying file attributes, and for renaming and deleting files. `FilenameFilter` is an interface that defines a method that accepts or rejects specified filenames. It is used by the `java.awt.FileDialog` dialog box and by the `File` class to specify what types of files should be included in directory listings. `RandomAccessFile` allows you to read or write from or to arbitrary locations of a file. Often, though, you'll prefer sequential access to a file and should use one of the stream classes.

`InputStream` and `OutputStream` are abstract classes that define methods for reading and writing data. Their subclasses allow data to be read from and written to a variety of sources and sinks. `FileInputStream` and `FileOutputStream` read from and write to files. `ByteArrayInputStream` and `ByteArrayOutputStream` read from and write to an array of bytes in memory. Similarly, `StringBufferInputStream` reads data from a `StringBuffer` object. `PipedInputStream` reads data from a `PipedOutputStream`, and `PipedOutputStream` writes data to a `PipedInputStream`. These classes work together to implement a "pipe" for communication between threads.

`FilterInputStream` and `FilterOutputStream` are special—they filter input and output data. When a `FilterInputStream` is created, an `InputStream` is specified for it to filter. When you call the `read()` method of a `FilterInputStream`, it calls the `read()` method of its specified stream, processes the data it reads somehow, and then returns it. Similarly, you specify an `OutputStream` to be

---

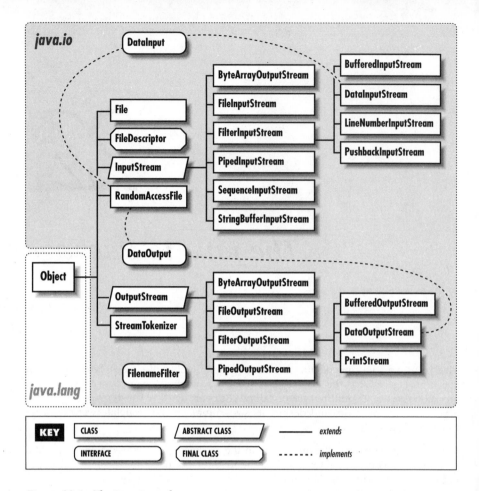

Figure 22-1: The java.io package

filtered when you create a FilterOutputStream. Calling the write() method of a FilterOutputStream causes it to process your data in some way and then pass that processed data to the write() method of its OutputStream.

FilterInputStream and FilterOutputStream do not perform any filtering themselves; this is done by their subclasses. BufferedInputStream and BufferedOutputStream provide input and output buffering and can increase I/O efficiency. DataInputStream reads raw bytes from a stream and interprets them in various formats. It has methods to read lines of text, and various methods to read Java primitive data types in their standard binary formats. This is probably the most commonly used input stream class. DataOutputStream allows you to write Java primitive data types in binary format. It isn't as commonly used as the PrintStream, however, which allows you to write lines of text and Java primitive data types in textual format.

One final note about filtered input and output streams is that they can be combined to any length. For example, you could connect a FileInputStream to a BufferedInputStream to provide buffering, and then connect the resulting stream to a DataInputStream so that you can easily read lines of text from it.

See Section 6, *Input and Output*, for some examples of input and output using the classes in `java.io`.

java.io.BufferedInputStream

This class is a `FilterInputStream` that provides input data buffering—efficiency is increased by reading in large amounts of data and storing them in an internal buffer. When data is requested, it is usually available from the buffer. Thus, most calls to read data do not have to make a (slow) call to actually read data from a disk. Create a `BufferedInputStream` by specifying the `InputStream` that is to have buffering applied in the call to the constructor.

```
public class BufferedInputStream extends FilterInputStream {
    // Public Constructors
        public BufferedInputStream(InputStream in);
        public BufferedInputStream(InputStream in, int size);
    // Protected Instance Variables
        protected byte[] buf;
        protected int count;
        protected int marklimit;
        protected int markpos;
        protected int pos;
    // Public Instance Methods
        public synchronized int available() throws IOException; // Overrides FilterInputStream.available()
        public synchronized void mark(int readlimit);  // Overrides FilterInputStream.mark()
        public boolean markSupported();  // Overrides FilterInputStream.markSupported()
        public synchronized int read() throws IOException; // Overrides FilterInputStream.read()
        public synchronized int read(byte[] b, int off, int len) throws IOException;
                                    // Overrides FilterInputStream.read()
        public synchronized void reset() throws IOException;  // Overrides FilterInputStream.reset()
        public synchronized long skip(long n) throws IOException;  // Overrides FilterInputStream.skip()

}
```

java.io.BufferedOutputStream

This class is a `FilterOutputStream` that provides output data buffering—output efficiency is increased by storing values to be written in a buffer and actually writing them out only when the buffer fills up or when the `flush()` method is called. Create a `BufferedOutputStream` by specifying the `OutputStream` that is to have buffering applied in the call to the constructor.

```
public class BufferedOutputStream extends FilterOutputStream {
    // Public Constructors
        public BufferedOutputStream(OutputStream out);
        public BufferedOutputStream(OutputStream out, int size);
    // Protected Instance Variables
        protected byte[] buf;
        protected int count;
    // Public Instance Methods
        public synchronized void flush() throws IOException; // Overrides FilterOutputStream.flush()
```

$\rightarrow$

```
public synchronized void write(int b) throws IOException; // OverridesFilterOutputStream.write( )
public synchronized void write(byte[ ] b, int off, int len) throws IOException;
                                    // Overrides FilterOutputStream.write( )
}
```

---

java.io.ByteArrayInputStream

This class is a subclass of InputStream in which input data comes from a specified array of byte values. This is useful when you want to read data in memory as if it were coming from a file or pipe or socket. This class is much like StringBuffer-InputStream.

```
public class ByteArrayInputStream extends InputStream {
    // Public Constructors
        public ByteArrayInputStream(byte[ ] buf);
        public ByteArrayInputStream(byte[ ] buf, int offset, int length);
    // Protected Instance Variables
        protected byte[ ] buf;
        protected int count;
        protected int pos;
    // Public Instance Methods
        public synchronized int available(); // Overrides InputStream.available( )
        public synchronized int read(); // Defines InputStream.read( )
        public synchronized int read(byte[ ] b, int off, int len); // Overrides InputStream.read( )
        public synchronized void reset(); // Overrides InputStream.reset( )
        public synchronized long skip(long n); // Overrides InputStream.skip( )
}
```

---

java.io.ByteArrayOutputStream

This class is a subclass of OutputStream in which data that is written is stored in an internal byte array. The internal array grows as necessary, and can be retrieved with toByteArray() or toString(). The reset() method discards any data currently stored in the internal array and begins storing data from the beginning again.

```
public class ByteArrayOutputStream extends OutputStream {
    // Public Constructors
        public ByteArrayOutputStream();
        public ByteArrayOutputStream(int size);
    // Protected Instance Variables
        protected byte[ ] buf;
        protected int count;
    // Public Instance Methods
        public synchronized void reset();
        public int size();
        public synchronized byte[ ] toByteArray();
```

```
        public String toString(); // Overrides Object.toString()
        public String toString(int hibyte);
        public synchronized void write(int b); // Defines OutputStream.write()
        public synchronized void write(byte[] b, int off, int len); // Overrides OutputStream.write()
        public synchronized void writeTo(OutputStream out) throws IOException;

}
```

java.io.DataInput

This interface defines the methods required for streams that can read character data or Java primitive data types in a machine-independent format. It is implemented by `DataInputStream` and `RandomAccessFile`. See `DataInputStream` for more information on the methods.

```
public abstract interface DataInput {
    // Public Instance Methods
        public abstract boolean readBoolean() throws IOException, EOFException;
        public abstract byte readByte() throws IOException, EOFException;
        public abstract char readChar() throws IOException, EOFException;
        public abstract double readDouble() throws IOException, EOFException;
        public abstract float readFloat() throws IOException, EOFException;
        public abstract void readFully(byte[] b) throws IOException, EOFException;
        public abstract void readFully(byte[] b, int off, int len) throws IOException, EOFException;
        public abstract int readInt() throws IOException, EOFException;
        public abstract String readLine() throws IOException;
        public abstract long readLong() throws IOException, EOFException;
        public abstract short readShort() throws IOException, EOFException;
        public abstract String readUTF() throws IOException;
        public abstract int readUnsignedByte() throws IOException, EOFException;
        public abstract int readUnsignedShort() throws IOException, EOFException;
        public abstract int skipBytes(int n) throws IOException, EOFException;

}
```

java.io.DataInputStream

This class is a type of `FilterInputStream` that allows you to read lines of text and Java primitive data types in a portable way. This is perhaps the most commonly used class for file input. Create a `DataInputStream` by specifying the `InputStream` that is to be filtered in the call to the constructor.

Many of this class's methods read and return a single Java primitive type, in binary format, from the stream. `readUnsignedByte()` and `readUnsignedShort()` read unsigned values and return them as `int` values, since unsigned `byte` and `short` types are not supported in Java. `read()` reads data into an array of bytes, blocking until at least some data is available. By contrast, `readFully()` reads data into an array of bytes, but blocks until all of the requested data becomes available.

→

java.io

readLine() reads characters from the stream until it encounters a newline, a carriage return, or a newline carriage return pair. The returned string is not terminated with a newline or carriage return. readUTF() reads a string of Unicode text encoded in the UTF-8 "transformation format." UTF-8 is an ASCII-compatible encoding of Unicode characters that is often used for the transmission and storage of Unicode text. The static version of the readUTF() method can be used to read a UTF-8 encoded string from any InputStream class. Finally, skipBytes() blocks until the specified number of bytes have been read and discarded.

```
public class DataInputStream extends FilterInputStream implements DataInput {
    // Public Constructor
        public DataInputStream(InputStream in);
    // Class Methods
        public final static String readUTF(DataInput in) throws IOException;
    // Public Instance Methods
        public final int read(byte[] b) throws IOException;        // Overrides FilterInputStream.read()
        public final int read(byte[] b, int off, int len) throws IOException;   // Overrides FilterInputStream.read()
        public final boolean readBoolean() throws IOException;
        public final byte readByte() throws IOException;
        public final char readChar() throws IOException;
        public final double readDouble() throws IOException;
        public final float readFloat() throws IOException;
        public final void readFully(byte[] b) throws IOException, EOFException;
        public final void readFully(byte[] b, int off, int len) throws IOException, EOFException;
        public final int readInt() throws IOException;
        public final String readLine() throws IOException;
        public final long readLong() throws IOException;
        public final short readShort() throws IOException;
        public final String readUTF() throws IOException;
        public final int readUnsignedByte() throws IOException;
        public final int readUnsignedShort() throws IOException;
        public final int skipBytes(int n) throws IOException;
}
```

java.io.DataOutput

This interface defines the methods required for streams that can write character data or Java primitive data types in a machine-independent format. It is implemented by DataOutputStream and RandomAccessFile. See DataOutputStream for more information on the methods.

```
public abstract interface DataOutput {
    // Public Instance Methods
        public abstract void write(int b) throws IOException;
        public abstract void write(byte[] b) throws IOException;
        public abstract void write(byte[] b, int off, int len) throws IOException;
        public abstract void writeBoolean(boolean v) throws IOException;
        public abstract void writeByte(int v) throws IOException;
        public abstract void writeBytes(String s) throws IOException;
        public abstract void writeChar(int v) throws IOException;
        public abstract void writeChars(String s) throws IOException;
```

```
    public abstract void writeDouble(double v) throws IOException;
    public abstract void writeFloat(float v) throws IOException;
    public abstract void writeInt(int v) throws IOException;
    public abstract void writeLong(long v) throws IOException;
    public abstract void writeShort(int v) throws IOException;
    public abstract void writeUTF(String str) throws IOException;

}
```

---

java.io.DataOutputStream

This class is a subclass of `FilterOutputStream` that allows you to write Java primitive data types in a portable way. Create a `DataOutputStream` by specifying the `OutputStream` that is to be filtered in the call to the constructor.

Many of this class's methods write a single Java primitive type, in binary format to the output stream. `write()` writes a single byte, an array, or a sub-array of bytes. `writeUTF()` outputs a Java string of Unicode characters using the UTF-8 "transformation format." UTF-8 is an ASCII-compatible encoding of Unicode characters that is often used for the transmission and storage of Unicode text. `flush()` forces any buffered data to be output. `size()` returns the number of bytes written so far. Note that this class does not provide any methods for writing strings. That is done by `Print-OutputStream`. Note also that the primitive Java types written by this class are written in their binary representation, not in an ASCII representation. Again, values may be written in ASCII form with the `PrintOutputStream` class.

```
public class DataOutputStream extends FilterOutputStream implements DataOutput {
    // Public Constructor
        public DataOutputStream(OutputStream out);
    // Protected Instance Variables
        protected int written;
    // Public Instance Methods
        public void flush() throws IOException;  // Overrides FilterOutputStream.flush()
        public final int size();
    // Overrides FilterOutputStream.write()
        public synchronized void write(int b) throws IOException;
    // Overrides FilterOutputStream.write()
        public synchronized void write(byte[]b, int off, intlen) throws IOException;
        public final void writeBoolean(boolean v) throws IOException;
        public final void writeByte(int v) throws IOException;
        public final void writeBytes(String s) throws IOException;
        public final void writeChar(int v) throws IOException;
        public final void writeChars(String s) throws IOException;
        public final void writeDouble(double v) throws IOException;
        public final void writeFloat(float v) throws IOException;
        public final void writeInt(int v) throws IOException;
        public final void writeLong(long v) throws IOException;
```

java.io

→

```
        public final void writeShort(int v) throws IOException;
        public final void writeUTF(String str) throws IOException;

}
```

java.io.File

This class provides a platform-independent definition of file and directory names. It also provides methods to list the files in a directory, to check the existence, readability, writeability, type, size, and modification time of files and directories, to make new directories, to rename files and directories, and to delete files and directories. The constants defined by this class are the platform-dependent directory and path separator characters, available as a String or char.

getName() returns the name of the File with any directory names omitted. get-Path() returns the full name of the file, including the directory name. get-Parent() returns the directory of the File. If the File is an absolute specification, then getAbsolutePath() returns the complete filename. Otherwise, if the File is a relative file specification, it returns the relative filename appended to the current working directory.

isAbsolute() tests whether the File is an absolute specification. exists(), canWrite(), canRead(), isFile(), and isDirectory() perform the obvious tests on the specified File. length() returns the length of the file. last-Modified() returns the modification time of the file (which should be used for comparison with other file times only, and not interpreted as any particular time format).

list() returns the name of all entries in a directory that are not rejected by an optional FilenameFilter. mkdir() creates a directory. mkdirs() creates all the directories in a File specification. renameTo() renames a file or directory. delete() deletes a file or directory. Note that there is no method to create a file; that is done with a FileOutputStream.

```
public class File extends Object {
    // Public Constructors
        public File(String path) throws NullPointerException;
        public File(String path, String name);
        public File(File dir, String name);
    // Constants
        public final static String pathSeparator;
        public final static char pathSeparatorChar;
        public final static String separator;
        public final static char separatorChar;
    // Public Instance Methods
        public boolean canRead();
        public boolean canWrite();
        public boolean delete();
        public boolean equals(Object obj); // Overrides Object.equals()
        public boolean exists();
```

```
        public String getAbsolutePath();
        public String getName();
        public String getParent();
        public String getPath();
        public int hashCode(); // Overrides Object.hashCode()
        public boolean isAbsolute();
        public boolean isDirectory();
        public boolean isFile();
        public long lastModified();
        public long length();
        public String[] list();
        public String[] list(FilenameFilter filter);
        public boolean mkdir();
        public boolean mkdirs();
        public boolean renameTo(File dest);
        public String toString(); // Overrides Object.toString()
}
```

java.io.FileDescriptor

This class is a platform-independent representation of a low-level handle to an open file or an open socket. The static in, out, and err variables are FileDescriptor objects that represent the system standard input, output, and error streams, respectively. There is no public constructor method to create a FileDescriptor object. You can obtain one with the getFD() method of FileInputStream, FileOutputStream, and RandomAccessFile.

```
public final class FileDescriptor extends Object {
    // Default Constructor: public FileDescriptor()
    // Constants
        public final static FileDescriptor err;
        public final static FileDescriptor in;
        public final static FileDescriptor out;
    // Public Instance Methods
        public boolean valid();
}
```

java.io.FileInputStream

This class is a subclass of InputStream that reads data from a file specified by name or by a File or FileDescriptor object. FileInputStream provides only a low-level interface to reading data; you would typically use a DataInputStream object to filter input from a FileInputStream and provide a higher-level interface for reading strings and binary data. Call close() to close the file when input is no

→

longer needed. Note that this class has a finalizer method that calls close() if necessary.

```
public class FileInputStream extends InputStream {
    // Public Constructors
        public FileInputStream(String name) throws FileNotFoundException, IOException;
        public FileInputStream(File file) throws FileNotFoundException, IOException;
        public FileInputStream(FileDescriptor fdObj);
    // Public Instance Methods
        public int available() throws IOException; // Overrides InputStream.available()
        public void close() throws IOException; // Overrides InputStream.close()
        public final FileDescriptor getFD() throws IOException;
        public int read() throws IOException; // Defines InputStream.read()
        public int read(byte[] b) throws IOException; // Overrides InputStream.read()
        public int read(byte[] b, int off, int len) throws IOException; // Overrides InputStream.read()
        public long skip(long n) throws IOException; // Overrides InputStream.skip()
    // Protected Instance Methods
        protected void finalize() throws IOException;
}
```

---

java.io.FileOutputStream

This class is a subclass of OutputStream that writes data to a file specified by name, or by a File or FileDescriptor object. FileOutputStream provides only a low-level interface to writing data; you would typically use a DataOutputStream or PrintOutputStream to filter output to a FileOutputStream and provide a higher-level interface for writing data. Use close() to close a FileOutputStream when no further output will be written to it. Note that this class has a finalizer method that will call close() if necessary.

```
public class FileOutputStream extends OutputStream {
    // Public Constructors
        public FileOutputStream(String name) throws IOException;
        public FileOutputStream(File file) throws IOException;
        public FileOutputStream(FileDescriptor fdObj);
    // Public Instance Methods
        public void close() throws IOException; // Overrides OutputStream.close()
        public final FileDescriptor getFD() throws IOException;
        public void write(int b) throws IOException; // Defines OutputStream.write()
        public void write(byte[] b) throws IOException; // Overrides OutputStream.write()
        public void write(byte[] b, int off, int len) throws IOException; // Overrides OutputStream.write()
    // Protected Instance Methods
        protected void finalize() throws IOException;
}
```

---

java.io.FilenameFilter

This interface defines the accept() method that must be implemented by any object that filters filenames (i.e., selects a subset of filenames from a list of filenames). There are no standard `FilenameFilter` classes implemented by Java, but objects that implement this interface are used by the `java.awt.FileDialog` object, and by the `File.list()` method. A typical `FilenameFilter` object might check that the specified `File` represents a file (not a directory), is readable (and possibly writable as well), and that its name ends with some desired extension.

```
public abstract interface FilenameFilter {
    // Public Instance Methods
        public abstract boolean accept(File dir, String name);

}
```

---

java.io.FilterInputStream

This class provides method definitions required to filter data obtained from the `InputStream` specified when the `FilterInputStream` is created. It must be sub-classed to perform some sort of filtering operation, and may not be instantiated directly. See the subclasses `BufferedInputStream`, `DataInputStream`, `Line-NumberInputStream`, and `PushbackInputStream`.

```
public class FilterInputStream extends InputStream {
    // Protected Constructor
        protected FilterInputStream(InputStream in);
    // Protected Instance Variables
        protected InputStream in;
    // Public Instance Methods
        public int available() throws IOException;  // Overrides InputStream.available()
        public void close() throws IOException;  // Overrides InputStream.close()
        public synchronized void mark(int readlimit);  // Overrides InputStream.mark()
        public boolean markSupported();  // Overrides InputStream.markSupported()
        public int read() throws IOException;  // Defines InputStream.read()
        public int read(byte[] b) throws IOException;  // Overrides InputStream.read()
        public int read(byte[] b, int off, int len) throws IOException;  // Overrides InputStream.read()
        public synchronized void reset() throws IOException;  // Overrides InputStream.reset()
        public long skip(long n) throws IOException;  // Overrides InputStream.skip()

}
```

---

java.io.FilterOutputStream

This class provides method definitions required to filter the data to be written to the `OutputStream` specified when the `FilterOutputStream` is created. It must be subclassed to perform some sort of filtering operation and may not be instantiated directly. See the subclasses `BufferedOutputStream`, `DataOutputStream`, and `PrintStream`.

```
public class FilterOutputStream extends OutputStream {
    // Public Constructor
        public FilterOutputStream(OutputStream out);
    // Protected Instance Variables
        protected OutputStream out;
    // Public Instance Methods
```

$\rightarrow$

java.io

```
        public void close() throws IOException; // Overrides OutputStream.close()
        public void flush() throws IOException; // Overrides OutputStream.flush()
        public void write(int b) throws IOException; // Defines OutputStream.write()
        public void write(byte[] b) throws IOException; // Overrides OutputStream.write()
        public void write(byte[] b, int off, int len) throws IOException; // Overrides OutputStream.write()
}
```

java.io.InputStream

This abstract class is the superclass of all input streams. It defines the basic input methods that all input stream classes provide.

read() reads a single byte or an array or subarray of bytes. skip() skips a specified number of bytes of input. available() returns the number of bytes that can be read without blocking. close() closes the input stream and frees up any system resources associated with it. The stream should not be used after close() has been called.

If markSupported() returns true for a given InputStream, then that stream supports the mark() and reset() methods. mark() marks the current position in the input stream so that reset() can return to that position as long as no more than the specified number of bytes have been read between the mark() and reset().

```
public abstract class InputStream extends Object {
    // Public Constructor
        public InputStream(); // Empty
    // Public Instance Methods
        public int available() throws IOException;
        public void close() throws IOException; // Empty
        public synchronized void mark(int readlimit); // Empty
        public boolean markSupported();
        public abstract int read() throws IOException;
        public int read(byte[] b) throws IOException;
        public int read(byte[] b, int off, int len) throws IOException;
        public synchronized void reset() throws IOException;
        public long skip(long n) throws IOException;
}
```

java.io.LineNumberInputStream

This class is a FilterInputStream that keeps track of the number of lines of data that have been read. getLineNumber() returns the current line number. setLine-Number() sets the line number of the current line. Subsequent lines are numbered starting from that number.

```
public class LineNumberInputStream extends FilterInputStream {
    // Public Constructor
    public LineNumberInputStream(InputStream in);
    // Public Instance Methods
    public int available() throws IOException; // Overrides FilterInputStream.available()
    public int getLineNumber();
    public void mark(int readlimit); // Overrides FilterInputStream.mark()
    public int read() throws IOException; // Overrides FilterInputStream.read()
    public int read(byte[] b, int off, int len) throws IOException; // Overrides FilterInputStream.read()
    public void reset() throws IOException; // Overrides FilterInputStream.reset()
    public void setLineNumber(int lineNumber);
    public long skip(long n) throws IOException; // Overrides FilterInputStream.skip()
}
```

java.io.OutputStream

This abstract class is the superclass of all output streams. It defines the basic output methods that all output stream classes provide.

write() writes a single byte or an array or subarray of bytes. flush() forces any buffered output to be written. close() closes the stream and frees up any system resources associated with it. The stream may not be used once close() has been called.

```
public abstract class OutputStream extends Object {
    // Public Constructor
    public OutputStream(); // Empty
    // Public Instance Methods
    public void close() throws IOException; // Empty
    public void flush() throws IOException; // Empty
    public abstract void write(int b) throws IOException;
    public void write(byte[] b) throws IOException;
    public void write(byte[] b, int off, int len) throws IOException;
}
```

java.io.PipedInputStream

This class is an InputStream that implements one-half of a pipe, and is useful for communication between threads. A PipedInputStream must be connected to a PipedOutputStream object, which may be specified when the PipedInput-Stream is created or with the connect() method. Data read from a PipedInput-Stream object is received from the PipedOutputStream to which it is connected.

See InputStream() for information on the low-level methods for reading data from a PipedInputStream. A FilterInputStream may be used to provide a higher-level interface for reading data from a PipedInputStream.

```
public class PipedInputStream extends InputStream {
    // Public Constructors
    public PipedInputStream(PipedOutputStream src) throws IOException;
```

$\rightarrow$

```
      public PipedInputStream(); // Empty
   // Public Instance Methods
      public void close() throws IOException; // Overrides InputStream.close()
      public void connect(PipedOutputStream src) throws IOException;
      public synchronized int read() throws IOException; // Defines InputStream.read()
      public synchronized int read(byte[] b, int off, int len) throws IOException; // Overrides InputStream.read()

}
```

java.io.PipedOutputStream

This class is an OutputStream that implements one half of a pipe, and is useful for communication between threads. A PipedOutputStream must be connected to a PipedInputStream, which may be specified when the PipedOutputStream is created or with the connect() method. Data written to the PipedOutputStream will be available for reading on the PipedInputStream.

See OutputStream() for information on the low-level methods for writing data to a PipedOutputStream. A FilterOutputStream may be used to provide a higher-level interface for writing data to a PipedOutputStream.

```
public class PipedOutputStream extends OutputStream {
   // Public Constructors
      public PipedOutputStream(PipedInputStream snk) throws IOException;
      public PipedOutputStream(); // Empty
   // Public Instance Methods
      public void close() throws IOException; // Overrides OutputStream.close()
      public void connect(PipedInputStream snk) throws IOException;
      public void write(int b) throws IOException; // Defines OutputStream.write()
      public void write(byte[] b, int off, int len) throws IOException; // Overrides OutputStream.write()

}
```

java.io.PrintStream

This class is a FilterOutputStream that implements a number of methods for displaying textual representation of Java primitive data types. The print() methods output a standard textual representation of each data type. The println() methods do the same, and follow that representation with a newline. The methods convert various Java primitive types to String representations and then output the resulting string. When an Object is passed to a print() or println(), it is converted to a String by calling its toString() method.

PrintStream is the OutputStream type that makes it easiest to output text. As such, it is the most commonly used of the output streams. The System.out variable is a PrintStream.

Note that this class does not handle Unicode—it discards the top 8 bits of all 16-bit Unicode characters, and thus displays only Latin-1 (ISO8859-1) characters.

Note that `PrintStream` outputs textual representations of Java data types, while the `DataOutputStream` outputs binary representations of data.

```
public class PrintStream extends FilterOutputStream {
    // Public Constructors
        public PrintStream(OutputStream out);
        public PrintStream(OutputStream out, boolean autoflush);
    // Public Instance Methods
        public boolean checkError();
        public void close();  // Overrides FilterOutputStream.close()
        public void flush();  // Overrides FilterOutputStream.flush()
        public void print(Object obj);
        public synchronized void print(String s);
        public synchronized void print(char[] s);
        public void print(char c);
        public void print(int i);
        public void print(long l);
        public void print(float f);
        public void print(double d);
        public void print(boolean b);
        public void println();
        public synchronized void println(Object obj);
        public synchronized void println(String s);
        public synchronized void println(char[] s);
        public synchronized void println(char c);
        public synchronized void println(int i);
        public synchronized void println(long l);
        public synchronized void println(float f);
        public synchronized void println(double d);
        public synchronized void println(boolean b);
        public void write(int b) throws IOException;  // Overrides FilterOutputStream.write()
        public void write(byte[] b, int off, int len) throws IOException;  // Overrides FilterOutputStream.write()
}
```

java.io.PushbackInputStream

This class is a `FilterInputStream` that implements a one-byte push back buffer. The `unread()` method "pushes" one character back into the stream—this character is the first one read by the next call to a `read()` method. This class is sometimes useful when writing parsers.

```
public class PushbackInputStream extends FilterInputStream {
    // Public Constructor
        public PushbackInputStream(InputStream in);
    // Protected Instance Variables
        protected int pushBack;
    // Public Instance Methods
        public int available() throws IOException;  // Overrides FilterInputStream.available()
        public boolean markSupported();  // Overrides FilterInputStream.markSupported()
```

$\rightarrow$

```
        public int read( ) throws IOException;  // Overrides FilterInputStream.read( )
        public int read(byte[] bytes, int offset, int length) throws IOException;
                        // Overrides FilterInputStream.read( )
        public void unread(int ch) throws IOException;

}
```

java.io.RandomAccessFile

This class allows reading and writing of arbitrary bytes, text, and primitive Java data types from or to any specified location in a file. Because this class provides random, rather than sequential, access to files it is neither a subclass of InputStream nor of OutputStream, but provides an entirely independent method for reading and writing data from or to files. RandomAccessFile implements the same interfaces as DataInputStream and DataOutputStream, and thus defines the same methods for reading and writing data as those classes do.

In addition, the seek() method provides random access to the file—it is used to select the position in the file from which or to which data should be read or written. The *mode* argument to the constructor methods should be "r" for a file that is to be read-only, and "rw" for a file that is to be written (and perhaps read as well).

```
public class RandomAccessFile extends Object implements DataOutput, DataInput {
        // Public Constructors
        public RandomAccessFile(String name, String mode) throws IOException;
        public RandomAccessFile(File file, String mode) throws IOException;
        // Public Instance Methods
        public void close( ) throws IOException;
        public final FileDescriptor getFD( ) throws IOException;
        public long getFilePointer( ) throws IOException;
        public long length( ) throws IOException;
        public int read( ) throws IOException;
        public int read(byte[] b, int off, int len) throws IOException;
        public int read(byte[] b) throws IOException;
        public final boolean readBoolean( ) throws IOException;
        public final byte readByte( ) throws IOException;
        public final char readChar( ) throws IOException;
        public final double readDouble( ) throws IOException;
        public final float readFloat( ) throws IOException;
        public final void readFully(byte[] b) throws IOException;
        public final void readFully(byte[] b, int off, int len) throws IOException;
        public final int readInt( ) throws IOException;
        public final String readLine( ) throws IOException;
        public final long readLong( ) throws IOException;
        public final short readShort( ) throws IOException;
        public final String readUTF( ) throws IOException;
        public final int readUnsignedByte( ) throws IOException;
        public final int readUnsignedShort( ) throws IOException;
        public void seek(long pos) throws IOException;
        public int skipBytes(int n) throws IOException;
```

```
        public void write(int b) throws IOException;
        public void write(byte[] b) throws IOException;
        public void write(byte[] b, int off, int len) throws IOException;
        public final void writeBoolean(boolean v) throws IOException;
        public final void writeByte(int v) throws IOException;
        public final void writeBytes(String s) throws IOException;
        public final void writeChar(int v) throws IOException;
        public final void writeChars(String s) throws IOException;
        public final void writeDouble(double v) throws IOException;
        public final void writeFloat(float v) throws IOException;
        public final void writeInt(int v) throws IOException;
        public final void writeLong(long v) throws IOException;
        public final void writeShort(int v) throws IOException;
        public final void writeUTF(String str) throws IOException;

}
```

java.io.SequenceInputStream

This class provides a way of seamlessly concatenating the data from two or more input streams. It provides an InputStream interface to a sequence of Input-Stream objects. Data is read from the streams in the order in which the streams are specified. When the end of one stream is reached, data is automatically read from the next stream. This class might be useful, for example, when implementing an "include file" facility for a parser of some sort.

```
public class SequenceInputStream extends InputStream {
    // Public Constructors
        public SequenceInputStream(Enumeration e);
        public SequenceInputStream(InputStream s1, InputStream s2);
    // Public Instance Methods
        public void close() throws IOException; // Overrides InputStream.close()
        public int read() throws IOException; // Defines InputStream.read()
        public int read(byte[] buf, int pos, int len) throws IOException; // Overrides InputStream.read()

}
```

java.io.StreamTokenizer

This class performs lexical analysis of a specified input stream and breaks the input up into tokens. It can be extremely useful when writing simple parsers.

nextToken() returns the next token in the stream—this is either one of the constants defined by the class, (which represent end-of-file, end-of-line, a parsed floating-point number, and a parsed word) or a character value. pushBack() "pushes" the token back onto the stream, so that it is returned by the next call to next-Token(). The public variables sval and nval contain the string and numeric values (if applicable) of the most recently read token. They are applicable when the

→

java.io

returned token is TT_WORD and TT_NUMBER. lineno() returns the current line number.

The remaining methods specify flags and characters that control how tokens are recognized. wordChars() specifies a range of characters that should be treated as parts of words. whitespaceChars() specifies a range of characters that serve to delimit tokens. eolIsSignificant() specifies whether end-of-line is significant. If so, the TT_EOL constant is returned for end-of-lines. Otherwise they are treated as whitespace.

ordinaryChars() and ordinaryChar() specify characters that are never part of tokens and should be returned as-is. resetChars() makes all characters "ordinary."

commentChar() specifies a character that begins a comment that lasts until the end of the line. No characters in the comment are returned. slashStarComments() and slashSlashComments() specify whether the StringTokenizer should recognize C and C++-style comments. If so, no part of the comments are returned as tokens.

quoteChar() specifies a character used to delimit strings. When a string token is parsed, the quote character is returned as the token value, and the body of the string is stored in the sval variable.

parseNumbers() specifies that the StringTokenizer should recognize and return double-precision floating-point number tokens.

lowerCaseMode() specifies whether TT_WORD tokens should be converted to all lowercase characters before being stored in sval.

```
public class StreamTokenizer extends Object {
    // Public Constructor
    public StreamTokenizer(InputStream I);
    // Constants
    public final static int TT_EOF;
    public final static int TT_EOL;
    public final static int TT_NUMBER;
    public final static int TT_WORD;
    // Public Instance Variables
    public double nval;
    public String sval;
    public int ttype;
    // Public Instance Methods
    public void commentChar(int ch);
    public void eolIsSignificant(boolean flag);
    public int lineno();
    public void lowerCaseMode(boolean fl);
    public int nextToken() throws IOException;
    public void ordinaryChar(int ch);
    public void ordinaryChars(int low, int hi);
    public void parseNumbers();
    public void pushBack();
    public void quoteChar(int ch);
    public void resetSyntax();
```

```
        public void slashSlashComments(boolean flag);
        public void slashStarComments(boolean flag);
        public String toString( ); // Overrides Object.toString( )
        public void whitespaceChars(int low, int hi);
        public void wordChars(int low, int hi);
}
```

java.io.StringBufferInputStream

This class is a subclass of `InputStream` in which input data comes from the characters of a specified `String` object. This is useful when you want to read data in memory as if it were coming from a file or pipe or socket. This class is much like `ByteArrayInputStream`.

```
public class StringBufferInputStream extends InputStream {
    // Public Constructor
        public StringBufferInputStream(String s);
    // Protected Instance Variables
        protected String buffer;
        protected int count;
        protected int pos;
    // Public Instance Methods
        public synchronized int available( ); // Overrides InputStream.available( )
        public synchronized int read( ); // Defines InputStream.read( )
        public synchronized int read(byte[] b, int off, int len); // Overrides InputStream.read( )
        public synchronized void reset( ); // Overrides InputStream.reset( )
        public synchronized long skip(long n); // Overrides InputStream.skip( )
}
```

java.io

The java.lang Package

The `java.lang` package contains the classes that are most central to the Java language. As you can see from Figure 23-1, the class hierarchy is broad rather than deep, which means that the classes are independent of each other.

`Object` is the ultimate superclass of all Java classes and is therefore at the top of all class hierarchies. `Class` is a class that describes a Java class. There is one `Class` object for each class that is loaded into Java.

`Boolean`, `Character`, `Double`, `Float`, `Integer`, and `Long` are class wrappers around primitive Java data types. These classes are useful when you need to pass a value by reference, and also contains useful utility methods.

`String` and `StringBuffer` are objects that represent strings. `String` is an immutable type; `StringBuffer` may have its string changed in place.

`Runtime` provides a number of low-level methods associated with the Java runtime system. `System` provides similar low-level system methods. All the `System` methods are class methods, and this class may not be instantiated. `Math` is a similar class that supports only class methods—its methods provide floating-point math support.

`Process` defines a platform-independent interface to processes running externally to the Java interpreter. The `Thread` class provides support for multiple threads of control running within the same Java interpreter.

`Throwable` is the root class of the exception and error hierarchy. `Throwable` objects are used with the Java `throw` and `catch` statements.

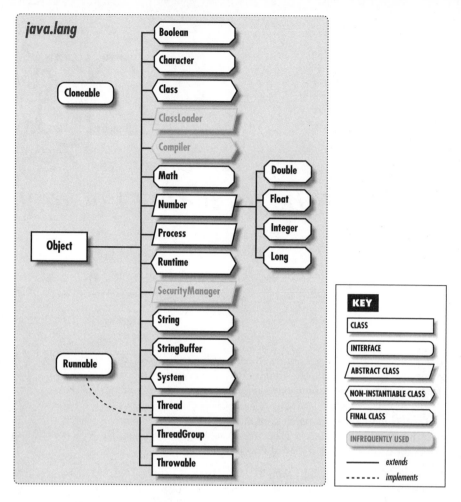

Figure 23-1: The java.lang package

---

java.lang.Boolean

This class provides an object wrapper around the boolean primitive type. It is use-ful when you need to pass a boolean value by reference. Note the TRUE and FALSE constants, which are Boolean objects; they are not the same as the true and false boolean values.

booleanValue() returns the boolean value of a Boolean object. The class method getBoolean() retrieves the boolean value of a named property. The class method valueOf() parses a string and returns the Boolean value it represents.

```
public final class Boolean extends Object {
    // Public Constructors
    public Boolean(boolean value);
    public Boolean(String s);
    // Constants
```

```
        public final static Boolean FALSE;
        public final static Boolean TRUE;
    // Class Methods
        public static boolean getBoolean(String name);
        public static Boolean valueOf(String s);
    // Public Instance Methods
        public boolean booleanValue();
        public boolean equals(Object obj); // Overrides Object.equals()
        public int hashCode(); // Overrides Object.hashCode()
        public String toString(); // Overrides Object.toString()

}
```

java.lang.Character

This class provides an object wrapper around the primitive char data type. It is useful when you need to pass a char value by reference. charValue() returns the char value of a Character object. A number of class methods provide the Java/Unicode equivalent of the C *<ctype.h>* character macros for checking the type of characters and converting to uppercase and lowercase letters. digit() returns the integer equivalent of a given character for a given radix (e.g., radix 16 for hexadecimal). forDigit() returns the character that corresponds to the specified value for the specified radix.

```
public final class Character extends Object {
    // Public Constructor
        public Character(char value);
    // Constants
        public final static int MAX_RADIX;
        public final static int MIN_RADIX;
    // Class Methods
        public static int digit(char ch, int radix);
        public static char forDigit(int digit, int radix);
        public static boolean isDigit(char ch);
        public static boolean isLowerCase(char ch);
        public static boolean isSpace(char ch);
        public static boolean isUpperCase(char ch);
        public static char toLowerCase(char ch);
        public static char toUpperCase(char ch);
    // Public Instance Methods
        public char charValue();
        public boolean equals(Object obj); // Overrides Object.equals()
        public int hashCode(); // Overrides Object.hashCode()
        public String toString(); // Overrides Object.toString()

}
```

java.lang

java.lang.Class

This class represents a Java class—there is a Class object for each class that is loaded into Java. There is no constructor for this class, but the class method for-Name() returns a Class object for a named class, or dynamically loads the class, if necessary. Once a class has been loaded, and its Class object created, new-Instance() creates an instance of a given class—this is the only way to create an object in Java without using new. These two methods allow the dynamic loading and instantiation of classes in Java.

getName() returns the name of the class. getSuperclass() returns its superclass. isInterface() tests whether the Class object represents an interface. getInterfaces() returns an array of the interfaces that this class implements.

```
public final class Class extends Object {
    // No Constructor
    // Class Methods
        public static Class forName(String className) throws ClassNotFoundException;
    // Public Instance Methods
        public ClassLoader getClassLoader();
        public Class[] getInterfaces();
        public String getName();
        public Class getSuperclass();
        public boolean isInterface();
        public Object newInstance() throws InstantiationException, IllegalAccessException;
        public String toString();  // Overrides Object.toString()
}
```

java.lang.ClassLoader

This abstract class defines the necessary hook for Java to load classes over the network, or from other sources. Normal applications do not need to use or subclass this class.

```
public abstract class ClassLoader extends Object {
    // Protected Constructor
        protected ClassLoader();
    // Protected Instance Methods
        protected final Class defineClass(byte[] data, int offset, int length) throws ClassFormatError;
        protected final Class findSystemClass(String name) throws ClassNotFoundException, NoClassDefFoundError;
        protected abstract Class loadClass(String name, boolean resolve) throws ClassNotFoundException;
        protected final void resolveClass(Class c);
}
```

java.lang.Cloneable

This interface defines no methods or variables, but indicates that the class that implements it may be cloned (i.e., copied) by calling the Object method clone().

Calling `clone()` for an object that does not implement this interface causes a `CloneNotSupportedException` to be thrown.

```
public interface Cloneable {

}
```

java.lang.Compiler

The static methods of this class provide an interface to the Java compiler.

```
public final class Compiler extends Object {
    // No Constructor
    // Class Methods
        public static Object command(Object any);
        public static boolean compileClass(Class clazz);
        public static boolean compileClasses(String string);
        public static void disable();
        public static void enable();

}
```

java.lang.Double

This class provides an object wrapper around the `double` primitive data type. This is useful when you need to pass a `double` by reference. `valueOf` converts a string to a `Double`, `doubleValue()` returns the primitive `double` value of a `Double` object, and there are other methods for returning a `Double` value as a variety of other primitive types.

This class also provides some useful constants and static methods for testing `double` values. `MIN_VALUE` and `MAX_VALUE` are the smallest (closest to zero) and largest representable `double` values. `isInfinite()` in class method and instance method forms tests whether a `double` or a `Double` has an infinite value. Similarly `isNaN()` tests whether a `double` or `Double` is not-a-number—this is a comparison that cannot be done directly because the `NaN` constant never tests equal to any other value, including itself. `doubleToLongBits()` and `longBitsToDouble()` allow you to manipulate the bit representation of a `double` directly.

```
public final class Double extends Number {
    // Public Constructors
        public Double(double value);
        public Double(String s) throws NumberFormatException;
    // Constants
        public final static double MAX_VALUE;
        public final static double MIN_VALUE;
        public final static double NEGATIVE_INFINITY;
        public final static double NaN;
        public final static double POSITIVE_INFINITY;
    // Class Methods
        public static long doubleToLongBits(double value);
        public static boolean isInfinite(double v);
```

→

```
          public static boolean isNaN(double v);
          public static double longBitsToDouble(long bits);
          public static String toString(double d);
          public static Double valueOf(String s) throws NumberFormatException;
    // Public Instance Methods
          public double doubleValue();  // Defines Number.doubleValue()
          public boolean equals(Object obj);  // Overrides Object.equals()
          public float floatValue();  // Defines Number.floatValue()
          public int hashCode();  // Overrides Object.hashCode()
          public int intValue();  // Defines Number.intValue()
          public boolean isInfinite();
          public boolean isNaN();
          public long longValue();  // Defines Number.longValue()
          public String toString();  // Overrides Object.toString()

}
```

java.lang.Float

This class provides an object wrapper around the `float` primitive data type. This is useful when you need to pass a `float` by reference. `valueOf` converts a string to a `Float`, `floatValue()` returns the primitive `float` value of a `Float` object, and there are methods for returning a `Float` value as a variety of other primitive types.

This class also provides some useful constants and static methods for testing `float` values. `MIN_VALUE` and `MAX_VALUE` are the smallest (closest to zero) and largest representable `double` values. `isInfinite()` in class method and instance method forms tests whether a `float` or a `Float` has an infinite value. Similarly `isNaN()` tests whether a `float` or `Float` is not-a-number—this is a comparison that cannot be done directly because the `NaN` constant never tests equal to any other value, including itself. `floatToIntBits()` and `intBitsToFloat()` allow you to manipulate the bit representation of a `float` directly.

```
public final class Float extends Number {
    // Public Constructors
          public Float(float value);
          public Float(double value);
          public Float(String s) throws NumberFormatException;
    // Constants
          public final static float MAX_VALUE;
          public final static float MIN_VALUE;
          public final static float NEGATIVE_INFINITY;
          public final static float NaN;
          public final static float POSITIVE_INFINITY;
    // Class Methods
          public static int floatToIntBits(float value);
          public static float intBitsToFloat(int bits);
          public static boolean isInfinite(float v);
          public static boolean isNaN(float v);
          public static String toString(float f);
```

```
        public static Float valueOf(String s) throws NumberFormatException;
    // Public Instance Methods
        public double doubleValue();  // Defines Number.doubleValue( )
        public boolean equals(Object obj);  // Overrides Object.equals( )
        public float floatValue();  // Defines Number.floatValue( )
        public int hashCode();  // Overrides Object.hashCode( )
        public int intValue();  // Defines Number.intValue( )
        public boolean isInfinite( );
        public boolean isNaN( );
        public long longValue();  // Defines Number.longValue( )
        public String toString();  // Overrides Object.toString( )

}
```

---

java.lang.Integer

This class provides an object wrapper around the `int` primitive data type. It is useful when you need to pass `int` values by reference. This class also contains useful minimum and maximum constants and useful conversion methods. `parseInt()` and `valueOf` convert a string to an `int` or to an `Integer`, respectively. Each can take a radix argument to specify the base that the value is represented in. `toString( )` converts in the other direction and may also take a radix argument. Other routines return the value of an `Integer` as various primitive types, and finally, the `getInteger()` methods return the integer value of a named property or the value of the specified default.

```
public final class Integer extends Number {
    // Public Constructors
        public Integer(int value);
        public Integer(String s) throws NumberFormatException;
    // Constants
        public final static int MAX_VALUE;
        public final static int MIN_VALUE;
    // Class Methods
        public static Integer getInteger(String nm);
        public static Integer getInteger(String nm, int val);
        public static Integer getInteger(String nm, Integer val);
        public static int parseInt(String s, int radix) throws NumberFormatException;
        public static int parseInt(String s) throws NumberFormatException;
        public static String toString(int i, int radix);
        public static String toString(int i);
        public static Integer valueOf(String s, int radix) throws NumberFormatException;
        public static Integer valueOf(String s) throws NumberFormatException;
    // Public Instance Methods
        public double doubleValue();  // Defines Number.doubleValue( )
        public boolean equals(Object obj);  // Overrides Object.equals( )
        public float floatValue();  // Defines Number.floatValue( )
        public int hashCode();  // Overrides Object.hashCode( )
        public int intValue();  // Defines Number.intValue( )
```

java.lang

→

```
        public long longValue( );  // Defines Number.longValue( )
        public String toString( );  // Overrides Object.toString( )

}
```

java.lang.Long

This class provides an object wrapper around the `long` primitive data type. It is useful when you need to pass `long` values by reference. This class also contains useful minimum and maximum constants and useful conversion methods. `parseLong()` and `valueOf` convert a string to a `long` or to a `Long`, respectively. Each can take a radix argument to specify the base that the value is represented in. `toString` converts in the other direction and may also take a radix argument. Other routines return the value of a `Long` as various primitive types, and finally, the `getLong()` methods return the `long` value of a named property or the value of the specified default.

```
public final class Long extends Number {
    // Public Constructors
        public Long(long value);
        public Long(String s) throws NumberFormatException;
    // Constants
        public final static long MAX_VALUE;
        public final static long MIN_VALUE;
    // Class Methods
        public static Long getLong(String nm);
        public static Long getLong(String nm, long val);
        public static Long getLong(String nm, Long val);
        public static long parseLong(String s, int radix) throws NumberFormatException;
        public static long parseLong(String s) throws NumberFormatException;
        public static String toString(long i, int radix);
        public static String toString(long i);
        public static Long valueOf(String s, int radix) throws NumberFormatException;
        public static Long valueOf(String s) throws NumberFormatException;
    // Public Instance Methods
        public double doubleValue( );  // Defines Number.doubleValue( )
        public boolean equals(Object obj);  // Overrides Object.equals( )
        public float floatValue( );  // Defines Number.floatValue( )
        public int hashCode( );  // Overrides Object.hashCode( )
        public int intValue( );  // Defines Number.intValue( )
        public long longValue( );  // Defines Number.longValue( )
        public String toString( );  // Overrides Object.toString( )

}
```

java.lang.Math

This class defines constants for the mathematical values e and π, and defines static methods for floating point trigonometry, exponentiation, and other operations. It is the equivalent of the C *<math.h>* functions. It also contains methods for computing minimum and maximum values and for generating pseudo-random numbers.

```
public final class Math extends Object {
    // No Constructor
    // Constants
        public final static double E;
        public final static double PI;
    // Class Methods
        public static double IEEEremainder(double f1, double f2);
        public static int abs(int a);
        public static long abs(long a);
        public static float abs(float a);
        public static double abs(double a);
        public static double acos(double a);
        public static double asin(double a);
        public static double atan(double a);
        public static double atan2(double a, double b);
        public static double ceil(double a);
        public static double cos(double a);
        public static double exp(double a);
        public static double floor(double a);
        public static double log(double a) throws ArithmeticException;
        public static int max(int a, int b);
        public static long max(long a, long b);
        public static float max(float a, float b);
        public static double max(double a, double b);
        public static int min(int a, int b);
        public static long min(long a, long b);
        public static float min(float a, float b);
        public static double min(double a, double b);
        public static double pow(double a, double b) throws ArithmeticException;
        public static synchronized double random();
        public static double rint(double a);
        public static int round(float a);
        public static long round(double a);
        public static double sin(double a);
        public static double sqrt(double a) throws ArithmeticException;
        public static double tan(double a);
}
```

java.lang.Number

This is an abstract class that is the superclass of Integer, Long, Float, and Double. It defines conversion functions that those types all implement.

```
public abstract class Number extends Object {
    // Public Constructor
        public Number(); // Empty
    // Public Instance Methods
        public abstract double doubleValue();
```

$\rightarrow$

```
        public abstract float floatValue( );
        public abstract int intValue( );
        public abstract long longValue( );

}
```

java.lang.Object

This is the root class in Java. All classes are subclasses of Object, and thus all objects can invoke the public and protected methods of this class. equals() tests whether two objects have the same value (i.e., not whether two variables refer to the same object, but whether two distinct objects contain the same values). For classes that implement the Cloneable interface, clone() makes a copy of an Object. getClass() returns the Class object associated with any Object, and the notify(), notifyAll(), and wait() methods are used for thread synchronization on a given Object.

A number of these Object methods should be overridden by subclasses of Object. Subclasses should provide their own definition of the toString() method so that they can be used with the string concatenation operator and with the Print-Stream.println() method. Defining the toString() method for all objects also helps with debugging.

Classes that contain references to other objects should override the equals() and clone() methods (for Cloneable objects). The equals() method should recursively call the equals() methods of all the objects the class refers to. Similarly, the clone() method should recursively call the clone() method of all objects the class refers to.

Classes that allocate system resources other than memory (such as file descriptors or windowing system graphic contexts) should override the finalize() method to release these resources when the object is no longer referred to.

Some classes may also want to override the hashCode() method to provide an appropriate hash code to be used when storing instances in a Hashtable data structure.

```
public class Object {
        // Public Constructor
        public Object( ); // Empty
        // Public Instance Methods
        public boolean equals(Object obj);
        public final Class getClass( );
        public int hashCode( );
        public final void notify( ) throws IllegalMonitorStateException;
        public final void notifyAll( ) throws IllegalMonitorStateException;
        public String toString( );
        public final void wait(long timeout) throws InterruptedException, IllegalMonitorStateException;
        public final void wait(long timeout, int nanos) throws InterruptedException, IllegalMonitorStateException;
        public final void wait( ) throws InterruptedException, IllegalMonitorStateException;
        // Protected Instance Methods
```

```
        protected Object clone( ) throws CloneNotSupportedException, OutOfMemoryError;
        protected void finalize( ) throws Throwable; // Empty

}
```

java.lang.Process

This class describes a process started by a `Runtime.exec()` method call that is running externally to the Java interpreter. Note that a `Process` is a very different thing than a `Thread`, though they can be operated on in similar ways. The `Process` class itself is abstract and may not be instantiated. The `System.exec()` methods return an internal subclass that implements the `Process` methods in a platform-dependent way.

```
public abstract class Process extends Object {
        // Default Constructor: public Process( )
        // Public Instance Methods
        public abstract void destroy( );
        public abstract int exitValue( ) throws IllegalThreadStateException;
        public abstract InputStream getErrorStream( );
        public abstract InputStream getInputStream( );
        public abstract OutputStream getOutputStream( );
        public abstract int waitFor( ) throws InterruptedException;

}
```

java.lang.Runnable

This interface specifies the `run()` method that is required for use with the `Thread` class. Any class that implements this interface can provide the "body" of a thread. See `Thread` for more information.

```
public abstract interface Runnable {
        // Public Instance Methods
        public abstract void run( );

}
```

java.lang.Runtime

This class encapsulates a number of platform-dependent system functions. The static method `getRuntime()` returns the `Runtime` object for the current platform, and this object can be used to perform system functions in a platform-independent way.

`exec()` starts a new process running externally to the interpreter. Note that any processes run outside of Java may be system-dependent.

→

java.lang

`exit()` causes the Java interpreter to exit and return a specified return code.

`freeMemory()` returns the approximate amount of free memory. `totalMemory()` returns the total amount of memory available to the Java interpreter. `gc()` forces the garbage collector to run synchronously, which may free up more memory. Similarly, `runFinalization()` forces the `finalize()` methods of unreferenced objects to be run immediately. This may free up system resources that those objects were holding.

`getLocalizedInputStream()` and `getLocalizedOutputStream()` return input and output streams that automatically translate the local character encoding to Unicode and Unicode to the local character encoding.

`load()` loads a dynamic library with a fully specified path name. `loadLibrary()` loads a dynamic library with only the library name specified; it looks in platform-dependent locations for the specified library. These libraries generally contain native code definitions for native methods.

`traceInstructions()` and `traceMethodCalls()` enable and disable tracing by the interpreter.

Note that some of the `Runtime` methods are more commonly called via the static methods of the `System` class.

```
public class Runtime extends Object {
    // No Constructor
    // Class Methods
        public static Runtime getRuntime();
    // Public Instance Methods
        public Process exec(String command) throws IOException;
        public Process exec(String command, String[] envp) throws IOException;
        public Process exec(String[] cmdarray) throws IOException;
        public Process exec(String[] cmdarray, String[] envp) throws IOException;
        public void exit(int status);
        public long freeMemory();
        public void gc();
        public InputStream getLocalizedInputStream(InputStream in);
        public OutputStream getLocalizedOutputStream(OutputStream out);
        public synchronized void load(String filename) throws UnsatisfiedLinkError;
        public synchronized void loadLibrary(String libname) throws UnsatisfiedLinkError;
        public void runFinalization();
        public long totalMemory();
        public void traceInstructions(boolean on);
        public void traceMethodCalls(boolean on);

}
```

java.lang.SecurityManager

This abstract class defines the methods necessary to implement a security policy for the execution of untrusted code. Before performing a large number of potentially sensitive operations, Java calls methods of the `SecurityManager` object currently in effect to determine whether the operation is permitted. These methods throw a `SecurityException` if the operation is not permitted.

Normal applications do not need to use or subclass the `SecurityManager` class. It is only used for Web browsers, applet viewers, or other programs that may run untrusted code.

```
public abstract class SecurityManager extends Object {
    // Protected Constructor
        protected SecurityManager() throws SecurityException;
    // Protected Instance Variables
        protected boolean inCheck;
    // Public Instance Methods
        public void checkAccept(String host, int port) throws SecurityException;
        public void checkAccess(Thread g) throws SecurityException;
        public void checkAccess(ThreadGroup g) throws SecurityException;
        public void checkConnect(String host, int port) throws SecurityException;
        public void checkConnect(String host, int port, Object context);
        public void checkCreateClassLoader() throws SecurityException;
        public void checkDelete(String file) throws SecurityException;
        public void checkExec(String cmd) throws SecurityException;
        public void checkExit(int status) throws SecurityException;
        public void checkLink(String lib) throws SecurityException;
        public void checkListen(int port) throws SecurityException;
        public void checkPackageAccess(String pkg);
        public void checkPackageDefinition(String pkg);
        public void checkPropertiesAccess() throws SecurityException;
        public void checkPropertyAccess(String key) throws SecurityException;
        public void checkPropertyAccess(String key, String def) throws SecurityException;
        public void checkRead(FileDescriptor fd) throws SecurityException;
        public void checkRead(String file) throws SecurityException;
        public void checkRead(String file, Object context) throws SecurityException;
        public void checkSetFactory();
        public boolean checkTopLevelWindow(Object window);
        public void checkWrite(FileDescriptor fd) throws SecurityException;
        public void checkWrite(String file) throws SecurityException;
        public boolean getInCheck();
        public Object getSecurityContext();
    // Protected Instance Methods
        protected int classDepth(String name);
        protected int classLoaderDepth();
        protected ClassLoader currentClassLoader();
        protected Class[] getClassContext();
        protected boolean inClass(String name);
        protected boolean inClassLoader();
}
```

java.lang.String

The `String` class represents a string of characters. A `String` object is created by the Java compiler whenever it encounters a string in double-quotes—this method of creation is usually simpler than using a constructor. The methods of this class provide the equivalents of the C library *<string.h>* functions. `String` objects are immutable—you may not change their contents. Use a `StringBuffer` if you want to

$\rightarrow$

manipulate the contents of a string. The + operator can be used to concatenate `String` objects.

```java
public final class String extends Object {
    // Public Constructors
    public String();
    public String(String value);
    public String(char[] value);
    public String(char[] value, int offset, int count) throws StringIndexOutOfBoundsException;
    public String(byte[] ascii, int hibyte, int offset, int count) throws StringIndexOutOfBoundsException;
    public String(byte[] ascii, int hibyte);
    public String(StringBuffer buffer);
    // Class Methods
    public static String copyValueOf(char[] data, int offset, int count);
    public static String copyValueOf(char[] data);
    public static String valueOf(Object obj);
    public static String valueOf(char[] data);
    public static String valueOf(char[] data, int offset, int count);
    public static String valueOf(boolean b);
    public static String valueOf(char c);
    public static String valueOf(int i);
    public static String valueOf(long l);
    public static String valueOf(float f);
    public static String valueOf(double d);
    // Public Instance Methods
    public char charAt(int index) throws StringIndexOutOfBoundsException;
    public int compareTo(String anotherString);
    public String concat(String str);
    public boolean endsWith(String suffix);
    public boolean equals(Object anObject);  // Overrides Object.equals()
    public boolean equalsIgnoreCase(String anotherString);
    public void getBytes(int srcBegin, int srcEnd, byte[] dst, int dstBegin);
    public void getChars(int srcBegin, int srcEnd, char[] dst, int dstBegin);
    public int hashCode();  // Overrides Object.hashCode()
    public int indexOf(int ch);
    public int indexOf(int ch, int fromIndex);
    public int indexOf(String str);
    public int indexOf(String str, int fromIndex);
    public String intern();
    public int lastIndexOf(int ch);
    public int lastIndexOf(int ch, int fromIndex);
    public int lastIndexOf(String str);
    public int lastIndexOf(String str, int fromIndex);
    public int length();
    public boolean regionMatches(int toffset, String other, int ooffset, int len);
    public boolean regionMatches(boolean ignoreCase, int toffset, String other, int ooffset, int len);
    public String replace(char oldChar, char newChar);
    public boolean startsWith(String prefix, int toffset);
    public boolean startsWith(String prefix);
    public String substring(int beginIndex);
    public String substring(int beginIndex, int endIndex) throws StringIndexOutOfBoundsException;
    public char[] toCharArray();
```

```
    public String toLowerCase( );
    public String toString( );  // Overrides Object.toString()
    public String toUpperCase( );
    public String trim( );

}
```

java.lang.StringBuffer

This class represents a string of characters. It differs from the String class in that its contents may be modified. A StringBuffer object grows in length as necessary. The string stored in a StringBuffer object may be modified in place with the setCharAt( ), append( ), and insert( ) methods.

After a string is processed in a StringBuffer object, it may be efficiently converted to a String object for subsequent use. The StringBuffer.toString( ) method does not copy the internal array of characters; instead it shares that array with the new String object, and makes a new copy for itself only when further modifications are made to the StringBuffer object.

```
public final class StringBuffer extends Object {
    // Public Constructors
        public StringBuffer( );
        public StringBuffer(int length);
        public StringBuffer(String str);
    // Public Instance Methods
        public synchronized StringBuffer append(Object obj);
        public synchronized StringBuffer append(String str);
        public synchronized StringBuffer append(char[] str);
        public synchronized StringBuffer append(char[] str, int offset, int len);
        public StringBuffer append(boolean b);
        public synchronized StringBuffer append(char c);
        public StringBuffer append(int i);
        public StringBuffer append(long l);
        public StringBuffer append(float f);
        public StringBuffer append(double d);
        public int capacity( );
        public synchronized char charAt(int index) throws StringIndexOutOfBoundsException;
        public synchronized void ensureCapacity(int minimumCapacity);
        public synchronized void getChars(int srcBegin, int srcEnd, char[] dst, int dstBegin)
                                throws StringIndexOutOfBoundsException;
        public synchronized StringBuffer insert(int offset, Object obj) throws StringIndexOutOfBoundsException;
        public synchronized StringBuffer insert(int offset, String str) throws StringIndexOutOfBoundsException;
        public synchronized StringBuffer insert(int offset, char[] str) throws StringIndexOutOfBoundsException;
        public StringBuffer insert(int offset, boolean b) throws StringIndexOutOfBoundsException;
        public synchronized StringBuffer insert(int offset, char c) throws StringIndexOutOfBoundsException;
        public StringBuffer insert(int offset, int i) throws StringIndexOutOfBoundsException;
        public StringBuffer insert(int offset, long l) throws StringIndexOutOfBoundsException;
        public StringBuffer insert(int offset, float f) throws StringIndexOutOfBoundsException;
        public StringBuffer insert(int offset, double d) throws StringIndexOutOfBoundsException;
        public int length( );
        public synchronized void setCharAt(int index, char ch) throws StringIndexOutOfBoundsException;
```

$\rightarrow$

```
        public synchronized void setLength(int newLength) throws StringIndexOutOfBoundsException;
        public String toString(); // Overrides Object.toString()

}
```

java.lang.System

This class defines methods that provide a platform-independent interface to system functions. All of the methods and variables of this class are static. The class may not be instantiated.

The in, out, and err variables are the system standard input, output, and error streams.

arraycopy() copies an array or a portion of an array into a destination array.

currentTimeMillis() returns the current time in milliseconds since midnight GMT on January 1, 1970.

getProperty() looks up a named property on the system properties list, returning the optionally specified default value if no property definition was found. get-Properties() returns the entire properties list. setProperties() sets a Pro-perties object on the properties list.

exit(), gc(), load(), loadLibrary() and runFinalization() invoke the methods of the same name in the Runtime object. See Runtime for details.

```
public final class System extends Object {
    // No Constructor
    // Class Variables
        public static PrintStream err;
        public static InputStream in;
        public static PrintStream out;
    // Class Methods
        public static void arraycopy(Object src, int src_position, Object dst, int dst_position, int length)
                                throws ArrayIndexOutOfBoundsException, ArrayStoreException;
        public static long currentTimeMillis();
        public static void exit(int status);
        public static void gc();
        public static Properties getProperties();
        public static String getProperty(String key);
        public static String getProperty(String key, String def);
        public static SecurityManager getSecurityManager();
        public static String getenv(String name); // Obsolete; throws an error
        public static void load(String filename) throws UnsatisfiedLinkError;
        public static void loadLibrary(String libname) throws UnsatisfiedLinkError;
        public static void runFinalization();
        public static void setProperties(Properties props);
        public static void setSecurityManager(SecurityManager s) throws SecurityException;

}
```

java.lang.Thread

This class encapsulates all the information about a single thread of control running on the Java interpreter. To create a thread, you must pass a Runnable object (i.e., an object that implements the Runnable interface by defining a run() method) to the Thread constructor, or you must subclass Thread so that it defines its own run() method.

The run() method of the Thread or of the specified Runnable object is the "body" of the thread. It begins executing when the start() method of the Thread object is called. The thread runs until the run() method returns or until the stop() method of its Thread object is called. The static methods of this class operate on the currently running thread. The instance methods may be called from one thread to operate on a different thread.

start() starts a thread running. stop() stops it by throwing a ThreadDeath error. suspend() temporarily halts a thread. resume() allows it to resume. sleep() makes the current thread stop for a specified amount of time. yield() makes the current thread give up control to any other threads of equal priority that are waiting to run. join() waits for a thread to die.

```
public class Thread extends Object implements Runnable {
    // Public Constructors
        public Thread();
        public Thread(Runnable target);
        public Thread(ThreadGroup group, Runnable target);
        public Thread(String name);
        public Thread(ThreadGroup group, String name);
        public Thread(Runnable target, String name);
        public Thread(ThreadGroup group, Runnable target, String name);
    // Constants
        public final static int MAX_PRIORITY;
        public final static int MIN_PRIORITY;
        public final static int NORM_PRIORITY;
    // Class Methods
        public static int activeCount();
        public static Thread currentThread();
        public static void dumpStack();
        public static int enumerate(Thread[] tarray);
        public static boolean interrupted(); // Not implemented; throws NoSuchMethodError
        public static void sleep(long millis) throws InterruptedException;
        public static void sleep(long millis, int nanos) throws InterruptedException;
        public static void yield();
    // Public Instance Methods
        public void checkAccess() throws SecurityException;
        public int countStackFrames() throws IllegalThreadStateException;
        public void destroy(); // Not implemented; throws NoSuchMethodError
        public final String getName();
        public final int getPriority();
        public final ThreadGroup getThreadGroup();
        public void interrupt(); // Not implemented; throws NoSuchMethodError
        public final boolean isAlive();
```

$\rightarrow$

java.lang

```
      public final boolean isDaemon();
      public boolean isInterrupted();  // Not implemented; throws NoSuchMethodError
      public final synchronized void join(long millis) throws InterruptedException;
      public final synchronized void join(long millis, int nanos) throws InterruptedException;
      public final void join() throws InterruptedException;
      public final void resume();
      public void run();
      public final void setDaemon(boolean on) throws IllegalThreadStateException;
      public final void setName(String name);
      public final void setPriority(int newPriority) throws IllegalArgumentException;
      public synchronized void start() throws IllegalThreadStateException;
      public final void stop();
      public final synchronized void stop(Throwable o);
      public final void suspend();
      public String toString();  // Overrides Object.toString()

}
```

---

java.lang.ThreadGroup

This class defines a group of threads and allows operations on the group as a whole. A ThreadGroup may contain Thread objects, as well as "child" ThreadGroup objects. All ThreadGroup objects are created as children of some other Thread-Group, and thus there is a parent/child hierarchy of ThreadGroup objects.

Some programs may find it convenient to define their own ThreadGroup, but generally thread groups will only be used by system-level applications.

```
public class ThreadGroup extends Object {
    // Public Constructors
        public ThreadGroup(String name);
        public ThreadGroup(ThreadGroup parent, String name) throws NullPointerException;
    // Public Instance Methods
        public synchronized int activeCount();
        public synchronized int activeGroupCount();
        public final void checkAccess() throws SecurityException;
        public final synchronized void destroy() throws IllegalThreadStateException;
        public int enumerate(Thread[] list);
        public int enumerate(Thread[] list, boolean recurse);
        public int enumerate(ThreadGroup[] list);
        public int enumerate(ThreadGroup[] list, boolean recurse);
        public final int getMaxPriority();
        public final String getName();
        public final ThreadGroup getParent();
        public final boolean isDaemon();
        public synchronized void list();
        public final boolean parentOf(ThreadGroup g);
        public final synchronized void resume();
        public final void setDaemon(boolean daemon);
        public final synchronized void setMaxPriority(int pri);
```

```
        public final synchronized void stop();
        public final synchronized void suspend();
        public String toString();  // Overrides Object.toString()
        public void uncaughtException(Thread t, Throwable e);

}
```

---

java.lang.Throwable

This is the root class of the Java exception and error hierarchy. All exceptions and errors that are thrown are subclasses of Throwable. The getMessage() method retrieves the error message usually associated with the exception or error. print-StackTrace() prints a stack trace that shows where the exception occurred. fillInStackTrace() extends the stack trace when the exception is partially handled, and then re-thrown.

```
public class Throwable extends Object {
    // Public Constructors
        public Throwable();
        public Throwable(String message);
    // Public Instance Methods
        public Throwable fillInStackTrace();
        public String getMessage();
        public void printStackTrace();
        public void printStackTrace(PrintStream s);
        public String toString();  // Overrides Object.toString()

}
```

java.lang

The java.net Package

The `java.net` package provides a powerful and flexible infrastructure for networking. Figure 24-1 shows the class hierarchy for this package. Many of the classes in this package are part of the networking infrastructure and are not used by normal applications; these complicated classes can make the package a difficult one to understand. In this overview we describe only the classes that an application might normally use.

The `URL` class represents an Internet Uniform Resource Locator. It provides a very simple interface to networking—the object referred to by the URL can be downloaded with a single call, or streams may be opened to read from or write to the object.

At a slightly more complex level, the `URLConnection` object may be obtained from a given `URL` object. The `URLConnection` class provides additional methods that allow you to work with URLs in more sophisticated ways.

If you want to do more than simply download an object referenced by a URL, you can do your own networking with the `Socket` class. This class allows you to connect to a specified port on a specified Internet host and read and write data using the `InputStream` and `OutputStream` classes of the `java.io` package. If you want to implement a server to accept connections from clients, you can use the related `ServerSocket` class. Both `Socket` and `ServerSocket` use the `InetAddress` address class, which represents an Internet address.

Finally, the `java.net` package allows you to do very low-level networking with `DatagramPacket` objects which may be sent and received over the network through a `DatagramSocket` object.

See Section 7, *Networking*, for some example applications that use classes from `java.net`.

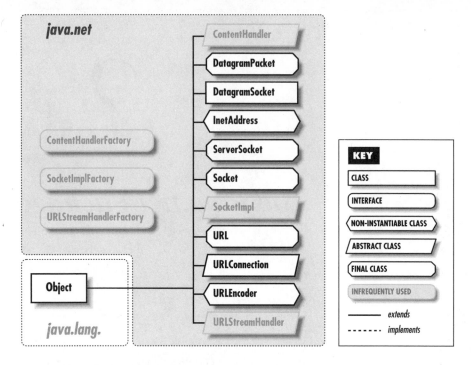

Figure 24-1: The java.net package

java.net.ContentHandler

This abstract class defines a method that reads data from a URLConnection and returns an object representing that data. Each subclass that implements this method is responsible for handling a different type of content (i.e., a different MIME type). Applications never create ContentHandler objects directly—they are created, when necessary, by the registered ContentHandlerFactory object. Applications should also never call ContentHandler methods directly—they should call URL.-getContent() or URLConnection.getContent() instead. The only time you would need to subclass ContentHandler is if you were writing a Web browser or similar application that needed to parse and understand some new content type.

```
public abstract class ContentHandler extends Object {
    // Default Constructor: public ContentHandler()
    // Public Instance Methods
        public abstract Object getContent(URLConnection urlc) throws IOException;
}
```

java.net.ContentHandlerFactory

This interface defines a method that creates and returns an appropriate Content-Handler object for a specified MIME type. A system-wide ContentHandler-

Factory interface may be specified by using the `URLConnection.setContent-HandlerFactory()` method.

Normal applications never need to use or implement this interface.

```
public abstract interface ContentHandlerFactory {
    // Public Instance Methods
        public abstract ContentHandler createContentHandler(String mimetype);

}
```

---

java.net.DatagramPacket

This class implements a "packet" of data that may be sent or received over the network through a `DatagramSocket`. One of the `DatagramPacket` constructors specifies an array of binary data to be sent with its destination address and port. A packet created with this constructor may then be sent with the `send()` method of a `DatagramSocket`. The other `DatagramPacket` constructor specifies an array of bytes into which data should be received. The `receive()` method of `Datagram-Socket` waits for data and stores it in a `DatagramPacket` created in this way. The contents and sender of a received packet may be queried with the `Datagram-Packet` instance methods.

```
public final class DatagramPacket extends Object {
    // Public Constructors
        public DatagramPacket(byte[] ibuf, int ilength);
        public DatagramPacket(byte[] ibuf, int ilength, InetAddress iaddr, int iport);
    // Public Instance Methods
        public InetAddress getAddress();
        public byte[] getData();
        public int getLength();
        public int getPort();

}
```

---

java.net.DatagramSocket

This class defines a socket that can receive and send unreliable datagram packets over the network. A datagram is a very low-level networking interface: it is simply an array of bytes sent over the network. A datagram does not implement any kind of stream-based communication protocol, and there is no semi-permanent "connection" established between the sender and the receiver. Datagram packets are called "unreliable" because the protocol does not make any attempt to ensure that they arrived or to resend them if they did not. Thus, packets sent through a `Datagram-Socket` are not guaranteed to arrive in the order sent, or to arrive at all. On the other hand, this low-overhead protocol makes datagram transmission very fast.

If a port is specified when the `DatagramSocket` is created, that port is be used; otherwise, the system assigns a port. `getLocalPort()` returns the port number in use. `send()` sends a `DatagramPacket` through the socket. The packet must contain the destination address to which it should be sent. `receive()` waits for data to arrive at the socket and stores it, along with the address of the sender, into the

$\rightarrow$

---

specified DatagramPacket. close() closes the socket and frees the port it used for reuse. Once close() has been called, the DatagramSocket should not be used again.

See Socket and URL for higher-level interfaces to networking.

```
public class DatagramSocket extends Object {
    // Public Constructors
        public DatagramSocket() throws SocketException;
        public DatagramSocket(int port) throws SocketException;
    // Public Instance Methods
        public synchronized void close();
        public int getLocalPort();
        public synchronized void receive(DatagramPacket p) throws IOException;
        public void send(DatagramPacket p) throws IOException;
    // Protected Instance Methods
        protected synchronized void finalize();

}
```

java.net.InetAddress

This class represents an Internet address, and is used when creating Datagram-Packet or Socket objects. The class does not have a public constructor function, but instead supports three static methods which return one or more instances of InetAddress. getLocalHost() returns an InetAddress for the local host. getByName() returns the InetAddress of a host specified by name. getAll-ByName() returns an array of InetAddress that represents all of the available addresses for a host specified by name. Instance methods are getHostName(), which returns the hostname of an InetAddress, and getAddress(), which returns the Internet IP address as an array of bytes, with the highest-order byte as the first element of the array.

```
public final class InetAddress extends Object {
    // No Constructor
    // Class Methods
        public static synchronized InetAddress[] getAllByName(String host) throws UnknownHostException;
        public static synchronized InetAddress getByName(String host) throws UnknownHostException;
        public static InetAddress getLocalHost() throws UnknownHostException;
    // Public Instance Methods
        public boolean equals(Object obj); // Overrides Object.equals()
        public byte[] getAddress();
        public String getHostName();
        public int hashCode(); // Overrides Object.hashCode()
        public String toString(); // Overrides Object.toString()

}
```

java.net.ServerSocket

This class is used by servers to listen for connection requests from clients. When you create a `ServerSocket`, it listens for connections on the specified port for an optionally specified amount of time. When a connection request arrives and the `ServerSocket` is returned, `getInetAddress()` returns the address of the connecting client, and `accept()` accepts the requested connection and returns a `Socket` for future communication between client and server.

```
public final class ServerSocket extends Object {
    // Public Constructors
        public ServerSocket(int port) throws IOException;
        public ServerSocket(int port, int count) throws IOException;
    // Class Methods
        public static synchronized void setSocketFactory(SocketImplFactory fac)
                                            throws IOException, SocketException;
    // Public Instance Methods
        public Socket accept() throws IOException;
        public void close() throws IOException;
        public InetAddress getInetAddress();
        public int getLocalPort();
        public String toString(); // Overrides Object.toString()

}
```

java.net.Socket

This class implements a socket for interprocess communication over the network. The constructor methods create the socket and connect it to the specified host and port. You may also optionally specify whether communication through the socket should be based on an underlying reliable connection-based stream protocol, or on an underlying unreliable (but faster) datagram protocol. A stream protocol is the default.

Once the socket is created, `getInputStream()` and `getOutputStream()` return `InputStream` and `OutputStream` objects that you can use just as you would for file input and output. `getInetAddress()` and `getPort()` return the address and port that the socket is connected to. `getLocalPort()` returns the local port that the socket is using.

```
public final class Socket extends Object {
    // Public Constructors
        public Socket(String host, int port) throws UnknownHostException, IOException;
        public Socket(String host, int port, boolean stream) throws IOException;
        public Socket(InetAddress address, int port) throws IOException;
        public Socket(InetAddress address, int port, boolean stream) throws IOException;
    // Class Methods
        public static synchronized void setSocketImplFactory(SocketImplFactory fac)
                                        throws IOException, SocketException;
    // Public Instance Methods
        public synchronized void close() throws IOException;
```

$\rightarrow$

```
        public InetAddress getInetAddress( );
        public InputStream getInputStream( ) throws IOException;
        public int getLocalPort( );
        public OutputStream getOutputStream( ) throws IOException;
        public int getPort( );
        public String toString( );  // Overrides Object.toString( )

}
```

---

java.net.SocketImpl

This abstract class defines the methods necessary to implement communication through sockets. Different subclasses of this class may provide different implementations suitable in different environments (such as behind firewalls). These socket implementations are used by the `Socket` and `ServerSocket` classes.

Normal applications never need to use or implement this interface.

```
public abstract class SocketImpl extends Object {
    // Default Constructor: public SocketImpl( )
    // Protected Instance Variables
        protected InetAddress address;
        protected FileDescriptor fd;
        protected int localport;
        protected int port;
    // Public Instance Methods
        public String toString( );  // Overrides Object.toString( )
    // Protected Instance Methods
        protected abstract void accept(SocketImpl s ) throws IOException;
        protected abstract int available( ) throws IOException;
        protected abstract void bind(InetAddress host, int port) throws IOException;
        protected abstract void close( ) throws IOException;
        protected abstract void connect(String host, int port) throws IOException;
        protected abstract void connect(InetAddress address, int port) throws IOException;
        protected abstract void create(boolean stream) throws IOException;
        protected FileDescriptor getFileDescriptor( );
        protected InetAddress getInetAddress( );
        protected abstract InputStream getInputStream( ) throws IOException;
        protected int getLocalPort( );
        protected abstract OutputStream getOutputStream( ) throws IOException;
        protected int getPort( );
        protected abstract void listen(int count) throws IOException;

}
```

java.net.SocketImplFactory

This interface defines a method that creates `SocketImpl` objects. `SocketImpl-Factory` objects may be registered to create `SocketImpl` objects for the `Socket` and `ServerSocket` classes.

Normal applications never need to use or implement this interface.

```
public abstract interface SocketImplFactory {
    // Public Instance Methods
        public abstract SocketImpl createSocketImpl();
}
```

java.net.URL

This class represents a URL (a Uniform Resource Locator) and allows the data referred to by the URL to be downloaded. A URL may be specified as a single string or with separate protocol, host, port, and file specifications. Relative URLs may also be specified with a `String` and the URL object that it is relative to.

`getFile()`, `getHost()`, `getPort()`, `getProtocol()`, and `getRef()` return the various portions of the URL specified by a URL object. `sameFile()` determines whether a URL object refers to the same file as this one.

The data or object referred to by a URL may be downloaded from the Internet in three ways: through a `URLConnection` created with `openConnection()`, through an `InputStream` created by `openStream()`, or through `getContent()`, which returns the URL contents directly.

```
public final class URL extends Object {
    // Public Constructors
        public URL(String protocol, String host, int port, String file) throws MalformedURLException;
        public URL(String protocol, String host, String file) throws MalformedURLException;
        public URL(String spec) throws MalformedURLException;
        public URL(URL context, String spec) throws MalformedURLException;
    // Class Methods
        public static synchronized void setURLStreamHandlerFactory(URLStreamHandlerFactory fac) throws Error;
    // Public Instance Methods
        public boolean equals(Object obj); // Overrides Object.equals()
        public final Object getContent() throws IOException;
        public String getFile();
        public String getHost();
        public int getPort();
        public String getProtocol();
        public String getRef();
        public int hashCode(); // Overrides Object.hashCode()
        public URLConnection openConnection() throws IOException;
        public final InputStream openStream() throws IOException;
        public boolean sameFile(URL other);
        public String toExternalForm();
        public String toString(); // Overrides Object.toString()
```

$\rightarrow$

java.net

// *Protected Instance Methods*
    protected void **set**(String *protocol*, String *host*, int *port*, String *file*, String *ref*);

}

---

java.net.URLConnection

This abstract class defines a network connection to an object specified by a URL. URL.openConnection() returns a URLConnection instance. You would use a URLConnection object when you want more control over the downloading data than is through the simpler URL methods.

connect() actually performs the network connection. Other methods that depend on being connected will call this method. getContent() returns the data referred to by the URL, parsed into an appropriate type of Object. If the URL protocol supports read and write operations then getInputStream() and getOutput-Stream() respectively return input and output streams to the object referred to by the URL.

getContentLength(), getContentType(), getContentEncoding(), get-Expiration(), getDate(), and getLastModified() return the appropriate information about the object referred to by the URL, if that information can be determined (e.g., from HTTP header fields). getHeaderField() returns an HTTP header field specified by name or by number. getHeaderFieldInt() and getHeader-FieldDate() return the value of a named header field parsed as an integer or a date.

There are a number of options that you may specify to control how the URLConnection behaves. These options are set with the various set() methods, and may be queried with corresponding get() methods. The options must be set before the connect() method is called.

setDoInput() and setDoOutput() allow you to specify whether you use the URLConnection for input and/or output. The default is input-only.

setAllowUserInteraction() specifies whether user-interaction (such as typing a password) is allowed during the data transfer. The initial default is false. set-DefaultAllowUserInteraction() is a class method that allows you to change the default value for user interaction.

setUseCaches() allows you to specify whether a cached version of the URL may be used. You can set this to false to force a URL to be reloaded. setDefault-UseCaches() sets the default value for setUseCaches().

setIfModifiedSince() allows you to specify that a URL should not be fetched (if it is possible to determine its modification date) unless it has been modified since a specified time.

public abstract class **URLConnection** extends Object {
    // *Protected Constructor*
      protected **URLConnection**(URL *url*);
    // *Protected Instance Variables*

```
        protected boolean allowUserInteraction;
        protected boolean connected;
        protected boolean doInput;
        protected boolean doOutput;
        protected long ifModifiedSince;
        protected URL url;
        protected boolean useCaches;
    // Class Methods
        public static boolean getDefaultAllowUserInteraction();
        public static String getDefaultRequestProperty(String key);
        protected static String guessContentTypeFromName(String fname);
        protected static String guessContentTypeFromStream(InputStream is) throws IOException;
        public static synchronized void setContentHandlerFactory(ContentHandlerFactory fac) throws Error;
        public static void setDefaultAllowUserInteraction(boolean defaultallowuserinteraction);
        public static void setDefaultRequestProperty(String key, String value);  // Empty
    // Public Instance Methods
        public abstract void connect() throws IOException;
        public boolean getAllowUserInteraction();
        public Object getContent() throws IOException, UnknownServiceException;
        public String getContentEncoding();
        public int getContentLength();
        public String getContentType();
        public long getDate();
        public boolean getDefaultUseCaches();
        public boolean getDoInput();
        public boolean getDoOutput();
        public long getExpiration();
        public String getHeaderField(String name);
        public String getHeaderField(int n);
        public long getHeaderFieldDate(String name, long Default);
        public int getHeaderFieldInt(String name, int Default);
        public String getHeaderFieldKey(int n);
        public long getIfModifiedSince();
        public InputStream getInputStream() throws IOException, UnknownServiceException;
        public long getLastModified();
        public OutputStream getOutputStream() throws IOException, UnknownServiceException;
        public String getRequestProperty(String key);
        public URL getURL();
        public boolean getUseCaches();
        public void setAllowUserInteraction(boolean allowuserinteraction);
        public void setDefaultUseCaches(boolean defaultusecaches);
        public void setDoInput(boolean doinput);
        public void setDoOutput(boolean dooutput);
        public void setIfModifiedSince(long ifmodifiedsince);
        public void setRequestProperty(String key, String value);
        public void setUseCaches(boolean usecaches);
        public String toString();  // Overrides Object.toString()

}
```

java.net

---

java.net.URLEncoder

This class defines a single static method which is used to convert a string to its URL-encoded form. That is, spaces are converted to '+', and non-alphanumeric characters other than underscore are output as two hexadecimal digits following a percent sign. Note that this technique only works for 8-bit characters. This method is used to "canonicalize" a URL specification so that it uses only characters from an extremely portable subset of ASCII which can be correctly handled by computers around the world.

```
public class URLEncoder extends Object {
    // No Constructor
    // Class Methods
        public static String encode(String s);

}
```

java.net.URLStreamHandler

This abstract class defines the method that creates a URLConnection for a given URL. A separate subclass of this class may be defined for various URL protocol types. A URLStreamHandler is created by a URLStreamHandlerFactory.

Normal applications never need to use or subclass this class.

```
public abstract class URLStreamHandler extends Object {
    // Default Constructor: public URLStreamHandler( )
    // Protected Instance Methods
        protected abstract URLConnection openConnection(URL u) throws IOException;
        protected void parseURL(URL u, String spec, int start, int limit);
        protected void setURL(URL u, String protocol, String host, int port, String file, String ref);
        protected String toExternalForm(URL u);

}
```

java.net.URLStreamHandlerFactory

This interface defines a method that creates a URLStreamHandler object for a specified protocol.

Normal applications never need to use or implement this interface.

```
public abstract interface URLStreamHandlerFactory {
    // Public Instance Methods
        public abstract URLStreamHandler createURLStreamHandler(String protocol);

}
```

The java.util Package

The java.util package defines a number of useful classes. This package should not be considered a "utility" package separate from the rest of the language; in fact, Java depends directly on several of the classes in this package. Figure 25-1 shows the class hierarchy of this package.

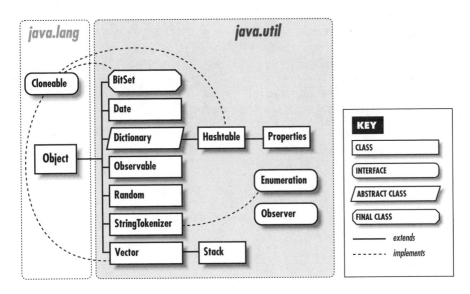

Figure 25-1: The java.util package

The `Hashtable` class is one of the most useful in the package—it implements a hashtable or associative array. It allows arbitrary objects to be stored and retrieved by arbitrary keys. The `Properties` subclass of `Hashtable` is used to store the Java system properties list.

`Vector` is another extremely useful class. It implements an array of objects that grows as necessary as objects are added.

The `Enumeration` interface provides a simple and consistent way to loop through all the elements contained within some kind of object or data structure.

The remaining classes are also useful. `BitSet` implements an arbitrary-size array of bits. `Date` represents a date/time value and provides many useful methods for manipulating dates and times. `Random` generates and returns pseudo-random numbers in a variety of forms. `StringTokenizer` parses a string into tokens. `Stack` implements a last-on-first-off stack on which objects may be pushed and from which they may be popped. And the `Observer` interface and `Observable` class provide infrastructure for implementing the object-oriented model-view paradigm in Java.

---

java.util.BitSet

This class defines an arbitrarily large set of bits. Instance methods allow you to set, clear, and query individual bits in the set, and also to perform bitwise boolean arithmetic on the bits in `BitSet` objects. This class can be used as an extremely compact array of boolean values, although reading and writing those values is slower than normal array access.

```
public final class BitSet extends Object implements Cloneable {
    // Public Constructors
        public BitSet();
        public BitSet(int nbits);
    // Public Instance Methods
        public void and(BitSet set);
        public void clear(int bit);
        public Object clone(); // Overrides Object.clone()
        public boolean equals(Object obj); // Overrides Object.equals()
        public boolean get(int bit);
        public int hashCode(); // Overrides Object.hashCode()
        public void or(BitSet set);
        public void set(int bit);
        public int size();
        public String toString(); // Overrides Object.toString()
        public void xor(BitSet set);
}
```

---

java.util.Date

This class represents dates and times. It lets you work with them in a system-independent way. You can create a `Date` by specifying the number of milliseconds from the epoch (midnight GMT, January 1st, 1970), or by specifying the year, month, date, and optionally, the hour, minute, and second. Years are specified as the number of years since 1900. If you call the `Date` constructor with no arguments, the `Date` is initialized to the current time and date. The instance methods of the class allow you to get and set the various date and time fields, to compare dates and times, and to convert dates to and from string representations.

```
public class Date extends Object {
    // Public Constructors
        public Date();
        public Date(long date);
        public Date(int year, int month, int date);
        public Date(int year, int month, int date, int hrs, int min);
        public Date(int year, int month, int date, int hrs, int min, int sec);
        public Date(String s);
    // Class Methods
        public static long UTC(int year, int month, int date, int hrs, int min, int sec);
        public static long parse(String s);
    // Public Instance Methods
        public boolean after(Date when);
        public boolean before(Date when);
        public boolean equals(Object obj); // Overrides Object.equals()
        public int getDate();
        public int getDay();
        public int getHours();
        public int getMinutes();
        public int getMonth();
        public int getSeconds();
        public long getTime();
        public int getTimezoneOffset();
        public int getYear();
        public int hashCode(); // Overrides Object.hashCode()
        public void setDate(int date);
        public void setHours(int hours);
        public void setMinutes(int minutes);
        public void setMonth(int month);
        public void setSeconds(int seconds);
        public void setTime(long time);
        public void setYear(int year);
        public String toGMTString();
        public String toLocaleString();
        public String toString(); // Overrides Object.toString()

}
```

java.util.Dictionary

This abstract class is the superclass of `Hashtable`. Other hashtable-like data structures might also extend this class. See `Hashtable` for more information.

```
public abstract class Dictionary extends Object {
    // Public Constructor
        public Dictionary(); // Empty
    // Public Instance Methods
```

$\rightarrow$

```
        public abstract Enumeration elements();
        public abstract Object get(Object key);
        public abstract boolean isEmpty();
        public abstract Enumeration keys();
        public abstract Object put(Object key, Object value) throws NullPointerException;
        public abstract Object remove(Object key);
        public abstract int size();

}
```

java.util.Enumeration

This interface defines the methods necessary to enumerate, or iterate through a set of values, such as the set of values contained in a hashtable or binary tree. It is particularly useful for data structures, like hashtables, for which elements cannot simply be looked up by index, as they can in arrays. An Enumeration is often not instantiated directly, but instead is created by the object that is to have its values enumerated. A number of classes, such as Vector and Hashtable, have methods that return Enumeration objects.

To use an Enumeration object, you use its two methods in a loop: hasMore-Elements() returns true if there are more values to be enumerated, and can be used to determine whether a loop should continue. Within a loop, a call to next-Element() returns a value from the enumeration. An Enumeration makes no guarantees about the order in which the values are returned. The values in an Enumeration may be iterated through only once—there is no way to reset it to the beginning.

```
public abstract interface Enumeration {
    // Public Instance Methods
        public abstract boolean hasMoreElements();
        public abstract Object nextElement() throws NoSuchElementException;

}
```

java.util.Hashtable

This class implements a hashtable data structure, which allows you to associate values with a key and to efficiently look up the value associated with a given key. A hashtable is essentially an associative array, which stores objects with non-numeric array indices.

put() associates a value with a key in a Hashtable. get() retrieves a value for a specified key. remove() deletes a key/value association. keys() and elements() return Enumeration objects that allow you to iterate through the complete set of keys and values stored in the table.

```
public class Hashtable extends Dictionary implements Cloneable {
    // Public Constructors
        public Hashtable(int initialCapacity, float loadFactor) throws IllegalArgumentException;
        public Hashtable(int initialCapacity);
        public Hashtable();
    // Public Instance Methods
        public synchronized void clear();
        public synchronized Object clone(); // Overrides Object.clone()
        public synchronized boolean contains(Object value) throws NullPointerException;
        public synchronized boolean containsKey(Object key);
        public synchronized Enumeration elements(); // Defines Dictionary.elements()
        public synchronized Object get(Object key); // Defines Dictionary.get()
        public boolean isEmpty(); // Defines Dictionary.isEmpty()
        public synchronized Enumeration keys(); // Defines Dictionary.keys()
        public synchronized Object put(Object key, Object value) throws NullPointerException;
                            // Defines Dictionary.put()
        public synchronized Object remove(Object key); // Defines Dictionary.remove()
        public int size(); // Defines Dictionary.size()
        public synchronized String toString(); // Overrides Object.toString()
    // Protected Instance Methods
        protected void rehash();

}
```

---

java.util.Observable

This class is the superclass of all "observable" objects to be used in an object-oriented model/view paradigm. The class methods allow you to add and delete Observer objects to and from an Observable's list, and to notify all of the Observer objects on the list. Observer objects are "notified" by invoking their update() method. Observable also maintains an internal "changed" flag, which may be set and cleared by the Observable, and which may be queried with has-Changed() by any interested observer.

```
public class Observable extends Object {
    // Default Constructor: public Observable()
    // Public Instance Methods
        public synchronized void addObserver(Observer o);
        public synchronized int countObservers();
        public synchronized void deleteObserver(Observer o);
        public synchronized void deleteObservers();
        public synchronized boolean hasChanged();
        public void notifyObservers();
        public synchronized void notifyObservers(Object arg);
    // Protected Instance Methods
        protected synchronized void clearChanged();
        protected synchronized void setChanged();

}
```

java.util.Observer

This interface defines the update() method required for an object to "observe" subclasses of Observable. An Observer registers interested in an Observable() by calling the Observable.addObserver() method. Observer objects that have been registered in this way will have their update() method invoked by the Observable when that object has changed.

```
public abstract interface Observer {
    // Public Instance Methods
        public abstract void update(Observable o, Object arg);

}
```

java.util.Properties

This class is an extension of Hashtable which allows key/value pairs to be read from and written to a stream. The Properties class is used to implement the system properties list, which supports user customization by allowing programs to look up the value of named resources.

Any Properties object may be created with another Properties object specified that contains default values. Keys (property names) and values are associated in a Properties object with the Hashtable method put(). Values are looked up with getProperty()—if this method does not find the key in the current Properties object, then it looks in the default Properties object that was passed to the constructor method. A default value may also be specified in case the key is not found at all.

propertyNames() returns an enumeration of all property names (keys) stored in the Properties object and (recursively) also all property names stored in the default Properties object associated with it. list() prints the properties stored in a Properties object. It is useful for debugging. save() writes a Properties object to a stream. load() reads key/value pairs from a stream and stores them in a Properties object.

```
public class Properties extends Hashtable {
    // Public Constructors
        public Properties();
        public Properties(Properties defaults);
    // Protected Instance Variables
        protected Properties defaults;
    // Public Instance Methods
        public String getProperty(String key);
        public String getProperty(String key, String defaultValue);
        public void list(PrintStream out);
        public synchronized void load(InputStream in) throws IOException;
        public Enumeration propertyNames();
        public synchronized void save(OutputStream out, String header);

}
```

java.util.Random

This class implements a pseudo-random number generator. The instance methods return random values for various Java primitive types. nextDouble() and next-Float() return a value between 0.0 and 1.0. nextLong() and nextInt() return long and int values distributed across the range of those data types. next-Gaussian() returns pseudo-random values with a Gaussian distribution—the mean of the values is 0.0, and the standard deviation is 1.0. You can use the setSeed() method or the optional constructor argument to initialize the pseudo-random number generator with some variable seed value other than the current time (the default), or with a constant to ensure a repeatable sequence of pseudo-randomness.

```
public class Random extends Object {
    // Public Constructors
        public Random();
        public Random(long seed);
    // Public Instance Methods
        public double nextDouble();
        public float nextFloat();
        public synchronized double nextGaussian();
        public int nextInt();
        public long nextLong();
        public synchronized void setSeed(long seed);
}
```

java.util.Stack

This class implements a last-in-first-out stack of objects. push() puts an object on the top of the stack. pop() removes and returns the top object from the stack. peek() returns the top object without removing it.

```
public class Stack extends Vector {
    // Default Constructor: public Stack()
    // Public Instance Methods
        public boolean empty();
        public Object peek() throws EmptyStackException;
        public Object pop() throws EmptyStackException;
        public Object push(Object item);
        public int search(Object o);
}
```

java.util.StringTokenizer

This class, when instantiated with a String, breaks the string up into tokens separated by any of the characters in the specified string of delimiters. (For example, words separated by space and tab characters are tokens.) The hasMoreTokens() and nextToken() methods can be used to obtain the tokens in order.

$\rightarrow$

When you create a `StringTokenizer` you may specify a string of delimiter characters to use for the entire string, or you may rely on the default whitespace delimiters. You may also specify whether the delimiters themselves should be returned as tokens. You may optionally specify a new string of delimiter characters when you call `nextToken()`.

`countTokens()` returns the number of tokens in the string. Note that `String-Tokenizer` implements the `Enumeration` interface, so you may also access the tokens with the familiar `hasMoreElements()` and `nextElement()` methods.

```
public class StringTokenizer extends Object implements Enumeration {
    // Public Constructors
        public StringTokenizer(String str, String delim, boolean returnTokens);
        public StringTokenizer(String str, String delim);
        public StringTokenizer(String str);
    // Public Instance Methods
        public int countTokens();
        public boolean hasMoreElements();
        public boolean hasMoreTokens();
        public Object nextElement() throws NoSuchElementException;
        public String nextToken() throws NoSuchElementException;
        public String nextToken(String delim);

}
```

---

java.util.Vector

This class implements an array of objects that grows in size as necessary. It is useful when you need to keep track of a number of objects but do not know in advance how many there will be. There are a number of methods for storing objects in and removing objects from the `Vector`. Other methods look up the object at specified positions in the `Vector`, or search for specified objects within the `Vector`. `elements()` returns an `Enumeration` of the objects stored in the `Vector`. `size()` returns the number of objects currently stored in the `Vector`. `capacity()` returns the number of elements that may be stored before the vector's internal storage must be reallocated.

```
public class Vector extends Object implements Cloneable {
    // Public Constructors
        public Vector(int initialCapacity, int capacityIncrement);
        public Vector(int initialCapacity);
        public Vector();
    // Protected Instance Variables
        protected int capacityIncrement;
        protected int elementCount;
        protected Object[] elementData;
    // Public Instance Methods
        public final synchronized void addElement(Object obj);
        public final int capacity();
        public synchronized Object clone(); // Overrides Object.clone()
        public final boolean contains(Object elem);
        public final synchronized void copyInto(Object[] anArray);
        public final synchronized Object elementAt(int index) throws ArrayIndexOutOfBoundsException;
```

```
        public final synchronized Enumeration elements( );
        public final synchronized void ensureCapacity(int minCapacity);
        public final synchronized Object firstElement( ) throws NoSuchElementException;
        public final int indexOf(Object elem);
        public final synchronized int indexOf(Object elem, int index);
        public final synchronized void insertElementAt(Object obj, int index)
                                                throws ArrayIndexOutOfBoundsException;
        public final boolean isEmpty( );
        public final synchronized Object lastElement( ) throws NoSuchElementException;
        public final int lastIndexOf(Object elem);
        public final synchronized int lastIndexOf(Object elem, int index);
        public final synchronized void removeAllElements( );
        public final synchronized boolean removeElement(Object obj);
        public final synchronized void removeElementAt(int index)
                                                throws ArrayIndexOutOfBoundsException;
        public final synchronized void setElementAt(Object obj, int index)
                                                throws ArrayIndexOutOfBoundsException;
        public final synchronized void setSize(int newSize);
        public final int size( );
        public final synchronized String toString( );  // Overrides Object.toString( )
        public final synchronized void trimToSize( );

}
```

java.util

Java Errors and Exceptions

This section lists the errors and exceptions thrown by the Java interpreter and by the methods of the Java API. The classes listed here are all subclasses of `java.lang.Error` and `java.lang.Exception`, but they are part of several different packages. Figure 26-1 and Figure 26-2 show the exception and error class hierarchy and also indicate the package each class belongs to.

An `Error` generally signals that a non-recoverable error has occurred. They should not be caught and usually cause the Java interpreter to display a message and exit. An exception is the `ThreadDeath` error which causes the thread in which it is thrown to stop running, but which does not print an error message or affect other threads.

An `Exception` signals an abnormal condition that must be specially handled to prevent program termination. Exceptions may be caught and handled. Exceptions that are not subclasses of `RuntimeException` must be caught or declared in the `throws` clause of any method that can throw them. These exception classes represent routine abnormal conditions that should be anticipated and caught to prevent program termination.

All errors and exceptions are subclasses of `Throwable`. As such, they may all have a message associated with them, which can be retrieved with the `getMessage()` method. You can use this to print a message describing the error or exception. You can also use `java.lang.Throwable` methods to display a stack trace of where the exception or error occurred.

Note that the classes listed in this section are alphabetized by class name, not by package name. Because both package name and class name appear in the headings, it may appear that they are out of order.

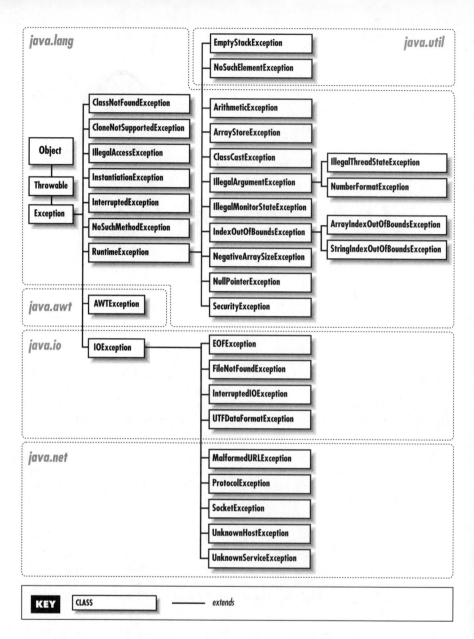

Figure 26-1: Java exception classes

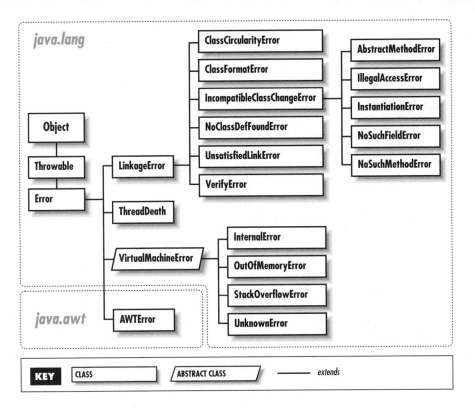

Figure 26-2: Java error classes

---

java.awt.AWTError

Signals that an error has occurred in the java.awt package.

```
public class AWTError extends Error {
    // Public Constructor
        public AWTError(String msg);

}
```

---

java.awt.AWTException

Signals that an exception has occurred in the java.awt package.

```
public class AWTException extends Exception {
    // Public Constructor
        public AWTException(String msg);

}
```

---

java.lang.AbstractMethodError

Signals an attempt to invoke an abstract method.

```
public class AbstractMethodError extends IncompatibleClassChangeError {
    // Public Constructors
        public AbstractMethodError( );
        public AbstractMethodError(String s );
}
```

java.lang.ArithmeticException

A RuntimeException that signals an exceptional arithmetic condition, such as integer division by zero.

```
public class ArithmeticException extends RuntimeException {
    // Public Constructors
        public ArithmeticException( );
        public ArithmeticException(String s );
}
```

java.lang.ArrayIndexOutOfBoundsException

Signals that an array index less than zero or greater than or equal to the array size has been used.

```
public class ArrayIndexOutOfBoundsException extends IndexOutOfBoundsException {
    // Public Constructors
        public ArrayIndexOutOfBoundsException( );
        public ArrayIndexOutOfBoundsException(int index );
        public ArrayIndexOutOfBoundsException(String s );
}
```

java.lang.ArrayStoreException

Signals an attempt to store the wrong type of object into an array.

```
public class ArrayStoreException extends RuntimeException {
    // Public Constructors
        public ArrayStoreException( );
        public ArrayStoreException(String s );
}
```

java.lang.ClassCastException

Signals an invalid cast of an object to a type of which it is not an instance.

```
public class ClassCastException extends RuntimeException {
    // Public Constructors
        public ClassCastException();
        public ClassCastException(String s);
}
```

java.lang.ClassCircularityError

Signals that a circular dependency has been detected while performing initialization for a class.

```
public class ClassCircularityError extends LinkageError {
    // Public Constructors
        public ClassCircularityError();
        public ClassCircularityError(String s);
}
```

java.lang.ClassFormatError

Signals an error in the binary format of a class file.

```
public class ClassFormatError extends LinkageError {
    // Public Constructors
        public ClassFormatError();
        public ClassFormatError(String s);
}
```

java.lang.ClassNotFoundException

Signals that a class to be loaded could not be found.

```
public class ClassNotFoundException extends Exception {
    // Public Constructors
        public ClassNotFoundException();
        public ClassNotFoundException(String s);
}
```

java.lang.CloneNotSupportedException

Signals that the `clone()` method has been called for an object of a class that does not implement the `Cloneable` interface.

```
public class CloneNotSupportedException extends Exception {
    // Public Constructors
        public CloneNotSupportedException();
        public CloneNotSupportedException(String s);

}
```

java.io.EOFException

An `IOException` that signals the end-of-file.

```
public class EOFException extends IOException {
    // Public Constructors
        public EOFException();
        public EOFException(String s);

}
```

java.util.EmptyStackException

Signals that a `Stack` object is empty.

```
public class EmptyStackException extends RuntimeException {
    // Public Constructor
        public EmptyStackException(); // Empty

}
```

java.lang.Error

A `Throwable` that forms the root of the error hierarchy. Subclasses of `Error`, unlike subclasses of `Exception`, should generally not be caught, and generally cause termination of the program. `getMessage()` returns a message associated with the error. See `Throwable` for other methods.

Subclasses of `Error` need not be declared in the `throws` clause of a method definition.

```
public class Error extends Throwable {
    // Public Constructors
        public Error();
        public Error(String s);

}
```

java.lang.Exception

A `Throwable` that forms the root of the exception hierarchy. Programs may catch subclasses of `Exception`, but generally should not catch subclasses of `Error`. `get-Message()` returns a message associated with the exception. See `Throwable` for other methods.

Subclasses of `Exception` that are not subclasses of `RuntimeException` must be declared in the `throws` clause of any method that can throw them.

```
public class Exception extends Throwable {
    // Public Constructors
        public Exception();
        public Exception(String s);
}
```

java.io.FileNotFoundException

An `IOException` that signals that a specified file was not found.

```
public class FileNotFoundException extends IOException {
    // Public Constructors
        public FileNotFoundException();
        public FileNotFoundException(String s);
}
```

java.io.IOException

Signals that an exceptional condition has occurred during input or output. This class has several more specific subclasses. See `EOFException`, `FileNotFound-Exception`, `InterruptedIOException`, and `UTFDataFormatException`.

```
public class IOException extends Exception {
    // Public Constructors
        public IOException();
        public IOException(String s);
}
```

java.lang.IllegalAccessError

Signals an attempted use of a class, method, or variable that is not accessible.

```
public class IllegalAccessError extends IncompatibleClassChangeError {
    // Public Constructors
        public IllegalAccessError();
        public IllegalAccessError(String s);
}
```

java.lang.IllegalAccessException

Signals that a class or initializer is not accessible. Thrown by Class.new-Instance().

```
public class IllegalAccessException extends Exception {
    // Public Constructors
        public IllegalAccessException();
        public IllegalAccessException(String s);
}
```

java.lang.IllegalArgumentException

Signals an illegal argument to a method. See subclasses IllegalThreadState-Exception and NumberFormatException.

```
public class IllegalArgumentException extends RuntimeException {
    // Public Constructors
        public IllegalArgumentException();
        public IllegalArgumentException(String s);
}
```

java.lang.IllegalMonitorStateException

Signals an illegal monitor state. It is thrown by the object notify() and wait() methods used for thread synchronization.

```
public class IllegalMonitorStateException extends RuntimeException {
    // Public Constructors
        public IllegalMonitorStateException();
        public IllegalMonitorStateException(String s);
}
```

java.lang.IllegalThreadStateException

Signals that a thread is not in the appropriate state for an attempted operation to succeed.

```
public class IllegalThreadStateException extends IllegalArgumentException {
    // Public Constructors
        public IllegalThreadStateException();
        public IllegalThreadStateException(String s);
}
```

java.lang.IncompatibleClassChangeError

This is the superclass of a group of related error types. It signals some kind of illegal use of a legal class.

```
public class IncompatibleClassChangeError extends LinkageError {
    // Public Constructors
        public IncompatibleClassChangeError();
        public IncompatibleClassChangeError(String s);
}
```

java.lang.IndexOutOfBoundsException

Signals that an index is out of bounds. See the subclasses ArrayIndexOut-OfBoundsException and StringIndexOutOfBoundsException.

```
public class IndexOutOfBoundsException extends RuntimeException {
    // Public Constructors
        public IndexOutOfBoundsException();
        public IndexOutOfBoundsException(String s);
}
```

java.lang.InstantiationError

Signals an attempt to instantiate an interface or abstract class.

```
public class InstantiationError extends IncompatibleClassChangeError {
    // Public Constructors
        public InstantiationError();
        public InstantiationError(String s);
}
```

java.lang.InstantiationException

Signals an attempt to instantiate an interface or an abstract class.

```
public class InstantiationException extends Exception {
    // Public Constructors
        public InstantiationException();
        public InstantiationException(String s);
}
```

Errors and Exceptions

java.lang.InternalError

Signals an internal error in the Java interpreter.

```
public class InternalError extends VirtualMachineError {
    // Public Constructors
        public InternalError();
        public InternalError(String s);
}
```

java.lang.InterruptedException

Signals that the thread has been interrupted.

```
public class InterruptedException extends Exception {
    // Public Constructors
        public InterruptedException();
        public InterruptedException(String s);
}
```

java.io.InterruptedIOException

An IOException that signals that an input or output operation was interrupted. The bytesTransferred variable contains the number of bytes read or written before the operation was interrupted.

```
public class InterruptedIOException extends IOException {
    // Public Constructors
        public InterruptedIOException();
        public InterruptedIOException(String s);
    // Public Instance Variables
        public int bytesTransferred;
}
```

java.lang.LinkageError

The superclass of a group of errors that signal problems linking a class or resolving dependencies between classes.

```
public class LinkageError extends Error {
    // Public Constructors
        public LinkageError();
        public LinkageError(String s);
}
```

java.net.MalformedURLException

Signals that an unparsable URL specification has been passed to a method.

```
public class MalformedURLException extends IOException {
    // Public Constructors
        public MalformedURLException(); // Empty
        public MalformedURLException(String msg);
}
```

java.lang.NegativeArraySizeException

Signals an attempt to allocate an array with fewer than zero elements.

```
public class NegativeArraySizeException extends RuntimeException {
    // Public Constructors
        public NegativeArraySizeException();
        public NegativeArraySizeException(String s);
}
```

java.lang.NoClassDefFoundError

Signals that the definition of a specified class could not be found.

```
public class NoClassDefFoundError extends LinkageError {
    // Public Constructors
        public NoClassDefFoundError();
        public NoClassDefFoundError(String s);
}
```

java.util.NoSuchElementException

Signals that there are no elements in an object (such as a `Vector`) or that there are no *more* elements in an object (such as an `Enumeration`).

```
public class NoSuchElementException extends RuntimeException {
    // Public Constructors
        public NoSuchElementException();
        public NoSuchElementException(String s);
}
```

java.lang.NoSuchFieldError

Signals that a specified field could not be found.

```
public class NoSuchFieldError extends IncompatibleClassChangeError {
    // Public Constructors
        public NoSuchFieldError( );
        public NoSuchFieldError(String s);

}
```

java.lang.NoSuchMethodError

Signals that a specified method could not be found.

```
public class NoSuchMethodError extends IncompatibleClassChangeError {
    // Public Constructors
        public NoSuchMethodError( );
        public NoSuchMethodError(String s);

}
```

java.lang.NoSuchMethodException

Signals that a specified method could not be found.

```
public class NoSuchMethodException extends Exception {
    // Public Constructors
        public NoSuchMethodException( );
        public NoSuchMethodException(String s);

}
```

java.lang.NullPointerException

Signals an attempt to access a field or invoke a method of a `null` object.

```
public class NullPointerException extends RuntimeException {
    // Public Constructors
        public NullPointerException( );
        public NullPointerException(String s);

}
```

java.lang.NumberFormatException

Signals an illegal number format.

```
public class NumberFormatException extends IllegalArgumentException {
    // Public Constructors
        public NumberFormatException();
        public NumberFormatException(String s);
}
```

java.lang.OutOfMemoryError

Signals that the interpreter has run out of memory (and that garbage collection is unable to free any memory).

```
public class OutOfMemoryError extends VirtualMachineError {
    // Public Constructors
        public OutOfMemoryError();
        public OutOfMemoryError(String s);
}
```

java.net.ProtocolException

Signals a protocol error in the Socket class.

```
public class ProtocolException extends IOException {
    // Public Constructors
        public ProtocolException(String host);
        public ProtocolException();  // Empty
}
```

java.lang.RuntimeException

This exception type is not used directly, but serves as a superclass of a group of run-time exceptions that need not be declared in the throws clause of a method definition. These exceptions need not be declared because they are run-time conditions that can generally occur in any Java method. Thus declaring them would be unduly burdensome, and Java does not require it.

```
public class RuntimeException extends Exception {
    // Public Constructors
        public RuntimeException();
        public RuntimeException(String s);
}
```

Errors and Exceptions

java.lang.SecurityException

Signals that an operation is not permitted for security reasons.

```
public class SecurityException extends RuntimeException {
    // Public Constructors
        public SecurityException();
        public SecurityException(String s);
}
```

java.net.SocketException

Signals an exceptional condition while using a socket.

```
public class SocketException extends IOException {
    // Public Constructors
        public SocketException(String msg);
        public SocketException(); // Empty
}
```

java.lang.StackOverflowError

Signals that a stack overflow has occurred within the Java interpreter.

```
public class StackOverflowError extends VirtualMachineError {
    // Public Constructors
        public StackOverflowError();
        public StackOverflowError(String s);
}
```

java.lang.StringIndexOutOfBoundsException

Signals that the index used to access a character of a `String` or `StringBuffer` is less than zero or is too large.

```
public class StringIndexOutOfBoundsException extends IndexOutOfBoundsException {
    // Public Constructors
        public StringIndexOutOfBoundsException();
        public StringIndexOutOfBoundsException(String s);
        public StringIndexOutOfBoundsException(int index);
}
```

java.lang.ThreadDeath

Signals that a thread should terminate. This error is thrown in a thread when the Thread.stop() method is called for that thread. This is an unusual Error type that simply causes a thread to be terminated, but does not print an error message or cause the interpreter to exit. You may catch ThreadDeath errors to do any necessary cleanup for a thread, but if you do, you must re-throw the error, so that the thread actually terminates.

```
public class ThreadDeath extends Error {
    // Default Constructor: public ThreadDeath()
}
```

java.io.UTFDataFormatException

An IOException that signals that a malformed UTF-8 string has been encountered by a class that implements the DataInput interface. UTF-8 is an ASCII-compatible "transformation format" for Unicode characters that is often used to store and transmit Unicode text.

```
public class UTFDataFormatException extends IOException {
    // Public Constructors
        public UTFDataFormatException();
        public UTFDataFormatException(String s);
}
```

java.lang.UnknownError

Signals that an unknown error has occurred at the level of the Java Virtual Machine.

```
public class UnknownError extends VirtualMachineError {
    // Public Constructors
        public UnknownError();
        public UnknownError(String s);
}
```

java.net.UnknownHostException

Signals that the name of a specified host could not be resolved.

```
public class UnknownHostException extends IOException {
    // Public Constructors
        public UnknownHostException(String host);
        public UnknownHostException(); // Empty
}
```

java.net.UnknownServiceException

Signals an attempt to use an unsupported service of a network connection.

```
public class UnknownServiceException extends IOException {
    // Public Constructors
        public UnknownServiceException( ); // Empty
        public UnknownServiceException(String msg);

}
```

java.lang.UnsatisfiedLinkError

Signals that Java cannot satisfy all of the links in a class that it has loaded.

```
public class UnsatisfiedLinkError extends LinkageError {
    // Public Constructors
        public UnsatisfiedLinkError( );
        public UnsatisfiedLinkError(String s);

}
```

java.lang.VerifyError

Signals that a class has not passed the byte-code verification procedures.

```
public class VerifyError extends LinkageError {
    // Public Constructors
        public VerifyError( );
        public VerifyError(String s);

}
```

java.lang.VirtualMachineError

An abstract error type that serves as superclass for a group of errors related to the Java Virtual Machine. See `InternalError`, `UnknownError`, `OutOfMemoryError`, and `StackOverflowError`.

```
public abstract class VirtualMachineError extends Error {
    // Public Constructors
        public VirtualMachineError( );
        public VirtualMachineError(String s);

}
```

Part V

API Cross References

Part V consists of cross-reference indexes to the API quick reference of Part IV. The *How to Use This Book* section at the beginning of the book explains how these indexes help you find information you can't look up directly in Part IV.

Class Defined-In Index

This index tells you in which package a given class is defined. It is useful when you encounter an unfamiliar class (specified without its fully-qualified package name) in Java source code, in the API quick reference, or in another one of the quick reference indexes. Once you've looked up the package name of a class, you'll know where in Part IV to find the class's documentation.

AbstractMethodError: java.lang
AppletContext: java.applet
AppletStub: java.applet
Applet: java.applet
ArithmeticException: java.lang
ArrayIndexOutOfBoundsException: java.lang
ArrayStoreException: java.lang
AudioClip: java.applet
AWTError: java.awt
AWTException: java.awt
BitSet: java.util
Boolean: java.lang
BorderLayout: java.awt
BufferedInputStream: java.io
BufferedOutputStream: java.io
ButtonPeer: java.awt.peer
Button: java.awt
ByteArrayInputStream: java.io
ByteArrayOutputStream: java.io
CanvasPeer: java.awt.peer
Canvas: java.awt
CardLayout: java.awt
Character: java.lang

CheckboxGroup: java.awt
CheckboxMenuItemPeer: java.awt.peer
CheckboxMenuItem: java.awt
CheckboxPeer: java.awt.peer
Checkbox: java.awt
ChoicePeer: java.awt.peer
Choice: java.awt
ClassCastException: java.lang
ClassCircularityError: java.lang
ClassFormatError: java.lang
ClassLoader: java.lang
ClassNotFoundException: java.lang
Class: java.lang
Cloneable: java.lang
CloneNotSupportedException: java.lang
ColorModel: java.awt.image
Color: java.awt
Compiler: java.lang
ComponentPeer: java.awt.peer
Component: java.awt
ContainerPeer: java.awt.peer
Container: java.awt
ContentHandlerFactory: java.net
ContentHandler: java.net

Class
Defined-In

CropImageFilter: java.awt.image
DatagramPacket: java.net
DatagramSocket: java.net
DataInputStream: java.io
DataInput: java.io
DataOutputStream: java.io
DataOutput: java.io
Date: java.util
DialogPeer: java.awt.peer
Dialog: java.awt
Dictionary: java.util
Dimension: java.awt
DirectColorModel: java.awt.image
Double: java.lang
EmptyStackException: java.util
Enumeration: java.util
EOFException: java.io
Error: java.lang
Event: java.awt
Exception: java.lang
FileDescriptor: java.io
FileDialogPeer: java.awt.peer
FileDialog: java.awt
FileInputStream: java.io
FilenameFilter: java.io
FileNotFoundException: java.io
FileOutputStream: java.io
File: java.io
FilteredImageSource: java.awt.image
FilterInputStream: java.io
FilterOutputStream: java.io
Float: java.lang
FlowLayout: java.awt
FontMetrics: java.awt
Font: java.awt
FramePeer: java.awt.peer
Frame: java.awt
Graphics: java.awt
GridBagConstraints: java.awt
GridBagLayout: java.awt
GridLayout: java.awt
Hashtable: java.util
IllegalAccessError: java.lang
IllegalAccessException: java.lang
IllegalArgumentException: java.lang
IllegalMonitorStateException: java.lang
IllegalThreadStateException: java.lang
ImageConsumer: java.awt.image
ImageFilter: java.awt.image
ImageObserver: java.awt.image
ImageProducer: java.awt.image
Image: java.awt

IncompatibleClassChangeError:
java.lang
IndexColorModel: java.awt.image
IndexOutOfBoundsException: java.lang
InetAddress: java.net
InputStream: java.io
Insets: java.awt
InstantiationError: java.lang
InstantiationException: java.lang
Integer: java.lang
InternalError: java.lang
InterruptedException: java.lang
InterruptedIOException: java.io
IOException: java.io
LabelPeer: java.awt.peer
Label: java.awt
LayoutManager: java.awt
LineNumberInputStream: java.io
LinkageError: java.lang
ListPeer: java.awt.peer
List: java.awt
Long: java.lang
MalformedURLException: java.net
Math: java.lang
MediaTracker: java.awt
MemoryImageSource: java.awt.image
MenuBarPeer: java.awt.peer
MenuBar: java.awt
MenuComponentPeer: java.awt.peer
MenuComponent: java.awt
MenuContainer: java.awt
MenuItemPeer: java.awt.peer
MenuItem: java.awt
MenuPeer: java.awt.peer
Menu: java.awt
NegativeArraySizeException: java.lang
NoClassDefFoundError: java.lang
NoSuchElementException: java.util
NoSuchFieldError: java.lang
NoSuchMethodError: java.lang
NoSuchMethodException: java.lang
NullPointerException: java.lang
NumberFormatException: java.lang
Number: java.lang
Object: java.lang
Observable: java.util
Observer: java.util
OutOfMemoryError: java.lang
OutputStream: java.io
PanelPeer: java.awt.peer
Panel: java.awt
PipedInputStream: java.io
PipedOutputStream: java.io

PixelGrabber: java.awt.image
Point: java.awt
Polygon: java.awt
PrintStream: java.io
Process: java.lang
Properties: java.util
ProtocolException: java.net
PushbackInputStream: java.io
RandomAccessFile: java.io
Random: java.util
Rectangle: java.awt
RGBImageFilter: java.awt.image
Runnable: java.lang
RuntimeException: java.lang
Runtime: java.lang
ScrollbarPeer: java.awt.peer
Scrollbar: java.awt
SecurityException: java.lang
SecurityManager: java.lang
SequenceInputStream: java.io
ServerSocket: java.net
SocketException: java.net
SocketImplFactory: java.net
SocketImpl: java.net
Socket: java.net
StackOverflowError: java.lang
Stack: java.util
StreamTokenizer: java.io
StringBufferInputStream: java.io
StringBuffer: java.lang
StringIndexOutOfBoundsException:
java.lang
StringTokenizer: java.util
String: java.lang
System: java.lang
TextAreaPeer: java.awt.peer
TextArea: java.awt
TextComponentPeer: java.awt.peer
TextComponent: java.awt
TextFieldPeer: java.awt.peer
TextField: java.awt
ThreadDeath: java.lang
ThreadGroup: java.lang
Thread: java.lang
Throwable: java.lang
Toolkit: java.awt
UnknownError: java.lang
UnknownHostException: java.net
UnknownServiceException: java.net
UnsatisfiedLinkError: java.lang
URLConnection: java.net
URLEncoder: java.net
URLStreamHandlerFactory: java.net

URLStreamHandler: java.net
URL: java.net
UTFDataFormatException: java.io
Vector: java.util
VerifyError: java.lang
VirtualMachineError: java.lang
WindowPeer: java.awt.peer
Window: java.awt

*Class
Defined-In*

Method Defined-In Index

This index allows you to look up a method name and find all the classes and interfaces that define that method. This is often useful when you want to look up documentation for some method of a class, but you don't know whether it is defined directly by the class or if it's inherited from one of the various superclasses.

Note that constructors are not included in this index; they are obviously defined in a class of the same name. Use Section 27, *Class Defined-In Index*, if you are unfamiliar with a class you find here and need to look up the package it is part of.

abs(): Math
accept(): FilenameFilter, ServerSocket, SocketImpl
acos(): Math
action(): Component
activeCount(): Thread, ThreadGroup
activeGroupCount(): ThreadGroup
add(): Container, Menu, MenuBar, Rectangle
addConsumer(): FilteredImageSource, ImageProducer, MemoryImage-Source
addElement(): Vector
addHelpMenu(): MenuBarPeer
addImage(): MediaTracker
addItem(): Choice, ChoicePeer, List, ListPeer, MenuPeer
addLayoutComponent(): BorderLayout, CardLayout, FlowLayout, GridBag-Layout, GridLayout, LayoutManager
addMenu(): MenuBarPeer

addNotify(): Button, Canvas, Checkbox, CheckboxMenuItem, Choice, Component, Container, Dialog, File-Dialog, Frame, Label, List, Menu, MenuBar, MenuItem, Panel, Scrollbar, TextArea, TextField, Window
addObserver(): Observable
addPoint(): Polygon
addSeparator(): Menu, MenuPeer
AdjustForGravity(): GridBagLayout
after(): Date
allowsMultipleSelections(): List
and(): BitSet
append(): StringBuffer
appendText(): TextArea
appletResize(): AppletStub
ArrangeGrid(): GridBagLayout
arraycopy(): System
asin(): Math
atan(): Math

Method
Defined-In

atan2(): Math
available(): BufferedInputStream, Byte-
ArrayInputStream, FileInputStream,
FilterInputStream, InputStream, Line-
NumberInputStream, PushbackInput-
Stream, SocketImpl, StringBuffer-
InputStream
before(): Date
bind(): SocketImpl
booleanValue(): Boolean
bounds(): Component
brighter(): Color
bytesWidth(): FontMetrics
canRead(): File
canWrite(): File
capacity(): StringBuffer, Vector
ceil(): Math
charAt(): String, StringBuffer
charsWidth(): FontMetrics
charValue(): Character
charWidth(): FontMetrics
checkAccept(): SecurityManager
checkAccess(): SecurityManager,
Thread, ThreadGroup
checkAll(): MediaTracker
checkConnect(): SecurityManager
checkCreateClassLoader(): Security-
Manager
checkDelete(): SecurityManager
checkError(): PrintStream
checkExec(): SecurityManager
checkExit(): SecurityManager
checkID(): MediaTracker
checkImage(): Component,
ComponentPeer, Toolkit
checkLink(): SecurityManager
checkListen(): SecurityManager
checkPackageAccess(): SecurityManager
checkPackageDefinition(): Security-
Manager
checkPropertiesAccess(): Security-
Manager
checkPropertyAccess(): Security-
Manager
checkRead(): SecurityManager
checkSetFactory(): SecurityManager
checkTopLevelWindow(): Security-
Manager
checkWrite(): SecurityManager
classDepth(): SecurityManager
classLoaderDepth(): SecurityManager
clear(): BitSet, Hashtable, List, ListPeer
clearChanged(): Observable

clearRect(): Graphics
clipRect(): Graphics
clone(): BitSet, GridBagConstraints,
Hashtable, ImageFilter, Insets,
Object, Vector
close(): DatagramSocket, FileInput-
Stream, FileOutputStream, Filter-
InputStream, FilterOutputStream,
InputStream, OutputStream, Piped-
InputStream, PipedOutputStream,
PrintStream, RandomAccessFile,
SequenceInputStream, ServerSocket,
Socket, SocketImpl
command(): Compiler
commentChar(): StreamTokenizer
compareTo(): String
compileClass(): Compiler
compileClasses(): Compiler
concat(): String
connect(): PipedInputStream, Piped-
OutputStream, SocketImpl, URLConnection
contains(): Hashtable, Vector
containsKey(): Hashtable
controlDown(): Event
copyArea(): Graphics
copyInto(): Vector
copyValueOf(): String
cos(): Math
countComponents(): Container
countItems(): Choice, List, Menu
countMenus(): MenuBar
countObservers(): Observable
countStackFrames(): Thread
countTokens(): StringTokenizer
create(): Graphics, SocketImpl
createButton(): Toolkit
createCanvas(): Toolkit
createCheckbox(): Toolkit
createCheckboxMenuItem(): Toolkit
createChoice(): Toolkit
createContentHandler(): Content-
HandlerFactory
createDialog(): Toolkit
createFileDialog(): Toolkit
createFrame(): Toolkit
createImage(): Component,
ComponentPeer, Toolkit
createLabel(): Toolkit
createList(): Toolkit
createMenu(): Toolkit
createMenuBar(): Toolkit
createMenuItem(): Toolkit

createPanel(): Toolkit
createScrollbar(): Toolkit
createSocketImpl(): SocketImplFactory
createTextArea(): Toolkit
createTextField(): Toolkit
createURLStreamHandler(): URLStream-
  HandlerFactory
createWindow(): Toolkit
currentClassLoader(): SecurityManager
currentThread(): Thread
currentTimeMillis(): System
darker(): Color
defineClass(): ClassLoader
delete(): File
deleteObserver(): Observable
deleteObservers(): Observable
delItem(): List, MenuPeer
delItems(): List, ListPeer
deliverEvent(): Component, Container
delMenu(): MenuBarPeer
deselect(): List, ListPeer
destroy(): Applet, Process, Thread,
  ThreadGroup
digit(): Character
disable(): Compiler, Component,
  ComponentPeer, MenuItem, Menu-
  ItemPeer
dispose(): ComponentPeer, Frame,
  Graphics, MenuComponentPeer,
  Window
doubleToLongBits(): Double
doubleValue(): Double, Float, Integer,
  Long, Number
draw3DRect(): Graphics
drawArc(): Graphics
drawBytes(): Graphics
drawChars(): Graphics
drawImage(): Graphics
drawLine(): Graphics
drawOval(): Graphics
drawPolygon(): Graphics
drawRect(): Graphics
drawRoundRect(): Graphics
drawString(): Graphics
DumpConstraints(): GridBagLayout
DumpLayoutInfo(): GridBagLayout
dumpStack(): Thread
echoCharIsSet(): TextField
elementAt(): Vector
elements(): Dictionary, Hashtable, Vector
empty(): Stack
enable(): Compiler, Component,

ComponentPeer, MenuItem, Menu-
  ItemPeer
encode(): URLEncoder
endsWith(): String
ensureCapacity(): StringBuffer, Vector
enumerate(): Thread, ThreadGroup
eolIsSignificant(): StreamTokenizer
equals(): BitSet, Boolean, Character,
  Color, Date, Double, File, Float,
  Font, InetAddress, Integer, Long,
  Object, Point, Rectangle, String, URL
equalsIgnoreCase(): String
exec(): Runtime
exists(): File
exit(): Runtime, System
exitValue(): Process
exp(): Math
fill3DRect(): Graphics
fillArc(): Graphics
fillInStackTrace(): Throwable
fillOval(): Graphics
fillPolygon(): Graphics
fillRect(): Graphics
fillRoundRect(): Graphics
filterIndexColorModel(): RGBImage-
  Filter
filterRGB(): RGBImageFilter
filterRGBPixels(): RGBImageFilter
finalize(): DatagramSocket, FileInput-
  Stream, FileOutputStream, Graphics,
  Object
findSystemClass(): ClassLoader
first(): CardLayout
firstElement(): Vector
floatToIntBits(): Float
floatValue(): Double, Float, Integer,
  Long, Number
floor(): Math
flush(): BufferedOutputStream, Data-
  OutputStream, FilterOutputStream,
  Image, OutputStream, PrintStream
forDigit(): Character
forName(): Class
freeMemory(): Runtime
gc(): Runtime, System
get(): BitSet, Dictionary, Hashtable
getAbsolutePath(): File
getAddress(): DatagramPacket, Inet-
  Address
getAlignment(): Label
getAllByName(): InetAddress
getAllowUserInteraction(): URLConnection

getAlpha(): ColorModel, DirectColor-
Model, IndexColorModel
getAlphaMask(): DirectColorModel
getAlphas(): IndexColorModel
getApplet(): AppletContext
getAppletContext(): Applet, AppletStub
getAppletInfo(): Applet
getApplets(): AppletContext
getAscent(): FontMetrics
getAudioClip(): Applet, AppletContext
getBackground(): Component
getBlue(): Color, ColorModel, Direct-
ColorModel, IndexColorModel
getBlueMask(): DirectColorModel
getBlues(): IndexColorModel
getBoolean(): Boolean
getBoundingBox(): Polygon
getByName(): InetAddress
getBytes(): String
getChars(): String, StringBuffer
getCheckboxGroup(): Checkbox
getClass(): Object
getClassContext(): SecurityManager
getClassLoader(): Class
getClipRect(): Graphics
getCodeBase(): Applet, AppletStub
getColor(): Color, Graphics
getColorModel(): Component,
ComponentPeer, Toolkit
getColumns(): TextArea, TextField
getComponent(): Container
getComponents(): Container
getConstraints(): GridBagLayout
getContent(): ContentHandler, URL,
URLConnection
getContentEncoding(): URLConnection
getContentLength(): URLConnection
getContentType(): URLConnection
getCurrent(): CheckboxGroup
getCursorType(): Frame
getData(): DatagramPacket
getDate(): Date, URLConnection
getDay(): Date
getDefaultAllowUserInteraction(): URL-
Connection
getDefaultRequestProperty(): URLConnection
getDefaultToolkit(): Toolkit
getDefaultUseCaches(): URLConnection
getDescent(): FontMetrics
getDirectory(): FileDialog
getDocumentBase(): Applet, AppletStub
getDoInput(): URLConnection

getDoOutput(): URLConnection
getEchoChar(): TextField
getenv(): System
getErrorsAny(): MediaTracker
getErrorsID(): MediaTracker
getErrorStream(): Process
getExpiration(): URLConnection
getFamily(): Font
getFD(): FileInputStream, FileOutput-
Stream, RandomAccessFile
getFile(): FileDialog, URL
getFileDescriptor(): SocketImpl
getFilenameFilter(): FileDialog
getFilePointer(): RandomAccessFile
getFilterInstance(): ImageFilter
getFont(): Component, Font, Font-
Metrics, Graphics, MenuComponent,
MenuContainer
getFontList(): Toolkit
getFontMetrics(): Component,
ComponentPeer, Graphics, Toolkit
getForeground(): Component
getGraphics(): Component,
ComponentPeer, Image
getGreen(): Color, ColorModel, Direct-
ColorModel, IndexColorModel
getGreenMask(): DirectColorModel
getGreens(): IndexColorModel
getHeaderField(): URLConnection
getHeaderFieldDate(): URLConnection
getHeaderFieldInt(): URLConnection
getHeaderFieldKey(): URLConnection
getHeight(): FontMetrics, Image
getHelpMenu(): MenuBar
getHost(): URL
getHostName(): InetAddress
getHours(): Date
getHSBColor(): Color
getIconImage(): Frame
getIfModifiedSince(): URLConnection
getImage(): Applet, AppletContext,
Toolkit
getInCheck(): SecurityManager
getInetAddress(): ServerSocket, Socket,
SocketImpl
getInputStream(): Process, Socket,
SocketImpl, URLConnection
getInteger(): Integer
getInterfaces(): Class
getItem(): Choice, List, Menu
getLabel(): Button, Checkbox, Menu-
Item
getLastModified(): URLConnection

getLayout(): Container
getLayoutDimensions(): GridBagLayout
GetLayoutInfo(): GridBagLayout
getLayoutOrigin(): GridBagLayout
getLayoutWeights(): GridBagLayout
getLeading(): FontMetrics
getLength(): DatagramPacket
getLineIncrement(): Scrollbar
getLineNumber(): LineNumberInput-
  Stream
getLocalHost(): InetAddress
getLocalizedInputStream(): Runtime
getLocalizedOutputStream(): Runtime
getLocalPort(): DatagramSocket, Server-
  Socket, Socket, SocketImpl
getLong(): Long
getMapSize(): IndexColorModel
getMaxAdvance(): FontMetrics
getMaxAscent(): FontMetrics
getMaxDecent(): FontMetrics
getMaxDescent(): FontMetrics
getMaximum(): Scrollbar
getMaxPriority(): ThreadGroup
getMenu(): MenuBar
getMenuBar(): Frame
getMessage(): Throwable
getMinimum(): Scrollbar
GetMinSize(): GridBagLayout
getMinutes(): Date
getMode(): FileDialog
getMonth(): Date
getName(): Class, File, Font, Thread,
  ThreadGroup
getOrientation(): Scrollbar
getOutputStream(): Process, Socket,
  SocketImpl, URLConnection
getPageIncrement(): Scrollbar
getParameter(): Applet, AppletStub
getParameterInfo(): Applet
getParent(): Component, File, Menu-
  Component, ThreadGroup
getPath(): File
getPeer(): Component, Menu-
  Component
getPixelSize(): ColorModel
getPort(): DatagramPacket, Socket,
  SocketImpl, URL
getPriority(): Thread
getProperties(): System
getProperty(): Image, Properties, System
getProtocol(): URL

getRed(): Color, ColorModel, Direct-
  ColorModel, IndexColorModel
getRedMask(): DirectColorModel
getReds(): IndexColorModel
getRef(): URL
getRequestProperty(): URLConnection
getRGB(): Color, ColorModel, Direct-
  ColorModel, IndexColorModel
getRGBdefault(): ColorModel
getRows(): List, TextArea
getRuntime(): Runtime
getScreenResolution(): Toolkit
getScreenSize(): Toolkit
getSeconds(): Date
getSecurityContext(): SecurityManager
getSecurityManager(): System
getSelectedIndex(): Choice, List
getSelectedIndexes(): List, ListPeer
getSelectedItem(): Choice, List
getSelectedItems(): List
getSelectedText(): TextComponent
getSelectionEnd(): TextComponent,
  TextComponentPeer
getSelectionStart(): TextComponent,
  TextComponentPeer
getSize(): Font
getSource(): Image
getState(): Checkbox, CheckboxMenu-
  Item
getStyle(): Font
getSuperclass(): Class
getText(): Label, TextComponent, Text-
  ComponentPeer
getThreadGroup(): Thread
getTime(): Date
getTimezoneOffset(): Date
getTitle(): Dialog, Frame
getToolkit(): Component, Component-
  Peer, Window
getTransparentPixel(): IndexColor-
  Model
getURL(): URLConnection
getUseCaches(): URLConnection
getValue(): Scrollbar
getVisible(): Scrollbar
getVisibleIndex(): List
getWarningString(): Window
getWidth(): Image
getWidths(): FontMetrics
getYear(): Date
gotFocus(): Component
grabPixels(): PixelGrabber
grow(): Rectangle

Method
Defined-In

guessContentTypeFromName(): URL-Connection

guessContentTypeFromStream(): URL-Connection

handleEvent(): Component, ComponentPeer

hasChanged(): Observable

hashCode(): BitSet, Boolean, Character, Color, Date, Double, File, Float, Font, InetAddress, Integer, Long, Object, Point, Rectangle, String, URL

hasMoreElements(): Enumeration, StringTokenizer

hasMoreTokens(): StringTokenizer

hide(): Component, ComponentPeer

HSBtoRGB(): Color

IEEEremainder(): Math

imageComplete(): ImageConsumer, ImageFilter, PixelGrabber

imageUpdate(): Component, Image-Observer

inClass(): SecurityManager

inClassLoader(): SecurityManager

indexOf(): String, Vector

init(): Applet

insert(): StringBuffer

insertElementAt(): Vector

insertText(): TextArea, TextAreaPeer

insets(): Container, ContainerPeer

inside(): Component, Polygon, Rectangle

intBitsToFloat(): Float

intern(): String

interrupt(): Thread

interrupted(): Thread

intersection(): Rectangle

intersects(): Rectangle

intValue(): Double, Float, Integer, Long, Number

invalidate(): Component

isAbsolute(): File

isActive(): Applet, AppletStub

isAlive(): Thread

isBold(): Font

isConsumer(): FilteredImageSource, ImageProducer, MemoryImage-Source

isDaemon(): Thread, ThreadGroup

isDigit(): Character

isDirectory(): File

isEditable(): TextComponent

isEmpty(): Dictionary, Hashtable, Rectangle, Vector

isEnabled(): Component, MenuItem

isErrorAny(): MediaTracker

isErrorID(): MediaTracker

isFile(): File

isInfinite(): Double, Float

isInterface(): Class

isInterrupted(): Thread

isItalic(): Font

isLowerCase(): Character

isModal(): Dialog

isNaN(): Double, Float

isPlain(): Font

isResizable(): Dialog, Frame

isSelected(): List

isShowing(): Component

isSpace(): Character

isTearOff(): Menu

isUpperCase(): Character

isValid(): Component

isVisible(): Component

join(): Thread

keyDown(): Component

keys(): Dictionary, Hashtable

keyUp(): Component

last(): CardLayout

lastElement(): Vector

lastIndexOf(): String, Vector

lastModified(): File

layout(): Component, Container

layoutContainer(): BorderLayout, CardLayout, FlowLayout, GridBagLayout, GridLayout, LayoutManager

length(): File, RandomAccessFile, String, StringBuffer

lineno(): StreamTokenizer

list(): Component, Container, File, Properties, ThreadGroup

listen(): SocketImpl

load(): Properties, Runtime, System

loadClass(): ClassLoader

loadLibrary(): Runtime, System

locate(): Component, Container

location(): Component, GridBagLayout

log(): Math

longBitsToDouble(): Double

longValue(): Double, Float, Integer, Long, Number

lookupConstraints(): GridBagLayout

loop(): AudioClip

lostFocus(): Component

lowerCaseMode(): StreamTokenizer

makeVisible(): List, ListPeer

mark(): BufferedInputStream, Filter-InputStream, InputStream, Line-NumberInputStream

markSupported(): BufferedInputStream, FilterInputStream, InputStream, PushbackInputStream

max(): Math

metaDown(): Event

min(): Math

minimumLayoutSize(): BorderLayout, CardLayout, FlowLayout, GridBag-Layout, GridLayout, LayoutManager

minimumSize(): Component, ComponentPeer, Container, List, List-Peer, TextArea, TextAreaPeer, Text-Field, TextFieldPeer

mkdir(): File

mkdirs(): File

mouseDown(): Component

mouseDrag(): Component

mouseEnter(): Component

mouseExit(): Component

mouseMove(): Component

mouseUp(): Component

move(): Component, Point, Rectangle

newInstance(): Class

next(): CardLayout

nextDouble(): Random

nextElement(): Enumeration, String-Tokenizer

nextFloat(): Random

nextFocus(): Component, Component-Peer

nextGaussian(): Random

nextInt(): Random

nextLong(): Random

nextToken(): StreamTokenizer, String-Tokenizer

notify(): Object

notifyAll(): Object

notifyObservers(): Observable

openConnection(): URL, URLStream-Handler

openStream(): URL

or(): BitSet

ordinaryChar(): StreamTokenizer

ordinaryChars(): StreamTokenizer

pack(): Window

paint(): Canvas, Component, ComponentPeer

paintAll(): Component

paintComponents(): Container

paramString(): Button, Checkbox,

CheckboxMenuItem, Choice, Com-ponent, Container, Dialog, Event, FileDialog, Frame, Label, List, Menu-Component, MenuItem, Scrollbar, TextArea, TextComponent, TextField

parentOf(): ThreadGroup

parse(): Date

parseInt(): Integer

parseLong(): Long

parseNumbers(): StreamTokenizer

parseURL(): URLStreamHandler

peek(): Stack

play(): Applet, AudioClip

pop(): Stack

postEvent(): Component, Menu-Component, MenuContainer

pow(): Math

preferredLayoutSize(): BorderLayout, CardLayout, FlowLayout, GridBag-Layout, GridLayout, LayoutManager

preferredSize(): Component, ComponentPeer, Container, List, List-Peer, TextArea, TextAreaPeer, Text-Field, TextFieldPeer

prepareImage(): Component, ComponentPeer, Toolkit

previous(): CardLayout

print(): Component, ComponentPeer, PrintStream

printAll(): Component

printComponents(): Container

println(): PrintStream

printStackTrace(): Throwable

propertyNames(): Properties

push(): Stack

pushBack(): StreamTokenizer

put(): Dictionary, Hashtable

quoteChar(): StreamTokenizer

random(): Math

read(): BufferedInputStream, ByteArray-InputStream, DataInputStream, File-InputStream, FilterInputStream, InputStream, LineNumberInput-Stream, PipedInputStream, PushbackInputStream, Random-AccessFile, SequenceInputStream, StringBufferInputStream

readBoolean(): DataInput, DataInput-Stream, RandomAccessFile

readByte(): DataInput, DataInputStream, RandomAccessFile

readChar(): DataInput, DataInput-Stream, RandomAccessFile

readDouble(): DataInput, DataInput-
Stream, RandomAccessFile
readFloat(): DataInput, DataInput-
Stream, RandomAccessFile
readFully(): DataInput, DataInput-
Stream, RandomAccessFile
readInt(): DataInput, DataInputStream,
RandomAccessFile
readLine(): DataInput, DataInputStream,
RandomAccessFile
readLong(): DataInput, DataInput-
Stream, RandomAccessFile
readShort(): DataInput, DataInput-
Stream, RandomAccessFile
readUnsignedByte(): DataInput, Data-
InputStream, RandomAccessFile
readUnsignedShort(): DataInput, Data-
InputStream, RandomAccessFile
readUTF(): DataInput, DataInputStream,
RandomAccessFile
receive(): DatagramSocket
regionMatches(): String
rehash(): Hashtable
remove(): Container, Dictionary, Frame,
Hashtable, Menu, MenuBar, Menu-
Container
removeAll(): Container
removeAllElements(): Vector
removeConsumer(): FilteredImage-
Source, ImageProducer, Memory-
ImageSource
removeElement(): Vector
removeElementAt(): Vector
removeLayoutComponent(): Border-
Layout, CardLayout, FlowLayout,
GridBagLayout, GridLayout, Layout-
Manager
removeNotify(): Component, Container,
List, Menu, MenuBar, Menu-
Component, TextComponent
renameTo(): File
repaint(): Component, ComponentPeer
replace(): String
replaceItem(): List
replaceText(): TextArea, TextAreaPeer
requestFocus(): Component,
ComponentPeer
requestTopDownLeftRightResend():
FilteredImageSource, ImageProducer,
MemoryImageSource
resendTopDownLeftRight(): ImageFilter
reset(): BufferedInputStream, Byte-
ArrayInputStream, ByteArrayOutput-

Stream, FilterInputStream, Input-
Stream, LineNumberInputStream,
StringBufferInputStream
resetSyntax(): StreamTokenizer
reshape(): Component, Component-
Peer, Rectangle
resize(): Applet, Component, Rectangle
resolveClass(): ClassLoader
resume(): Thread, ThreadGroup
RGBtoHSB(): Color
rint(): Math
round(): Math
run(): Runnable, Thread
runFinalization(): Runtime, System
sameFile(): URL
save(): Properties
search(): Stack
seek(): RandomAccessFile
select(): Choice, ChoicePeer, List, List-
Peer, TextComponent, Text-
ComponentPeer
selectAll(): TextComponent
send(): DatagramSocket
set(): BitSet, URL
setAlignment(): Label, LabelPeer
setAllowUserInteraction(): URLConnection
setBackground(): Component,
ComponentPeer
setChanged(): Observable
setCharAt(): StringBuffer
setCheckboxGroup(): Checkbox,
CheckboxPeer
setColor(): Graphics
setColorModel(): ImageConsumer,
ImageFilter, PixelGrabber,
RGBImageFilter
setConstraints(): GridBagLayout
setContentHandlerFactory(): URLConnection
setCurrent(): CheckboxGroup
setCursor(): Frame, FramePeer
setDaemon(): Thread, ThreadGroup
setDate(): Date
setDefaultAllowUserInteraction(): URL-
Connection
setDefaultRequestProperty(): URLConnection
setDefaultUseCaches(): URLConnection
setDimensions(): CropImageFilter,
ImageConsumer, ImageFilter, Pixel-
Grabber

setDirectory(): FileDialog, FileDialog-
Peer
setDoInput(): URLConnection
setDoOutput(): URLConnection
setEchoCharacter(): TextField, Text-
FieldPeer
setEditable(): TextComponent, Text-
ComponentPeer
setElementAt(): Vector
setFile(): FileDialog, FileDialogPeer
setFilenameFilter(): FileDialog, File-
DialogPeer
setFont(): Component, ComponentPeer,
Graphics, MenuComponent
setForeground(): Component,
ComponentPeer
setHelpMenu(): MenuBar
setHints(): ImageConsumer, Image-
Filter, PixelGrabber
setHours(): Date
setIconImage(): Frame, FramePeer
setIfModifiedSince(): URLConnection
setLabel(): Button, ButtonPeer, Checkbox, CheckboxPeer, MenuItem,
MenuItemPeer
setLayout(): Container
setLength(): StringBuffer
setLineIncrement(): Scrollbar, Scrollbar-
Peer
setLineNumber(): LineNumberInput-
Stream
setMaxPriority(): ThreadGroup
setMenuBar(): Frame, FramePeer
setMinutes(): Date
setMonth(): Date
setMultipleSelections(): List, ListPeer
setName(): Thread
setPageIncrement(): Scrollbar,
ScrollbarPeer
setPaintMode(): Graphics
setPixels(): CropImageFilter, Image-
Consumer, ImageFilter, Pixel-
Grabber, RGBImageFilter
setPriority(): Thread
setProperties(): CropImageFilter,
ImageConsumer, ImageFilter, Pixel-
Grabber, System
setRequestProperty(): URLConnection
setResizable(): Dialog, DialogPeer,
Frame, FramePeer
setSeconds(): Date
setSecurityManager(): System
setSeed(): Random

setSize(): Vector
setSocketFactory(): ServerSocket
setSocketImplFactory(): Socket
setState(): Checkbox, CheckboxMenu-
Item, CheckboxMenuItemPeer,
CheckboxPeer
setStub(): Applet
setText(): Label, LabelPeer, Text-
Component, TextComponentPeer
setTime(): Date
setTitle(): Dialog, DialogPeer, Frame,
FramePeer
setURL(): URLStreamHandler
setURLStreamHandlerFactory(): URL
setUseCaches(): URLConnection
setValue(): Scrollbar, ScrollbarPeer
setValues(): Scrollbar, ScrollbarPeer
setXORMode(): Graphics
setYear(): Date
shiftDown(): Event
show(): CardLayout, Component,
ComponentPeer, Window
showDocument(): AppletContext
showStatus(): Applet, AppletContext
sin(): Math
size(): BitSet, ByteArrayOutputStream,
Component, DataOutputStream, Dictionary, Hashtable, Vector
skip(): BufferedInputStream, ByteArray-
InputStream, FileInputStream, Filter-
InputStream, InputStream, Line-
NumberInputStream, StringBuffer-
InputStream
skipBytes(): DataInput, DataInput-
Stream, RandomAccessFile
slashSlashComments(): Stream-
Tokenizer
slashStarComments(): StreamTokenizer
sleep(): Thread
sqrt(): Math
start(): Applet, Thread
startProduction(): FilteredImageSource,
ImageProducer, MemoryImage-
Source
startsWith(): String
status(): PixelGrabber
statusAll(): MediaTracker
statusID(): MediaTracker
stop(): Applet, AudioClip, Thread,
ThreadGroup
stringWidth(): FontMetrics
substituteColorModel(): RGBImageFilter
substring(): String

Method
Defined-In

suspend(): Thread, ThreadGroup
sync(): Toolkit
tan(): Math
toBack(): Window, WindowPeer
toByteArray(): ByteArrayOutputStream
toCharArray(): String
toExternalForm(): URL, URLStream-
    Handler
toFront(): Window, WindowPeer
toGMTString(): Date
toLocaleString(): Date
toLowerCase(): Character, String
toString(): BitSet, Boolean, Border-
    Layout, ByteArrayOutputStream,
    CardLayout, Character, Checkbox-
    Group, Class, Color, Component,
    Date, Dimension, Double, Event,
    File, Float, FlowLayout, Font, Font-
    Metrics, Graphics, GridBagLayout,
    GridLayout, Hashtable, InetAddress,
    Insets, Integer, Long, Menu-
    Component, Object, Point, Rectan-
    gle, ServerSocket, Socket, Socket-
    Impl, StreamTokenizer, String, String-
    Buffer, Thread, ThreadGroup,
    Throwable, URL, URLConnection,
    Vector
totalMemory(): Runtime
toUpperCase(): Character, String
traceInstructions(): Runtime
traceMethodCalls(): Runtime
translate(): Event, Graphics, Point, Rec-
    tangle
trim(): String
trimToSize(): Vector
uncaughtException(): ThreadGroup
union(): Rectangle
unread(): PushbackInputStream
update(): Component, Observer
UTC(): Date
valid(): FileDescriptor
validate(): Component, Container
valueOf(): Boolean, Double, Float, Inte-
    ger, Long, String
wait(): Object
waitFor(): Process
waitForAll(): MediaTracker
waitForID(): MediaTracker
whitespaceChars(): StreamTokenizer
wordChars(): StreamTokenizer
write(): BufferedOutputStream, Byte-
    ArrayOutputStream, DataOutput,
    DataOutputStream, FileOutput-

Stream, FilterOutputStream, Output-
    Stream, PipedOutputStream, Print-
    Stream, RandomAccessFile
writeBoolean(): DataOutput, Data-
    OutputStream, RandomAccessFile
writeByte(): DataOutput, DataOutput-
    Stream, RandomAccessFile
writeBytes(): DataOutput, DataOutput-
    Stream, RandomAccessFile
writeChar(): DataOutput, DataOutput-
    Stream, RandomAccessFile
writeChars(): DataOutput, DataOutput-
    Stream, RandomAccessFile
writeDouble(): DataOutput, Data-
    OutputStream, RandomAccessFile
writeFloat(): DataOutput, DataOutput-
    Stream, RandomAccessFile
writeInt(): DataOutput, DataOutput-
    Stream, RandomAccessFile
writeLong(): DataOutput, DataOutput-
    Stream, RandomAccessFile
writeShort(): DataOutput, DataOutput-
    Stream, RandomAccessFile
writeTo(): ByteArrayOutputStream
writeUTF(): DataOutput, DataOutput-
    Stream, RandomAccessFile
xor(): BitSet
yield(): Thread

Subclass Index

This index allows you to look up a class (or interface) and find a list of classes (or interfaces) that extend it. The API documentation lets you look up the superclass of a class; this index lets you look up its subclasses. This index is useful in the same way that a class-hierarchy diagram is.

If you do not know what package a class listed here is defined in, use Section 27, *Class Defined-In Index*, to look it up.

ColorModel: DirectColorModel, Index-ColorModel

Component: Button, Canvas, Checkbox, Choice, Container, Label, List, Scrollbar, TextComponent

ComponentPeer: ButtonPeer, CanvasPeer, CheckboxPeer, ChoicePeer, ContainerPeer, LabelPeer, ListPeer, ScrollbarPeer, TextComponentPeer

Container: Panel, Window

ContainerPeer: PanelPeer, WindowPeer

Dialog: FileDialog

DialogPeer: FileDialogPeer

Dictionary: Hashtable

Error: AWTError, LinkageError, ThreadDeath, VirtualMachineError

Exception: AWTException, ClassNotFoundException, CloneNotSupportedException, IllegalAccessException, InstantiationException, InterruptedException, IOException, NoSuchMethodException, RuntimeException

FilterInputStream: BufferedInputStream, DataInputStream, LineNumberInputStream, PushbackInputStream

FilterOutputStream: BufferedOutputStream, DataOutputStream, PrintStream

Hashtable: Properties

IllegalArgumentException: IllegalThreadStateException, NumberFormatException

ImageFilter: CropImageFilter, RGBImageFilter

IncompatibleClassChangeError: AbstractMethodError, IllegalAccessError, InstantiationError, NoSuchFieldError, NoSuchMethodError

IndexOutOfBoundsException: ArrayIndexOutOfBoundsException, StringIndexOutOfBoundsException

Subclass

InputStream: ByteArrayInputStream, FileInputStream, FilterInputStream, PipedInputStream, SequenceInputStream, StringBufferInputStream

IOException: EOFException, FileNotFoundException, InterruptedIOException, MalformedURLException, ProtocolException, SocketException, UnknownHostException, UnknownServiceException, UTFDataFormatException

LinkageError: ClassCircularityError, ClassFormatError, IncompatibleClassChangeError, NoClassDefFoundError, UnsatisfiedLinkError, VerifyError

MenuComponent: MenuBar, MenuItem

MenuComponentPeer: MenuBarPeer, MenuItemPeer

MenuItem: CheckboxMenuItem, Menu

MenuItemPeer: CheckboxMenuItemPeer, MenuPeer

Number: Double, Float, Integer, Long

Object: BitSet, Boolean, BorderLayout, CardLayout, Character, CheckboxGroup, Class, ClassLoader, Color, ColorModel, Compiler, Component, ContentHandler, DatagramPacket, DatagramSocket, Date, Dictionary, Dimension, Event, File, FileDescriptor, FilteredImageSource, FlowLayout, Font, FontMetrics, Graphics, GridBagConstraints, GridBagLayout, GridLayout, Image, ImageFilter, InetAddress, InputStream, Insets, Math, MediaTracker, MemoryImageSource, MenuComponent, Number, Observable, OutputStream, PixelGrabber, Point, Polygon, Process, Random, RandomAccessFile, Rectangle, Runtime, SecurityManager, ServerSocket, Socket, SocketImpl, StreamTokenizer, String, StringBuffer, StringTokenizer, System, Thread, ThreadGroup, Throwable, Toolkit, URL, URLConnection, URLEncoder, URLStreamHandler, Vector

OutputStream: ByteArrayOutputStream, FileOutputStream, FilterOutputStream, PipedOutputStream

Panel: Applet

RuntimeException: ArithmeticException, ArrayStoreException, ClassCastException, EmptyStackException, IllegalArgumentException, IllegalMonitorStateException, IndexOutOfBoundsException, NegativeArraySizeException, NoSuchElementException, NullPointerException, SecurityException

TextComponent: TextArea, TextField

TextComponentPeer: TextAreaPeer, TextFieldPeer

Throwable: Error, Exception

Vector: Stack

VirtualMachineError: InternalError, OutOfMemoryError, StackOverflowError, UnknownError

Window: Dialog, Frame

WindowPeer: DialogPeer, FramePeer

Implemented-By Index

This index allows you to look up an interface and find a list of classes that implement the interface. This is useful when you know you want to work with an instance of the interface, but don't know what possible classes you can use.

Note that not all interfaces in the Java API appear in this index—those that are not implemented by a public class in the API do not appear. It is the nature of interfaces to be useful for referring to instances of non-public classes. Since interfaces are frequently used in this way by the Java API, many interfaces do not appear here. For example, while a fair number of Java classes implement an `Enumeration` object, only one of the classes that implements that interface is public.

Cloneable:
  BitSet
  GridBagConstraints
  Hashtable
  ImageFilter
  Insets
  Vector
DataInput:
  DataInputStream
  RandomAccessFile
DataOutput:
  DataOutputStream
  RandomAccessFile
Enumeration:
  StringTokenizer
ImageConsumer:
  ImageFilter
  PixelGrabber

ImageObserver:
  Component
ImageProducer:
  FilteredImageSource
  MemoryImageSource
LayoutManager:
  BorderLayout
  CardLayout
  FlowLayout
  GridBagLayout
  GridLayout
MenuContainer:
  Frame
  Menu
  MenuBar
Runnable:
  Thread

Returned-By Index

This index allows you to look up a class or interface type and find out which methods return objects of that type. This index is useful when you know you want to work with an object of a particular type, but you're not sure of the best way to obtain an object of that type.

Constructor methods have been omitted from this index, as it is obvious what type of object they return. Methods with no return value, and those that return a primitive type have been omitted. Methods that return String or Dimension have also been omitted since there are too many of them to be useful for this index.

Return types and method names are specified without package names in this index. If you do not know what package a class listed here is defined in, use Section 27, *Class Defined-In Index*, to look it up.

Applet:
  AppletContext.getApplet()
AppletContext:
  Applet.getAppletContext()
  AppletStub.getAppletContext()
AudioClip:
  Applet.getAudioClip()
  AppletContext.getAudioClip()
Boolean:
  Boolean.valueOf()
ButtonPeer:
  Toolkit.createButton()
CanvasPeer:
  Toolkit.createCanvas()
Checkbox:
  CheckboxGroup.getCurrent()

CheckboxGroup:
  Checkbox.getCheckboxGroup()
CheckboxMenuItemPeer:
  Toolkit.createCheckboxMenuItem()
CheckboxPeer:
  Toolkit.createCheckbox()
ChoicePeer:
  Toolkit.createChoice()
Class:
  Class.forName()
  Class.getSuperclass()
  ClassLoader.defineClass()
  ClassLoader.findSystemClass()
  ClassLoader.loadClass()
  Object.getClass()

Class[]:
    Class.getInterfaces()
    SecurityManager.getClassContext()
ClassLoader:
    Class.getClassLoader()
    SecurityManager.currentClass-
    Loader()
Color:
    Color.brighter()
    Color.darker()
    Color.getColor()
    Color.getHSBColor()
    Component.getBackground()
    Component.getForeground()
    Graphics.getColor()
ColorModel:
    ColorModel.getRGBdefault()
    Component.getColorModel()
    ComponentPeer.getColorModel()
    Toolkit.getColorModel()
Component:
    Component.locate()
    Container.add()
    Container.getComponent()
    Container.locate()
Component[]:
    Container.getComponents()
ComponentPeer:
    Component.getPeer()
Container:
    Component.getParent()
ContentHandler:
    ContentHandlerFactory.create-
    ContentHandler()
DialogPeer:
    Toolkit.createDialog()
Double:
    Double.valueOf()
Enumeration:
    AppletContext.getApplets()
    Dictionary.elements()
    Dictionary.keys()
    Hashtable.elements()
    Hashtable.keys()
    Properties.propertyNames()
    Vector.elements()
FileDescriptor:
    FileInputStream.getFD()
    FileOutputStream.getFD()
    RandomAccessFile.getFD()
    SocketImpl.getFileDescriptor()
FileDialogPeer:
    Toolkit.createFileDialog()

FilenameFilter:
    FileDialog.getFilenameFilter()
Float:
    Float.valueOf()
Font:
    Component.getFont()
    Font.getFont()
    FontMetrics.getFont()
    Graphics.getFont()
    MenuComponent.getFont()
    MenuContainer.getFont()
FontMetrics:
    Component.getFontMetrics()
    ComponentPeer.getFontMetrics()
    Graphics.getFontMetrics()
    Toolkit.getFontMetrics()
FramePeer:
    Toolkit.createFrame()
Graphics:
    Component.getGraphics()
    ComponentPeer.getGraphics()
    Graphics.create()
    Image.getGraphics()
GridBagConstraints:
    GridBagLayout.getConstraints()
    GridBagLayout.lookupConstraints()
GridBagLayoutInfo:
    GridBagLayout.GetLayoutInfo()
Image:
    Applet.getImage()
    AppletContext.getImage()
    Component.createImage()
    ComponentPeer.createImage()
    Frame.getIconImage()
    Toolkit.createImage()
    Toolkit.getImage()
ImageFilter:
    ImageFilter.getFilterInstance()
ImageProducer:
    Image.getSource()
IndexColorModel:
    RGBImageFilter.filterIndexColor-
    Model()
InetAddress:
    DatagramPacket.getAddress()
    InetAddress.getByName()
    InetAddress.getLocalHost()
    ServerSocket.getInetAddress()
    Socket.getInetAddress()
    SocketImpl.getInetAddress()
InetAddress[]:
    InetAddress.getAllByName()

InputStream:
Process.getErrorStream()
Process.getInputStream()
Runtime.getLocalizedInputStream()
Socket.getInputStream()
SocketImpl.getInputStream()
URL.openStream()
URLConnection.getInputStream()
Insets:
Container.insets()
ContainerPeer.insets()
Integer:
Integer.getInteger()
Integer.valueOf()
LabelPeer:
Toolkit.createLabel()
LayoutManager:
Container.getLayout()
ListPeer:
Toolkit.createList()
Long:
Long.getLong()
Long.valueOf()
Menu:
MenuBar.add()
MenuBar.getHelpMenu()
MenuBar.getMenu()
MenuBar:
Frame.getMenuBar()
MenuBarPeer:
Toolkit.createMenuBar()
MenuComponentPeer:
MenuComponent.getPeer()
MenuContainer:
MenuComponent.getParent()
MenuItem:
Menu.add()
Menu.getItem()
MenuItemPeer:
Toolkit.createMenuItem()
MenuPeer:
Toolkit.createMenu()
Object:
BitSet.clone()
Class.newInstance()
Compiler.command()
ContentHandler.getContent()
Dictionary.get()
Dictionary.put()
Dictionary.remove()
Enumeration.nextElement()
GridBagConstraints.clone()
Hashtable.clone()

Hashtable.get()
Hashtable.put()
Hashtable.remove()
Image.getProperty()
ImageFilter.clone()
Insets.clone()
Object.clone()
SecurityManager.getSecurityContext()
Stack.peek()
Stack.pop()
Stack.push()
StringTokenizer.nextElement()
URL.getContent()
URLConnection.getContent()
Vector.clone()
Vector.elementAt()
Vector.firstElement()
Vector.lastElement()
Object[]:
MediaTracker.getErrorsAny()
MediaTracker.getErrorsID()
OutputStream:
Process.getOutputStream()
Runtime.getLocalizedOutputStream()
Socket.getOutputStream()
SocketImpl.getOutputStream()
URLConnection.getOutputStream()
PanelPeer:
Toolkit.createPanel()
Point:
Component.location()
GridBagLayout.getLayoutOrigin()
GridBagLayout.location()
Process:
Runtime.exec()
Properties:
System.getProperties()
Rectangle:
Component.bounds()
Graphics.getClipRect()
Polygon.getBoundingBox()
Rectangle.intersection()
Rectangle.union()
Runtime:
Runtime.getRuntime()
ScrollbarPeer:
Toolkit.createScrollbar()
SecurityManager:
System.getSecurityManager()
Socket:
ServerSocket.accept()

Returned-By

SocketImpl:
SocketImplFactory.createSocket-
Impl()
TextAreaPeer:
Toolkit.createTextArea()
TextFieldPeer:
Toolkit.createTextField()
Thread:
Thread.currentThread()
ThreadGroup:
Thread.getThreadGroup()
ThreadGroup.getParent()
Throwable:
Throwable.fillInStackTrace()
Toolkit:
Component.getToolkit()
ComponentPeer.getToolkit()
Toolkit.getDefaultToolkit()
Window.getToolkit()
URL:
Applet.getCodeBase()
Applet.getDocumentBase()
AppletStub.getCodeBase()
AppletStub.getDocumentBase()
URLConnection.getURL()
URLConnection:
URL.openConnection()
URLStreamHandler.open-
Connection()
URLStreamHandler:
URLStreamHandlerFactory.create-
URLStreamHandler()
WindowPeer:
Toolkit.createWindow()

Passed-To Index

This index allows you to look up a class or interface type and find out which methods take objects of that type as arguments. This index is useful when you want to use an object of a particular type, and need to find out what possible operations you can perform on it. (You should of course also look up the methods defined by the object's class and all of its superclasses.)

Primitive types, and the `String` class, have been omitted from this index, as there are far too many methods that accept arguments of those types to be included in an index like this one.

Argument types and method names are specified without package names in this index. If you do not know what package a class listed here is defined in, use Section 27, *Class Defined-In Index*, to look it up.

AppletStub:
    Applet.setStub()
BitSet:
    BitSet.and()
    BitSet.or()
    BitSet.xor()
Button:
    Toolkit.createButton()
Canvas:
    Toolkit.createCanvas()
Checkbox:
    CheckboxGroup.setCurrent()
    Toolkit.createCheckbox()
CheckboxGroup:
    Checkbox.Checkbox()
    Checkbox.setCheckboxGroup()
    CheckboxPeer.setCheckboxGroup()

CheckboxMenuItem:
    Toolkit.createCheckboxMenuItem()
Choice:
    Toolkit.createChoice()
Class:
    ClassLoader.resolveClass()
    Compiler.compileClass()
Color:
    Color.getColor()
    Component.setBackground()
    Component.setForeground()
    ComponentPeer.setBackground()
    ComponentPeer.setForeground()
    Graphics.drawImage()
    Graphics.setColor()
    Graphics.setXORMode()

ColorModel:
CropImageFilter.setPixels()
ImageConsumer.setColorModel()
ImageConsumer.setPixels()
ImageFilter.setColorModel()
ImageFilter.setPixels()
MemoryImageSource.MemoryImage-Source()
PixelGrabber.setColorModel()
PixelGrabber.setPixels()
RGBImageFilter.setColorModel()
RGBImageFilter.setPixels()
RGBImageFilter.substituteColor-Model()

Component:
BorderLayout.addLayout-Component()
BorderLayout.removeLayout-Component()
CardLayout.addLayoutComponent()
CardLayout.removeLayout-Component()
Container.add()
Container.remove()
FlowLayout.addLayoutComponent()
FlowLayout.removeLayout-Component()
GridBagLayout.addLayout-Component()
GridBagLayout.getConstraints()
GridBagLayout.lookupConstraints()
GridBagLayout.removeLayout-Component()
GridBagLayout.setConstraints()
GridLayout.addLayoutComponent()
GridLayout.removeLayout-Component()
LayoutManager.addLayout-Component()
LayoutManager.removeLayout-Component()
MediaTracker.MediaTracker()

Container:
BorderLayout.layoutContainer()
BorderLayout.minimumLayoutSize()
BorderLayout.preferredLayoutSize()
CardLayout.first()
CardLayout.last()
CardLayout.layoutContainer()
CardLayout.minimumLayoutSize()
CardLayout.next()
CardLayout.preferredLayoutSize()
CardLayout.previous()

CardLayout.show()
FlowLayout.layoutContainer()
FlowLayout.minimumLayoutSize()
FlowLayout.preferredLayoutSize()
GridBagLayout.ArrangeGrid()
GridBagLayout.GetLayoutInfo()
GridBagLayout.GetMinSize()
GridBagLayout.layoutContainer()
GridBagLayout.minimumLayout-Size()
GridBagLayout.preferredLayoutSize()
GridLayout.layoutContainer()
GridLayout.minimumLayoutSize()
GridLayout.preferredLayoutSize()
LayoutManager.layoutContainer()
LayoutManager.minimumLayout-Size()
LayoutManager.preferredLayout-Size()

ContentHandlerFactory:
URLConnection.setContentHandler-Factory()

DatagramPacket:
DatagramSocket.receive()
DatagramSocket.send()

DataInput:
DataInputStream.readUTF()

Date:
Date.after()
Date.before()

Dialog:
Toolkit.createDialog()

Dimension:
Applet.resize()
Component.resize()
Dimension.Dimension()
Rectangle.Rectangle()

Enumeration:
SequenceInputStream.Sequence-InputStream()

Event:
Component.action()
Component.deliverEvent()
Component.gotFocus()
Component.handleEvent()
Component.keyDown()
Component.keyUp()
Component.lostFocus()
Component.mouseDown()
Component.mouseDrag()
Component.mouseEnter()
Component.mouseExit()
Component.mouseMove()

Component.mouseUp()
Component.postEvent()
ComponentPeer.handleEvent()
Container.deliverEvent()
MenuComponent.postEvent()
MenuContainer.postEvent()

File:
File.File()
File.renameTo()
FileInputStream.FileInputStream()
FilenameFilter.accept()
FileOutputStream.FileOutputStream()
RandomAccessFile.RandomAccess-
File()

FileDescriptor:
FileInputStream.FileInputStream()
FileOutputStream.FileOutputStream()
SecurityManager.checkRead()
SecurityManager.checkWrite()

FileDialog:
Toolkit.createFileDialog()

FilenameFilter:
File.list()
FileDialog.setFilenameFilter()
FileDialogPeer.setFilenameFilter()

Font:
Component.getFontMetrics()
Component.setFont()
ComponentPeer.getFontMetrics()
ComponentPeer.setFont()
Font.getFont()
FontMetrics.FontMetrics()
Graphics.getFontMetrics()
Graphics.setFont()
MenuComponent.setFont()
Toolkit.getFontMetrics()

Frame:
Dialog.Dialog()
FileDialog.FileDialog()
Toolkit.createFrame()
Window.Window()

Graphics:
Canvas.paint()
Component.paint()
Component.paintAll()
Component.print()
Component.printAll()
Component.update()
ComponentPeer.paint()
ComponentPeer.print()
Container.paintComponents()
Container.printComponents()

GridBagConstraints:
GridBagLayout.AdjustForGravity()
GridBagLayout.DumpConstraints()
GridBagLayout.setConstraints()

GridBagLayoutInfo:
GridBagLayout.DumpLayoutInfo()
GridBagLayout.GetMinSize()

Hashtable:
CropImageFilter.setProperties()
ImageConsumer.setProperties()
ImageFilter.setProperties()
MemoryImageSource.MemoryImage-
Source()
PixelGrabber.setProperties()

Image:
Component.checkImage()
Component.imageUpdate()
Component.prepareImage()
ComponentPeer.checkImage()
ComponentPeer.prepareImage()
Frame.setIconImage()
FramePeer.setIconImage()
Graphics.drawImage()
ImageObserver.imageUpdate()
MediaTracker.addImage()
PixelGrabber.PixelGrabber()
Toolkit.checkImage()
Toolkit.prepareImage()

ImageConsumer:
FilteredImageSource.addConsumer()
FilteredImageSource.isConsumer()
FilteredImageSource.remove-
Consumer()
FilteredImageSource.requestTop-
DownLeftRightResend()
FilteredImageSource.start-
Production()
ImageFilter.getFilterInstance()
ImageProducer.addConsumer()
ImageProducer.isConsumer()
ImageProducer.removeConsumer()
ImageProducer.requestTopDown-
LeftRightResend()
ImageProducer.startProduction()
MemoryImageSource.addConsumer()
MemoryImageSource.isConsumer()
MemoryImageSource.remove-
Consumer()
MemoryImageSource.requestTop-
DownLeftRightResend()
MemoryImageSource.start-
Production()

Passed-To

ImageFilter:
    FilteredImageSource.FilteredImage-
    Source()
ImageObserver:
    Component.checkImage()
    Component.prepareImage()
    ComponentPeer.checkImage()
    ComponentPeer.prepareImage()
    Graphics.drawImage()
    Image.getHeight()
    Image.getProperty()
    Image.getWidth()
    Toolkit.checkImage()
    Toolkit.prepareImage()
ImageProducer:
    Component.createImage()
    ComponentPeer.createImage()
    FilteredImageSource.FilteredImage-
    Source()
    ImageFilter.resendTopDownLeft-
    Right()
    PixelGrabber.PixelGrabber()
    Toolkit.createImage()
IndexColorModel:
    RGBImageFilter.filterIndexColor-
    Model()
InetAddress:
    DatagramPacket.DatagramPacket()
    Socket.Socket()
    SocketImpl.bind()
    SocketImpl.connect()
InputStream:
    BufferedInputStream.BufferedInput-
    Stream()
    DataInputStream.DataInputStream()
    FilterInputStream.FilterInputStream()
    LineNumberInputStream.Line-
    NumberInputStream()
    Properties.load()
    PushbackInputStream.Pushback-
    InputStream()
    Runtime.getLocalizedInputStream()
    SequenceInputStream.Sequence-
    InputStream()
    StreamTokenizer.StreamTokenizer()
    URLConnection.guessContentType-
    FromStream()
Integer:
    Integer.getInteger()
Label:
    Toolkit.createLabel()
LayoutManager:
    Container.setLayout()

List:
    Toolkit.createList()
Long:
    Long.getLong()
Menu:
    MenuBar.add()
    MenuBar.setHelpMenu()
    MenuBarPeer.addHelpMenu()
    MenuBarPeer.addMenu()
    Toolkit.createMenu()
MenuBar:
    Frame.setMenuBar()
    FramePeer.setMenuBar()
    Toolkit.createMenuBar()
MenuComponent:
    Frame.remove()
    Menu.remove()
    MenuBar.remove()
    MenuContainer.remove()
MenuItem:
    Menu.add()
    MenuPeer.addItem()
    Toolkit.createMenuItem()
Object:
    BitSet.equals()
    Boolean.equals()
    Character.equals()
    Color.equals()
    Compiler.command()
    Component.action()
    Component.gotFocus()
    Component.lostFocus()
    Date.equals()
    Dictionary.get()
    Dictionary.put()
    Dictionary.remove()
    Double.equals()
    Event.Event()
    File.equals()
    Float.equals()
    Font.equals()
    Hashtable.contains()
    Hashtable.containsKey()
    Hashtable.get()
    Hashtable.put()
    Hashtable.remove()
    InetAddress.equals()
    Integer.equals()
    Long.equals()
    Object.equals()
    Observable.notifyObservers()
    Observer.update()
    Point.equals()

PrintStream.print()
PrintStream.println()
Rectangle.equals()
SecurityManager.checkConnect()
SecurityManager.checkRead()
SecurityManager.checkTopLevel-
Window()
Stack.push()
Stack.search()
String.equals()
String.valueOf()
StringBuffer.append()
StringBuffer.insert()
System.arraycopy()
URL.equals()
Vector.addElement()
Vector.contains()
Vector.indexOf()
Vector.insertElementAt()
Vector.lastIndexOf()
Vector.removeElement()
Vector.setElementAt()
Object[]:
Vector.copyInto()
Observable:
Observer.update()
Observer:
Observable.addObserver()
Observable.deleteObserver()
OutputStream:
BufferedOutputStream.Buffered-
OutputStream()
ByteArrayOutputStream.writeTo()
DataOutputStream.DataOutput-
Stream()
FilterOutputStream.FilterOutput-
Stream()
PrintStream.PrintStream()
Properties.save()
Runtime.getLocalizedOutputStream()
Panel:
Toolkit.createPanel()
PipedInputStream:
PipedOutputStream.connect()
PipedOutputStream.PipedOutput-
Stream()
PipedOutputStream:
PipedInputStream.connect()
PipedInputStream.PipedInput-
Stream()
Point:
Rectangle.add()
Rectangle.Rectangle()

Polygon:
Graphics.drawPolygon()
Graphics.fillPolygon()
PrintStream:
Component.list()
Container.list()
Properties.list()
Throwable.printStackTrace()
Properties:
Properties.Properties()
System.setProperties()
Rectangle:
GridBagLayout.AdjustForGravity()
Rectangle.add()
Rectangle.intersection()
Rectangle.intersects()
Rectangle.union()
Runnable:
Thread.Thread()
Scrollbar:
Toolkit.createScrollbar()
SecurityManager:
System.setSecurityManager()
SocketImpl:
SocketImpl.accept()
SocketImplFactory:
ServerSocket.setSocketFactory()
Socket.setSocketImplFactory()
TextArea:
Toolkit.createTextArea()
TextField:
Toolkit.createTextField()
Thread:
SecurityManager.checkAccess()
ThreadGroup.uncaughtException()
Thread[]:
Thread.enumerate()
ThreadGroup.enumerate()
ThreadGroup:
SecurityManager.checkAccess()
Thread.Thread()
ThreadGroup.parentOf()
ThreadGroup.ThreadGroup()
ThreadGroup[]:
ThreadGroup.enumerate()
Throwable:
Thread.stop()
ThreadGroup.uncaughtException()
URL:
Applet.getAudioClip()
Applet.getImage()
Applet.play()
AppletContext.getAudioClip()

Passed-To

AppletContext.getImage()
AppletContext.showDocument()
Toolkit.getImage()
URL.sameFile()
URL.URL()
URLConnection.URLConnection()
URLStreamHandler.open-
Connection()
URLStreamHandler.parseURL()
URLStreamHandler.setURL()
URLStreamHandler.toExternalForm()
URLConnection:
ContentHandler.getContent()
URLStreamHandlerFactory:
URL.setURLStreamHandlerFactory()
Window:
Toolkit.createWindow()

Thrown-By Index

This index allows you to look up the name of an exception or an error and find a list of all methods (with their classes) that throw that exception or error. This can sometimes be useful when debugging Java programs.

Methods are specified without package names in this index. If you do not know what package a class listed here is defined in, use Section 27, *Class Defined-In Index*, to look it up.

AWTError:
  Toolkit.getDefaultToolkit()
ArithmeticException:
  Math.log()
  Math.pow()
  Math.sqrt()
ArrayIndexOutOfBoundsException:
  Container.getComponent()
  System.arraycopy()
  Vector.elementAt()
  Vector.insertElementAt()
  Vector.removeElementAt()
  Vector.setElementAt()
ArrayStoreException:
  System.arraycopy()
ClassFormatError:
  ClassLoader.defineClass()
ClassNotFoundException:
  Class.forName()
  ClassLoader.findSystemClass()
  ClassLoader.loadClass()

CloneNotSupportedException:
  Object.clone()
EOFException:
  DataInput.readBoolean()
  DataInput.readByte()
  DataInput.readChar()
  DataInput.readDouble()
  DataInput.readFloat()
  DataInput.readFully()
  DataInput.readInt()
  DataInput.readLong()
  DataInput.readShort()
  DataInput.readUnsignedByte()
  DataInput.readUnsignedShort()
  DataInput.skipBytes()
  DataInputStream.readFully()
EmptyStackException:
  Stack.peek()
  Stack.pop()

Thrown-By

PipedInputStream.close()
PipedInputStream.connect()
PipedInputStream.read()
PipedOutputStream.PipedOutput-
Stream()
PipedOutputStream.close()
PipedOutputStream.connect()
PipedOutputStream.write()
PrintStream.write()
Properties.load()
PushbackInputStream.available()
PushbackInputStream.read()
PushbackInputStream.unread()
RandomAccessFile.RandomAccess-
File()
RandomAccessFile.close()
RandomAccessFile.getFD()
RandomAccessFile.getFilePointer()
RandomAccessFile.length()
RandomAccessFile.read()
RandomAccessFile.readBoolean()
RandomAccessFile.readByte()
RandomAccessFile.readChar()
RandomAccessFile.readDouble()
RandomAccessFile.readFloat()
RandomAccessFile.readFully()
RandomAccessFile.readInt()
RandomAccessFile.readLine()
RandomAccessFile.readLong()
RandomAccessFile.readShort()
RandomAccessFile.readUTF()
RandomAccessFile.readUnsigned-
Byte()
RandomAccessFile.readUnsigned-
Short()
RandomAccessFile.seek()
RandomAccessFile.skipBytes()
RandomAccessFile.write()
RandomAccessFile.writeBoolean()
RandomAccessFile.writeByte()
RandomAccessFile.writeBytes()
RandomAccessFile.writeChar()
RandomAccessFile.writeChars()
RandomAccessFile.writeDouble()
RandomAccessFile.writeFloat()
RandomAccessFile.writeInt()
RandomAccessFile.writeLong()
RandomAccessFile.writeShort()
RandomAccessFile.writeUTF()
Runtime.exec()
SequenceInputStream.close()
SequenceInputStream.read()
ServerSocket.ServerSocket()

ServerSocket.accept()
ServerSocket.close()
ServerSocket.setSocketFactory()
Socket.Socket()
Socket.close()
Socket.getInputStream()
Socket.getOutputStream()
Socket.setSocketImplFactory()
SocketImpl.accept()
SocketImpl.available()
SocketImpl.bind()
SocketImpl.close()
SocketImpl.connect()
SocketImpl.create()
SocketImpl.getInputStream()
SocketImpl.getOutputStream()
SocketImpl.listen()
StreamTokenizer.nextToken()
URL.getContent()
URL.openConnection()
URL.openStream()
URLConnection.connect()
URLConnection.getContent()
URLConnection.getInputStream()
URLConnection.getOutputStream()
URLConnection.guessContentType-
FromStream()
URLStreamHandler.open-
Connection()
IllegalAccessException:
  Class.newInstance()
IllegalArgumentException:
  Choice.select()
  GridLayout.GridLayout()
  Hashtable.Hashtable()
  Label.setAlignment()
  Scrollbar.Scrollbar()
  Thread.setPriority()
IllegalMonitorStateException:
  Object.notify()
  Object.notifyAll()
  Object.wait()
IllegalThreadStateException:
  Process.exitValue()
  Thread.countStackFrames()
  Thread.setDaemon()
  Thread.start()
  ThreadGroup.destroy()
InstantiationException:
  Class.newInstance()
InterruptedException:
  MediaTracker.waitForAll()
  MediaTracker.waitForID()

Thrown-By

Object.wait()
PixelGrabber.grabPixels()
Process.waitFor()
Thread.join()
Thread.sleep()

MalformedURLException:
URL.URL()

NoClassDefFoundError:
ClassLoader.findSystemClass()

NoSuchElementException:
Enumeration.nextElement()
StringTokenizer.nextElement()
StringTokenizer.nextToken()
Vector.firstElement()
Vector.lastElement()

NullPointerException:
Choice.addItem()
Dictionary.put()
File.File()
Hashtable.contains()
Hashtable.put()
ThreadGroup.ThreadGroup()

NumberFormatException:
Double.Double()
Double.valueOf()
Float.Float()
Float.valueOf()
Integer.Integer()
Integer.parseInt()
Integer.valueOf()
Long.Long()
Long.parseLong()
Long.valueOf()

OutOfMemoryError:
Object.clone()

SecurityException:
SecurityManager.SecurityManager()
SecurityManager.checkAccept()
SecurityManager.checkAccess()
SecurityManager.checkConnect()
SecurityManager.checkCreateClass-
Loader()
SecurityManager.checkDelete()
SecurityManager.checkExec()
SecurityManager.checkExit()
SecurityManager.checkLink()
SecurityManager.checkListen()
SecurityManager.checkProperties-
Access()
SecurityManager.checkProperty-
Access()
SecurityManager.checkRead()
SecurityManager.checkWrite()

System.setSecurityManager()
Thread.checkAccess()
ThreadGroup.checkAccess()

SocketException:
DatagramSocket.DatagramSocket()
ServerSocket.setSocketFactory()
Socket.setSocketImplFactory()

StringIndexOutOfBoundsException:
String.String()
String.charAt()
String.substring()
StringBuffer.charAt()
StringBuffer.getChars()
StringBuffer.insert()
StringBuffer.setCharAt()
StringBuffer.setLength()

Throwable:
Object.finalize()

UnknownHostException:
InetAddress.getAllByName()
InetAddress.getByName()
InetAddress.getLocalHost()
Socket.Socket()

UnknownServiceException:
URLConnection.getContent()
URLConnection.getInputStream()
URLConnection.getOutputStream()

UnsatisfiedLinkError:
Runtime.load()
Runtime.loadLibrary()
System.load()
System.loadLibrary()

Glossary

This glossary lists all of the keywords in the Java language and gives examples of using them. It also defines a number of object-oriented programing concepts and other terms that arise frequently when programming with Java.

abstract

The abstract keyword is used to declare abstract methods and classes. An abstract method has no implementation defined—it is declared with arguments and a return type as usual, but the body enclosed in curly braces is replaced with a semicolon. An abstract method cannot be declared static, private, or final. The implementation of an abstract method is provided by a subclass of the class in which it is defined. If an abstract method appears in a class, the class is also abstract. Abstract classes cannot be instantiated. Only a non-abstract subclass that provides an implementation for all the abstract methods may be instantiated. A class cannot be declared both final and abstract.

```
abstract public class Graphics {
    public abstract void draw_rectangle(int x, int y, int w, int h);
    public abstract void draw_circle(int x, int y, int r);
}
```

API (Application Programming Interface)

An API consists of the functions and variables that programmers are allowed to use in their applications. The Java API consists of all public and protected methods of all public classes in the java.applet, java.awt, java.awt.image, java.awt.peer, java.io, java.-lang, java.net, and java.util packages.

assignable

An object is assignable to a variable if it has the same type as the variable or if it is a subclass of the type of the variable. If the variable is of an interface type, then the object is assignable to the variable if it is an instance of a class that implements the interface. A primitive type is assignable to a variable if it can be converted to the variable's type without casting.

AWT (Abstract Windowing Toolkit)

This is the name for Java's platform-independent windowing, graphics, and user-interface toolkit.

`boolean`

`boolean` is a primitive Java data type that contains a truth value. The two possible values of a `boolean` variable are `true` and `false`. In Java, `boolean` values cannot be cast to or from any other type, including numeric types. The result of a comparison operator is a `boolean` value and control structures like `if` statements and `while` loops use a `boolean` value to determine how they execute.

```
boolean b;
int i = 5;

b = (i > 3);        // comparisons yield boolean values
if (b) i = 0;       // booleans are used in if statements
b = (i != 0)        // "convert" a number to a boolean by comparing it
i = b?1:0;          // "convert" a boolean to a number with the ?: operator
```

`break`

The `break` statement, without a label, transfers control out of ("breaks out of" or terminates) the nearest enclosing `for`, `while`, `do`, or `switch` statement. If the `break` keyword is followed by an identifier that is the label of an arbitrary enclosing statement, then execution transfers out of that enclosing statement. After the `break` statement is executed, any required `finally` clauses are executed, and control resumes at the statement following the terminated statement.

```
main_loop: for(int i=0; i < 10; i++) {
    try {
            for(int j=0; j < 10; j++) {
                if (j > i) break;// terminate just this loop
                if (a[i][j] == null)
                break main_loop;// do the finally clause and
                }// terminate both loops.
    }
    finally { cleanup(a, i, j); }
}
```

`byte`

`byte` is a primitive Java data type. It is an 8-bit two's-complement signed number (in all implementations). The minimum value is -128 and the maximum value is 127. It can be cast to and from other numeric types.

```
byte[] octet_buffer = new byte[1024];
byte lookup_table[] = {1, 2, 4, 8, 16, 32, 64};
```

`byvalue`

`byvalue` is a reserved keyword in Java. It is not currently used but may be defined by future versions of the language.

---

case

case is used to provide numeric labels for statements within a switch statement block. See switch for an example.

cast

cast is a reserved keyword in Java. It is not currently used, but may be defined by future versions of the language.

catch

The catch statement introduces an exception handling block of code following a try statement. The catch keyword is followed by an exception type and argument name in parentheses, and a block of code within curly braces. When an exception object that is assignable to the specified type is thrown, the object is assigned to the named argument, and the code within the block is executed to handle the exceptional condition. See try for an example.

char

char is a primitive Java data type. A variable of type char holds a single 16-bit Unicode character. char values may be cast to and from numeric values, but because character data is implicitly unsigned, casts of char to byte or short may result in a negative number. Note that strings in Java are *not* null-terminated arrays of char.

```
String s = "This is a test";
char last = s.charAt(s.length() - 1);
```

class

An encapsulated collection of data and methods to operate on the data. A class may be instantiated to produce an object that is an instance of the class. See class for a description of declaring a class in Java.

class

The class keyword is used to declare a class, thereby defining a new object type. Its syntax is similar to the struct keyword in C. (Note, though, that Java does not support C struct or union keywords.) The class keyword is preceded by zero or more class modifiers. It is followed by: the name of the class, an optional extends clause, an optional implements clause, an open curly brace, a series of variable and method declarations, and a close curly brace.

```
public class Screwdriver extends Tool implements Torque {
    private int head_type, shaft_length, handle_diameter;
    public void apply_torque(Torqueable screw) {
            // method definition here
    }
    // more variable and methods declarations here.
}
```

class method

A method declared static. Methods of this type are not passed implicit this references and may only refer to class variables and invoke other class methods of the current class. A class method may be invoked through the class name, rather than through an instance of the class.

---

class variable

A variable declared `static`. Variables of this type are associated with the class, rather than with a particular instance of the class. There is only one copy of a static variable, regardless of the number of instances of the class that are created.

component

Any of the GUI primitives implemented in the `java.awt` package as subclasses of `Component`. The classes `Button`, `Choice`, and `Text-Field` (among many others) are components.

const

`const` is a reserved keyword in Java. It is not currently used, but may be defined by future versions of the language.

constructor

A method that is invoked automatically when a new instance of a class is created. Constructors are used to initialize the variables of the newly created object. The constructor method has the same name as the class.

Container

One of the `java.awt` classes that can "contain" GUI components. Components contained in a container appear within the boundaries of the container. The classes `Dialog`, `Frame`, `Panel`, and `Window` are containers.

continue

The `continue` keyword is optionally followed by an identifier that names the label of an enclosing iteration statement. A `continue` statement stops the iteration in progress and causes execution to resume after the last statement in the `while`, `do`, or `for` loop just before the loop iteration is to begin again. If the `continue` statement specifies an enclosing labelled loop, execution skips to the end of that loop (even though the label appears at the top of the loop). Otherwise, execution skips to the end of the nearest enclosing loop. If there are any `finally` clauses between the `continue` statement and the end of the appropriate loop, these clauses are executed before control is transferred to the end of the loop.

```
big_loop: while(!done) {
    if (test(a,b) == 0) continue;// control goes to point 2.
    try {
                for(int i=0; i < 10; i++) {
                    if (a[i] == null)
                    continue;// control goes to point 1.
                    else if (b[i] == null)
                    continue big_loop;// control goes to point 2,
                    // after doing the finally block.
                    doit(a[i],b[i]);
                    // point 1. Increment and start loop again with the test.
                }
    }
    finally { cleanup(a,b); }
    // point 2.  Start loop again with the !done test.
}
```

data hiding

An object-oriented programming technique that makes an object's data `private` or `protected` (i.e., hidden) and allows programmers to access and manipulate that data only through method calls. Done well, data hiding can reduce bugs and it promotes reusability and modularity of classes. This technique is also commonly known as encapsulation.

default

The `default` keyword is used only within a `switch` statement block. It labels the statements to be executed by default, i.e., when the value of the `switch` expression does not match any of the `case` labels within the `switch` statement block. See `switch` for an example.

do

The `do` keyword introduces a `do/while` loop and has exactly the same syntax as in C. The `do/while` construct is far less common than the regular `while` loop. Don't forget that a semicolon is required after the condition in a `do/while` loop.

```
int i = 10;
do {
    do_it(i--);
} while (i != 0);
```

double

`double` is a Java primitive data type. A `double` value is a 64-bit ("double-precision") floating-point number represented in IEEE 754 format. The maximum positive and negative values that can be represented by a `double` are ±1.79769313486231570E+308, and the smallest (closest to zero) representable values are ±4.94065645841246544E-324. The constants `java.lang.Double.MAX_VALUE` and `java.lang.Double.-MIN_VALUE` also have these values. When writing a floating-point literal value, you can indicate that it should be treated as a `double` (instead of a `float`) by appending a `d` or `D`. There are four `double` values with special behavior:

positive infinity

This is a special value generated when a positive floating-point value becomes larger than the largest representable value. In arithmetic and comparison operations it behaves like infinity should—it is greater than any other number. The constant `java.lang.Double.POSITIVE_INFINITY` has this value.

negative infinity

This value is like positive infinity, except generated when a negative floating-point number overflows. It is more negative than any other number. The constant `java.lang.Double.NEGATIVE_INFINITY` has this value.

negative zero

This value is generated when a very small negative value underflows and becomes effectively zero. Direct comparison (with `==`) of negative zero to "regular" (i.e., positive) zero does not distinguish the two. One way to distinguish these two zero values, however, is

---

to divide by them: one divided by positive zero yields positive infinity, while one divided by negative zero yields negative infinity.

not a number

This value, also commonly known as NaN, is interpreted literally as "not a number." NaN is generated by mathematical operations that do not have defined values, such as zero divided by zero. Most operations that involve NaN as an argument return NaN as their value. The constant `java.lang.Double.NaN` is NaN. Note, though, that comparing NaN for equality with itself always returns `false`, so in order to test whether a number is NaN, use the method `java.lang.Double.isNaN()`.

else

The `else` keyword introduces the (optional) alternative clause of an `if` statement. If the expression evaluated by the `if` statement is `false`, then the statements within the `else` block are executed. With nested `if` statements, it is important to pay attention to be sure which `if` an `else` clause refers to. In Java, as in most languages, an `else` clause is part of the nearest `if` statement that does not have an `else`. Of course the easiest way to make this clear is to use curly braces to mark the `if` and `else` blocks, even when they contain only a single statement.

```
if (i == j)
    if (j == k)
                System.out.println("i == k");
    else  // this else goes with if (j == k)
                System.out.println("i != k");
else // this else goes with  if (i == j)
    System.out.println("i != j");
```

encapsulation

See data hiding.

exception

A signal that some unexpected condition has occurred in the program. In Java, exceptions are objects that are subclasses of `Exception` or `Error` (which themselves are subclasses of `Throwable`). Exceptions in Java are "raised" with the `throw` keyword and received with the `catch` keyword. See `throw`, `throws`, and `catch`.

extends

The `extends` keyword is used in a `class` declaration to specify the superclass of the class being defined. `extends` must be followed by the name of a class. This class is known as the superclass. The class being defined has access to all the `public` and `protected` variables and methods of the superclass (or, if the class being defined is in the same package, it has access to all non-`private` variables and methods). If a class definition omits the `extends` clause, its superclass is taken to be `java.lang.Object`.

An `extends` clause may also be used in `interface` declarations. In this case, the `extends` clause is followed by one or more comma-separated interface names. The interface being defined implicitly includes all the constants and abstract methods of each of the interfaces it extends. A class that implements this newly defined interface must provide an implementation for all the abstract methods of each of the interfaces that were extended, as well as any abstract methods defined in the new interface.

```
public class Complex extends Number {
    double x, y;
    ....
}
public class bicycle extends vehicle implements wheel {
    ...
}
public interface bicycle_wheel extends wheel, spokes, rubber_tire {
    ...
}
```

false

false is one of the two possible boolean values. Strictly speaking false is not a keyword of the Java language, but a literal value like an integer or a character value.

```
boolean done = false;
while(!done) {
    if (test()) done = true;
}
```

final

The final keyword is a modifier that may be applied to classes, methods, and variables. It has a similar, but not identical meaning in each case. When final is applied to a class, it means that the class may never be subclassed. java.lang.System is an example of a final class.

When the final modifier is applied to a method, it means that the method may never be overridden (i.e., hidden by a subclass method with the same name, arguments, and return type). static and private methods are implicitly final, as are all methods of a final class. If a method is implicitly or explicitly final, the compiler can perform certain optimizations, such as inlining the method, and the interpreter can invoke the method without the overhead of dynamic method lookup.

If final is applied to a variable, it means that the variable has a constant value. The definition of a final variable must include an initializer to assign a value to the variable; no assignments after initialization are permitted. static final variables are used in Java as constants, in much the same way that #define is used in C to define constants. If a final variable has a constant expression as its initializer, the compiler can treat the variable as a constant itself and perform computations with it at compile-time, rather than at run-time.

```
// A final class: can't be subclassed.
public final class Buffer {
    // A constant: this variable can't be assigned to.
    // Note the capital letters--a convention for constants.
    protected static final int DEFAULT_SIZE = 2048;

    // A final method: a subclass couldn't override this method
    // even if the class were non-final and allowed subclassing.
    public final read(Stream s, int n)
}
```

finalize

finalize is not actually a Java keyword, but a reserved method name. If a class contains an instance method named finalize that has no arguments and returns no value then this method is a finalizer:

```
void finalize()
```

The finalizer is called when an object is no longer being used (i.e., when there are no further references to it), but before the object's memory is actually reclaimed by the system. A finalizer should perform cleanup tasks and free system resources that are not handled by Java's garbage collection system. These may include closing open files or network connections, removing any lock files created on the system, and so on. A finalizer should invoke any superclass finalizer methods by calling super.finalize() as its last statement.

finalizer

A method that is called just before an object is reclaimed by the garbage collector. A finalizer method should release any system resources (other than memory) held by the object. See finalize.

finally

This keyword introduces the finally block of a try/catch/finally construct. catch and finally blocks provide exception handling and routine cleanup for the code in a try block. The finally block is optional, and appears after the try block and after zero or more catch blocks. The code in a finally block is executed once, regardless of how the code in the try block executes. In normal execution, control reaches the end of the try block and then proceeds to the finally block, which generally performs any necessary cleanup.

If control leaves the try block because of a return, continue, or break statement, the contents of the finally block are executed before control transfers to its new destination.

If an exception occurs in the try block, and there is a catch block to handle the exception, control transfers first to the catch block, and then to the finally block. If there is not a local catch block to handle the exception, control transfers first to the finally block, and then propagates up to the nearest catch block that can handle the exception.

Note that if a finally block itself transfers control with a return, continue, or break statement, or by raising an exception, the pending control transfer is abandoned, and this new transfer is processed.

See try for an example.

float

float is a Java primitive data type. A float value is a 32-bit ("single-precision") floating-point number represented in IEEE 754 format. The maximum positive and negative values that can be represented by a float are ±3.40282347E+38, and the smallest (i.e., closest to zero) representable values are ±1.40239846E-45. The class java.lang.Float serves as an object wrapper for primitive float types, and defines these minimum and maximum values as constants. When writing a floating-point literal value, you can indicate that it should be treated as a float (instead of a double) by appending f or F. There are four special values for the type `float`: positive infinity, negative infinity, negative zero, and NaN or not-a-number. These special `float` values have a different representation than the corresponding `double` values, but have the same meanings. See `double` for more information.

for

The `for` statement is perhaps the most useful looping construct available in Java. It is identical to the `for` loop in C, with the addition of the C++ ability to declare local loop variables in the initialization section of the loop. Java does not support the C comma operator that allows multiple expressions to be joined into a single expression, but the Java `for` loop does allow multiple comma-separated expressions to appear in the initialization and increment sections (but not the test section) of the loop. Note that because variable declaration syntax also uses the comma, the Java syntax allows you to specify either multiple comma-separated initialization expressions or the declaration (with initializer) of multiple (comma-separated) variables of the same type. You may not mix variable declarations with other expressions.

```
int i;
String s;
for(i=0, s = "testing";// initialize variables
    (i < 10) && (s.length() >= 1);// test for continuation
    i++, s = s.substring(1))// increment variables
{
    System.out.println(s);// loop body
}

// for loop with local loop variable declaration
for(int i = 0, j=10; i < j; i++, j--) System.out.println("k = " + i*j);
```

future

`future` is a reserved keyword in Java. It is not currently used but may be defined by future versions of the language.

garbage collection

The process of reclaiming the memory of objects that are no longer in use. An object is no longer in use when there are no references to it from any other objects in the system and no references in any local variables on the method call stack.

GC

An abbreviation for garbage collection or garbage collector. (Or occasionally "graphics context.")

generic

`generic` is a reserved keyword in Java. It is not currently used, but may be defined by future versions of the language.

goto

`goto` is a reserved keyword in Java. It is not currently used, but may be defined by future versions of the language.

GUI (graphical user interface)

A GUI is a user interface constructed from graphical push buttons, text fields, pulldown menus, dialog boxes, and other standard interface components. In Java, GUIs are implemented with the classes in the `java.awt` package.

if

The `if` statement is exactly the same in Java as in C: it executes a given statement (or block of statements) if a given expression is `true`. Alternatively, if the expression evaluates to `false`, then the statement or statements in the optional `else` clause are executed. See `else` for an example; see `switch` for a language construct that chooses among more than two alternatives.

implements

The `implements` keyword must be followed by one or more (comma-separated) interface names. It is used in class declarations to indicate that the class implements the named interface or interfaces. The `implements` clause is optional in class declarations; if it appears, it must follow the `extends` clause (if any). If an `implements` clause appears in the declaration of a non-`abstract` class, every method from each specified interface must be implemented by the class or by one of its superclasses.

```
public class GinsuKnife extends Knife implements Slices, Dices {
    ...
}
```

import

The `import` statement makes Java classes available to the current class under an abbreviated name. (Java classes are always available by their fully qualified name, assuming that the appropriate class file can be found relative to the CLASSPATH environment variable and that the class file is readable. `import` doesn't make the class available; it just saves typing and makes your code more legible). Any number of `import` statements may appear in a Java program. They must appear, however, after the optional `package` statement at the top of the file, and before the first class or interface definition in the file.

There are three forms of the `import` statement:

```
import package ;
import package.class ;
import package.* ;
```

The first form allows the specified package to be known by the name of its last component. For example:

```
import java.awt.image;
```

allows `java.awt.image.ImageFilter` to be called `image.Image-Filter`.

The second form allows the specified class in the specified package to be known by its class name alone. Thus:

```
import java.util.Hashtable;
```

allows you to type `Hashtable` instead of `java.util.Hashtable`.

Finally, the third form of the `import` statement makes all classes in a package available by their class name. For example, the following import statement is implicit (you need not specify it yourself) in every Java program:

```
import java.lang.*;
```

It makes the core classes of the language available by their unqualified class name. If two packages imported with this form of the statement contain classes with the same name, those classes must be referred to by their qualified name to resolve the conflict.

inheritance

An important feature of object-oriented programming: Subclasses inherit the non-`private` variables and methods of all their superclasses. That is, an object implicitly contains all the non-`private` variables of its superclass, and can invoke all the non-`private` methods of its superclass.

inner

`inner` is a reserved keyword in Java. It is not currently used, but may be defined by future versions of the language.

instance

An object. When a class is instantiated to produce an object, we say that the object is an instance of the class.

instanceof

`instanceof` is a Java operator that returns `true` if the object on its left-hand side is an instance of the class (or implements the interface) specified on its right-hand side. `instanceof` returns `false` if the object is not an instance of the specified class or does not implement the specified interface. It also returns `false` if the specified object is `null`.

```
if (tools[i] instanceof Screwdriver) {
    Screwdriver s = (Screwdriver) tools[i];
    s.torque(screws[j]);
}
else if (tools[i] instanceof Hammer) {
    ((Hammer)tools[i]).drive(nails[j]);
}
```

instance method

A non-`static` method of a class. Such a method is passed an implicit `this` reference to the object that invoked it. See also class method, `static`.

instance variable

A non-`static` variable of a class. Copies of such variables occur in every instance of the class that is created. See also class variable, `static`.

int

`int` is a primitive Java data type. It is a 32-bit two's-complement signed number (in all implementations). The minimum value is -2147483648 and the maximum value is 2147483647. It can be cast to and from other numeric types.

```
int j;
for(int i = 0; i < 10; i++) out.print(i + ", ");
```

interface

The `interface` keyword is used to declare an interface. Declaring an interface is very similar to declaring a class, except for the following differences:

- The only modifiers that may be used with an interface are `public` and `abstract`. All interfaces are implicitly `abstract`, so use of this modifier is optional.

- The `extends` clause of an interface specification may contain one or more (comma-separated) interface names. The interface being declared implicitly contains the constants and methods of each of the interfaces it extends.

- No `implements` clause is permitted in an interface declaration.

- An interface body may not contain any constructors, static class initializers, instance variables, or class methods.

- All variables declared in an interface are implicitly `static` and `final`, and these modifiers may optionally appear in the declaration. All variables must be initialized to a constant expression. All variables in a public interface are implicitly `public`. The `public` modifier is optional. Variables in an interface may not be `transient` or `volatile`.

- All methods in an interface are implicitly `abstract` and must have a semicolon in place of a body. The `abstract` modifier is optional. All methods in a public interface are implicitly `public`. The `public` modifier is optional. Methods in an interface may not be `final`, `native`, `static`, or `synchronized`.

```
public interface Hammer extends Tool {
    // Some constants describing possible shaft
    // materials for a Hammer
    static final byte WOODEN = 1;
    static final byte STEEL  = 2;
    static final byte FIBER  = 3;
    // abstract methods defined by this interface
    public abstract drive(Nail n) ;
    public abstract pull(Nail n) ;
}
```

ISO8859-1

An eight-bit character encoding standardized by the ISO. This encoding is also known as Latin-1 and contains characters from the Latin alphabet suitable for English and most languages of western Europe.

ISO 10646

A four-byte character encoding that includes all of the world's national standard character encodings. Also known as UCS. The two-byte Unicode character set maps to the range 0x00000000 to 0x0000FFFF of ISO 10646.

JDK (Java Developers Kit)

A package of software distributed by Sun Microsystems for Java developers. It includes the Java interpreter, Java classes, and Java development tools: compiler, debugger, disassembler, appletviewer, stub file generator, and documentation generator.

Latin-1

A nickname for ISO8859-1.

`long`

`long` is a primitive Java data type. It is a 64-bit two's-complement signed number (in all implementations). The minimum value is -9223372036854775808 and the maximum value is 9223372036854775807. It can be cast to and from other numeric types.

method

The object-oriented programming term for a function or procedure.

NaN (not-a-number)

This is a special value of the `double` and `float` data types that represents an undefined result of a mathematical operation, such as zero divided by zero. See `double`.

`native`

`native` is a modifier that may be applied to method declarations. It indicates that the method is implemented (elsewhere) in C, or in some other platform-dependent fashion. A `native` method should have a semicolon instead of a body. A `native` method cannot be `abstract`, but all other method modifiers may be used with `native` methods.

`new`

`new` is a unary operator that creates a new object or array (or raises an `OutOfMemoryException` if there is not enough memory available). The `new` syntax to create a new object is:

new *classname* (*argument-list*)

When invoked like this, `new` creates a dynamic instance of the specified class (which must be a non-`abstract` class), initializes all of its instance variables to their default values (0, 0.0, \u0000, `false`, or `null`), and then invokes the appropriate constructor to do any further initialization of the object. The "appropriate constructor" is the one that expects arguments with types matching those specified in the argument list (which may be empty). The `new` operator and the `newInstance()` method of the `java.lang.Class` class are the only ways to create new objects.

```
Complex c = new Complex(2.0, 3.0);
Button b = new Button("Quit");
```

The `new` operator can also be used to allocate arrays with the following syntax:

new *typename* [*dimension*] *other-dimensions*

When invoked in this form, `new` allocates an array with *dimension* elements. (*dimension* may be a constant integer, or an expression that evaluates to an integer.) For single-dimensional arrays, each element of the array is of the type specified by *typename*, and may be a primitive type, a class (abstract or not) or an interface. Once the array has been allocated, the elements of the array are initialized to their default values.

Note that objects are not created as the array elements, and that no object constructors are called. If additional dimensions are specified for the array, these subarrays are recursively created.

```
byte[] buffer = new byte[1024];
Font[][] fonts = new Font[5][4];
String[][][] = new String[20][][];
```

null

null is a special value that indicates that a variable does not refer to any object. The value null may be assigned to any class or interface variable. It cannot be cast to any integral type, and should not be considered equal to zero, as in C.

object

An instance of a class. A class models a group of things; an object models a particular member of that group.

operator

operator is a reserved keyword in Java. It is not currently used, but may be defined by future versions of the language.

outer

outer is a reserved keyword in Java. It is not currently used, but may be defined by future versions of the language.

overload

To provide definitions of more than one method with the same name but with different argument lists or return values. We call this process "method overloading" and say that the method name is "overloaded." When an overloaded method is called, the compiler determines which one is intended by examining the supplied argument types.

override

To define a method that exactly matches (i.e., same name, same argument types, and same return type) a method defined in a superclass. When an overridden method is invoked, the interpreter uses "dynamic method lookup" to determine which definition of the method is applicable to the current object.

package

The package statement must be the first statement in a Java file. It specifies which package the code in the file is part of. Java code that is part of a particular package has access to all classes (public and non-public) in the package, and all non-private methods and fields in all those classes. When Java code is part of a named package, the compiled class file must be placed at the appropriate position in the CLASSPATH directory hierarchy before it can be accessed by the Java interpreter or other utilities.

If the package statement is omitted from a file, the code in that file is part of an unnamed default package. This is convenient for small test programs, or during development because it means that the code can be interpreted from the current directory.

primitive type

One of the Java data types: `boolean`, `char`, `byte`, `short`, `int`, `long`, `float`, `double`. Primitive types are manipulated, assigned, and passed to methods "by value"—i.e., the actual bytes of the data are copied. See also "reference type."

`private`

The `private` keyword is a visibility modifier that can be applied to method and field variables of classes. A `private` field is not visible outside of its class definition.

`private protected`

When the `private` and `protected` visibility modifiers are both applied to a variable or method in a class, they indicate that the field is visible only within the class itself and within subclasses of the class. Note that subclasses can only access `private protected` fields within themselves or within other objects that are subclasses; they cannot access those fields within instances of the superclass.

`protected`

The `protected` keyword is a visibility modifier that can be applied to method and field variables of classes. A `protected` field is only visible within its class, within subclasses, or within the package of which its class is a part. Note that subclasses in different packages can only access `protected` fields within themselves or within other objects that are subclasses; they cannot access protected fields within instances of the superclass.

`public`

The `public` keyword is a visibility modifier that can be applied to classes and interfaces and to the method and field variables of classes and interfaces. A `public` class or interface is visible everywhere. A non-`public` class or interface is visible only within its package. A `public` method or variable is visible everywhere that its class is visible. When none of the `private`, `protected` or `public` modifiers is specified, a field is visible only within the package of which its class is a part.

reference type

Any object or array. Reference types are manipulated, assigned, and passed to methods "by reference." In other words, the underlying value is not copied; only a reference to it is. See also "primitive type."

`rest`

`rest` is a reserved keyword in Java. It is not currently used, but may be defined by future versions of the language.

`return`

The `return` statement in a method, constructor, or static class initializer causes control to return to the caller. Before control returns to the caller, the `finally` clauses (if any) of any `try` statements that the `return` is nested within are executed.

Static initializers, constructors, and methods that are declared to return `void` use the `return` statement alone:

```
if (done) return;
```

Methods that return a value follow the `return` statement with an expression. The value of this expression must be assignable to the return type of the method, and is returned as the value of the method call.

```
return sorted_array;
```

shadow

To declare a variable with the same name as a variable defined in a superclass. We say that the variable "shadows" the superclass's variable. You can use the `super` keyword to refer to the shadowed variable, or can refer to it by casting the object to the type of the superclass.

`short`

`short` is a primitive Java data type. It is a 16-bit two's-complement signed number (in all implementations). The minimum value is -32768 and the maximum value is 32767. It can be cast to and from other numeric types.

```
public class MousePosition { short x, y; }
```

`static`

The `static` keyword is a modifier that may be applied to method and variable declarations within a class. A `static` variable is also known as a "class variable" as opposed to non-`static` "instance variables." While each instance of a class has a full set of its own instance variables, there is only one copy of each `static` class variable, regardless of the number of instances of the class (perhaps zero) that are created. `static` variables may be accessed by class name or through an instance. Non-`static` variables can only be accessed through an instance.

A `static` method is also known as a "class method." Class methods are not passed an implicit `this` pointer to an instance of the class, and thus can not use or call non-`static` variables and methods of the class. A class method may be invoked through an instance of the class, or through the class itself, even if no instances of the class have been created. A non-`static` "instance method" can only be invoked through an instance of the class.

```
public class TypeA {
    public static int j;
    public static void f(int i) {}
    public static void g(int i) {
        f(i+j);         // a static method can call another static method
    }                   // and use static variables.
}
TypeA.g(A.j);           // We can refer to static methods and variables by class name.
TypeA a = new TypeA();
a.g(a.j);               // Or through an instance.
```

static initializer

A block of code that appears, within curly braces, following the `static` keyword, in a class definition. When a class is first loaded by Java, the class initializers are invoked, in the order in which they appear, in order to initialize the class. This may involve initializing the value of class variables or loading a library of native methods, for example.

subclass

A class that extends another. The subclass inherits the `public` and `protected` methods and variables of its superclass. See `extends`.

super

The keyword `super` refers to the same value as `this`—the instance of the class for which the current method (these keywords are only valid within non-`static` methods) was invoked. While the type of `this` is the type of the class in which the method appears, the type of `super` is the type of the superclass of the class in which the method appears. `super` is usually used to refer to superclass variables that have been shadowed by variables in the current class. Using `super` in this way is equivalent to casting `this` to the type of the superclass.

There are two additional special uses of the `super` keyword. The first is to invoke a function in the immediate superclass that has been overridden in the current class. Note that because of the definition of function overriding and dynamic method lookup, casting `this` to the type of the superclass and invoking the method through that cast object still invokes the overriding method in the subclass. To invoke overridden methods in the immediate superclass, you need to use `super`.

The second special use of the `super` keyword is as the first statement (and only the first statement) of a constructor. If `super` appears as the first statement of a constructor and is followed by a parenthesized (possibly empty) argument list, then it is interpreted as a call to a constructor of the immediate superclass. If `super` doesn't appear as the first statement of a constructor body, the Java compiler inserts an implicit call—`super()`—to the immediate superclass constructor.

```
class A {
    public A() { System.out.println("Constructor A(void)"); }
    public A(int i) { System.out.println("Constructor A(int)"); }
    public String name = "A";
    public void f() { System.out.println("A: " + name); }
}

class B extends A {
    public B() {
                // implicit super(); call automatically inserted here.
        System.out.println("Constructor B(void)");
    }
    public B(int i) {
        super(i);    // explicit call to a (non-default) superclass constructor.
        System.out.println("Constructor B(int)");
    }
    public String name = "B";// shadows name in class A.
    public void f() {// overrides method f() in class A.
        System.out.println("B: " + name);
    }
```

```
public void test() {
    String name = "local";

    System.out.println(name);// local name
    System.out.println(this.name);// name in B
    System.out.println(super.name);// name in A
    System.out.println(((A)this).name);// name in A

    f();        // calls f() in class B.
    this.f();   // calls f() in class B.
    super.f();  // calls f() in class A.
    ((A)this).f(); // calls f() in class B (dynamic lookup)
    }
}
```

superclass

A class that is extended by some other class. The superclass's `public` and `protected` methods and variables are available to the subclass. See `extends`.

`switch`

The `switch` statement is exactly the same in Java as it is in C. It is a way of selecting among an arbitrary number of code fragments based on the value of an expression. The `switch` keyword is followed by an integral-valued expression in parentheses and a block of code in curly braces. The statement block should contain one or more `case` and `default` keywords which serve to label sections of the code. When the `switch` statement is executed, the expression in parentheses is evaluated, and control jumps to the statement which has a `case` label that has the same value as the expression, or to the statement with the `default` label if no `case` label matches. The `break` statement is usually used within the body of a `switch` statement to terminate the statement when the appropriate code fragment has been executed. Without `break` statements, control would "fall through" from one labelled fragment to the next.

```
switch (font.getStyle()) {
    case Font.ITALIC:
            s = "italic"; break;
    case Font.BOLD:
            s = "bold"; break;
    case Font.BOLD + Font.ITALIC:
            s = "bolditalic"; break;
    default:
    case Font.PLAIN:
            s = ""; break;
}
```

`synchronized`

The `synchronized` keyword is used in two related ways in Java: as a modifier and as a statement. First, it is a modifier that can be applied to class or instance methods. It indicates that the method modifies the internal state of the class or the internal state of an instance of the class in a way that is not thread-safe. Before running a `synchronized` class method, Java obtains a lock on the class, to ensure that no other threads can be modifying the class concurrently. Before running a synchronized instance method, Java obtains a lock on the instance that invoked the method, ensuring that no other thread can be modifying the object at the same time.

Java also supports a synchronized statement that serves to specify a "critical section" of code. The synchronized keyword is followed by an expression in parentheses and a statement or block of statements. The expression must evaluate to an object or array. Java obtains a lock on the specified object or array before executing the statements.

this

Within an instance method or constructor of a class, this refers to "this object"—the instance currently being operated on. It is useful to refer to an instance variable of the class that has been shadowed by a local variable or method argument. It is also useful to pass the current object as an argument to static methods or methods of other classes.

There is one additional use of this. When this appears as the very first statement in a constructor method, it refers to one of the other constructors of the class.

```
class Point {
    public int x,y;
    public Point(x,y) { this.x = x; this.y = y; }
    public Point() { this(0,0); }
}
```

thread

A single independent stream of execution within a program. Since Java is a "multithreaded" programming language, more than one thread may be running within the Java interpreter at a time. Threads in Java are represented and controlled through the Thread object.

throw

The throw statement signals that an exceptional condition has occurred by throwing a specified exception object. This statement causes program execution to stop and resume at the nearest containing catch statement that can handle the specified exception object. Note that the throw keyword must be followed by an exception object, not an exception class.

```
if (font == null) throw new NullPointerException("null font specified");
```

throws

The throws keyword is used in a method declaration to list the exceptions that the method can throw. Any exceptions that a method can raise that are not subclasses of Error or RuntimeException must either be caught within the method or declared in the method's throws clause.

```
public void readfile(File f) throws FileNotFoundException {
    ...
}
```

transient

The transient keyword is a modifier that may be applied to variables in a class. It specifies that the variable is not part of the persistent state of the object. (This modifier is not currently used by any part of Java.)

true

true is one of the two possible `boolean` values. Strictly speaking, `true` is not a keyword of the Java language, but a literal value like an integer or a character value.

try

The `try` keyword is used to indicate a block of code to which subsequent `catch` and `finally` clauses apply. The `try` statement itself performs no special action. See `catch` and `finally` for more information on the `try/catch/finally` construct.

```
try {
    // do stuff here that may raise exceptions or
    // terminate in various ways
}
catch (SomeException e1) {
    // Handle one kind of exception here
}
catch (AnotherException e2) {
    // Handle another kind here.
}
finally {
    // Always execute this code, no matter what happens.
}
```

UCS (universal character set)

A synonym for ISO-10646.

Unicode

A 16-bit character encoding that includes all of the world's commonly used alphabets and ideographic character sets in a "unified" form (i.e., a form from which duplications among national standards have been removed). ASCII and Latin-1 characters may be trivially mapped to Unicode characters. Java uses Unicode for its `char` and `String` types.

UTF-8 (UCS transformation format 8-bit form)

This is an encoding for Unicode characters (and more generally, UCS characters) commonly used for transmission and storage. It is a multibyte format in which different characters require different numbers of bytes to be represented.

var

var is a reserved keyword in Java. It is not currently used, but may be defined by future versions of the language.

void

The `void` keyword is used to indicate that a method returns no value. The only methods that are declared without a return type or `void` specified are constructor functions. Java differs from C in that methods that take no arguments are declared with empty parentheses, not with the `void` keyword. Also unlike C, Java does not have any `void *` type, nor does it require a `(void)` cast in order to correctly ignore the result returned by a call to a non-`void` method.

```
public class Complex extends Number {
    double x, y;
    // A constructor: not void, but we don't have to declare
```

```
    // the implicit return value
    Complex(double x, double y) { ... }
    // A method with no arguments and no return value.
    // Note void as return type, but not between the parentheses.
    void swap_components() { ... }
}
```

volatile

The volatile keyword is a modifier that may be applied to variables. It specifies that the variable changes asynchronously (e.g., it may be a memory-mapped hardware register on a peripheral device), and that the compiler should not attempt to perform optimizations with it. For example, it should read the variable's value from memory every time and not attempt to save a copy of it in registers.

while

The while loop performs exactly in Java as it does in C. The expression in parentheses is evaluated, and if the boolean result is true, the statements within curly braces are executed. This process repeats until the value of the expression becomes false.

Index

---

getFontList( ), 269
getGraphics( ), 253
getHeaderField( ), 336
getImage( ), 95, 235-236, 271
getInputStream( ), getOutputStream( ), 333
getInteger( ), 315
getInterfaces( ), 312
getLineNumber( ), 300
getLocalHost( ), 332
getLocalizedInputStream( ), getLocalizedOutputStream( ), 320
getLocalPort( ), 331
getLong( ), 316
getMessage( ), 40, 327
getName( ), 296
getParameter( ), 191
getParameterInfo( ), 92, 234
getParent( ), 163, 244, 296
getPath( ), 296
getProperties( ), 191
getProperty( ), 16, 324, 344
getRef( ), 335
getRGBDefault( ), 272
getRuntime( ), 319
getScreenResolution( ), 269
getScreenSize( ), 269
getSelectedText( ), 268
getSource( ), 258, 271
getSuperclass( ), 312
getText( ), 268
getThreadGroup( ), 163
global variables, 17, 56
gotFocus( ), 106
GOT_FOCUS event, 244
goto statements, 38, 407
grabPixels( ), 278
graphical user interfaces (GUIs),
    103, 103-123, 237, 407
    components of, 237-270
        custom, 120-123
    handling events of, 114-117
    scrollbars, 117-120
    (see also layout managers)
graphics (see images)
Graphics class, 237, 253
    (see also java.awt package)
graying out
    inactive buttons, 157-159
    menu items, 264
GrepInputFilter class, 133-135

GridBagConstraints class,
    255-256
GridBagLayout layout manager,
    108-114, 256-257
GridLayout layout manager, 257
gridwidth
    gridheight fields, 255
gridx, gridy fields, 255
GUIs (see graphic user interfaces)

H

hand cursor, 190
handleEvent( ), 116
handling
    events (see events, handling)
    exceptions (see exceptions)
hashCode( ), 318
Hashtable class, 340, 342
hasMoreElements( ), 342, 346
hasMoreTokens( ), 345
header files, generating (see
    javah)
HEIGHT HTML attribute, 202
help command (jdb), 227
Help menus, 262
Helvetica (see fonts)
hide( ), 106, 244
hiding data (see encapsulation)
–host (jdb option), 226
hourglass cursor, 191
HSPACE HTML attribute, 202
HTML (Hypertext Markup Language), 181, 201-204
    ALIGN attribute, 202
    ALT attribute, 202
    <APPLET> tags, 86, 201-203
    CODE attribute, 202
    CODEBASE attribute, 202
    <EMBED> tag, 203
    HEIGHT attribute, 202
    HSPACE attribute, 202
    NAME attribute, 202
    <PARAM> tag, 194, 202
    VALUE attribute, 202
    VSPACE attribute, 202
    WIDTH attribute, 202
HTTP (Hypertext Transfer Protocol), 203

void (keyword), 46, 418
volatile (keyword), 47, 180, 419
VSPACE HTML attribute, 202
vulture threads, 165

W

wait( ), 165-169
wait cursor, 191
waitForID( ), 155, 261
warning messages, 219
weightx, weighty constraints,
     113, 255
where command (jdb), 229
while statements, 36, 403, 419
     (see also break statements;
     continue statements)
whitespaceChars( ), 306
WIDTH HTML attribute, 202
Window class, 270
WindowPeer interface, 287
windows, 101, 237, 237-270
     (see also java.awt package)

wordChars( ), 306
wristwatch cursor, 191
write( ), 301
writeUTF( ), 208
writing in Java (see program-
     ming in Java)
WWW, interacting with, 141-150

Y

yes( ) (dialogs), 106
YesNoDialog class, 106
yield( ), 325

Z

ZapfDingbats font, 187
zero
     division by, 25
     negative, 25, 403

About the Author

David Flanagan is a consulting computer programmer, user interface designer, and trainer. His previous books with O'Reilly & Associates include *X Toolkit Intrinsics Reference Manual* and *Motif Tools: Streamlined GUI Design and Programming with the Xmt Library*. David has a degree in computer science and engineering from the Massachusetts Institute of Technology.

Colophon

Our look is the result of reader comments, our own experimentation, and feedback from distribution channels. Distinctive covers complement our distinctive approach to technical topics, breathing personality and life into potentially dry subjects.

The illustrations featured on the cover of *Java in a Nutshell* are American football referees (or "refs," as they are frequently called). The referee poses, from left to right, are: first down, offsides, touchdown, pass interference, and timeout.

Edie Freedman designed this cover from illustrations drawn by Arthur Saarinen. The referees were created in Adobe Illustrator. Supporting artwork was done in QuarkXPress.

The fonts used in the book are Garamond and Garamond book. Text was prepared using the troff text formatter and FrameMaker. Figures were created by Chris Reilley in Macromedia Freehand 5.0 and Adobe Photoshop.

INTERNET
Books from O'Reilly & Associates, Inc.
WINTER 1995-96

The Whole Internet User's Guide & Catalog

By Ed Krol
2nd Edition April 1994
574 pages, ISBN 1-56592-063-5

Still the best book on the Internet! This is the second edition of our comprehensive—and bestselling—introduction to the Internet, the international network that includes virtually every major computer site in the world. In addition to email, file transfer, remote login, and network news, this book pays special attention to some new tools for helping you find information. Useful to beginners and veterans alike, this book will help you explore what's possible on the Net. Also includes a pull-out quick-reference card.

"An ongoing classic."
—*Rochester Business Journal*

"The book against which all subsequent Internet guides are measured, Krol's work has emerged as an indispensable reference to beginners and seasoned travelers alike as they venture out on the data highway."
—*Microtimes*

"*The Whole Internet User's Guide & Catalog* will probably become the Internet user's bible because it provides comprehensive, easy instructions for those who want to get the most from this valuable electronic tool."
—David J. Buerger, Editor, *Communications Week*

The Whole Internet for Windows 95

By Ed Krol & Paula Ferguson
1st Edition October 1995 (est.)
650 pages (est.), ISBN 1-56592-155-0

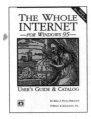

The best book on the Internet...now updated for Windows 95! *The Whole Internet for Windows 95* is the most comprehensive introduction to the Internet available today. For Windows users who in the past have struggled to take full advantage of the Internet's powerful utilities, Windows 95's built-in Internet support is a cause for celebration. And when you get online with Windows 95, this new edition of *The Whole Internet* will guide you every step of the way.

This book shows you how to use Microsoft Internet Explorer (the World Wide Web multimedia browser) and Microsoft Exchange (an email program). It also covers Netscape Navigator, the most popular Web browser on the market, and shows you how to use Usenet readers, file transfer tools, and database searching software.

But it does much more. You'll also want to take advantage of alternative popular free software programs that are downloadable from the Net. This book shows you where to find them and how to use them to save you time and money.

Using Email Effectively

By Linda Lamb & Jerry Peek
1st Edition April 1995
160 pages, ISBN 1-56592-103-8

After using email for a few years, you learn from your own mistakes and from reading other people's mail. You learn how to include a message but leave in only the sections that make your point, how to recognize if a network address "looks right," how to successfully subscribe and unsubscribe to a mailing list, how to save mail so that you can find it again. This book shortens the learning-from-experience curve for all mailers, so you can quickly be productive and send email that looks intelligent to others.

Bandits on the Information Superhighway

By Daniel J. Barrett
1st Edition February 1996
246 pages, ISBN 1-56592-156-9

Most people on the Internet behave honestly, but there are always some troublemakers. *Bandits* provides a crash course in Internet "street smarts," describing practical risks that every user should know about. Filled with anecdotes, technical tips, and the advice of experts from diverse fields, *Bandits* helps you identify and avoid risks online, so you can have a more productive and enjoyable time on the Internet.

The USENET Handbook

By Mark Harrison
1st Edition May 1995
388 pages, ISBN 1-56592-101-1

How to get the most out of network news! This book unlocks USENET, the world's largest discussion forum. It includes tutorials on the most popular newsreaders for UNIX and Windows (*tin, nn,* GNUS, and Trumpet). It's also a guide to the culture of the Net, giving you an introduction to etiquette, the private language, and some of the history.

World Wide Web Journal

Edited by O'Reilly & Associates and Web Consortium (W3C)
Special Issue January 1996
748 pages, ISBN 1-56592-169-0

The *World Wide Web Journal* is a quarterly publication that provides timely, in-depth coverage of the issues, techniques, and research developments in the World Wide Web. This special issue contains the Conference Proceeding papers that were chosen for the 4th International World Wide Web Conference in Boston, MA.

MH & xmh: Email for Users & Programmers

By Jerry Peek
3rd Edition April 1995
782 pages, ISBN 1-56592-093-7

This book explains how to make MH do things you never thought an email program could do. It covers all the MH commands as well as three interfaces to MH: *xmh* (for the X environment), *exmh* (written with tcl/tk), and *mh-e* (for GNU Emacs users). Also features configuration tips, customization and programming examples, and a description of the Multipurpose Internet Mail Extensions (MIME) and how to use it with MH.

The Computer User's Survival Guide

By Joan Stigliani
1st Edition October 1995
296 pages, ISBN 1-56592-030-9

The bad news: You can be hurt by working at a computer. The good news: Many of the factors that pose a risk are within your control. This book looks squarely at all the factors that affect your health on the job, including positioning, equipment, work habits, lighting, stress, radiation, and general health.

Internet In A Box,™ Version 2.0

Published by SPRY, Inc.
(Product good only in U.S. and Canada)
2nd Edition June 1995
UPC 799364 012001
Two diskettes & a 528-page version of **The Whole**
Internet Users Guide & Catalog *as documentation*

Now there are more ways to connect to the Internet—and you get to choose the most economical plan based on your dialing habits.

What will Internet In A Box do for me?

Internet In A Box is for PC users who want to connect to the Internet. Quite simply, it solves Internet access problems for individuals and small businesses without dedicated lines and/or UNIX machines. Internet In A Box provides instant connectivity, a multimedia Windows interface, and a full suite of applications. This product is so easy to use, you need to know only two things to get started: how to load software onto your PC and how to use a mouse.

New features of version 2.0 include:

- More connectivity options with the CompuServe Network.

- With Spry Mosaic and Progressive Image Rendering, browsing the Internet has never been easier.

- SPRY Mail provides MIME support and a built-in spell checker. Mail and News are now available within the Mosaic Toolbar.

- You'll enjoy safe and secure shopping online with Secure HTTP.

- SPRY News offers offline support for viewing and sending individual articles.

- A Network File Manager means there's an improved interface for dealing with various Internet hosts.

Marketing on the Internet

By Linda Lamb, Tim O'Reilly, Dale Dougherty,
& Brian Erwin
1st Edition June 1996 (est.)
170 pages (est.), ISBN 1-56592-105-4

Marketing on the Internet tells you what you need to know to successfully use this new communication and sales channel to put product and sales information online, build relationships with customers, send targeted announcements, and answer product support questions. In short, how to use the Internet as part of your overall marketing mix. Written from a marketing, not technical perspective.

WebSite™ 1.1

By O'Reilly & Associates, Inc.
Documentation by Susan Peck
2nd Edition January 1996
ISBN 1-56592-173-9, UPC 9-781565-921733
Includes four diskettes, 494-page book, and WebSite T-shirt

WebSite 1.1 now makes it easier than ever to start publishing on the Internet. WebSite is a 32-bit multi-threaded World Wide Web server that combines the power and flexibility of a UNIX server with the ease of use of a Windows application. Its intuitive graphical interface and easy install make it a natural for both Windows NT and Windows 95 users.

WebSite provides a tree-like display of all the documents and links on your server, with a simple solution for finding and fixing broken links. Using CGI, you can run a desktop application like Excel or Visual Basic from within a Web document on WebSite. Its access authentication lets you control which users have access to different parts of your Web server. WebSite is a product of O'Reilly & Associates, Inc. It is created in cooperation with Bob Denny and Enterprise Integration Technologies, Inc. (EIT).

New features of WebSite 1.1 include: HTML editor, multiple indexes, WebFind wizard, CGI with Visual Basic 4 framework and server push support, graphical interface for creating virtual servers, Windows 95 style install, logging reports for individual documents, HTML-2 and -3 support, external image map support, self-registration of users, and EMosaic 2.1 Web browser.

Designing for the Web: Basics for a New Medium

By Jennifer Niederst with Edie Freedman
1st Edition April 1996 (est.)
150 pages (est.), ISBN: 1-56592-165-8

This book is for designers who need to hone their skills for the Web. It explains how to work with HTML documents from a designer's point of view, outlines special problems with presenting information online, and walks through incorporating images into Web pages, with emphasis on resolution and improving efficiency. Also discusses the different browsers available and how to make sure a document is most effective for a broad spectrum of browsers and platforms.

Providing Web Content

Using HTML: The Definitive Guide

By Chuck Musciano & Bill Kennedy
1st Edition April 1996 (est.)
350 pages (est.), ISBN 1-56592-175-5

Using HTML helps you become fluent in HTML, fully versed in the language's syntax, semantics, and elements of style. The book covers the most up-to-date version of the HTML standard, plus all the common extensions and, in particular, Netscape extensions. The authors cover each and every element of the currently accepted version of the language in detail, explaining how each element works and how it interacts with all the other elements. They've also included a style guide that helps you decide how to best use HTML to accomplish a variety of tasks, from simple online documentation to complex marketing and sales presentations.

CGI Scripting on the World Wide Web

By Shishir Gundavaram
1st Edition March 1996 (est.)
375 pages (est.), ISBN 1-56592-168-2

This book offers a comprehensive explanation of CGI and related techniques for people who hold on to the dream of providing their own information servers on the Web. Gundavaram starts at the beginning, explaining the value of CGI and how it works, then moves swiftly into the subtle details of programming. The book offers a comprehensive look at the job of providing information dynamically on the Web.

Perl 5 Desktop Reference

By Johan Vromans
1st Edition February 1996
56 pages, ISBN: 1-56592-187-9

This is the standard quick-reference guide for the Perl programming language. It provides a complete overview of the language, from variables to input and output, from flow control to regular expressions, from functions to document formats —all packed into a convenient, carry-around booklet.

Java in a Nutshell: A Desktop Quick Reference for Java Programmers

By David Flanagan
1st Edition February 1996
450 pages (est.), ISBN 1-56592-183-6

Java in a Nutshell is a complete quick reference guide to the Java API, the hot new programming language from Sun Microsystems. This comprehensive volume contains descriptions of all of the Java classes and their related calls and an introduction to important Java concepts.

Exploring Java

By Pat Niemeyer & Josh Peck
1st Edition April 1996 (est.)
250 pages (est.), ISBN 1-56592-184-4

The first book in our new Java documentation series, Exploring Java introduces the basics of Java, the new object-oriented programming language for networked applications. This book shows you how to get up to speed writing Java applets and other applications, including networking programs, content and protocol handlers, and security managers.

Learning Perl

By Randal L. Schwartz, Foreword by Larry Wall
1st Edition November 1993
274 pages, ISBN 1-56592-042-2

Learning Perl is a step-by-step, hands-on tutorial designed to get you writing useful Perl scripts as quickly as possible. In addition to countless code examples, there are numerous programming exercises, with full answers. For a comprehensive and detailed guide to advanced programming with Perl, read the companion book, Programming perl.

Programming perl

By Larry Wall & Randal L. Schwartz
1st Edition January 1991
482 pages, ISBN 0-937175-64-1

An authoritative guide to the hottest new UNIX utility in years, coauthored by its creator, Larry Wall. Perl is a language for easily manipulating text, files, and processes. Programming perl covers Perl syntax, functions, debugging, efficiency, the Perl library, and more.

PGP: Pretty Good Privacy

By Simson Garfinkel
1st Edition December 1994
430 pages, ISBN 1-56592-098-8

PGP is a freely available encryption program that protects the privacy of files and electronic mail. It uses powerful public key cryptography and works on virtually every platform. This book is both a readable technical user's guide and a fascinating behind-the-scenes look at cryptography and privacy.

It describes how to use PGP and provides background on cryptography, PGP's history, battles over public key cryptography patents and U.S. government export restrictions, and public debates about privacy and free speech.

"I even learned a few things about PGP from Simson's informative book."—Phil Zimmermann, Author of PGP

"Since the release of PGP 2.0 from Europe in the fall of 1992, PGP's popularity and usage has grown to make it the de-facto standard for email encyrption. Simson's book is an excellent overview of PGP and the history of cryptography in general. It should prove a useful addition to the resource library for any computer user, from the UNIX wizard to the PC novice."
—Derek Atkins, PGP Development Team, MIT

Building Internet Firewalls

By D. Brent Chapman & Elizabeth D. Zwicky
1st Edition September 1995
544 pages, ISBN 1-56592-124-0

Everyone is jumping on the Internet bandwagon, despite the fact that the security risks associated with connecting to the Net have never been greater. This book is a practical guide to building firewalls on the Internet. It describes a variety of firewall approaches and architectures and discusses how you can build packet filtering and proxying solutions at your site. It also contains a full discussion of how to configure Internet services (e.g., FTP, SMTP, Telnet) to work with a firewall, as well as a complete list of resources, including the location of many publicly available firewall construction tools.

Practical UNIX and Internet Security

By Simson Garfinkel & Gene Spafford
2nd Edition April 1996 (est.)
800 pages (est.), ISBN 1-56592-148-8

A complete revision of the first edition, this new guide spells out the threats, system vulnerabilities, and counter-measures you can adopt to protect your UNIX system, network, and Internet connection. It's complete—covering both host and network security—and doesn't require that you be a programmer or a UNIX guru to use it.

This edition contains hundreds of pages of new information on Internet security, including new security tools and approaches. Covers many platforms, both System V and Berkeley-based (i.e. Sun, DEC, HP, IBM, SCO, NeXT, Linux, and other UNIX systems).

Computer Crime

By David Icove, Karl Seger & William VonStorch
1st Edition August 1995
464 pages, ISBN 1-56592-086-4

Computer crime is a growing threat. Attacks on computers, networks, and data range from terrorist threats to financial crimes to pranks. *Computer Crime: A Crimefighters Handbook* is aimed at those who need to understand, investigate, and prosecute computer crimes of all kinds.

This book discusses computer crimes, criminals, and laws, and profiles the computer criminal (using techniques developed for the FBI and other law enforcement agencies). It outlines the the risks to computer systems and personnel, operational, physical, and communications measures that can be taken to prevent computer crimes. It also discusses how to plan for, investigate, and prosecute computer crimes, ranging from the supplies needed for criminal investigation, to the detection and audit tools used in investigation, to the presentation of evidence to a jury.

Contains a compendium of computer-related federal statutes, all statutes of individual states, a resource summary, and detailed papers on computer crime.

Internet Administration

Getting Connected: 56K and Up

By Kevin Dowd
1st Edition May 1996 (est.)
450 pages (est.), ISBN 1-56592-154-2

A complete guide for businesses, schools, and other organizations who want to connect their computers to the Internet. This book covers everything you need to know to make informed decisions, from helping you figure out which services you really need to providing down-to-earth explanations of telecommunication options, such as frame relay, ISDN, and leased lines. Once you're online, it shows you how to set up basic Internet services, such as a World Wide Web server. Tackles issues for the PC, Macintosh, and UNIX platforms.

DNS and BIND

By Paul Albitz & Cricket Liu
1st Edition October 1992
418 pages, ISBN 1-56592-010-4

DNS and BIND contains all you need to know about the Internet's Domain Name System (DNS) and the Berkeley Internet Name Domain (BIND), its UNIX implementation. The Domain Name System is the Internet's "phone book"; it's a database that tracks important information (in particular, names and addresses) for every computer on the Internet. If you're a system administrator, this book will show you how to set up and maintain the DNS software on your network.

sendmail

By Bryan Costales, with Eric Allman & Neil Rickert
1st Edition November 1993
830 pages, ISBN 1-56592-056-2

This Nutshell Handbook® is far and away the most comprehensive book ever written on sendmail, the program that acts like a traffic cop in routing and delivering mail on UNIX-based networks. Although sendmail is used on almost every UNIX system, it's one of the last great uncharted territories—and most difficult utilities to learn—in UNIX system administration. This book provides a complete sendmail tutorial, plus extensive reference material on every aspect of the program. It covers IDA sendmail, the latest version (V8) from Berkeley, and the standard versions available on most systems.

Managing Internet Information Services

By Cricket Liu, Jerry Peek, Russ Jones, Bryan Buus, & Adrian Nye
1st Edition December 1994
668 pages, ISBN 1-56592-062-7

This comprehensive guide describes how to set up information services and make them available over the Internet. It discusses why a company would want to offer Internet services, provides complete coverage of all popular services, and tells how to select which ones to provide. Most of the book describes how to set up Gopher, World Wide Web, FTP, and WAIS servers and email services.

Networking Personal Computers with TCP/IP

By Craig Hunt
1st Edition July 1995
408 pages, ISBN 1-56592-123-2

This book offers practical information as well as detailed instructions for attaching PCs to a TCP/IP network and its UNIX servers. It discusses the challenges you'll face and offers general advice on how to deal with them, provides basic TCP/IP configuration information for some of the popular PC operating systems, covers advanced configuration topics and configuration of specific applications such as email, and includes a chapter on NetWare, the most popular PC LAN system software.

TCP/IP Network Administration

By Craig Hunt
1st Edition August 1992
502 pages, ISBN 0-937175-82-X

A complete guide to setting up and running a TCP/IP network for practicing system administrators. *TCP/IP Network Administration* covers setting up your network, configuring important network applications including sendmail, and issues in troubleshooting and security. It covers both BSD and System V TCP/IP implementations.

TO ORDER: **800-889-8969** (CREDIT CARD ORDERS ONLY); **ORDER@ORA.COM**

At Your Fingertips—
A COMPLETE GUIDE TO O'REILLY'S ONLINE SERVICES

O'Reilly & Associates offers extensive product and customer service information online. We invite you to come and explore our little neck-of-the-woods.

For product information and insight into new technologies, visit the O'Reilly Resource Center

Most comprehensive among our online offerings is the O'Reilly Resource Center. You'll find detailed information on all O'Reilly products, including titles, prices, tables of contents, indexes, author bios, software contents, and reviews. You can also view images of all our products. In addition, watch for informative articles that provide perspective on the technologies we write about. Interviews, excerpts, and bibliographies are also included.

After browsing online, it's easy to order, too, with GNN Direct or by sending email to **order@ora.com**. The O'Reilly Resource Center shows you how. Here's how to visit us online:

☞ *Via the World Wide Web*

If you are connected to the Internet, point your Web browser (e.g., `mosaic`, `netscape`, or `lynx`) to:

`http://www.ora.com/`

For the plaintext version, `telnet` to:
`www.ora.com` (login: `oraweb`)

☞ *Via Gopher*

If you have a Gopher program, our Gopher server has information in a menu format that some people prefer to the Web.

Connect your `gopher` to: `gopher.ora.com`

Or, point your Web browser to:
`gopher://gopher.ora.com/`

Or, you can `telnet` to: `gopher.ora.com`
(login: `gopher`)

A convenient way to stay informed: email mailing lists

An easy way to learn of the latest projects and products from O'Reilly & Associates is to subscribe to our mailing lists. We have email announcements and discussions on various topics, for example "ora-news," our electronic news service. Subscribers receive email as soon as the information breaks.

☞ *To join a mailing list:*

Send email to:

listproc@online.ora.com

Leave the message "subject" empty if possible.

If you know the name of the mailing list you want to subscribe to, put the following information on the first line of your message: `subscribe` "listname" "your name" `of` "your company."

For example: `subscribe ora-news Kris Webber of Fine Enterprises`

If you don't know the name of the mailing list, listproc will send you a listing of all the mailing lists. Put this word on the first line of the body: `lists`

To find out more about a particular list, send a message with this word as the first line of the body: `info` "listname"

For more information and help, send this message: `help`

For specific help, email to:
listmaster@online.ora.com

The complete O'Reilly catalog is now available via email

You can now receive a text-only version of our complete catalog via email. It contains detailed information about all our products, so it's mighty big: over 200 kbytes, or 200,000 characters.

To get the whole catalog in one message, send an empty email message to: **catalog@online.ora.com**

If your email system can't handle large messages, you can get the catalog split into smaller messages. Send email to: **catalog-split@online.ora.com**

To receive a print catalog, send your snail mail address to: **catalog@ora.com**

Check out Web Review, our new publication on the Web

Web Review is our new magazine that offers fresh insights into the Web. The editorial mission of Web Review is to answer the question: How and where do you BEST spend your time online? Each issue contains reviews that look at the most interesting and creative sites on the Web. Visit us at **http://gnn.com/wr/**

Web Review is the product of the recently formed Songline Studios, a venture between O'Reilly and America Online.

Get the files you want with FTP

We have an archive of example files from our books, the covers of our books, and much more available by anonymous FTP.

ftp to:

ftp.ora.com (login: **anonymous** – use your email address as the password.)

Or, if you have a WWW browser, point it to:

ftp://ftp.ora.com/

FTPMAIL

The ftpmail service connects to O'Reilly's FTP server and sends the results (the files you want) by email. This service is for people who can't use FTP—but who can use email.

For help and examples, send an email message to:

ftpmail@online.ora.com

(In the message body, put the single word: **help**)

Helpful information is just an email message away

Many customer services are provided via email. Here are a few of the most popular and useful:

info@online.ora.com
> For a list of O'Reilly's online customer services.

info@ora.com
> For general questions and information.

bookquestions@ora.com
> For technical questions, or corrections, concerning book contents.

order@ora.com
> To order books online and for ordering questions.

catalog@online.ora.com
> To receive an online copy of our catalog.

catalog@ora.com
> To receive a free copy of *ora.com*, our combination magazine and catalog. Please include your snail mail address.

international@ora.com
> Comments or questions about international ordering or distribution.

proposals@ora.com
> To submit book proposals.

info@gnn.com
> To receive information about America Online's GNN (Global Network Navigator).™

O'Reilly & Associates, Inc.

103A Morris Street, Sebastopol, CA 95472

Inquiries: **707-829-0515, 800-998-9938**

Credit card orders: **800-889-8969**
(Weekdays 6 A.M.- 5 P.M. PST)

FAX: **707-829-0104**

O'Reilly & Associates—
LISTING OF TITLES

INTERNET

CGI Scriptin on the World Wide Web (Winter '95-96 est.)
Designing for the Web (Winter '95-96 est.)
Exploring Java (Spring '96 est.)
Getting Connected (Spring '96 est.)
Java in a Nutshell
Smileys
The USENET Handbook
The Whole Internet User's Guide & Catalog
The Whole Internet for Windows 95
The World Wide Web Journal

SOFTWARE

Internet In A Box™
WebSite™ 1.1
WebBoard™

WHAT YOU NEED TO KNOW SERIES

Bandits on the Information Superhighway
Using Email Effectively
Marketing on the Internet (Spring '96 est.)
When You Can't Find Your System Administrator

HEALTH, CAREER & BUSINESS

Building a Successful Software Business
The Computer User's Survival Guide
Dictionary of PC hardware and Data Communication Terms (Winter '95-96 est.)
The Future Does Not Compute
Love Your Job!
TWI Day Calendar - 1996

USING UNIX

BASICS

Learning GNU Emacs
Learning the bash Shell
Learning the Korn Shell
Learning the UNIX Operating System
Learning the vi Editor
MH & xmh: Email for Users & Programmers
SCO UNIX in a Nutshell
UNIX in a Nutshell: System V Ed.
Using and Managing UUCP (Spring'96 est.)
Using csh and tcsh

ADVANCED

Exploring Expect
The Frame Handbook
Learning Perl
Making TeX Work
Perl 5 Quick Reference Guide
Programming perl
Running Linux
Running Linux Companion CD-ROM (Winter '95-96 est.)
sed & awk
UNIX Power Tools (with CD-ROM)

SYSTEM ADMINISTRATION

Building Internet Firewalls
Computer Crime: A Crimefighter's Handbook
Computer Security Basics
DNS and BIND
Essential System Administration
Linux Network Administrator's Guide
Managing Internet Information Services
Managing NFS and NIS
Networking Personal Computers with TCP/IP
Practical UNIX & Internet Security (Spring '96 est.)
PGP: Pretty Good Privacy
sendmail
System Performance Tuning
TCP/IP Network Administration
termcap & terminfo
Volume 8 : X Window System Administrator's Guide

PROGRAMMING

Applying RCS and SCCS
C++: The Core Language
Checking C Programs with lint
DCE Security Programming
Distributing Applications Across DCE and Windows NT
Encyclopedia of Graphics File Formats
Guide to Writing DCE Applications
High Performance Computing
lex & yacc
Managing Projects with make
Microsoft RPC Programming Guide
Migrating to Fortran 90
Multi-Platform Code Management
ORACLE Performance Tuning
ORACLE PL/SQL Programming
Porting UNIX Software
POSIX Programmer's Guide
POSIX.4: Programming for the Real World
Power Programming with RPC
Practical C Programming
Practical C++ Programming
Programming with curses
Programming with GNU Software (Winter '95-96 est.)
Programming with Pthreads (Winter '95-96 est.)
Software Portability with imake
Understanding DCE
Understanding Japanese Information Processing
Using C on the UNIX System

BERKELEY 4.4 SOFTWARE DISTRIBUTION

4.4BSD System Manager's Manual
4.4BSD User's Reference Manual
4.4BSD User's Supp. Documents
4.4BSD Programmer's Reference Manual
4.4BSD Programmer's Supplementary Documents
4.4BSD-Lite CD Companion
4.4BSD-Lite CD Companion: International Version

X WINDOW SYSTEM

Volume 0: X Protocol Reference Manual
Volume 1: Xlib Programming Manual
Volume 2: Xlib Reference Manual:
Volume 3: X Window System User's Guide
Volume. 3M: X Window System User's Guide, Motif Ed
Volume 4M: X Toolkit Intrinsics Programming Manual, Motif Ed.
Volume 5: X Toolkit Intrinsics Reference Manual
Volume 6A: Motif Programming Manual
Volume 6B: Motif Reference Manual
Volume 6C: Motif Tools
Volume 8 : X Window System Administrator's Guide
Volume 9: X Window Programming Extentions (Spring '96 est.)
Programmer's Supplement for Release 6
X User Tools (with CD-ROM)
The X Window System in a Nutshell

THE X RESOURCE

A QUARTERLY WORKING JOURNAL FOR X PROGRAMMERS

The X Resource: Issues 16 and Issue 17

TRAVEL

Travelers' Tales France
Travelers' Tales Hong Kong
Travelers' Tales India
Travelers' Tales Mexico
Travelers' Tales Spain
Travelers' Tales Thailand
Travelers' Tales: A Woman's World

O'Reilly & Associates—
INTERNATIONAL DISTRIBUTORS

Customers outside North America can now order O'Reilly & Associates books through the following distributors. They offer our international customers faster order processing, more bookstores, increased representation at tradeshows worldwide, and the high-quality, responsive service our customers have come to expect.

EUROPE, MIDDLE EAST, AND AFRICA
(except Germany, Switzerland, and Austria)

INQUIRIES
International Thomson Publishing Europe
Berkshire House
168-173 High Holborn
London WC1V 7AA, United Kingdom
Telephone: 44-71-497-1422
Fax: 44-71-497-1426
Email: itpint@itps.co.uk

ORDERS
International Thomson Publishing Services, Ltd.
Cheriton House, North Way
Andover, Hampshire SP10 5BE, United Kingdom
Telephone: 44-264-342-832 (UK orders)
Telephone: 44-264-342-806 (outside UK)
Fax: 44-264-364418 (UK orders)
Fax: 44-264-342761 (outside UK)

GERMANY, SWITZERLAND, AND AUSTRIA

International Thomson Publishing GmbH
O'Reilly-International Thomson Verlag
Königswinterer Straße 418
53227 Bonn, Germany
Telephone: 49-228-97024 0
Fax: 49-228-441342
Email: anfragen@ora.de

ASIA *(except Japan)*
INQUIRIES
International Thomson Publishing Asia
221 Henderson Road
#08-03 Henderson Industrial Park
Singapore 0315
Telephone: 65-272-6496
Fax: 65-272-6498

ORDERS
Telephone: 65-268-7867
Fax: 65-268-6727

JAPAN
O'Reilly & Associates, Inc.
103A Morris Street
Sebastopol, CA 95472 U.S.A.
Telephone: 707-829-0515
Telephone: 800-998-9938 (U.S. & Canada)
Fax: 707-829-0104
Email: order@ora.com

AUSTRALIA
WoodsLane Pty. Ltd.
7/5 Vuko Place, Warriewood NSW 2102
P.O. Box 935, Mona Vale NSW 2103
Australia
Telephone: 02-970-5111
Fax: 02-970-5002
Email: woods@tmx.mhs.oz.au

NEW ZEALAND
WoodsLane New Zealand Ltd.
21 Cooks Street (P.O. Box 575)
Wanganui, New Zealand
Telephone: 64-6-347-6543
Fax: 64-6-345-4840
Email: woods@tmx.mhs.oz.au

THE AMERICAS
O'Reilly & Associates, Inc.
103A Morris Street
Sebastopol, CA 95472 U.S.A.
Telephone: 707-829-0515
Telephone: 800-998-9938 (U.S. & Canada)
Fax: 707-829-0104
Email: order@ora.com